Shojo Beat

Beauty is the Beast ™

3

Story & Art by Tomo Matsumoto

Table of Contents

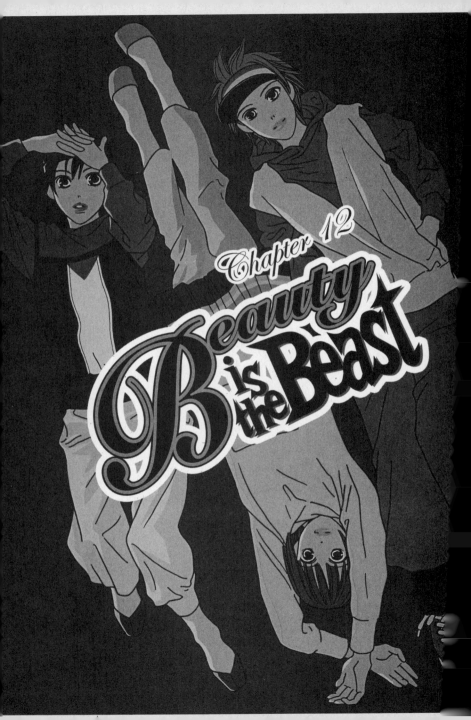

Chapter 12

Beauty is the Beast

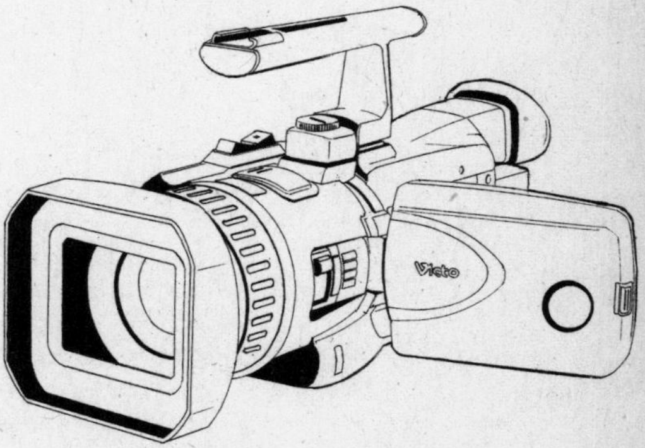
Victo

BEAUTY IS THE BEAST

Do you understand how something like this can happen?

WHAT'RE YOU TAPING?

HUH?

Hello. I'm Tomo Matsumoto. To people who've been reading my work and to first-time readers, hello. I'm happy to able to meet you. For this volume, I thought I'd write about the music I listen to while I'm drawing. Sometimes I receive letters saying, "I get the same BGM and listen to them. What do you listen to nowadays?" ☆ I will write things as they come into my mind, but I'll be happy if you come with me. Thanks!

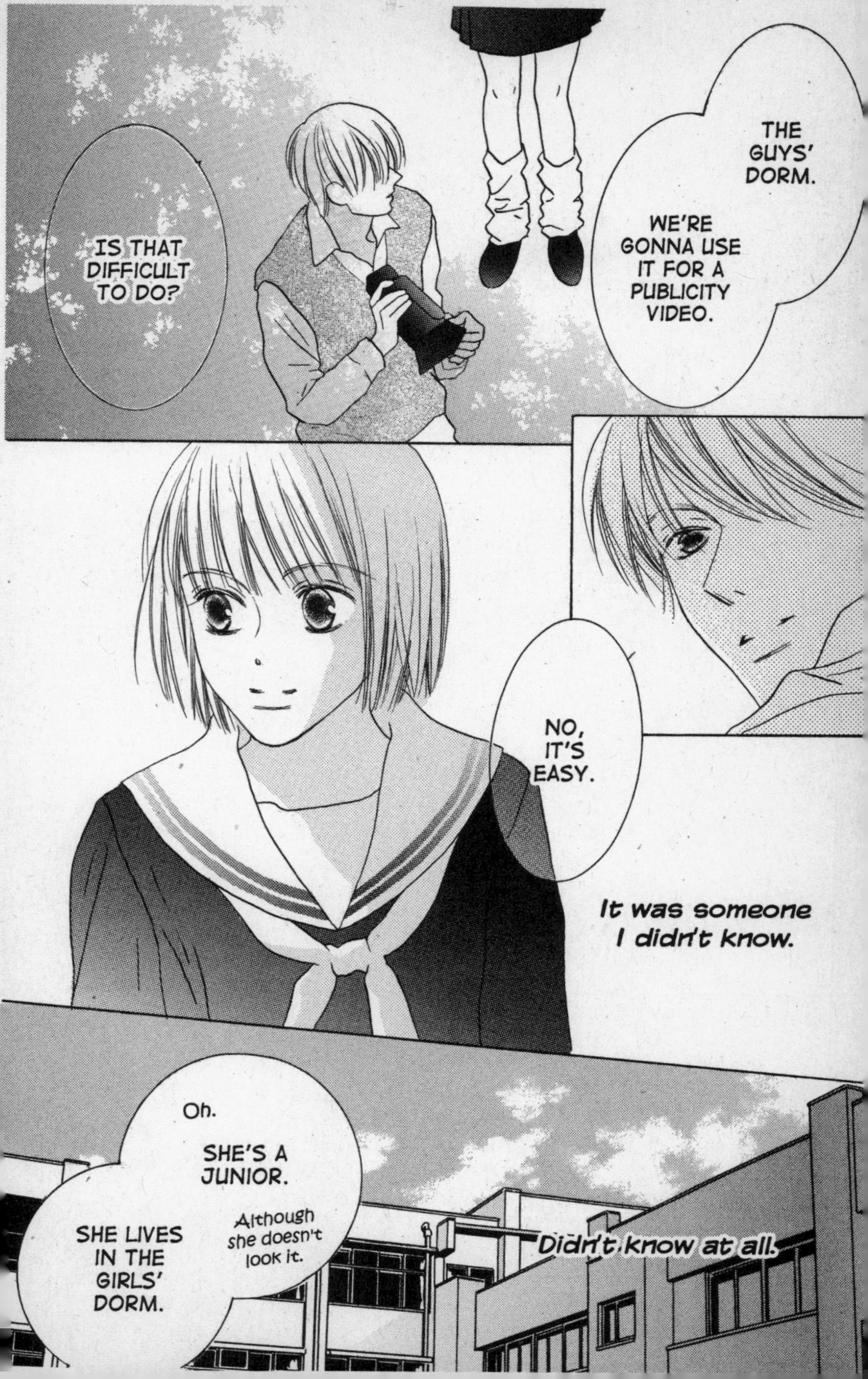
THE GUYS' DORM.
WE'RE GONNA USE IT FOR A PUBLICITY VIDEO.
IS THAT DIFFICULT TO DO?
NO, IT'S EASY.
It was someone I didn't know.
Didn't know at all.
Oh.
SHE'S A JUNIOR.
Although she doesn't look it.
SHE LIVES IN THE GIRLS' DORM.

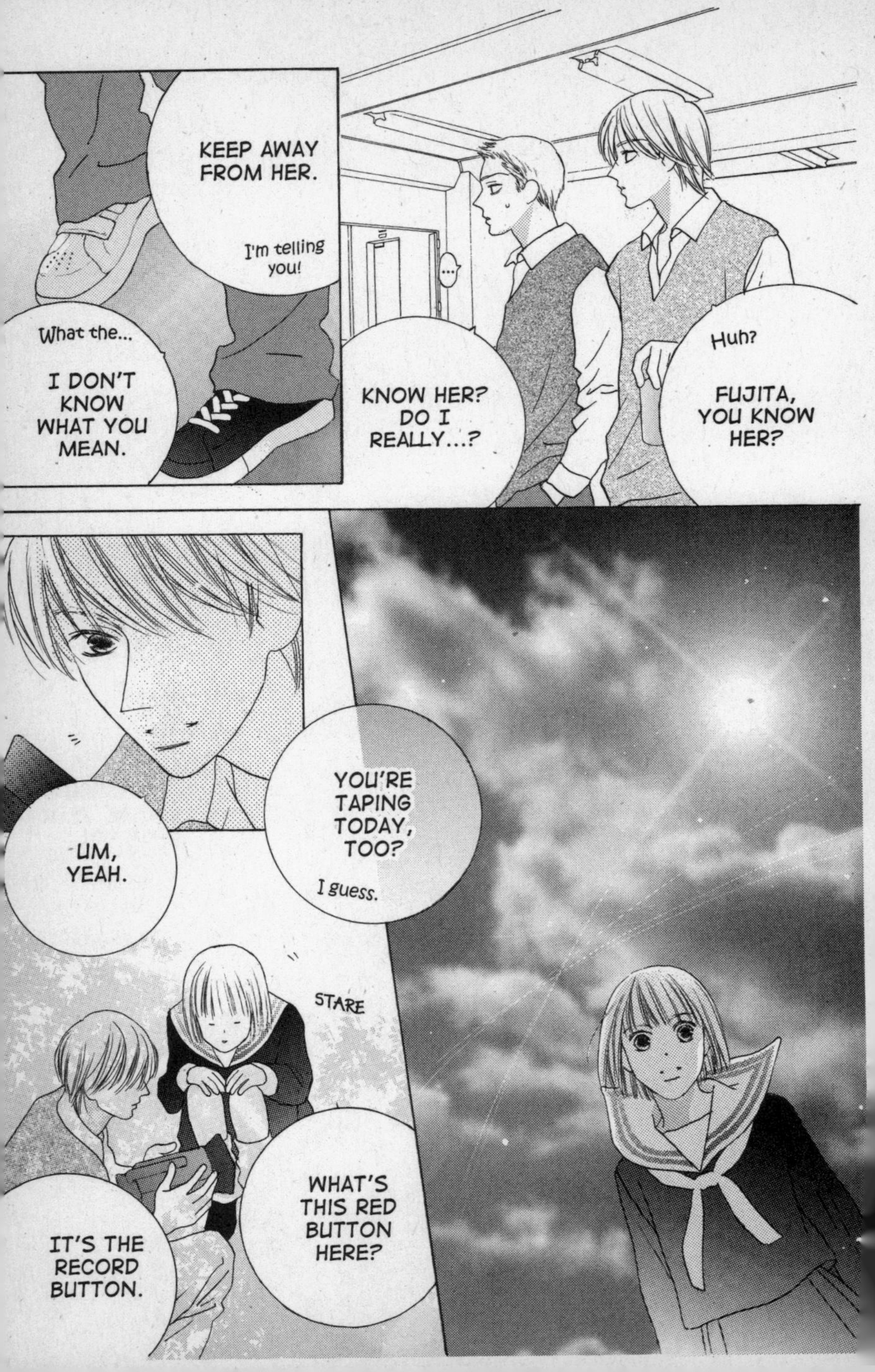
Huh?
FUJITA, YOU KNOW HER?
...
KNOW HER? DO I REALLY...?
KEEP AWAY FROM HER.
I'm telling you!
What the...
I DON'T KNOW WHAT YOU MEAN.
YOU'RE TAPING TODAY, TOO?
I guess.
UM, YEAH.
STARE
WHAT'S THIS RED BUTTON HERE?
IT'S THE RECORD BUTTON.

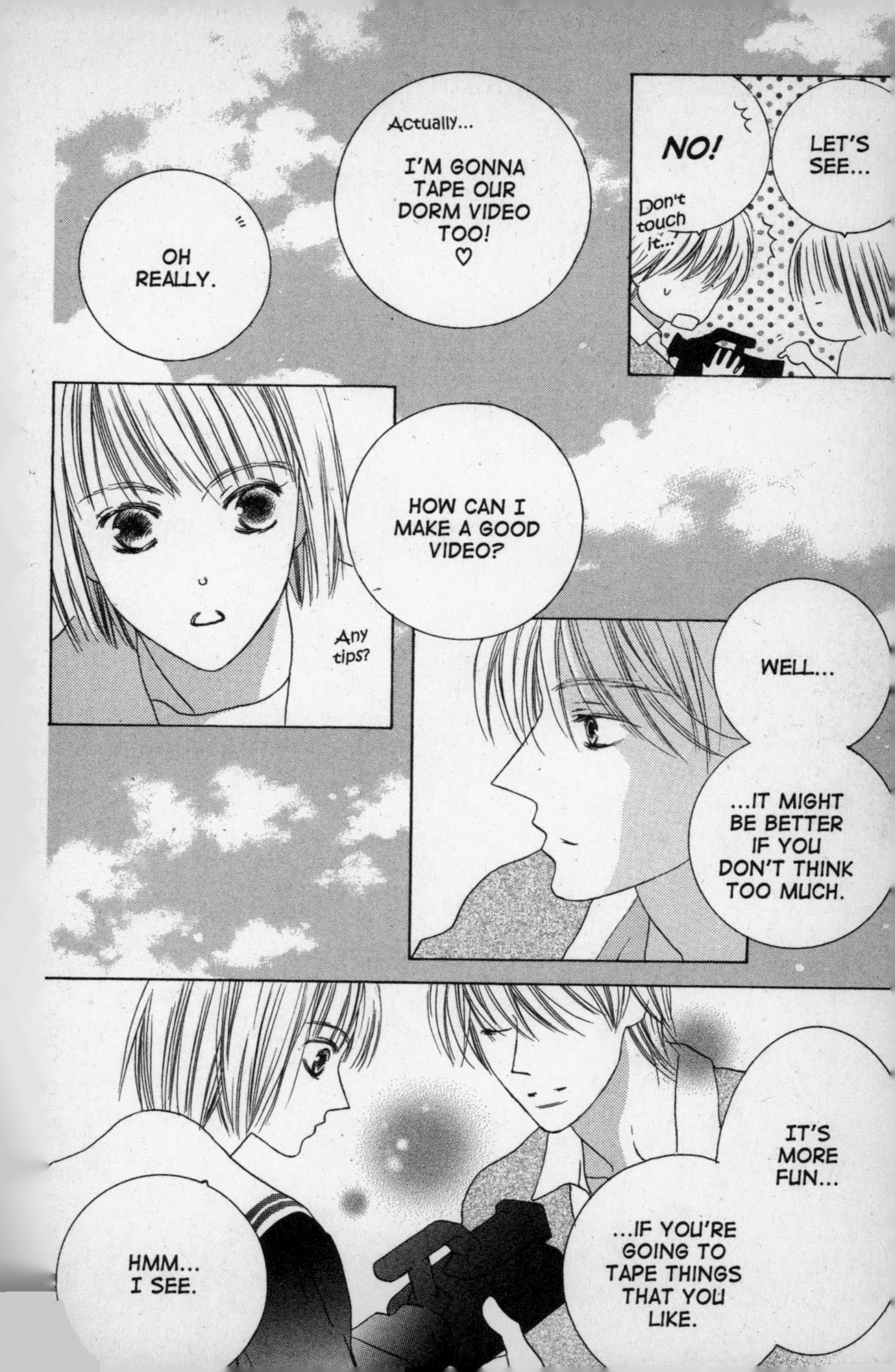
LET'S SEE...
NO!
Don't touch it...
Actually...
I'M GONNA TAPE OUR DORM VIDEO TOO! ♡
OH REALLY.
HOW CAN I MAKE A GOOD VIDEO?
Any tips?
WELL...
...IT MIGHT BE BETTER IF YOU DON'T THINK TOO MUCH.
IT'S MORE FUN...
...IF YOU'RE GOING TO TAPE THINGS THAT YOU LIKE.
HMM... I SEE.

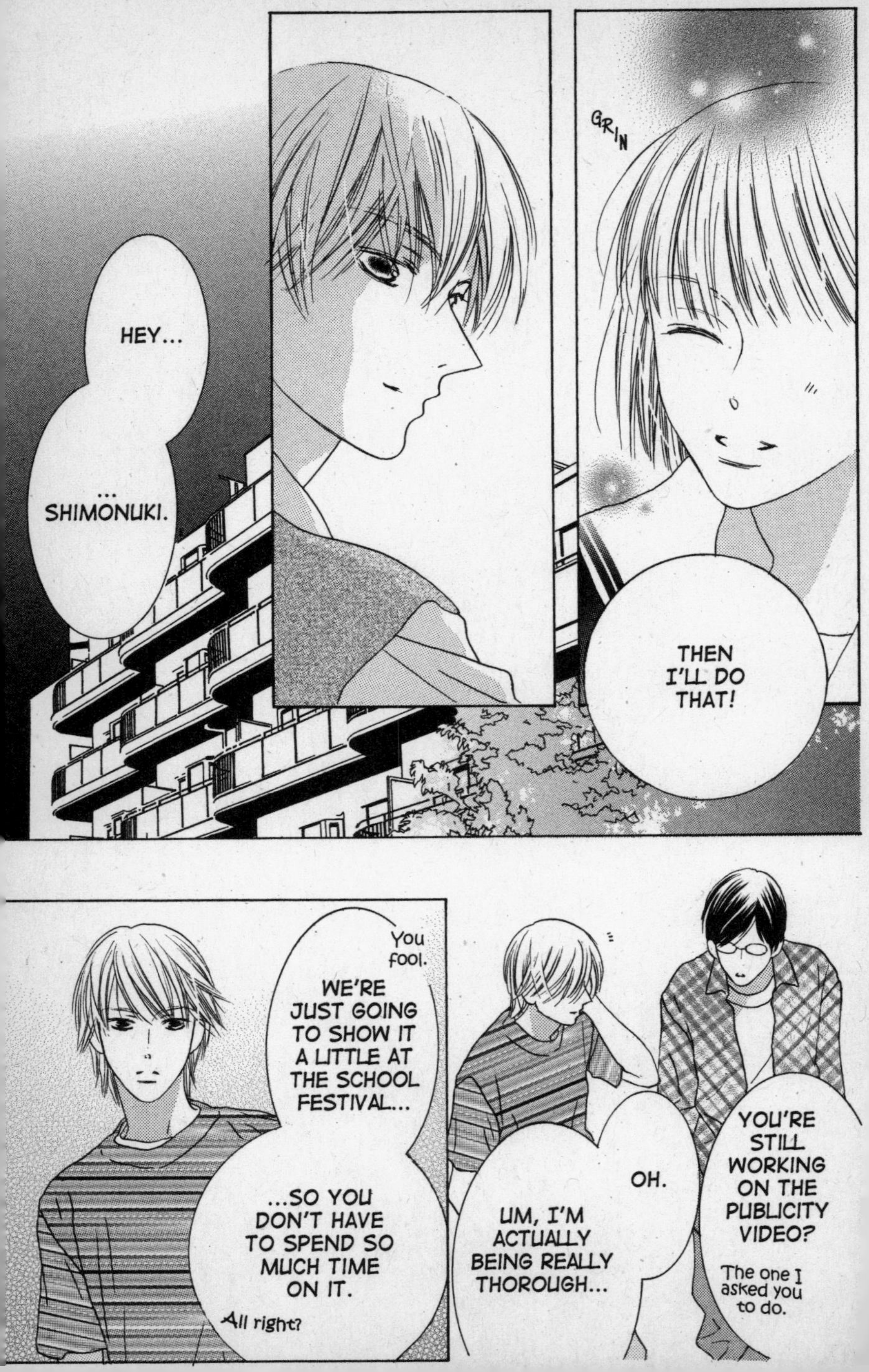
GRIN
THEN I'LL DO THAT!
HEY...
...SHIMONUKI.
YOU'RE STILL WORKING ON THE PUBLICITY VIDEO?
The one I asked you to do.
OH.
UM, I'M ACTUALLY BEING REALLY THOROUGH...
You fool.
WE'RE JUST GOING TO SHOW IT A LITTLE AT THE SCHOOL FESTIVAL...
...SO YOU DON'T HAVE TO SPEND SO MUCH TIME ON IT.
All right?

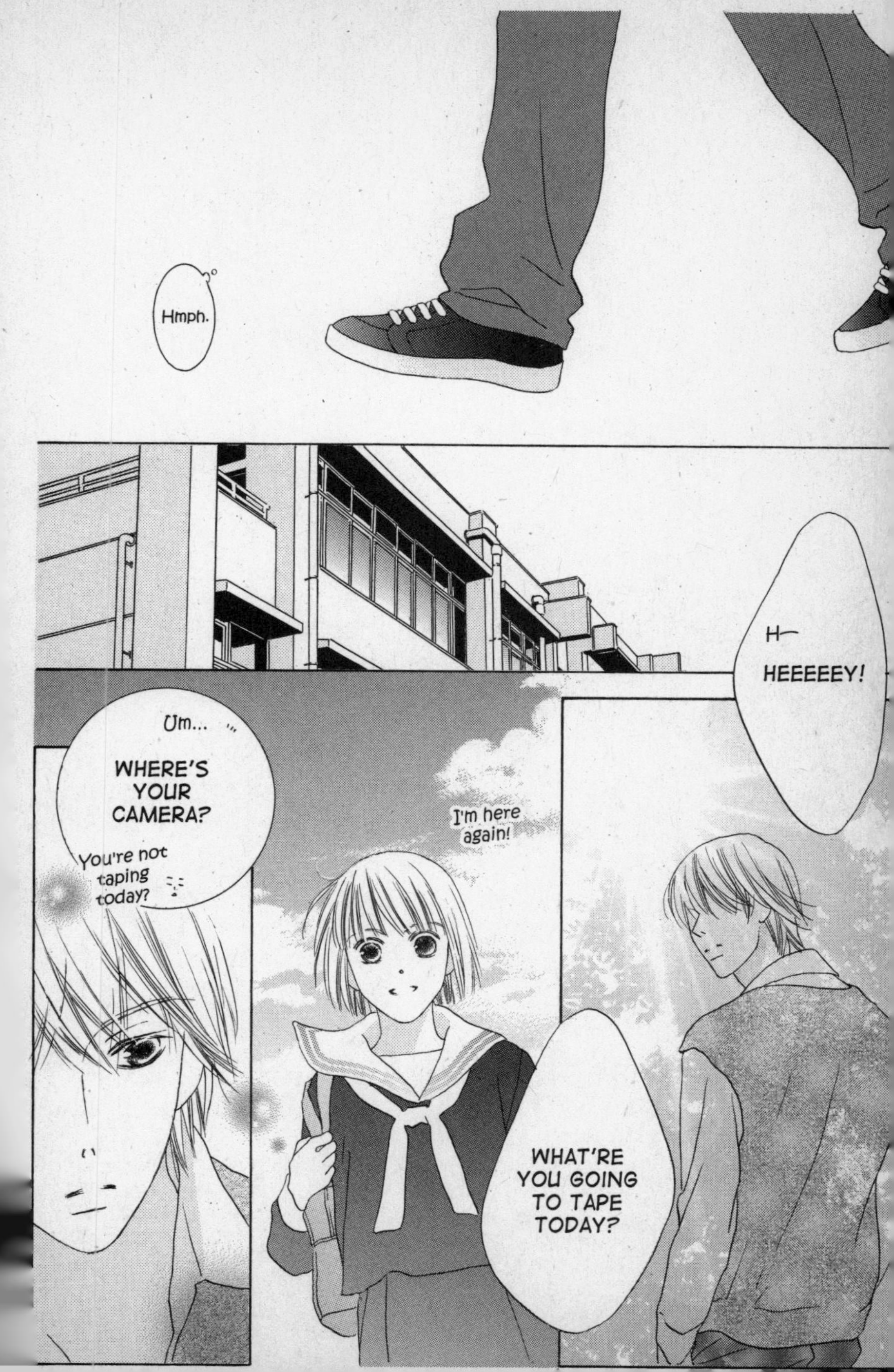
Hmph.
H—
HEEEEEY!
I'm here again!
WHAT'RE YOU GOING TO TAPE TODAY?
Um...
WHERE'S YOUR CAMERA?
You're not taping today?

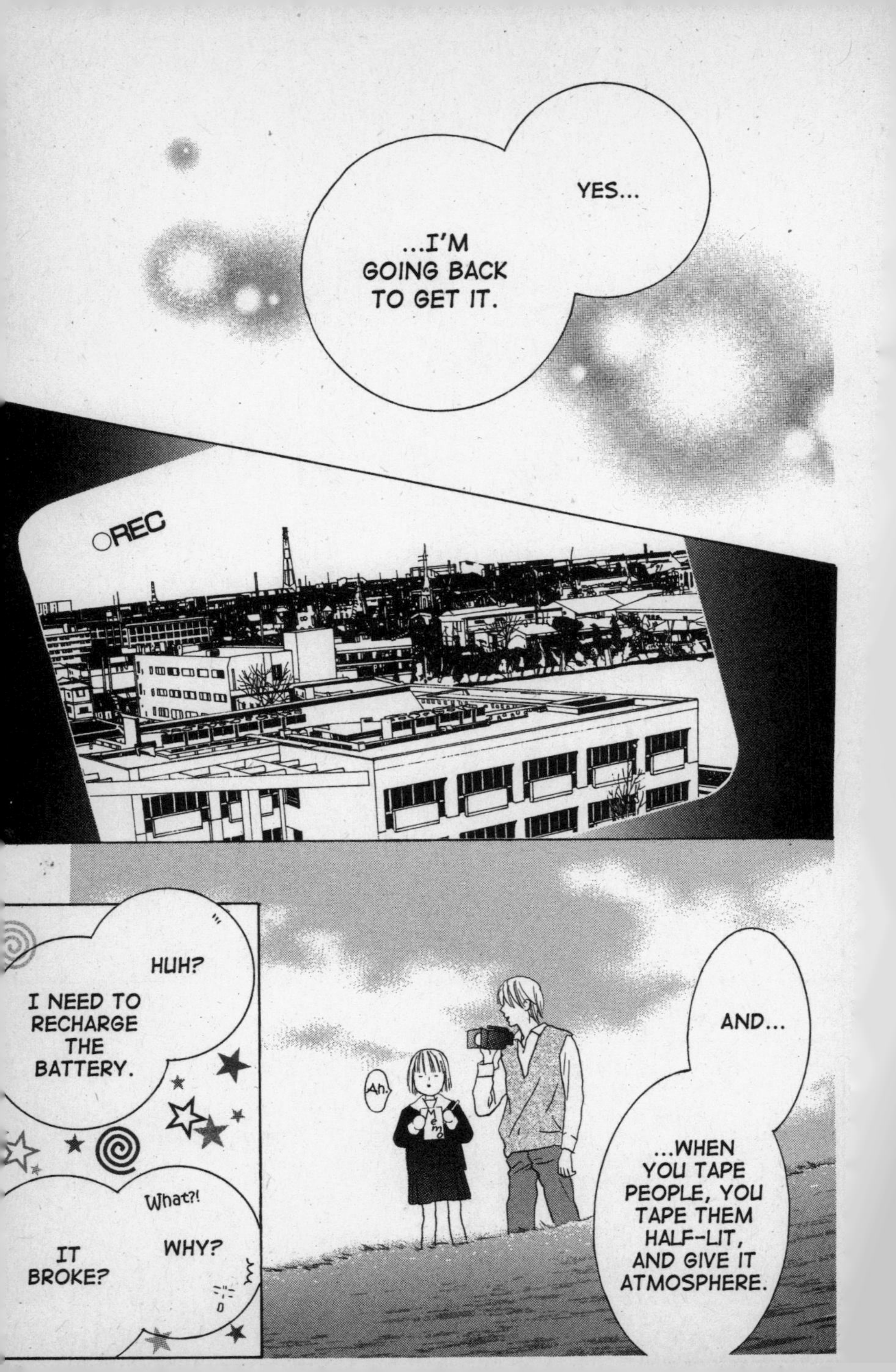
YES...
...I'M GOING BACK TO GET IT.
REC
AND...
...WHEN YOU TAPE PEOPLE, YOU TAPE THEM HALF-LIT, AND GIVE IT ATMOSPHERE.
Ah.
Memo
HUH?
I NEED TO RECHARGE THE BATTERY.
What?!
WHY?
IT BROKE?

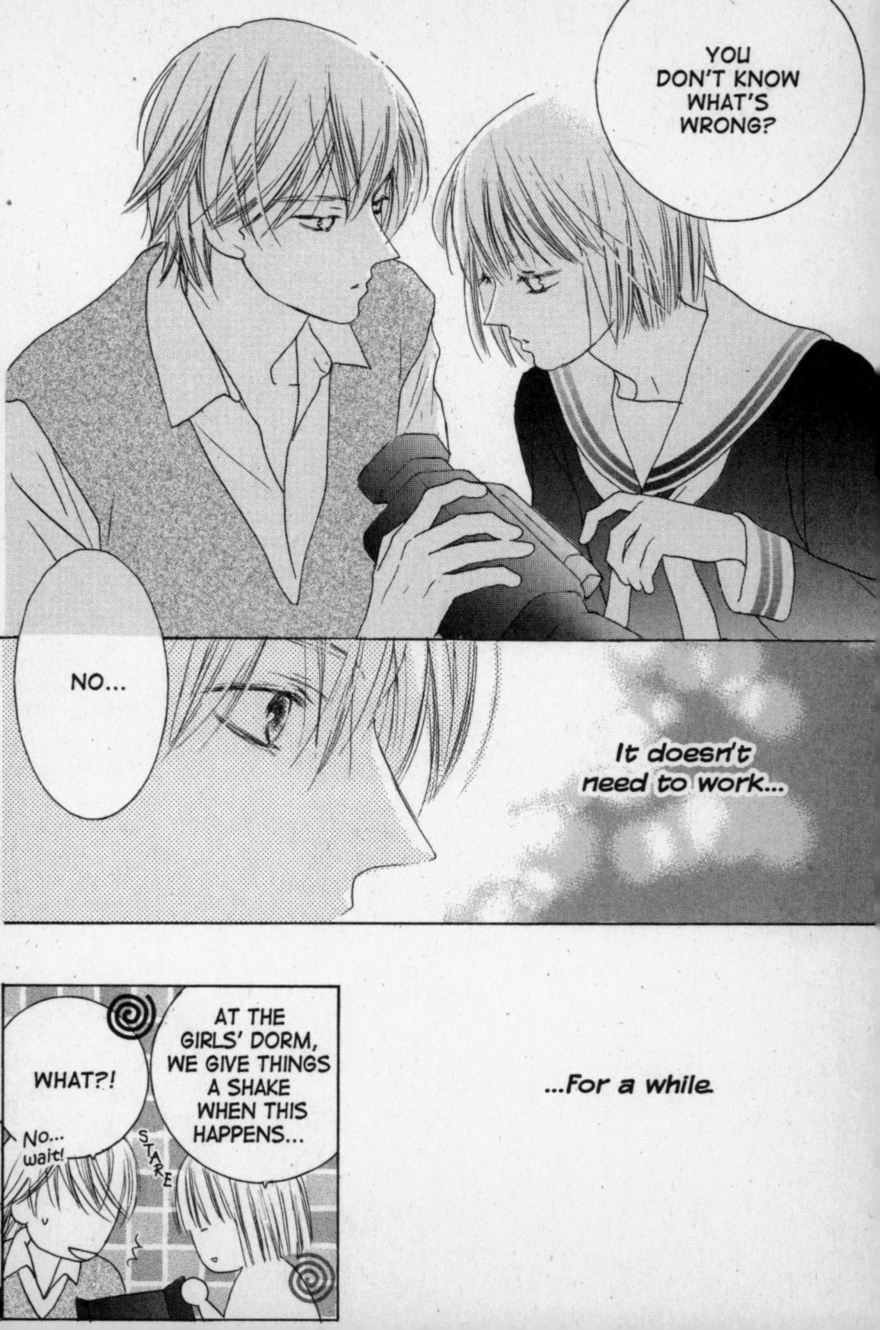
YOU DON'T KNOW WHAT'S WRONG?
NO...
It doesn't need to work...
...For a while.
AT THE GIRLS' DORM, WE GIVE THINGS A SHAKE WHEN THIS HAPPENS...
WHAT?!
STARE
No... wait!

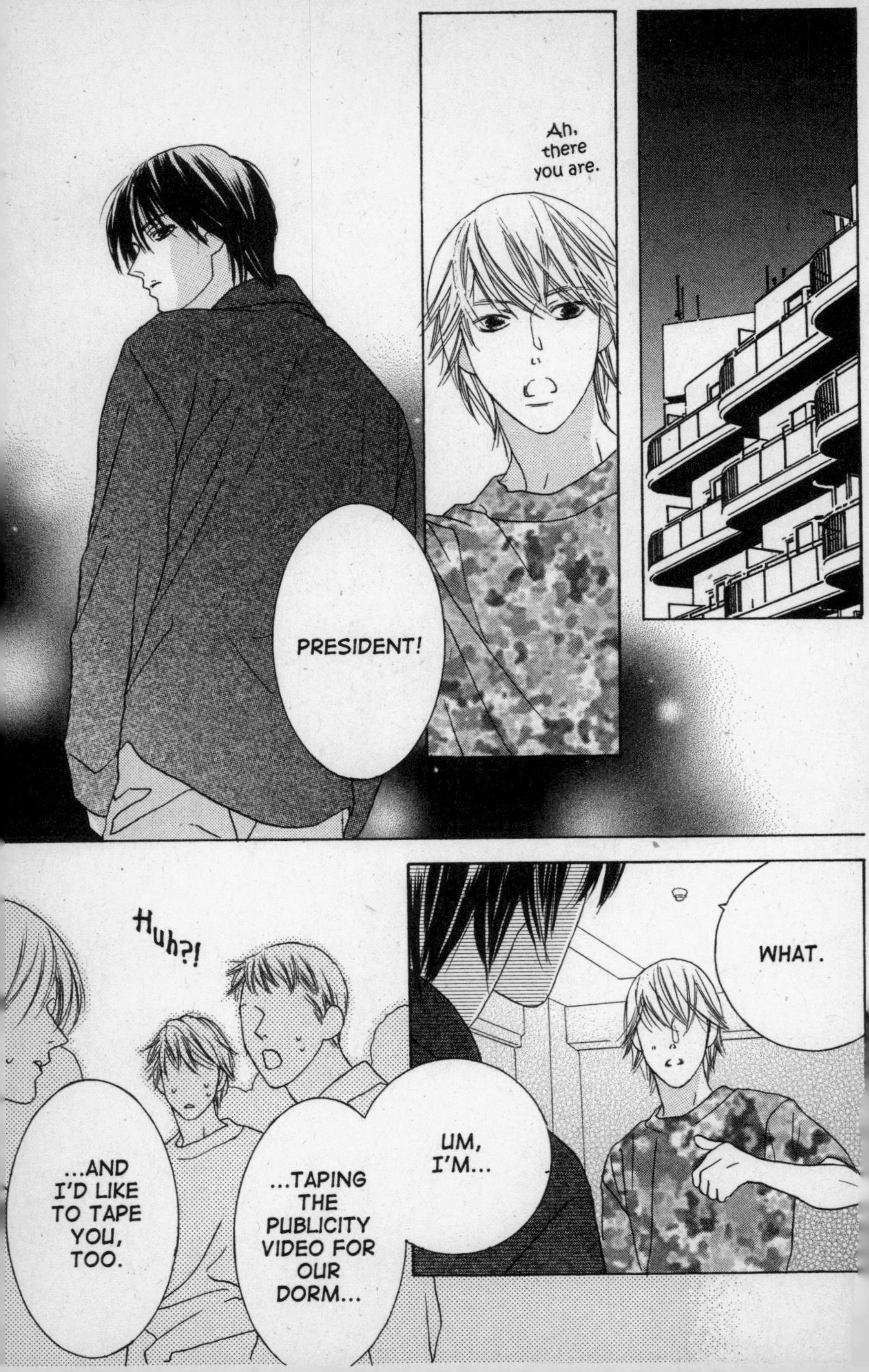

Ah, there you are.
PRESIDENT!
WHAT.
Huh?!
UM, I'M...
...TAPING THE PUBLICITY VIDEO FOR OUR DORM...
...AND I'D LIKE TO TAPE YOU, TOO.

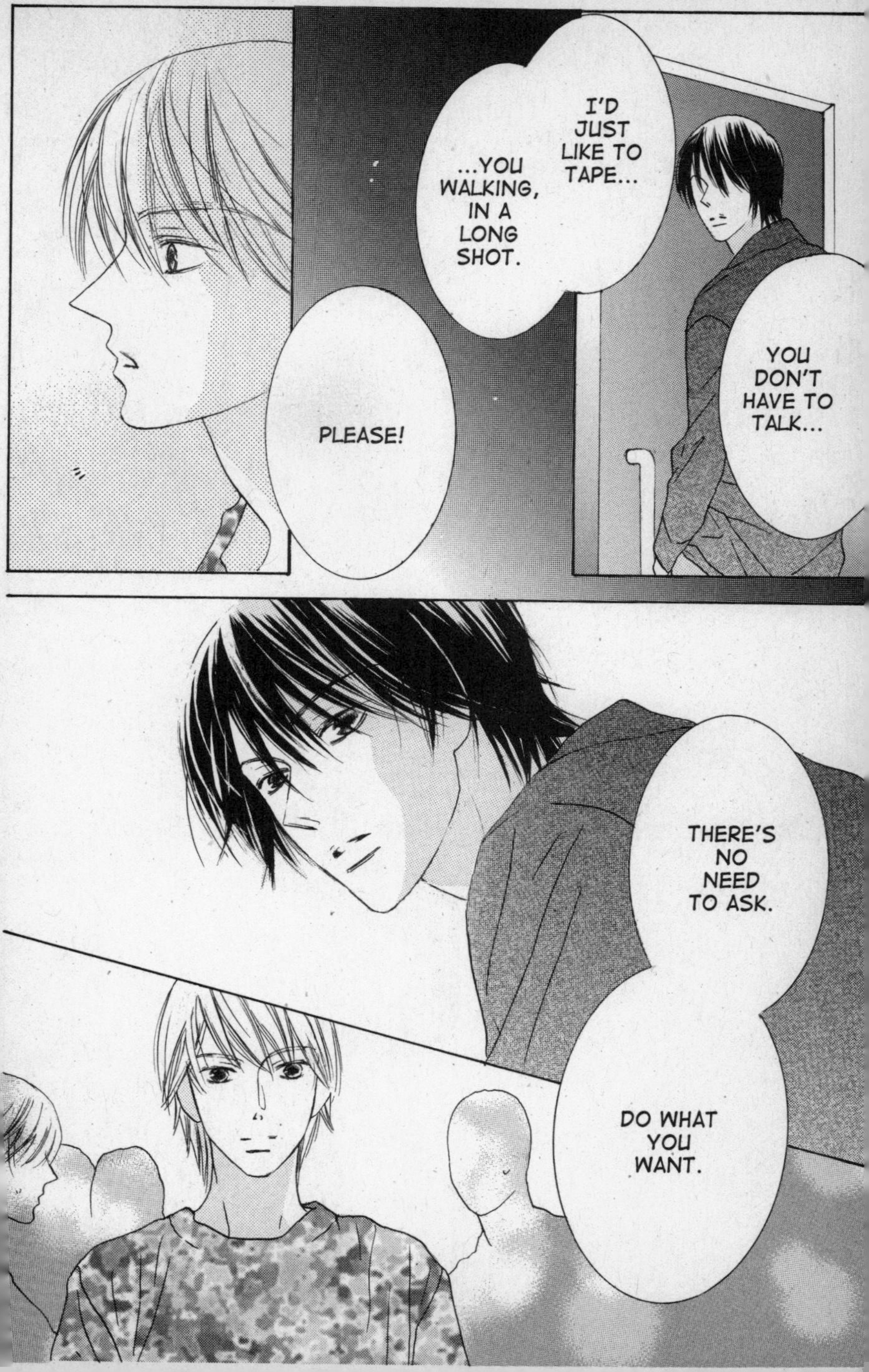
I'D JUST LIKE TO TAPE...
...YOU WALKING, IN A LONG SHOT.
PLEASE!
YOU DON'T HAVE TO TALK...
THERE'S NO NEED TO ASK.
DO WHAT YOU WANT.

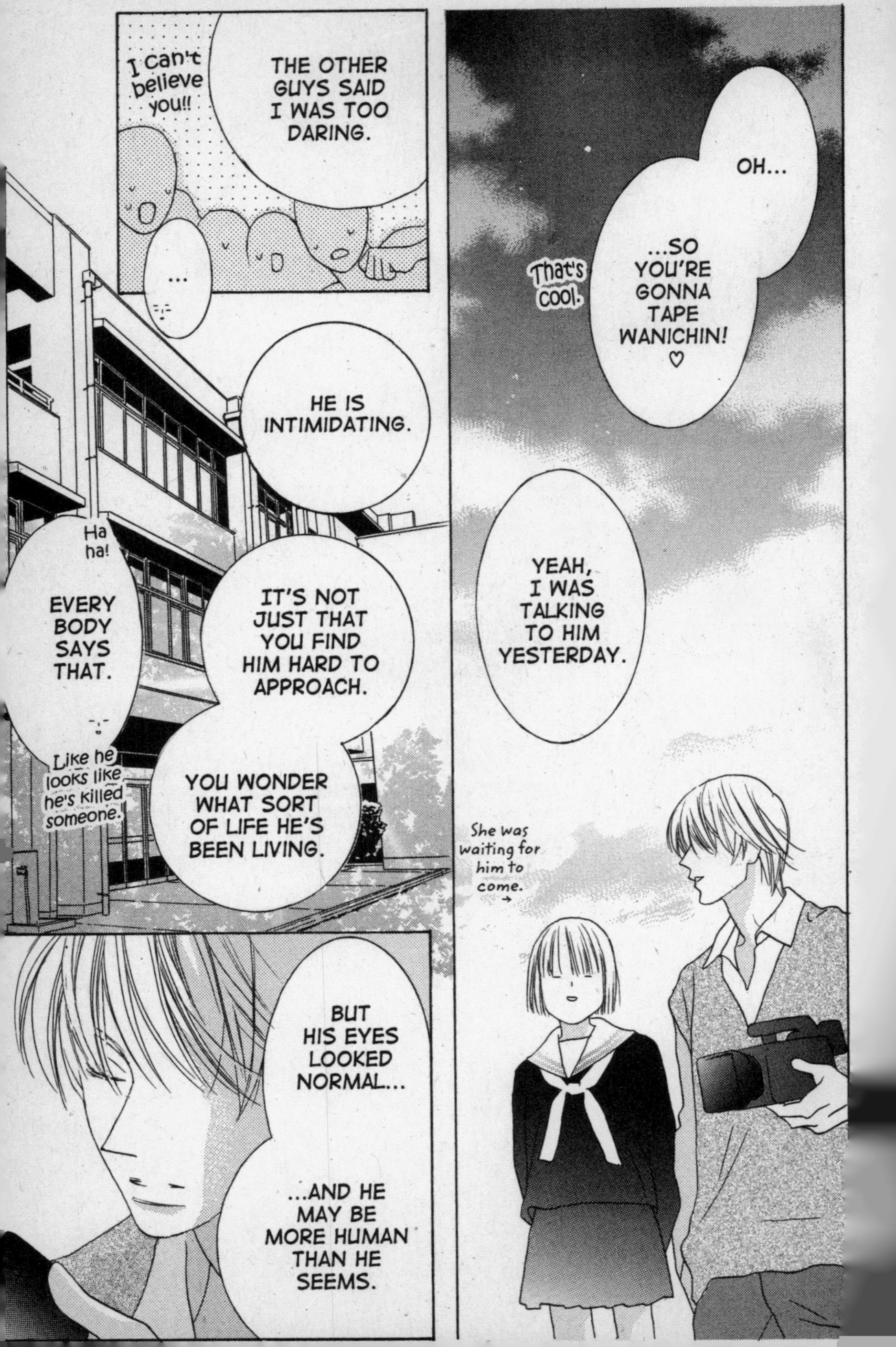
OH...
...SO YOU'RE GONNA TAPE WANICHIN! ♡
That's cool.
YEAH, I WAS TALKING TO HIM YESTERDAY.
She was waiting for him to come.
THE OTHER GUYS SAID I WAS TOO DARING.
I can't believe you!!
...
HE IS INTIMIDATING.
IT'S NOT JUST THAT YOU FIND HIM HARD TO APPROACH.
YOU WONDER WHAT SORT OF LIFE HE'S BEEN LIVING.
Ha ha!
EVERY BODY SAYS THAT.
Like he looks like he's killed someone.
BUT HIS EYES LOOKED NORMAL...
...AND HE MAY BE MORE HUMAN THAN HE SEEMS.

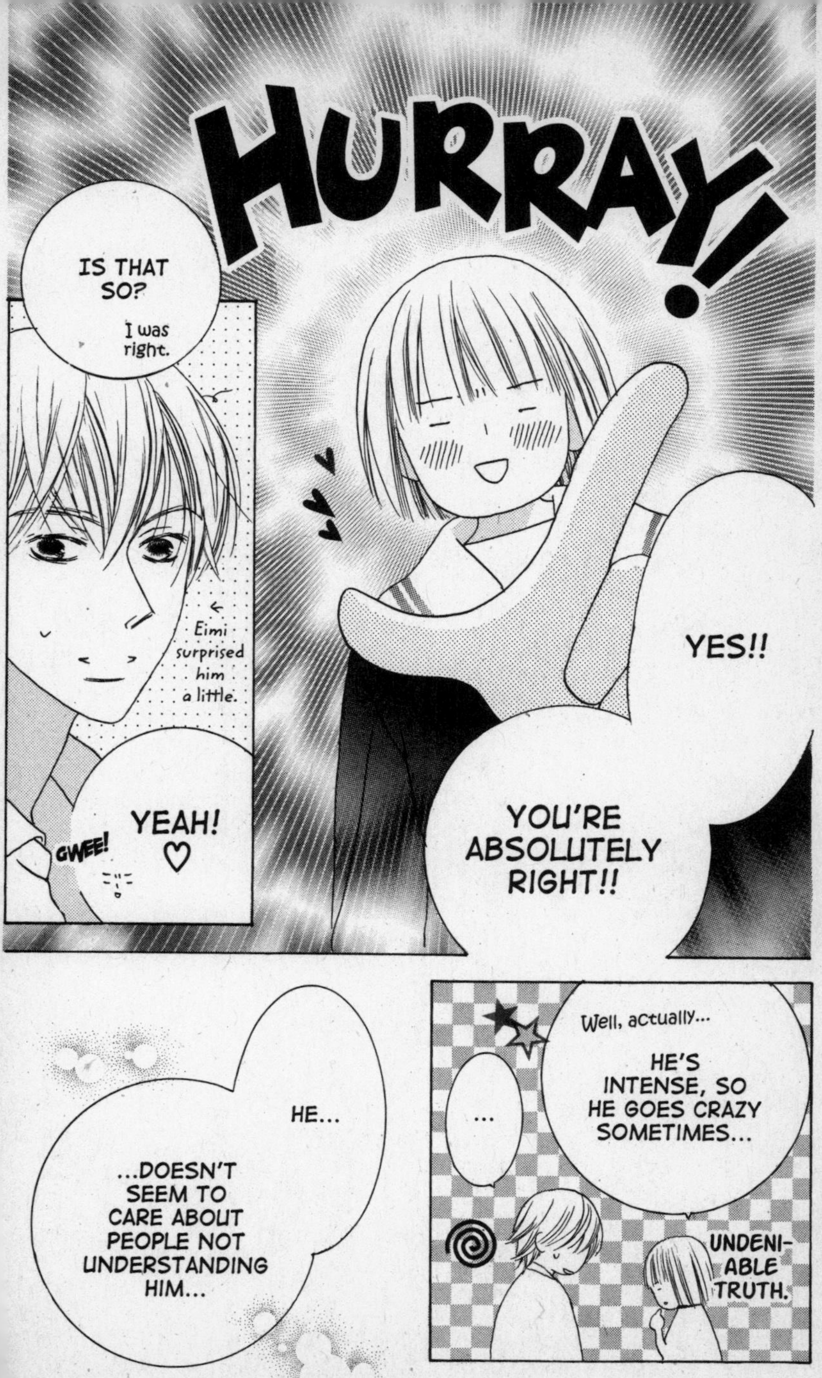
HURRAY!
YES!!
YOU'RE ABSOLUTELY RIGHT!!
IS THAT SO?
I was right.
Eimi surprised him a little.
YEAH! ♡
GWEE!
Well, actually...
HE'S INTENSE, SO HE GOES CRAZY SOMETIMES...
...
UNDENI-ABLE TRUTH.
HE...
...DOESN'T SEEM TO CARE ABOUT PEOPLE NOT UNDERSTANDING HIM...

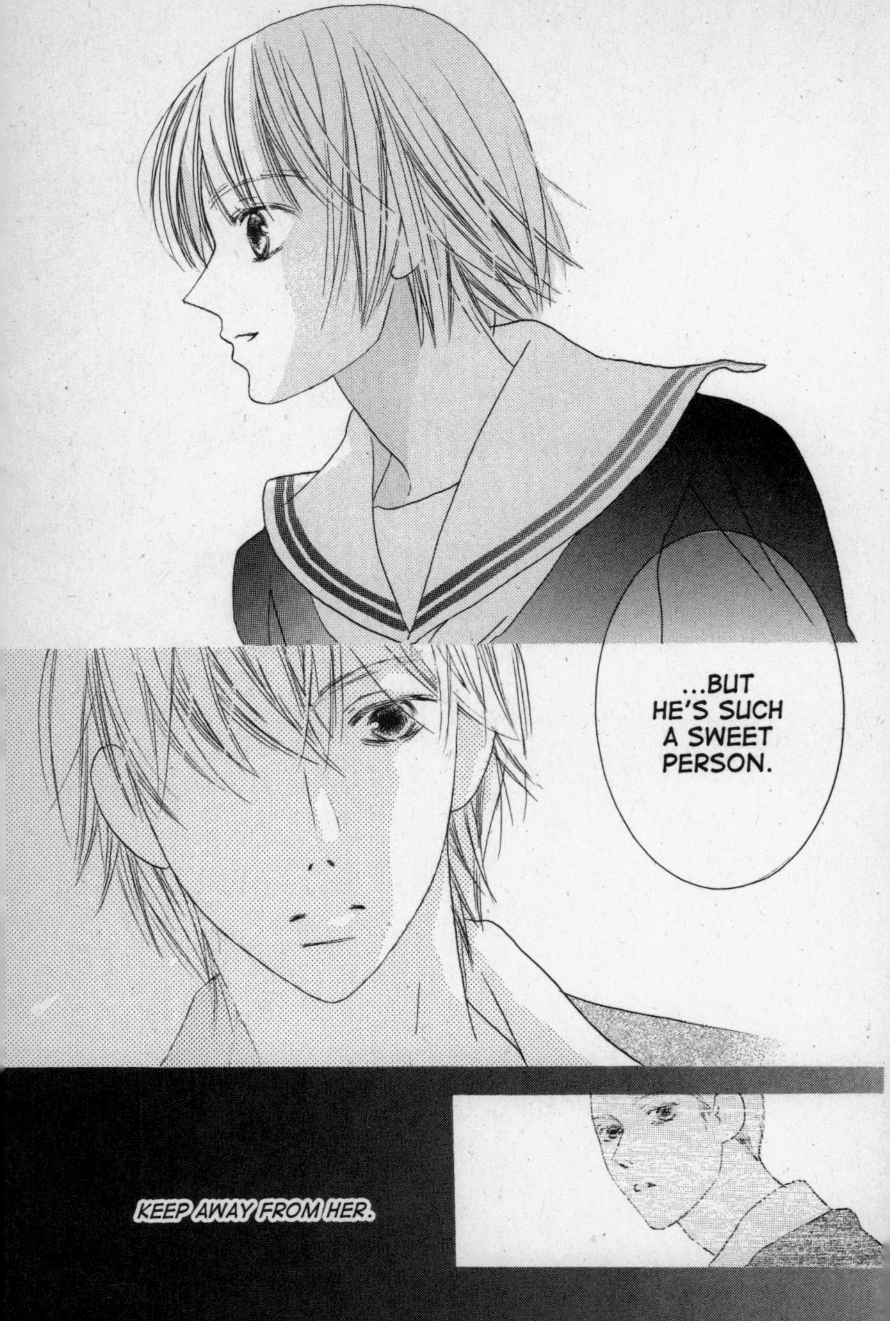
...BUT HE'S SUCH A SWEET PERSON.
KEEP AWAY FROM HER.

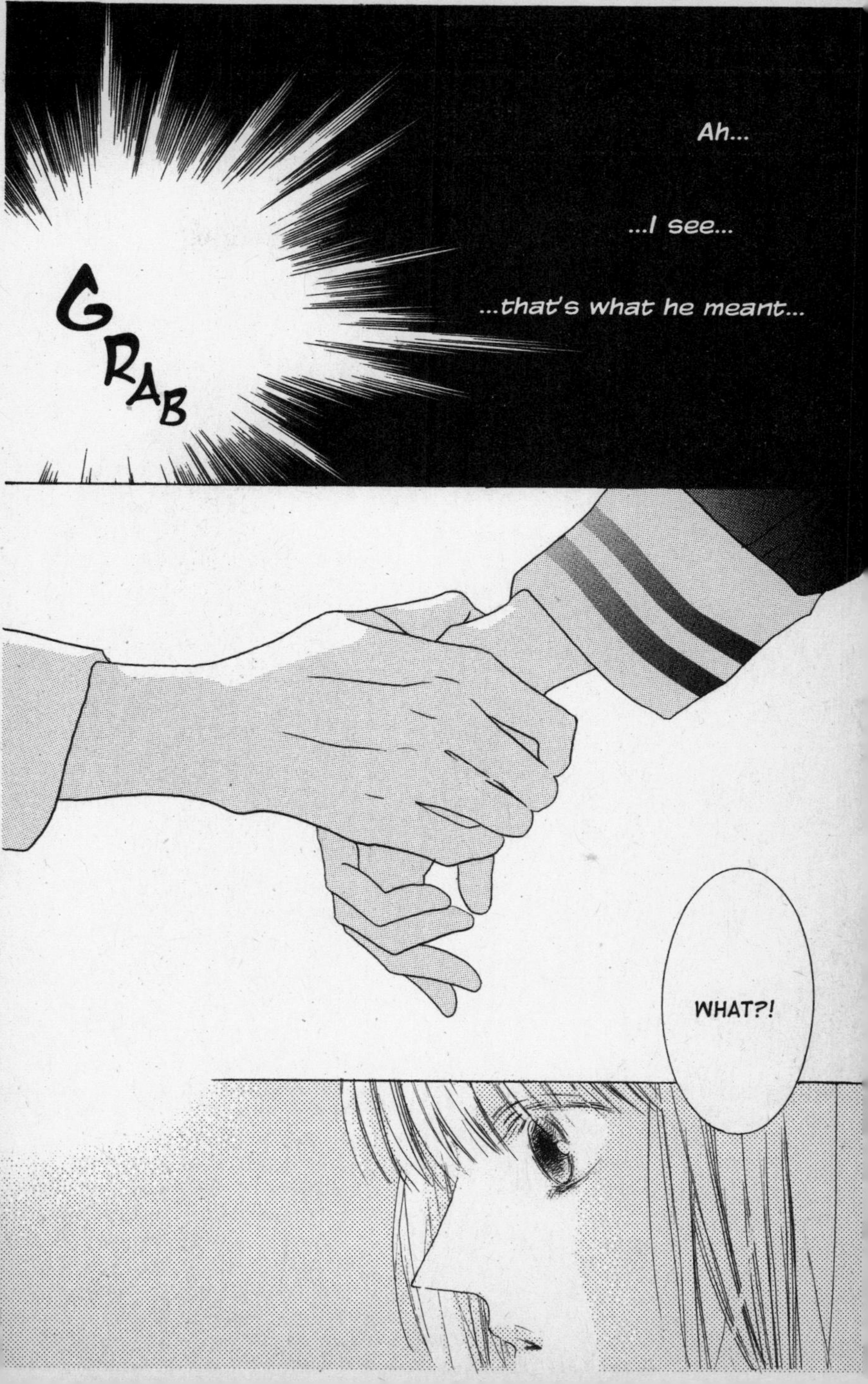
Ah...
...I see...
...that's what he meant...
GRAB
WHAT?!

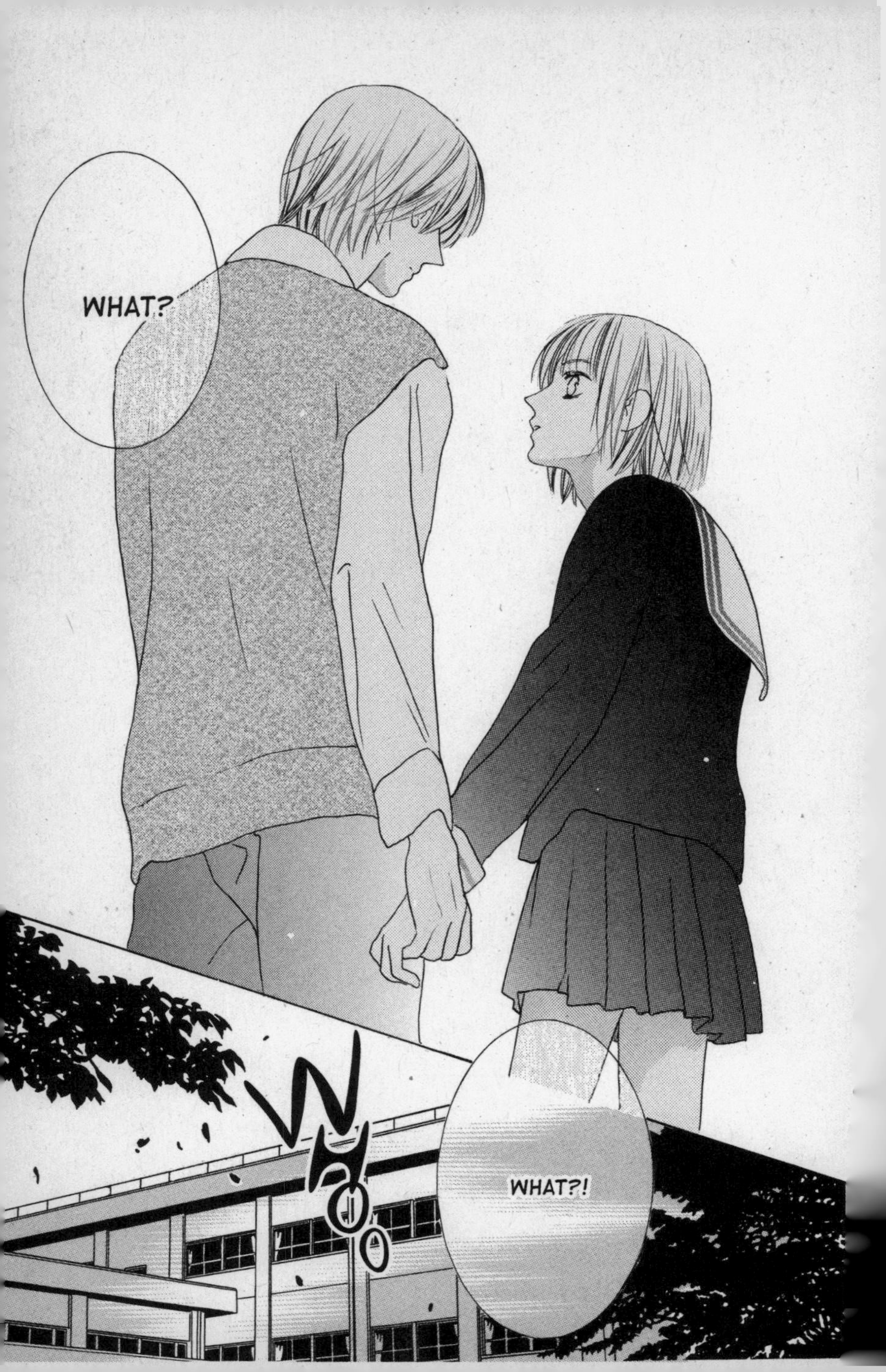
WHAT?
WHAT?!
WHOO

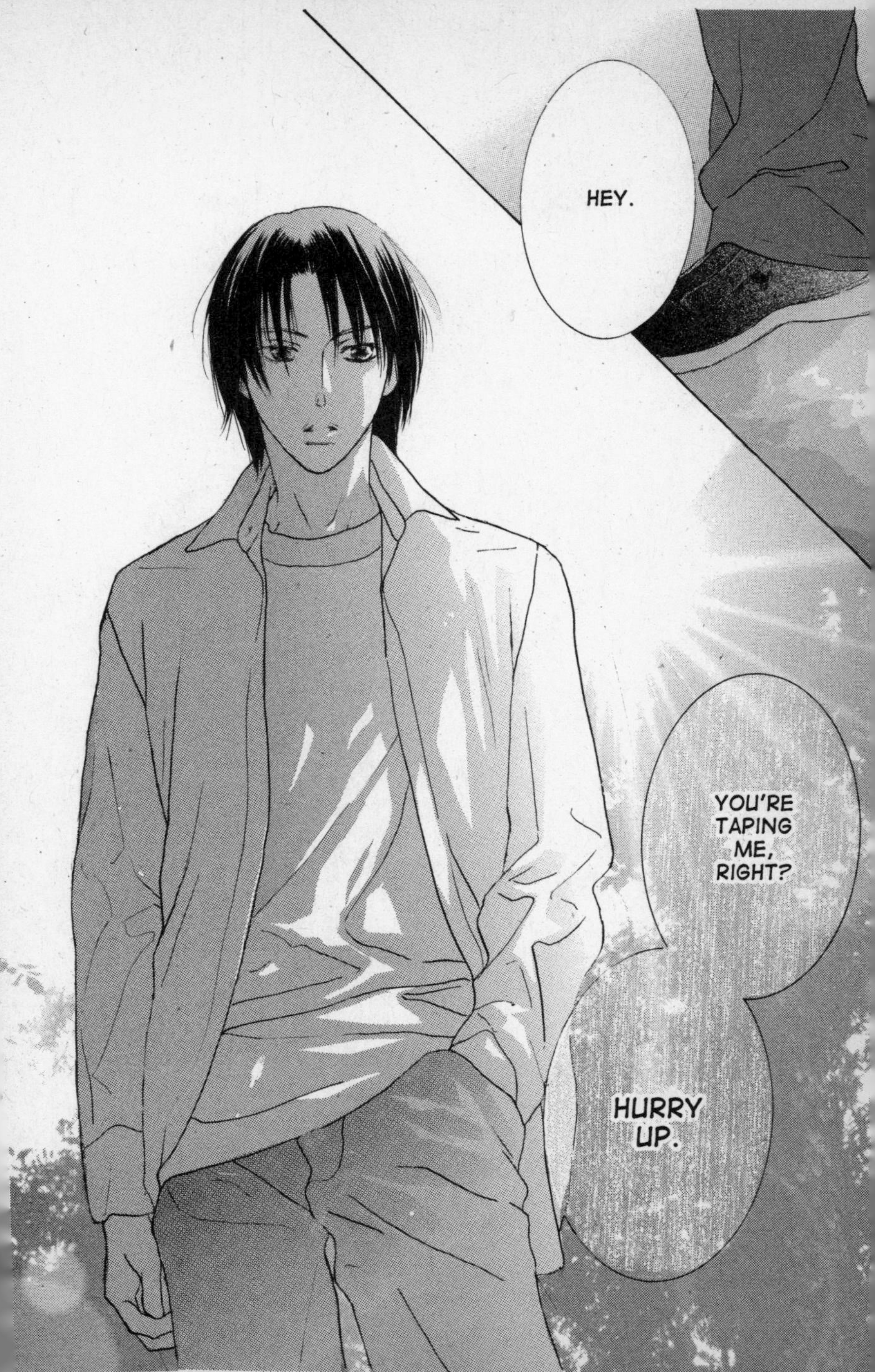
HEY.
YOU'RE TAPING ME, RIGHT?
HURRY UP.

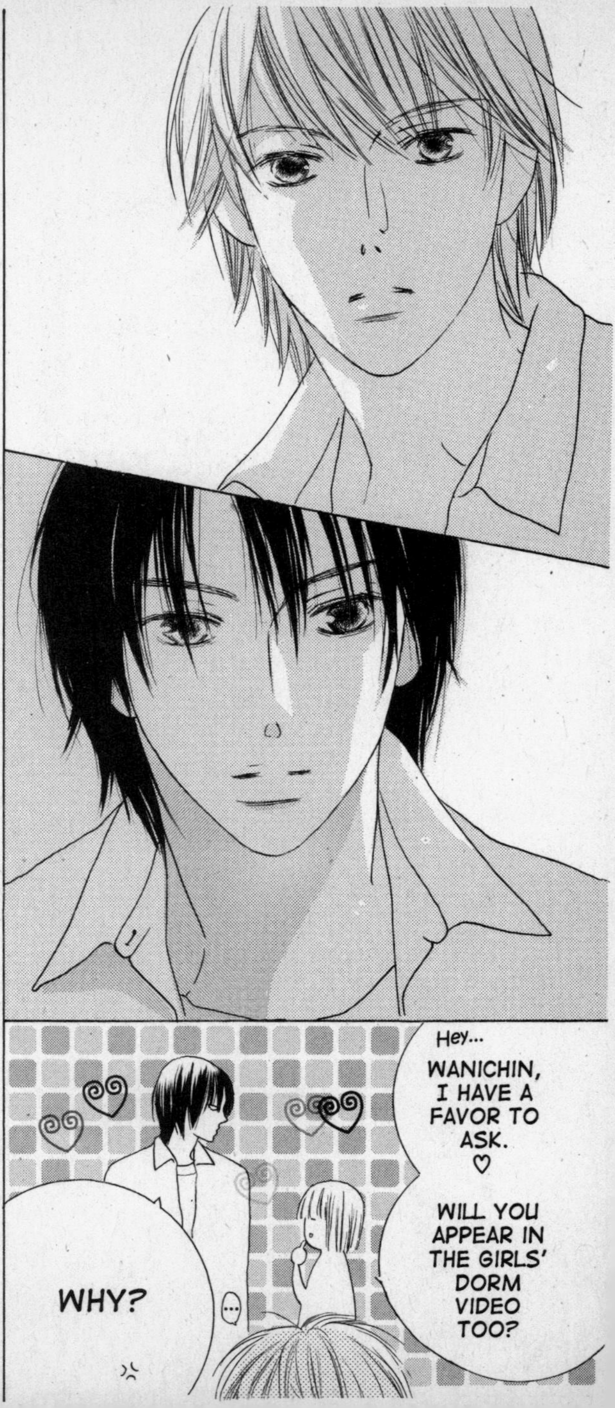
Hey...
WANICHIN, I HAVE A FAVOR TO ASK. ♡
WILL YOU APPEAR IN THE GIRLS' DORM VIDEO TOO?
...
WHY?

The new character, Shimonuki has appeared.

I had him appear because Wanibuu just doesn't do anything, but for some reason, he is very popular. Really. In some cases, Shimonuki may be more popular than Wanibuu.

Is it because he's such a good person overall? Wow, Simone. For me, a perfect, nice guy is a little difficult to draw, but I can't take my eyes off him because he's having so much trouble... It turns out now that he's the hottest character. Ha ha ha.

Eimi is the most popular character. "She's so cute! I want a younger sister like that!" are the comments I get. Your family will be really fatigued dealing with her, so I don't recommend it. Yes.

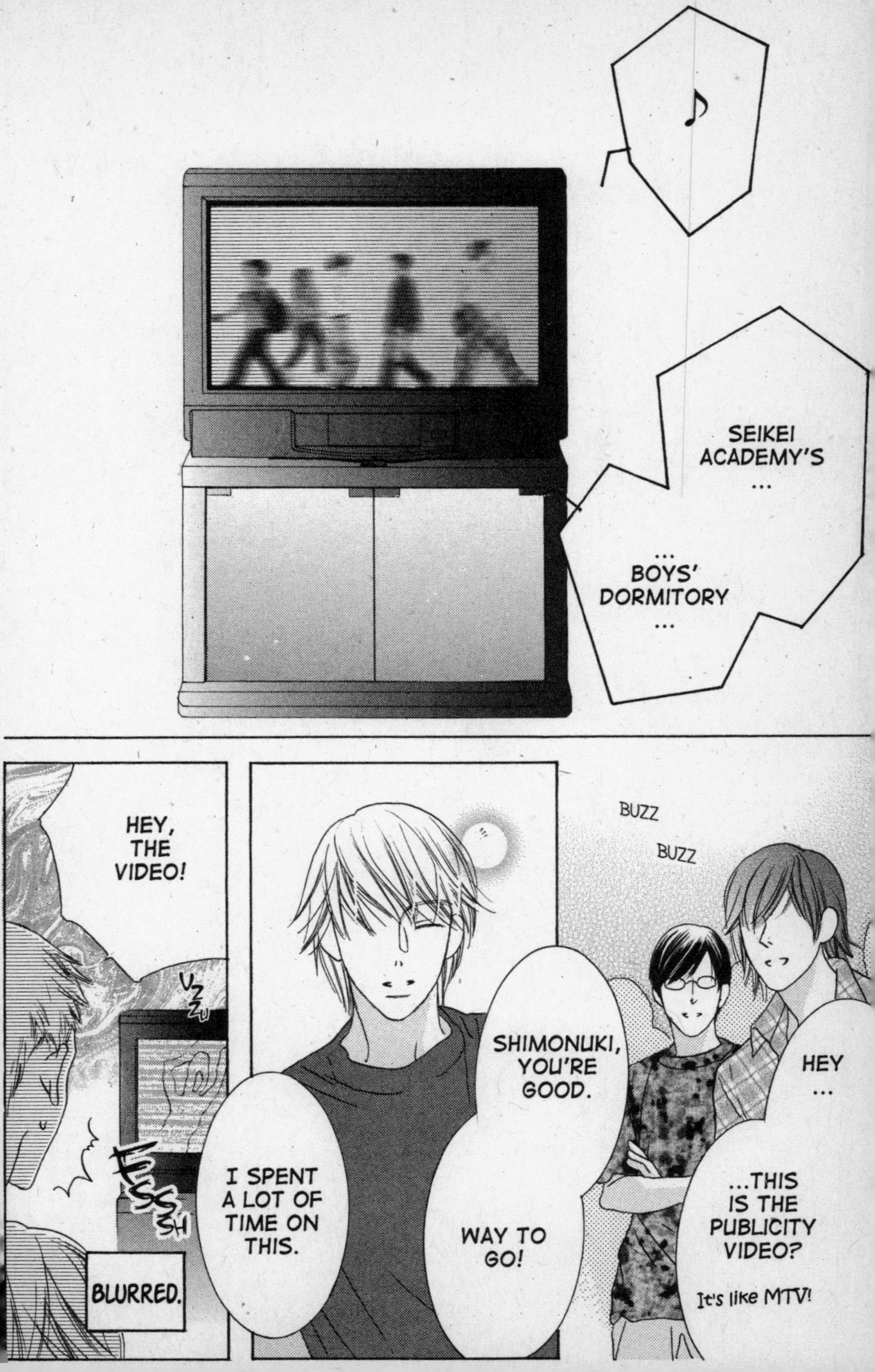
♪
SEIKEI ACADEMY'S ...
... BOYS' DORMITORY ...
BUZZ
BUZZ
HEY ...
...THIS IS THE PUBLICITY VIDEO?
It's like MTV!
SHIMONUKI, YOU'RE GOOD.
WAY TO GO!
I SPENT A LOT OF TIME ON THIS.
HEY, THE VIDEO!
BLURRED.

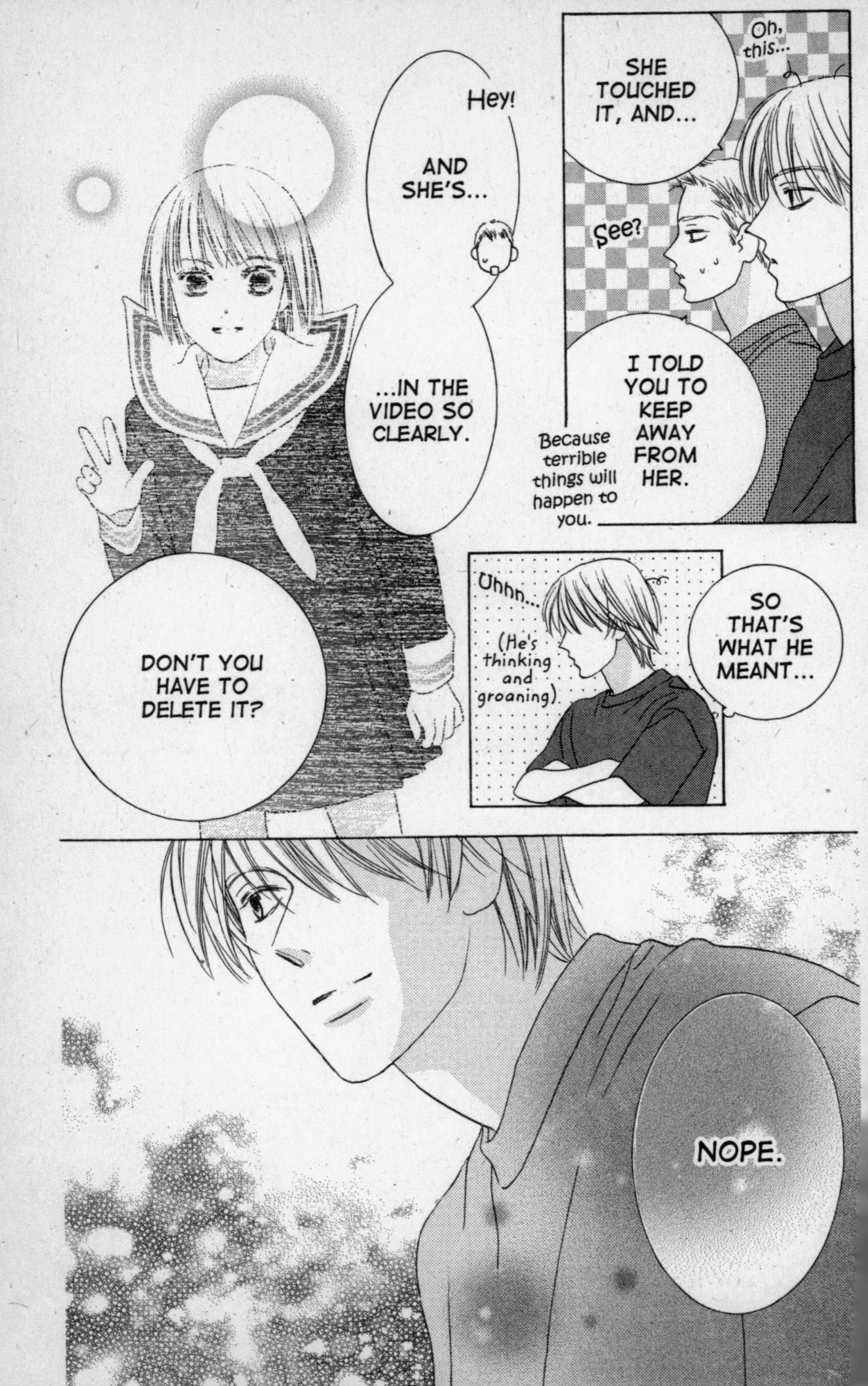
Oh, this...
SHE TOUCHED IT, AND...
See?
I TOLD YOU TO KEEP AWAY FROM HER.
Because terrible things will happen to you.
SO THAT'S WHAT HE MEANT...
Uhhn...
(He's thinking and groaning)
Hey!
AND SHE'S...
...IN THE VIDEO SO CLEARLY.
DON'T YOU HAVE TO DELETE IT?
NOPE.

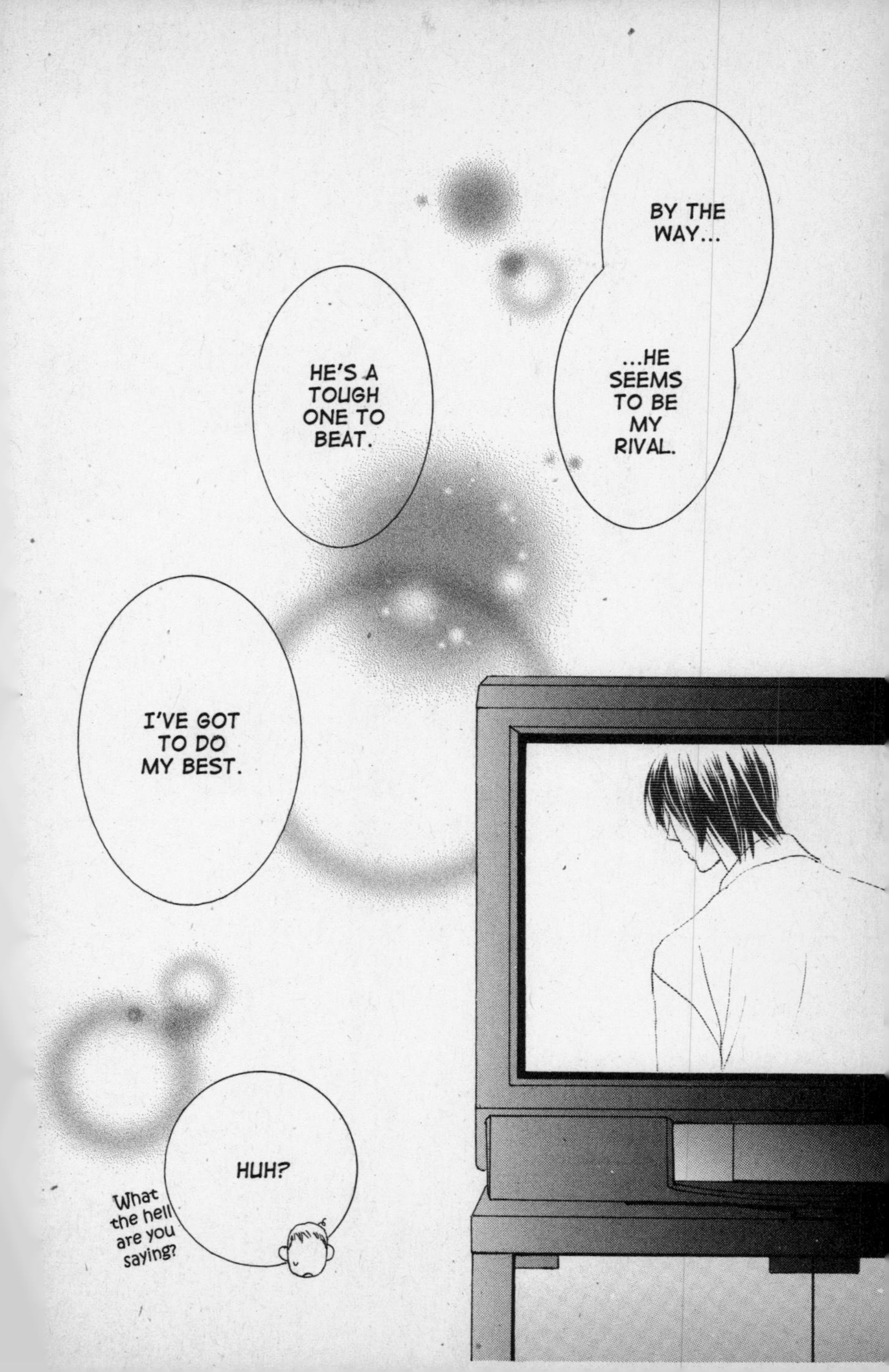
BY THE WAY...
...HE SEEMS TO BE MY RIVAL.
HE'S A TOUGH ONE TO BEAT.
I'VE GOT TO DO MY BEST.
HUH?
What the hell are you saying?

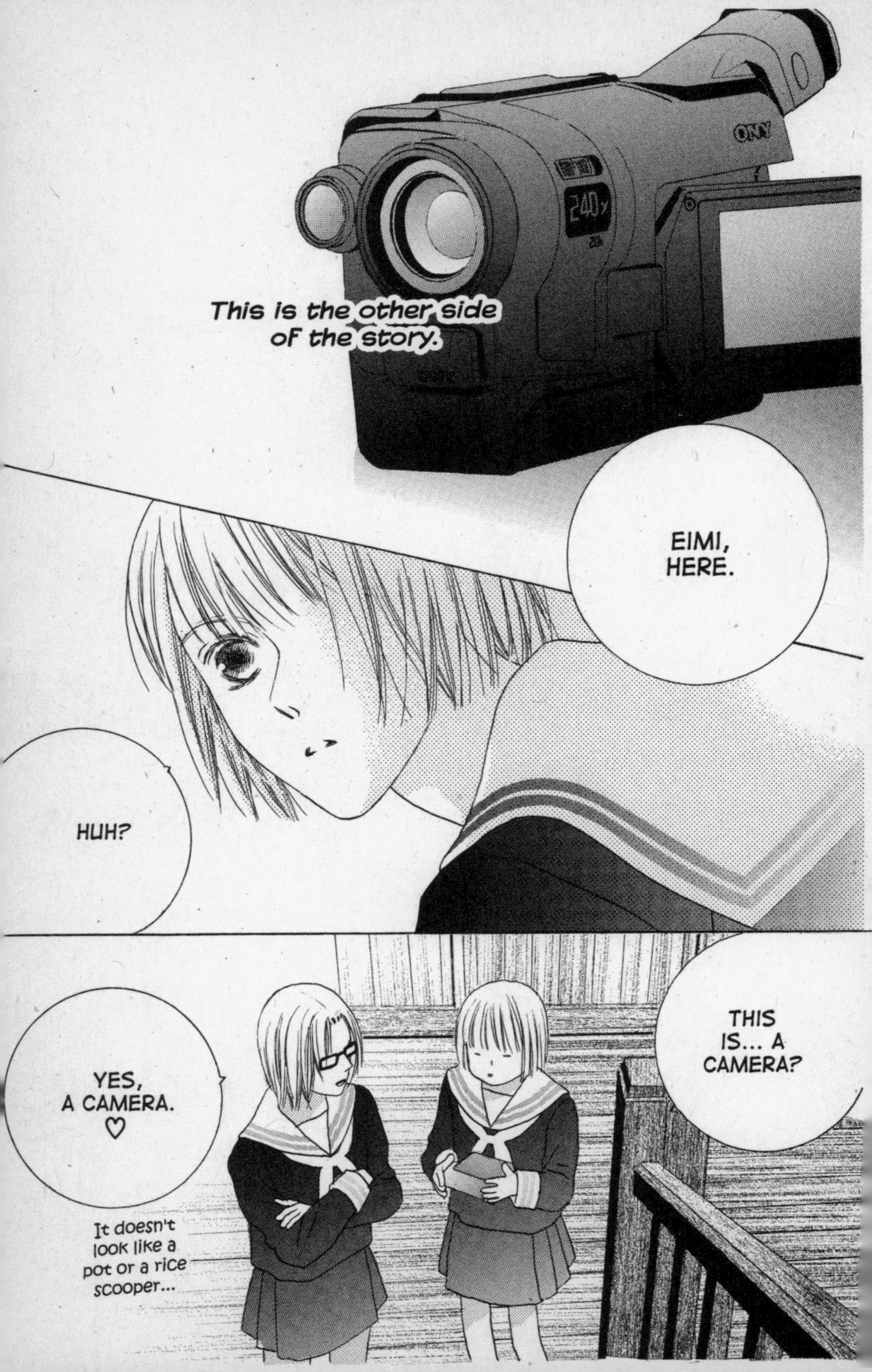
This is the other side of the story.
EIMI, HERE.
HUH?
THIS IS... A CAMERA?
YES, A CAMERA. ♡
It doesn't look like a pot or a rice scooper...

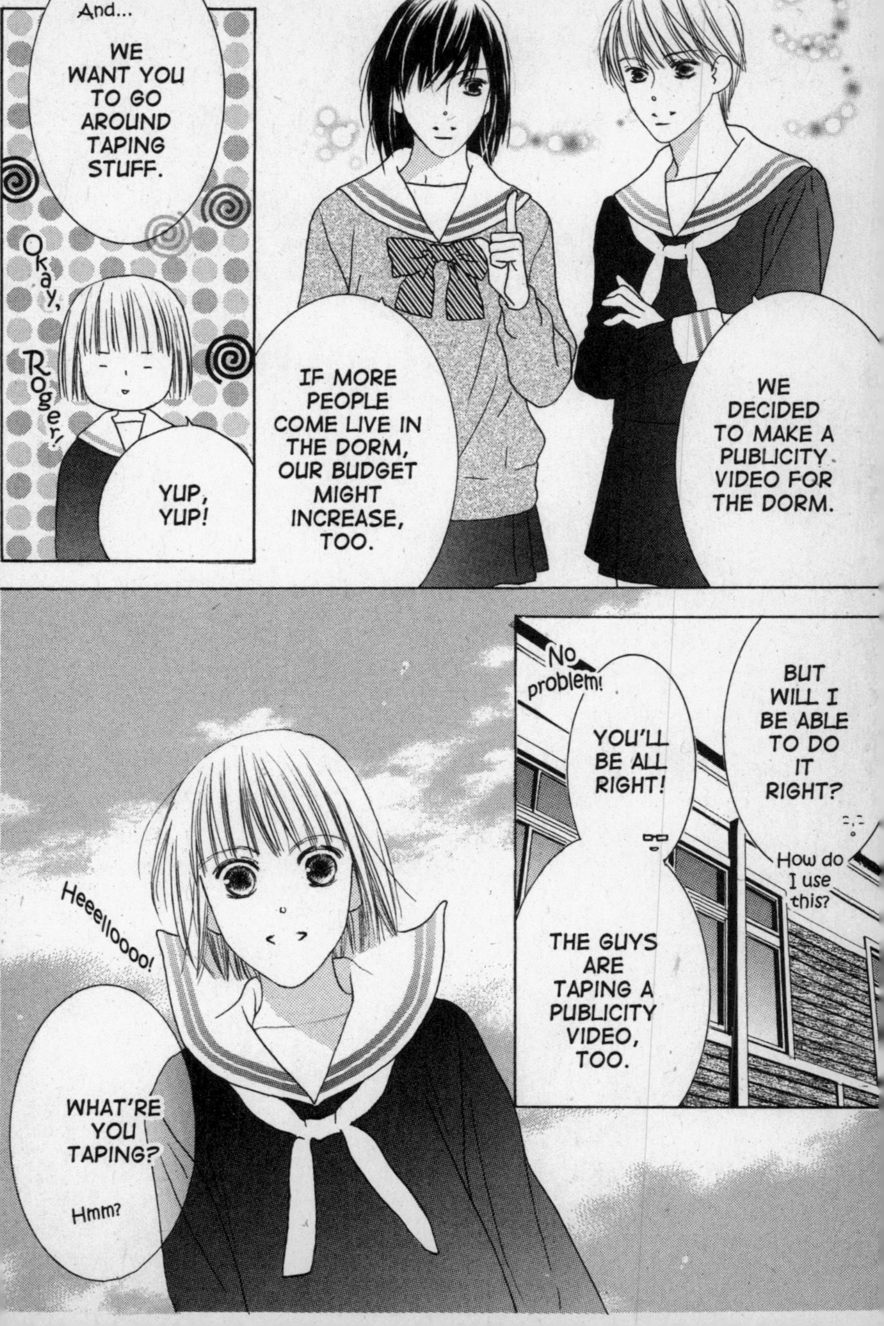
WE DECIDED TO MAKE A PUBLICITY VIDEO FOR THE DORM.
IF MORE PEOPLE COME LIVE IN THE DORM, OUR BUDGET MIGHT INCREASE, TOO.
And... WE WANT YOU TO GO AROUND TAPING STUFF.
Okay, Roger!
YUP, YUP!
BUT WILL I BE ABLE TO DO IT RIGHT?
How do I use this?
No problem!
YOU'LL BE ALL RIGHT!
THE GUYS ARE TAPING A PUBLICITY VIDEO, TOO.
Heeellooooo!
WHAT'RE YOU TAPING?
Hmm?

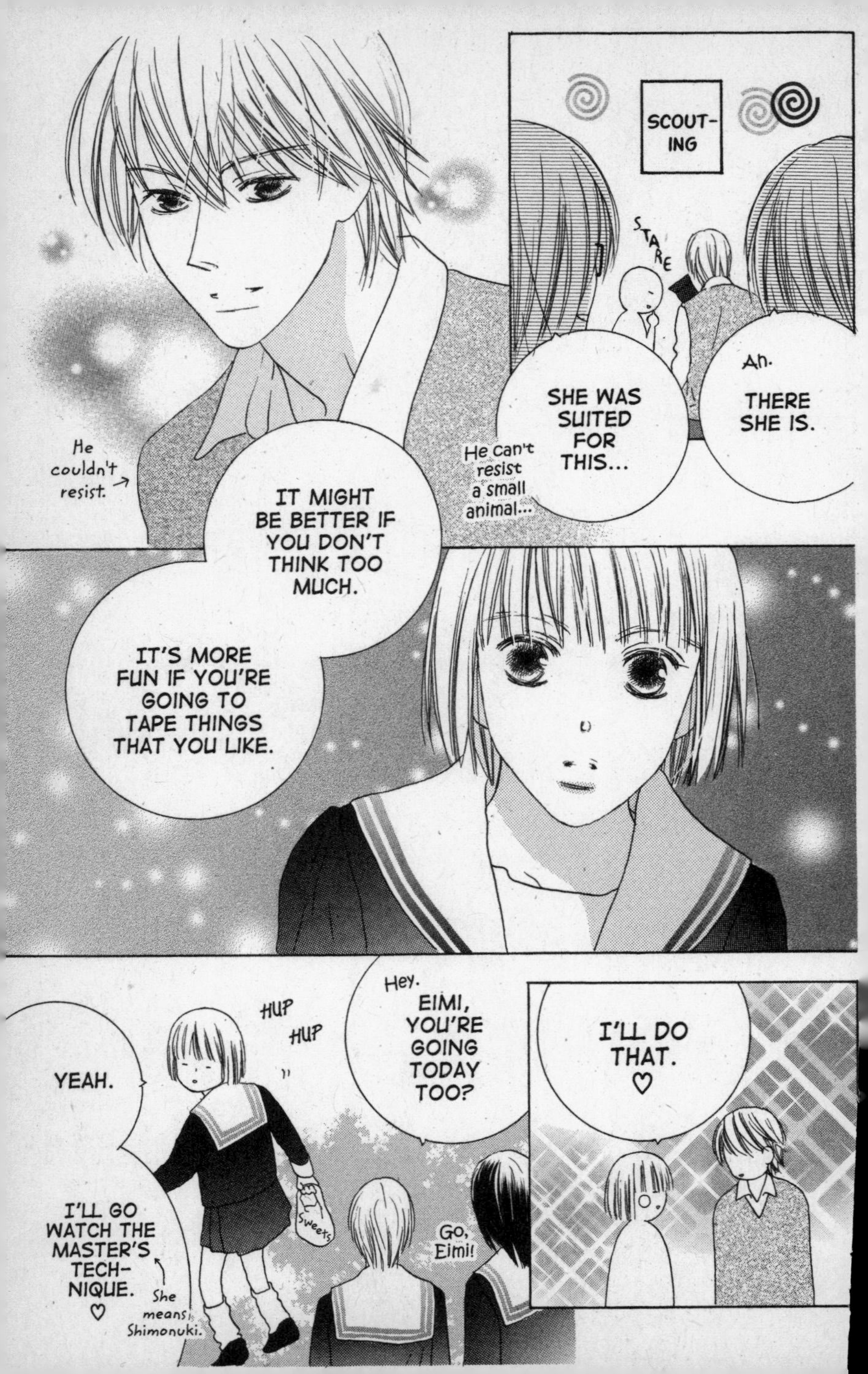
SCOUTING
STARE
Ah.
THERE SHE IS.
SHE WAS SUITED FOR THIS...
He can't resist a small animal...
He couldn't resist.
IT MIGHT BE BETTER IF YOU DON'T THINK TOO MUCH.
IT'S MORE FUN IF YOU'RE GOING TO TAPE THINGS THAT YOU LIKE.
I'LL DO THAT. ♡
Hey.
EIMI, YOU'RE GOING TODAY TOO?
HUP HUP
YEAH.
Go, Eimi!
Sweets
I'LL GO WATCH THE MASTER'S TECHNIQUE. ♡
She means Shimonuki.

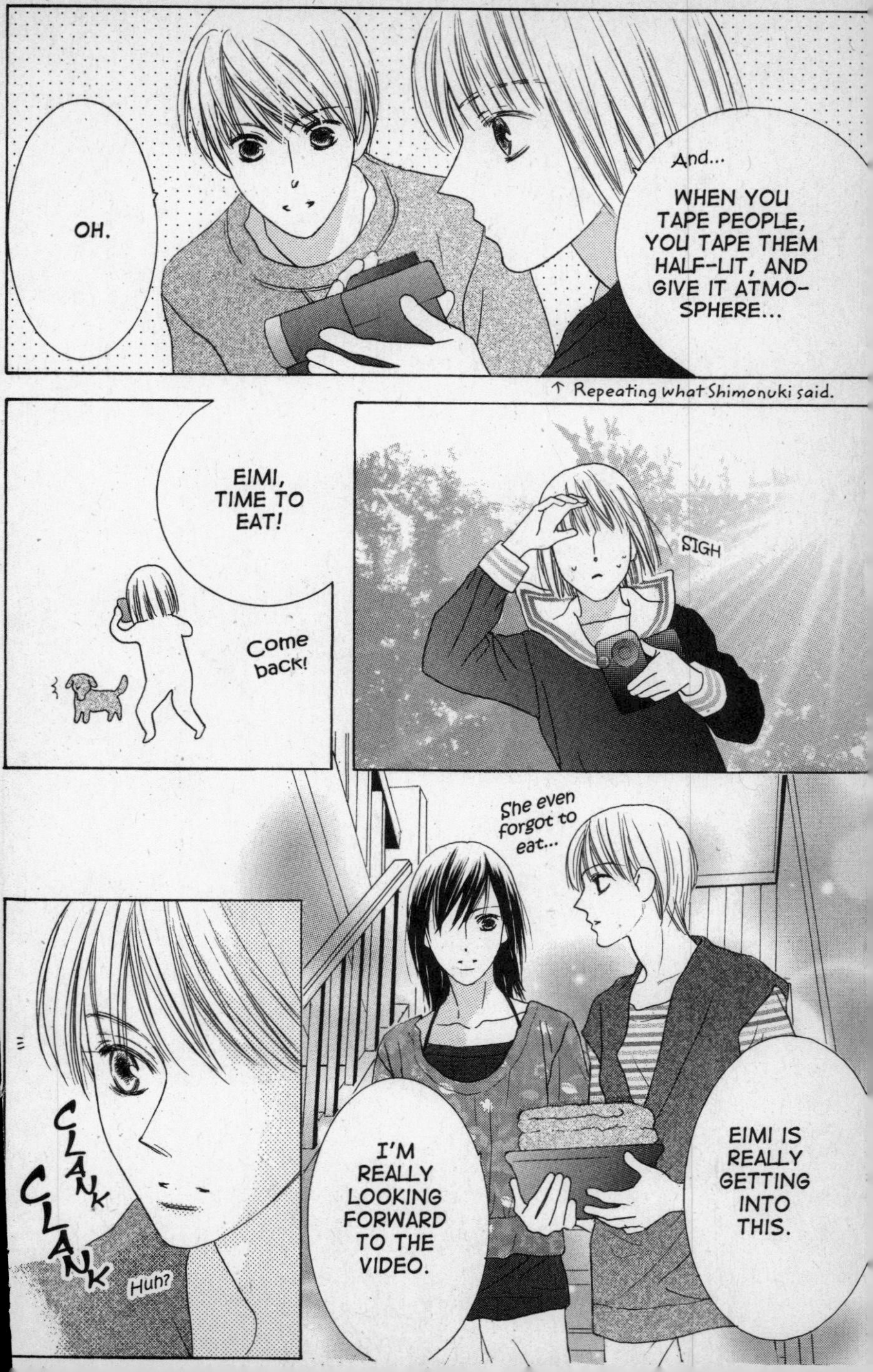
And...
WHEN YOU TAPE PEOPLE, YOU TAPE THEM HALF-LIT, AND GIVE IT ATMO-SPHERE...
OH.
↑ Repeating what Shimonuki said.
SIGH
EIMI, TIME TO EAT!
Come back!
She even forgot to eat...
EIMI IS REALLY GETTING INTO THIS.
I'M REALLY LOOKING FORWARD TO THE VIDEO.
CLANK
CLANK
Huh?

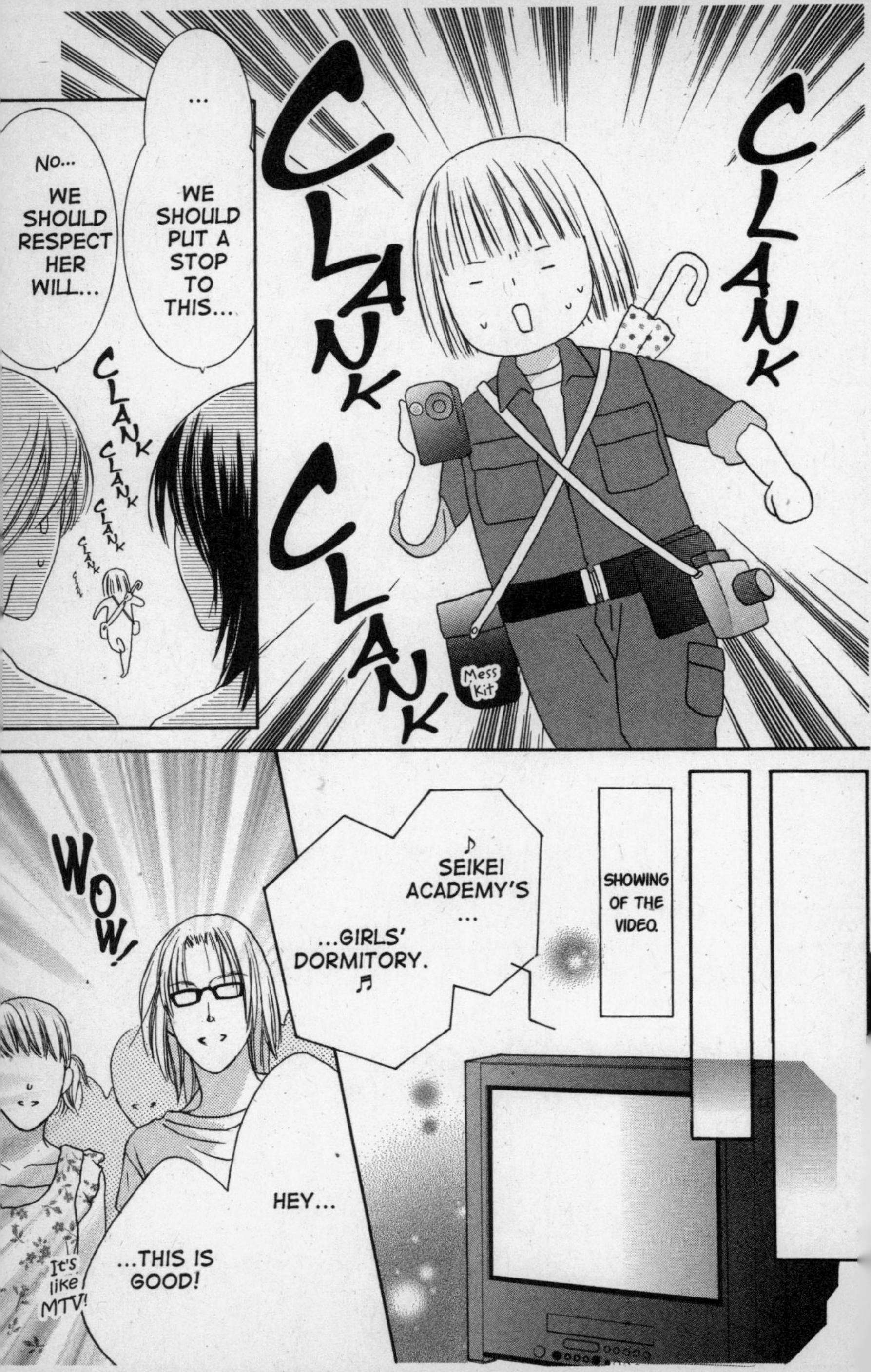
CLANK
CLANK
CLANK
Mess Kit
...
WE SHOULD PUT A STOP TO THIS...
No...
WE SHOULD RESPECT HER WILL...
CLANK
CLANK
CLANK
SHOWING OF THE VIDEO.
♪ SEIKEI ACADEMY'S ...
...GIRLS' DORMITORY. ♬
WOW!
HEY...
...THIS IS GOOD!
It's like MTV!

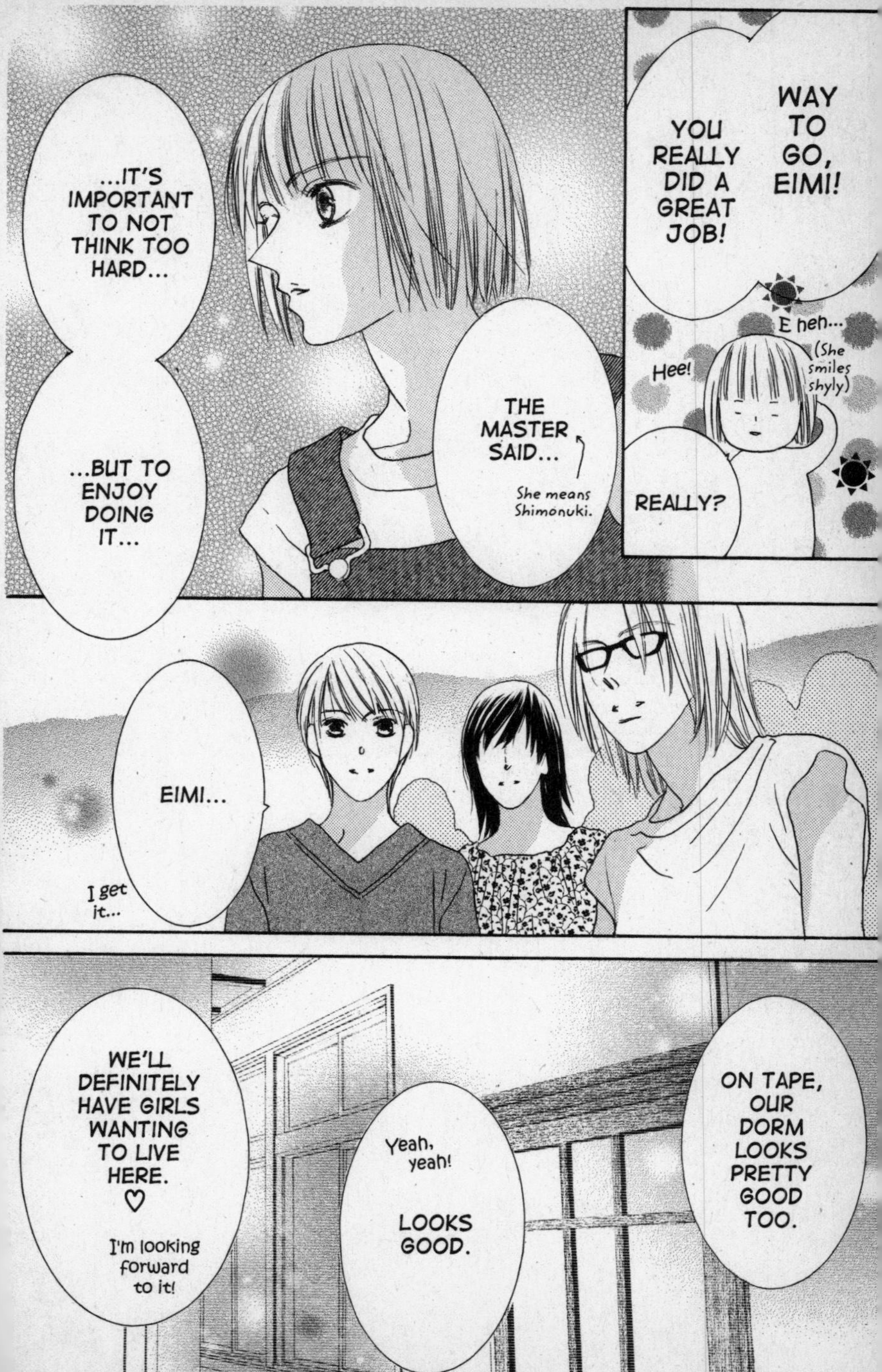
WAY TO GO, EIMI!
YOU REALLY DID A GREAT JOB!
E heh...
(She smiles shyly)
Hee!
REALLY?
THE MASTER SAID...
She means Shimonuki.
...IT'S IMPORTANT TO NOT THINK TOO HARD...
...BUT TO ENJOY DOING IT...
EIMI...
I get it...
ON TAPE, OUR DORM LOOKS PRETTY GOOD TOO.
Yeah, yeah!
LOOKS GOOD.
WE'LL DEFINITELY HAVE GIRLS WANTING TO LIVE HERE. ♡
I'm looking forward to it!

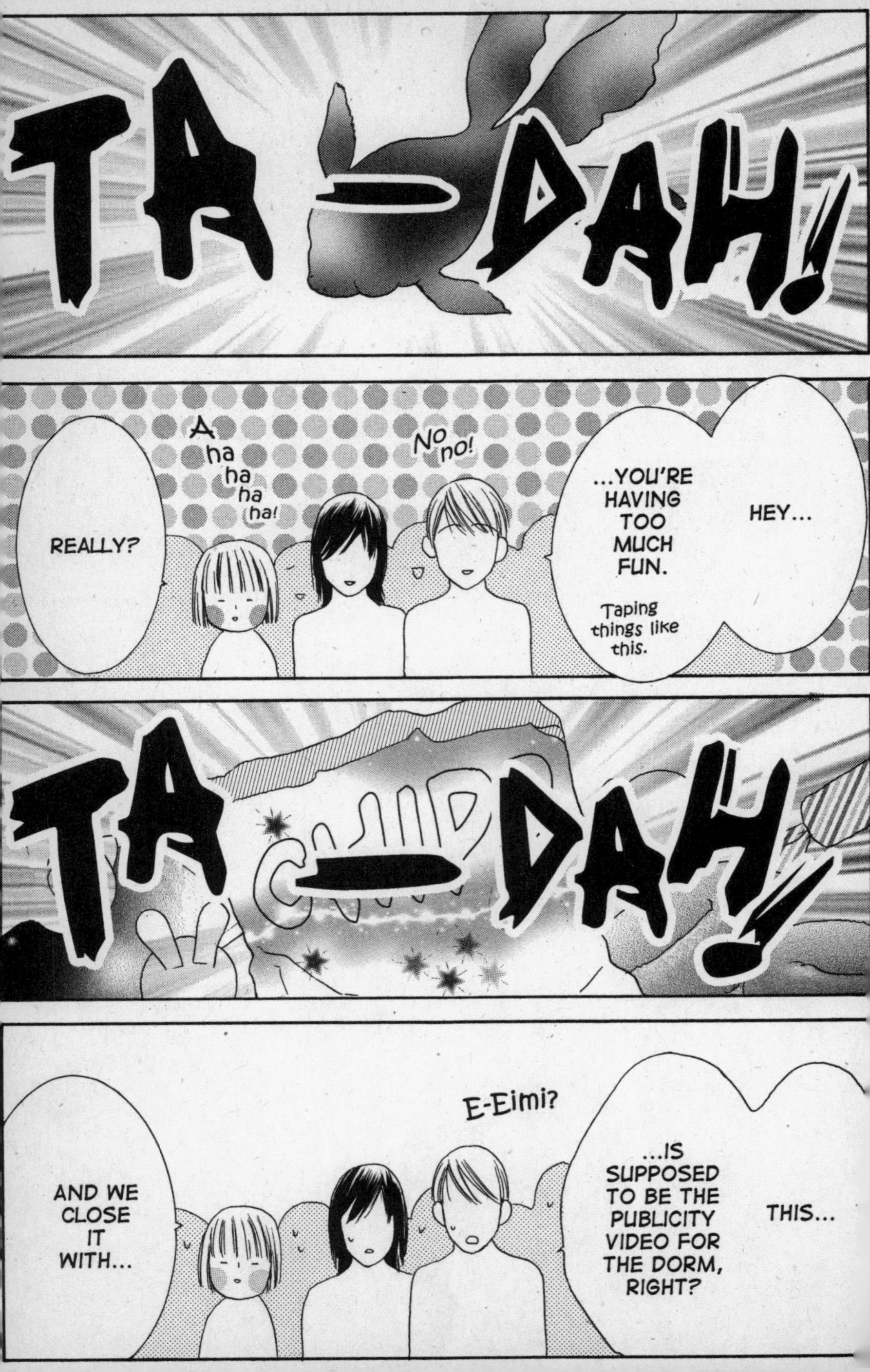
TA-DAH!
HEY...
...YOU'RE HAVING TOO MUCH FUN.
Taping things like this.
No no!
A ha ha ha ha!
REALLY?
TA-DAH!
THIS...
...IS SUPPOSED TO BE THE PUBLICITY VIDEO FOR THE DORM, RIGHT?
E-Eimi?
AND WE CLOSE IT WITH...

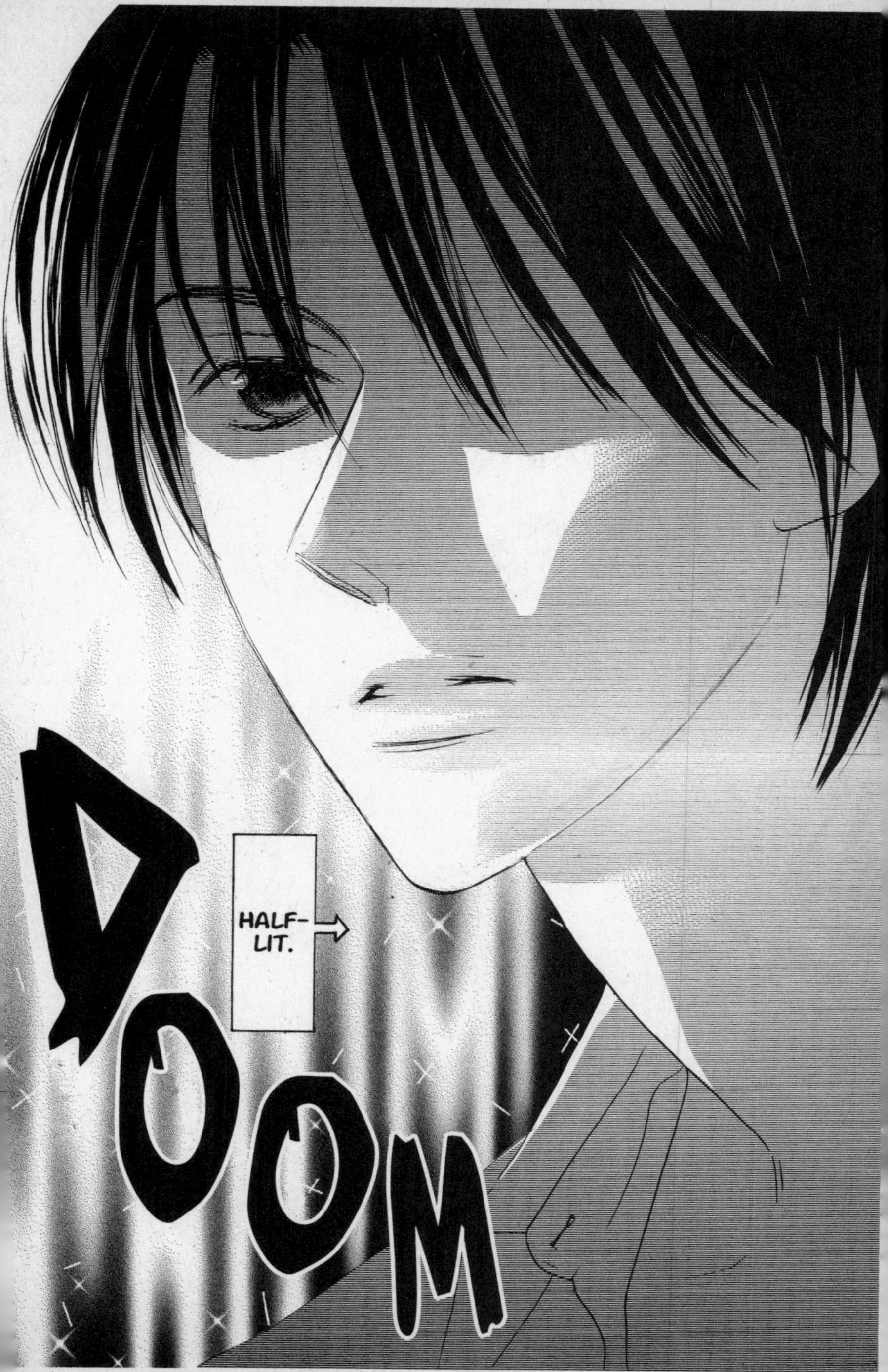
HALF-LIT.
DOOM

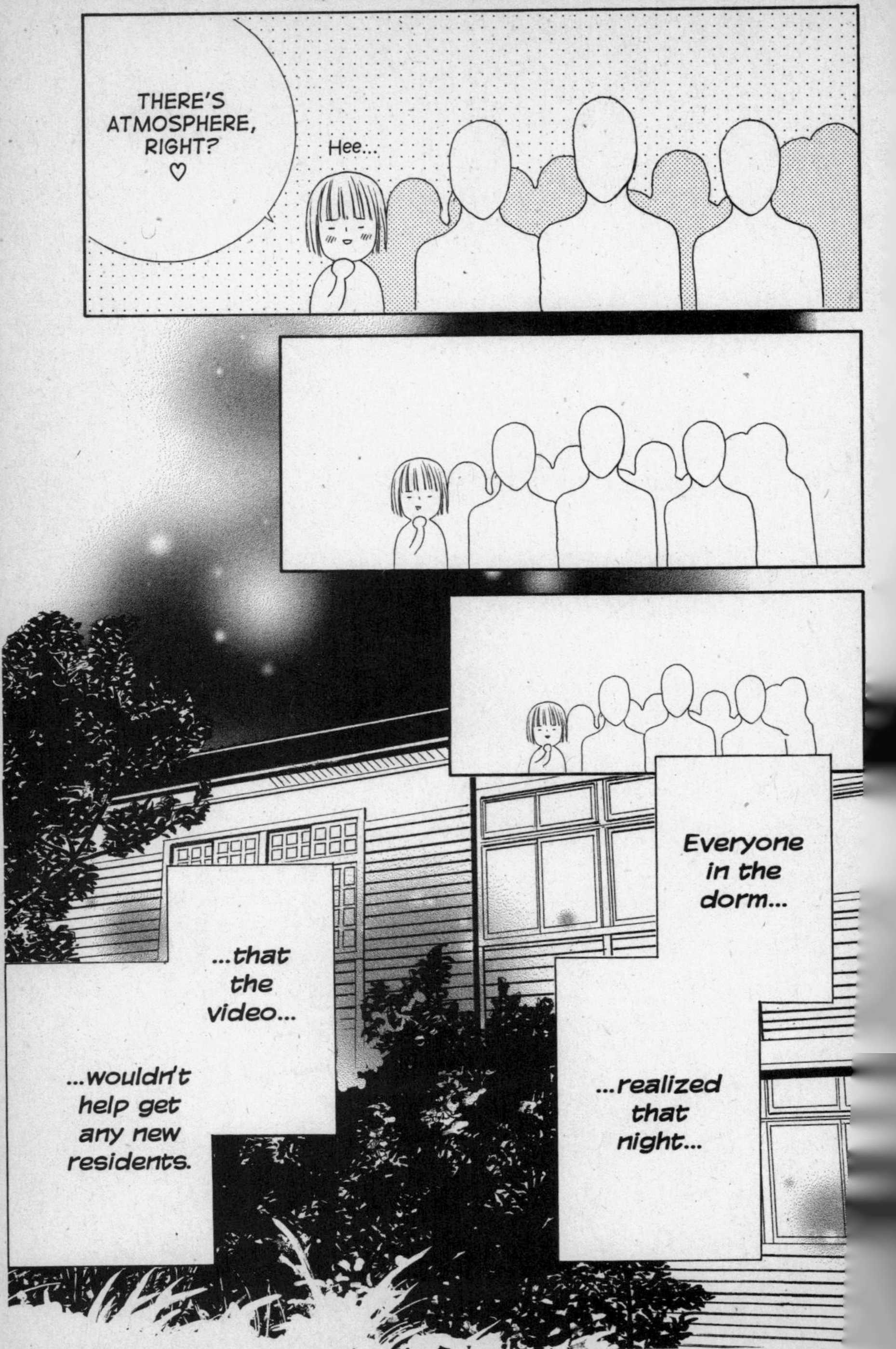
THERE'S ATMOSPHERE, RIGHT? ♡
Hee...
Everyone in the dorm...
...realized that night...
...that the video...
...wouldn't help get any new residents.

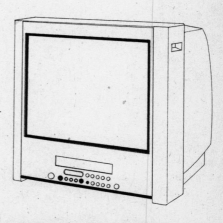

BEAUTY IS THE BEAST

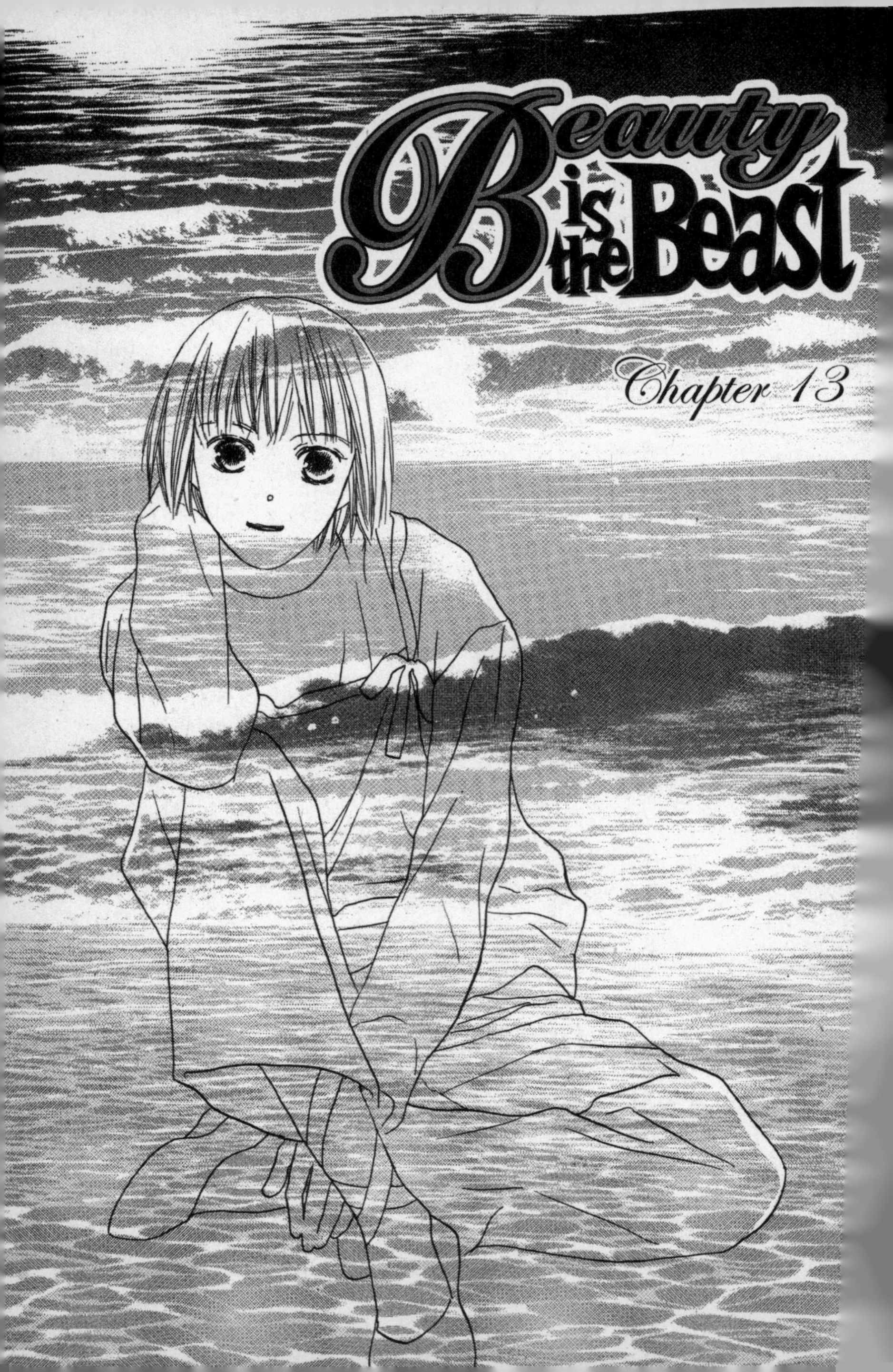
Beauty is the Beast
Chapter 13

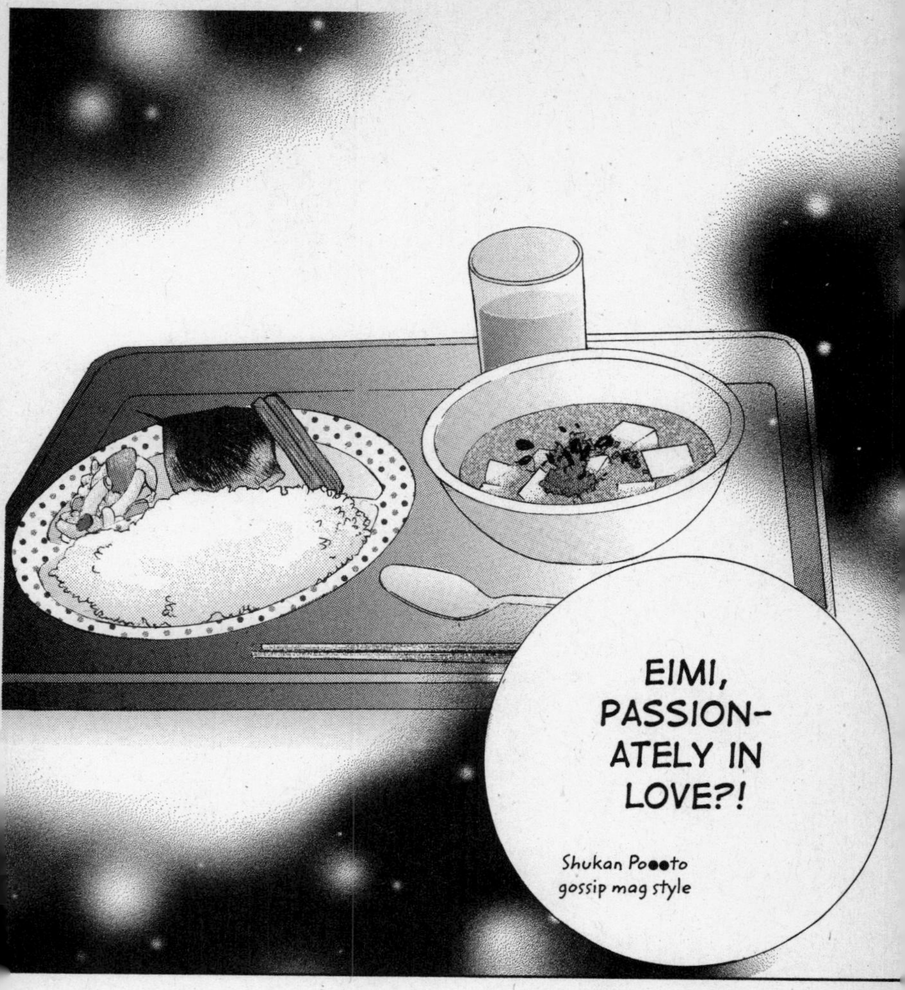
EIMI, PASSION-ATELY IN LOVE?!
Shukan Po●●to gossip mag style

Aaliyah/MISS YOU

I still can't draw Wanibuchi-kun well, and I always have trouble with the storyboards where he appears. I get impatient and impatient, and when I think "What should I do?!" I listen to this. Then, for some reason, I calm down.
I call this Wanichin's theme (...)
The song is like the quiet time right before sunrise.

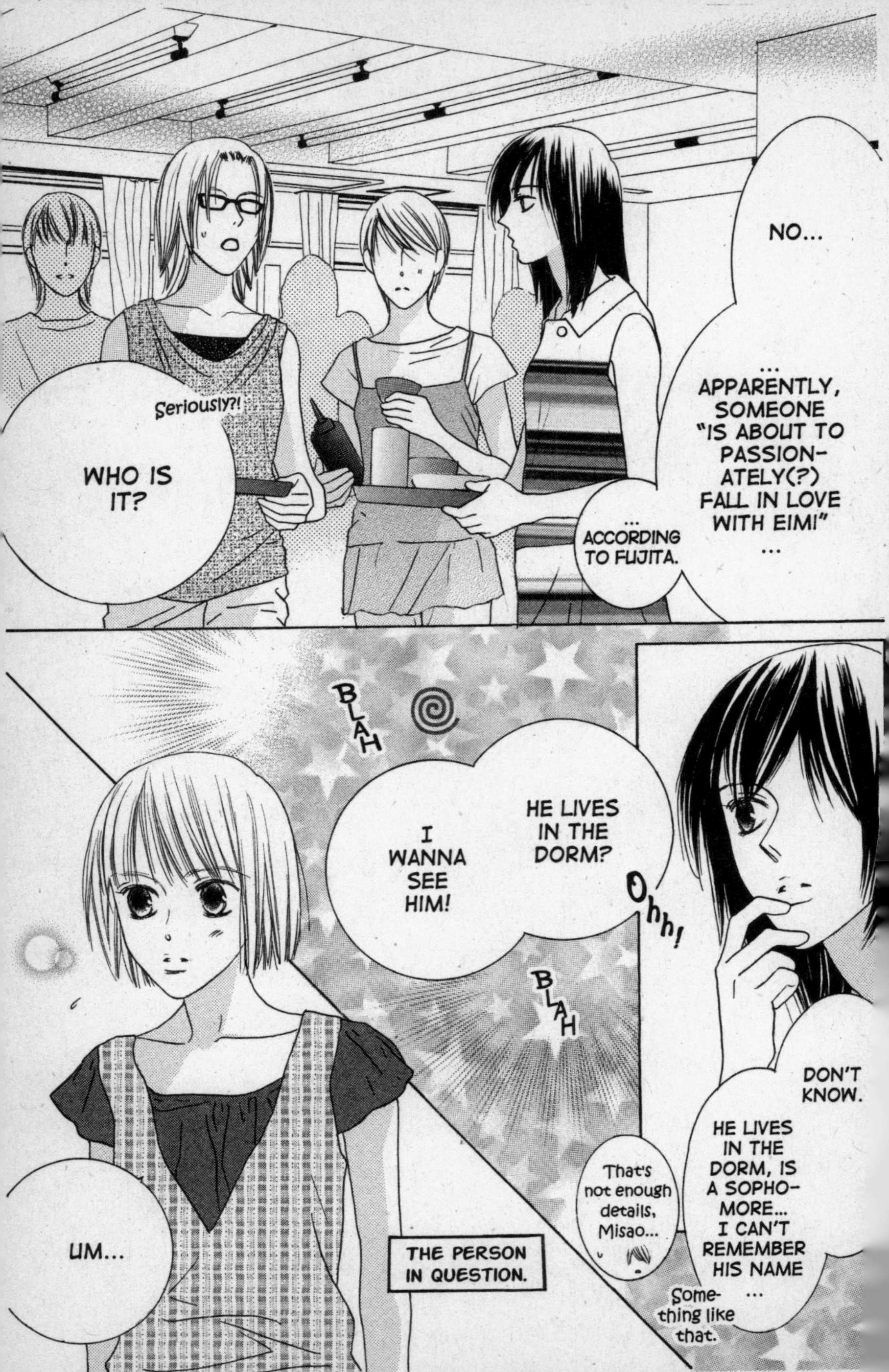
NO...
... APPARENTLY, SOMEONE "IS ABOUT TO PASSION-ATELY(?) FALL IN LOVE WITH EIMI" ...
... ACCORDING TO FUJITA.
Seriously?!
WHO IS IT?
DON'T KNOW.
HE LIVES IN THE DORM, IS A SOPHO-MORE... I CAN'T REMEMBER HIS NAME ...
Some-thing like that.
That's not enough details, Misao...
Ohh!
HE LIVES IN THE DORM?
I WANNA SEE HIM!
BLAH
BLAH
THE PERSON IN QUESTION.
UM...

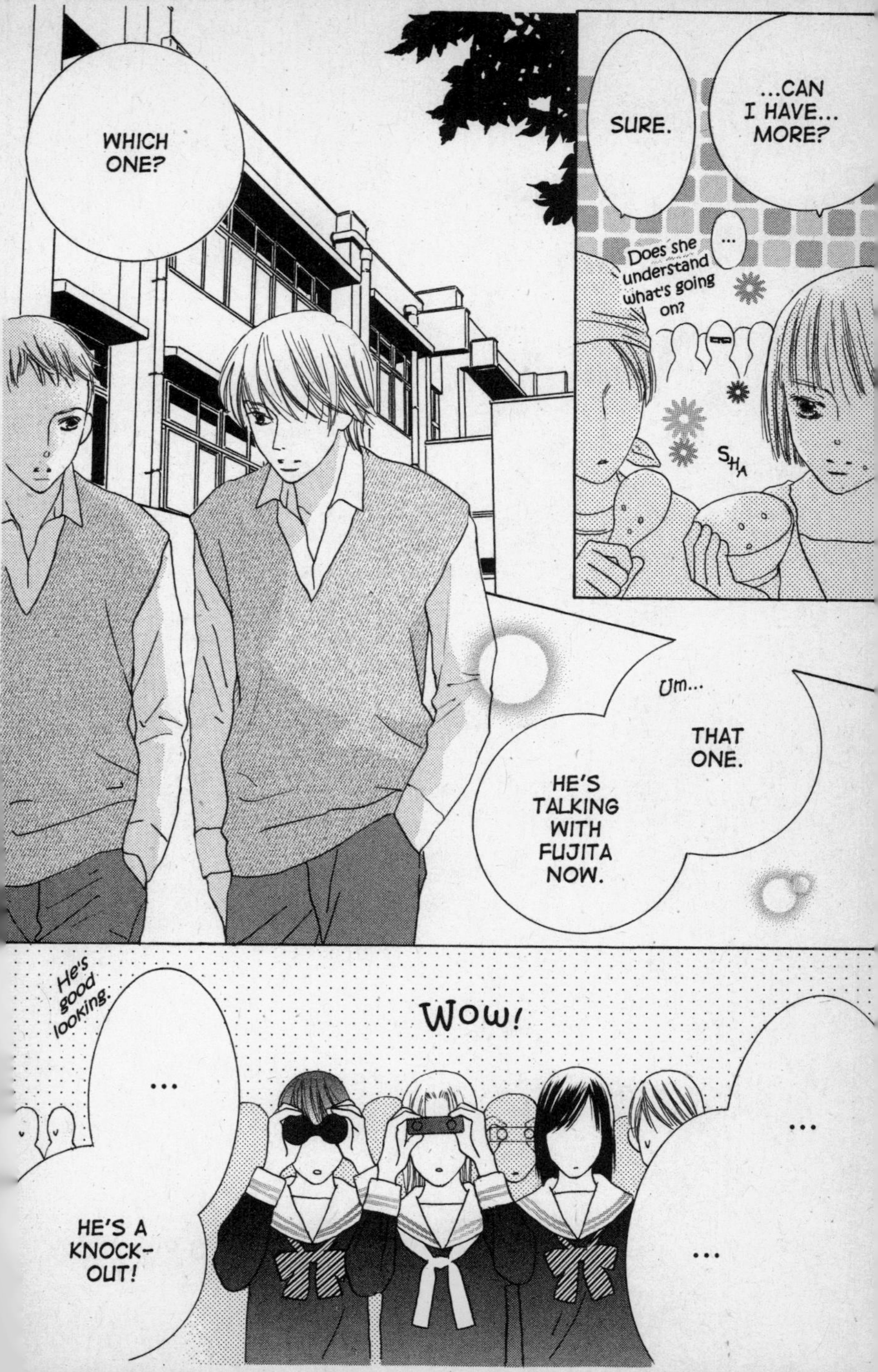
...CAN I HAVE... MORE?
SURE.
...
Does she understand what's going on?
SHA
WHICH ONE?
Um...
THAT ONE.
HE'S TALKING WITH FUJITA NOW.
...
...
WOW!
...
HE'S A KNOCKOUT!
He's good looking.

The clothes Eimi is wearing (worn-out T-shirt and pants) are just what I wear. Ha ha ha.

But I really love looking at and wearing clothes!! I may be the type to try out different clothes.
I look at what the salespeople are wearing and do research on how to dress up (long and hard), and when I decide that I'll buy a mini-skirt, I walk around so much I feel like throwing up (geez). But I have fun. My personality is slovenly, but I don't shop like "all right, I'll compromise with this." I don't buy things until I find the ones that I really want!! (Pant pant)

I say all this, but I usually wear worn-out T-shirts and pants... because I'm slovenly?

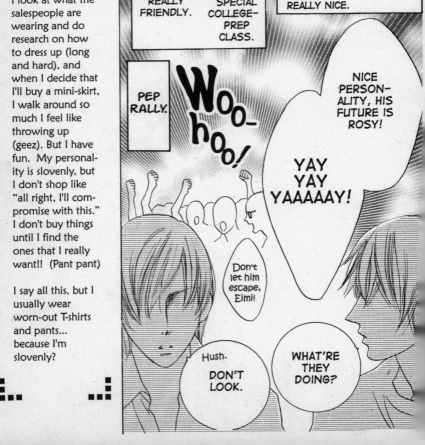

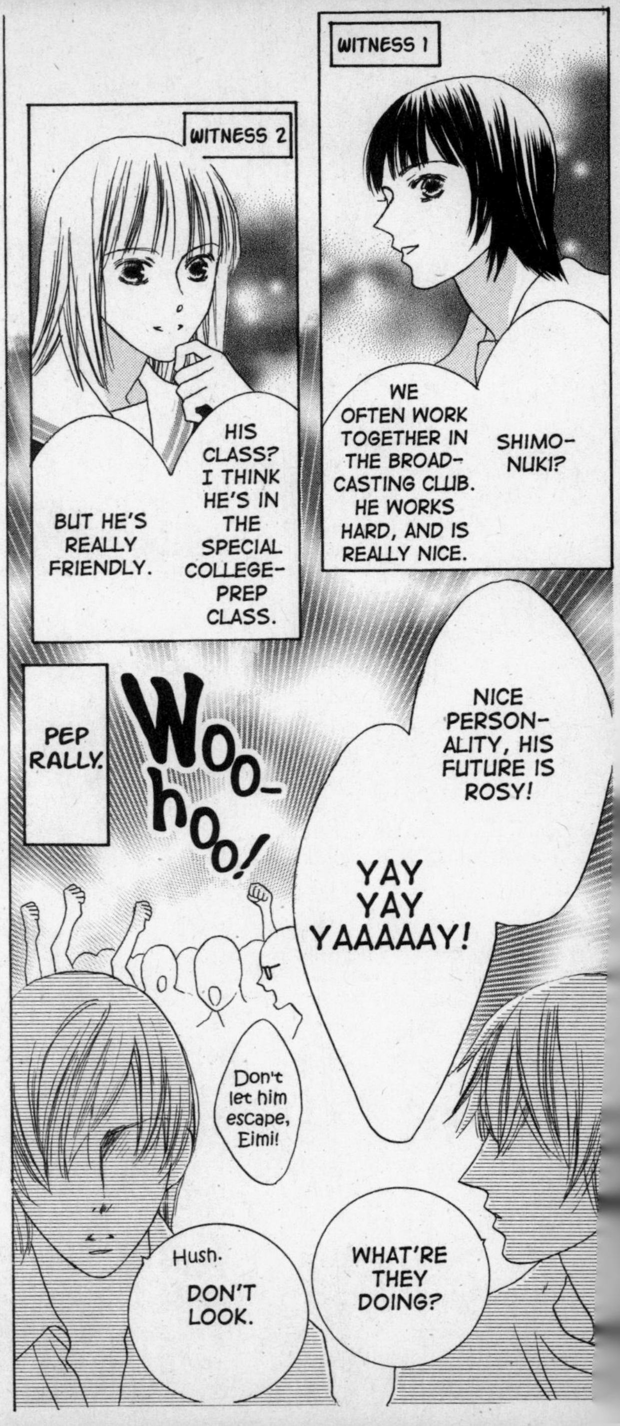
WITNESS 1
SHIMO-NUKI?
WE OFTEN WORK TOGETHER IN THE BROAD-CASTING CLUB. HE WORKS HARD, AND IS REALLY NICE.
WITNESS 2
HIS CLASS? I THINK HE'S IN THE SPECIAL COLLEGE-PREP CLASS.
BUT HE'S REALLY FRIENDLY.
NICE PERSON-ALITY, HIS FUTURE IS ROSY!
YAY YAY YAAAAAY!
Woo-hoo!
PEP RALLY.
WHAT'RE THEY DOING?
Don't let him escape, Eimi!
Hush.
DON'T LOOK.

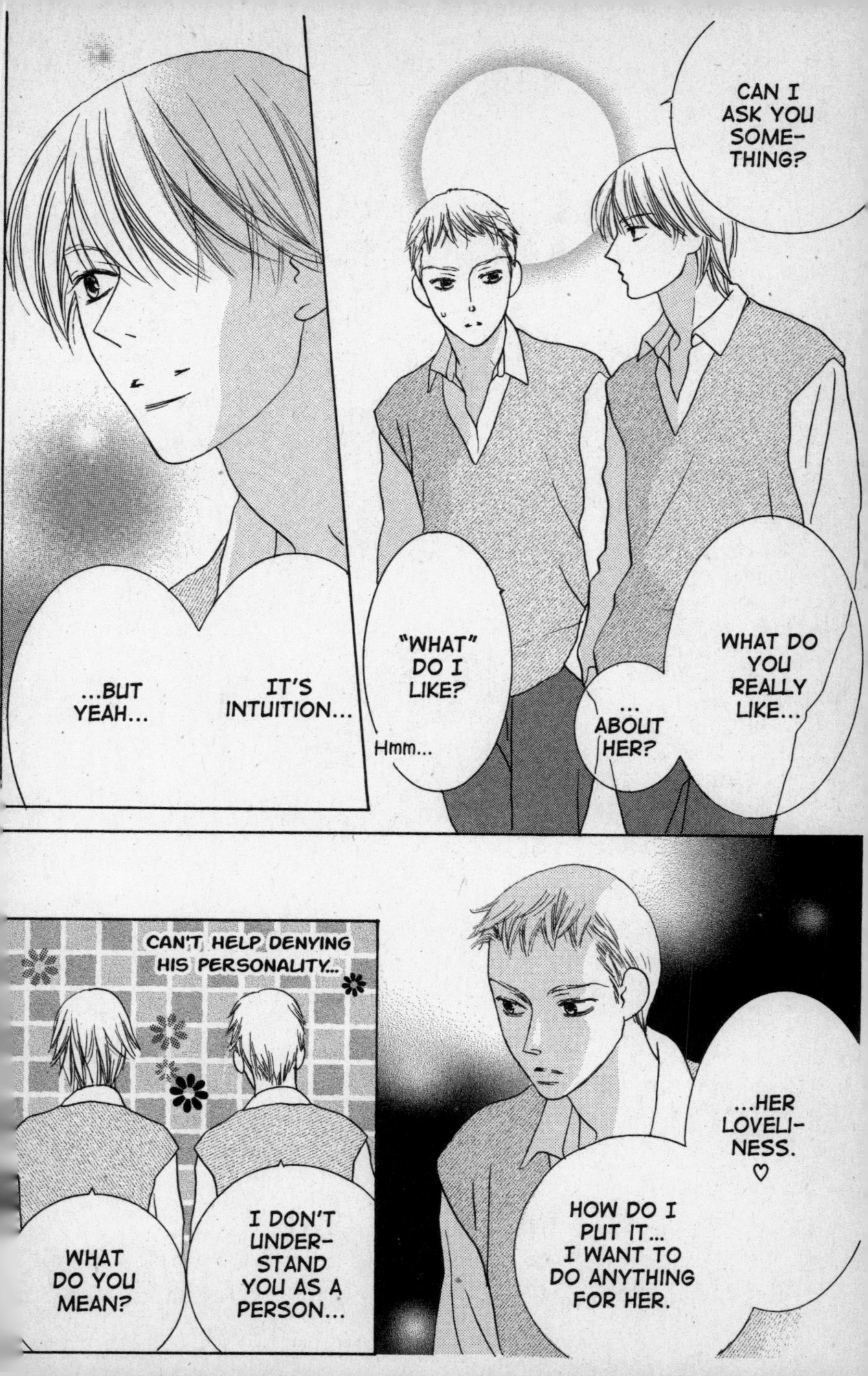
CAN I ASK YOU SOME-THING?
WHAT DO YOU REALLY LIKE...
... ABOUT HER?
"WHAT" DO I LIKE?
Hmm...
IT'S INTUITION...
...BUT YEAH...
...HER LOVELI-NESS. ♡
HOW DO I PUT IT... I WANT TO DO ANYTHING FOR HER.
CAN'T HELP DENYING HIS PERSONALITY...
I DON'T UNDER-STAND YOU AS A PERSON...
WHAT DO YOU MEAN?

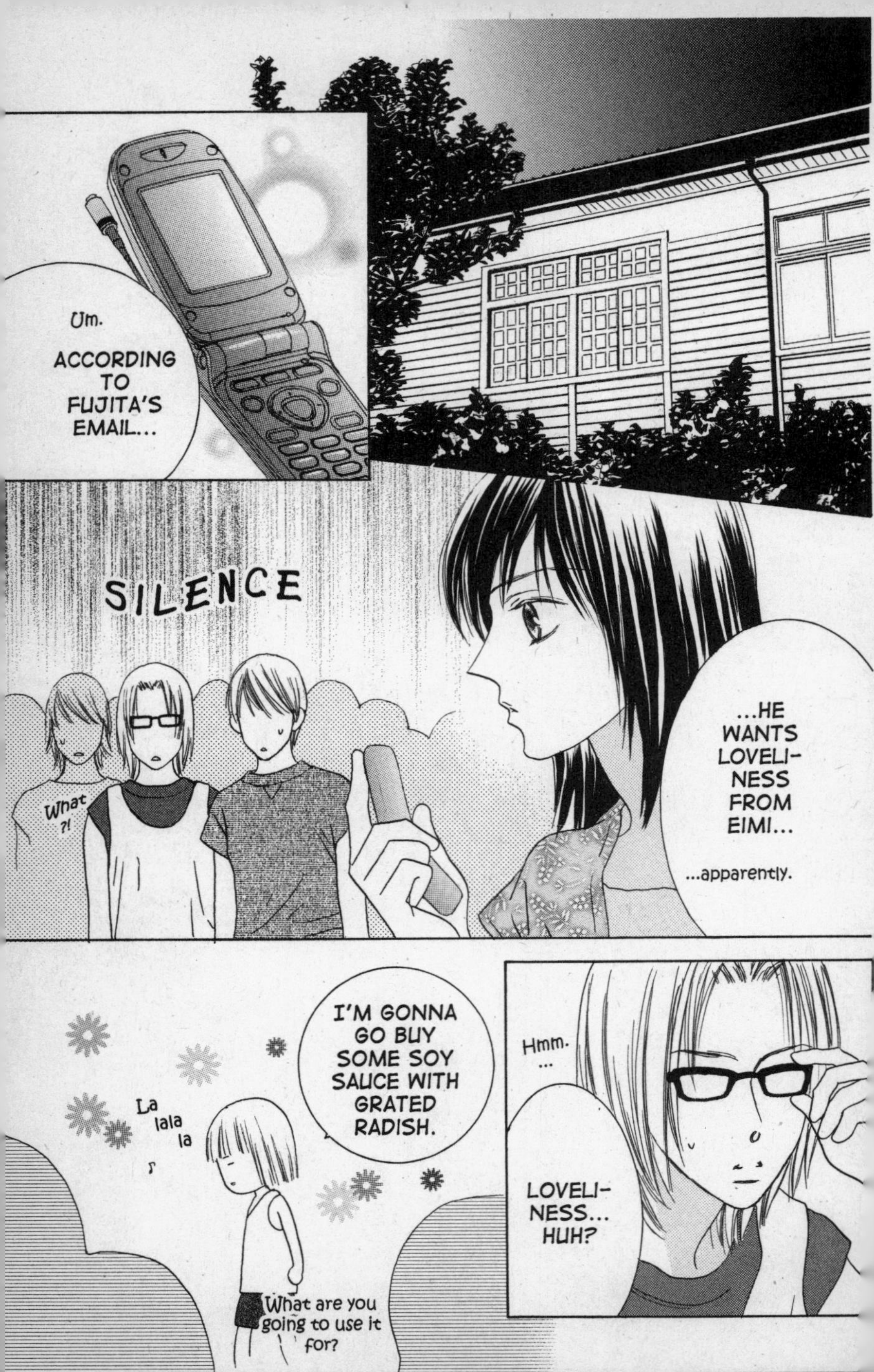
Um.
ACCORDING TO FUJITA'S EMAIL...
...HE WANTS LOVELI-NESS FROM EIMI...
...apparently.
SILENCE
What ?!
Hmm. ...
LOVELI-NESS... HUH?
I'M GONNA GO BUY SOME SOY SAUCE WITH GRATED RADISH.
La lala la ♪
What are you going to use it for?

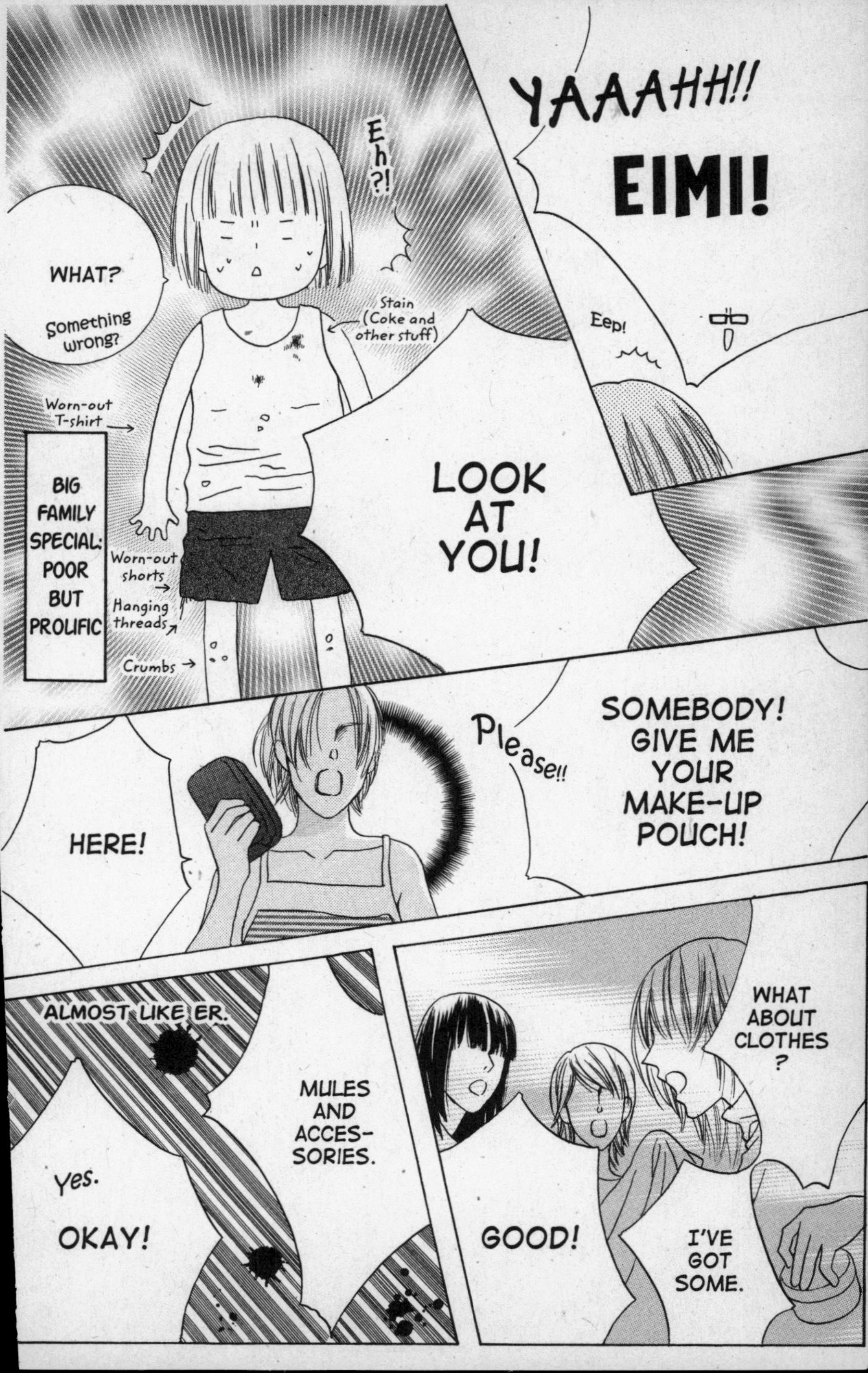
YAAAHH!!
EIMI!
Eep!
LOOK AT YOU!
Eh?!
WHAT?
Something wrong?
Stain (Coke and other stuff)
Worn-out T-shirt
Worn-out shorts
Hanging threads
Crumbs
BIG FAMILY SPECIAL: POOR BUT PROLIFIC
SOMEBODY! GIVE ME YOUR MAKE-UP POUCH!
Please!!
HERE!
WHAT ABOUT CLOTHES?
I'VE GOT SOME.
GOOD!
ALMOST LIKE ER.
MULES AND ACCES-SORIES.
Yes.
OKAY!

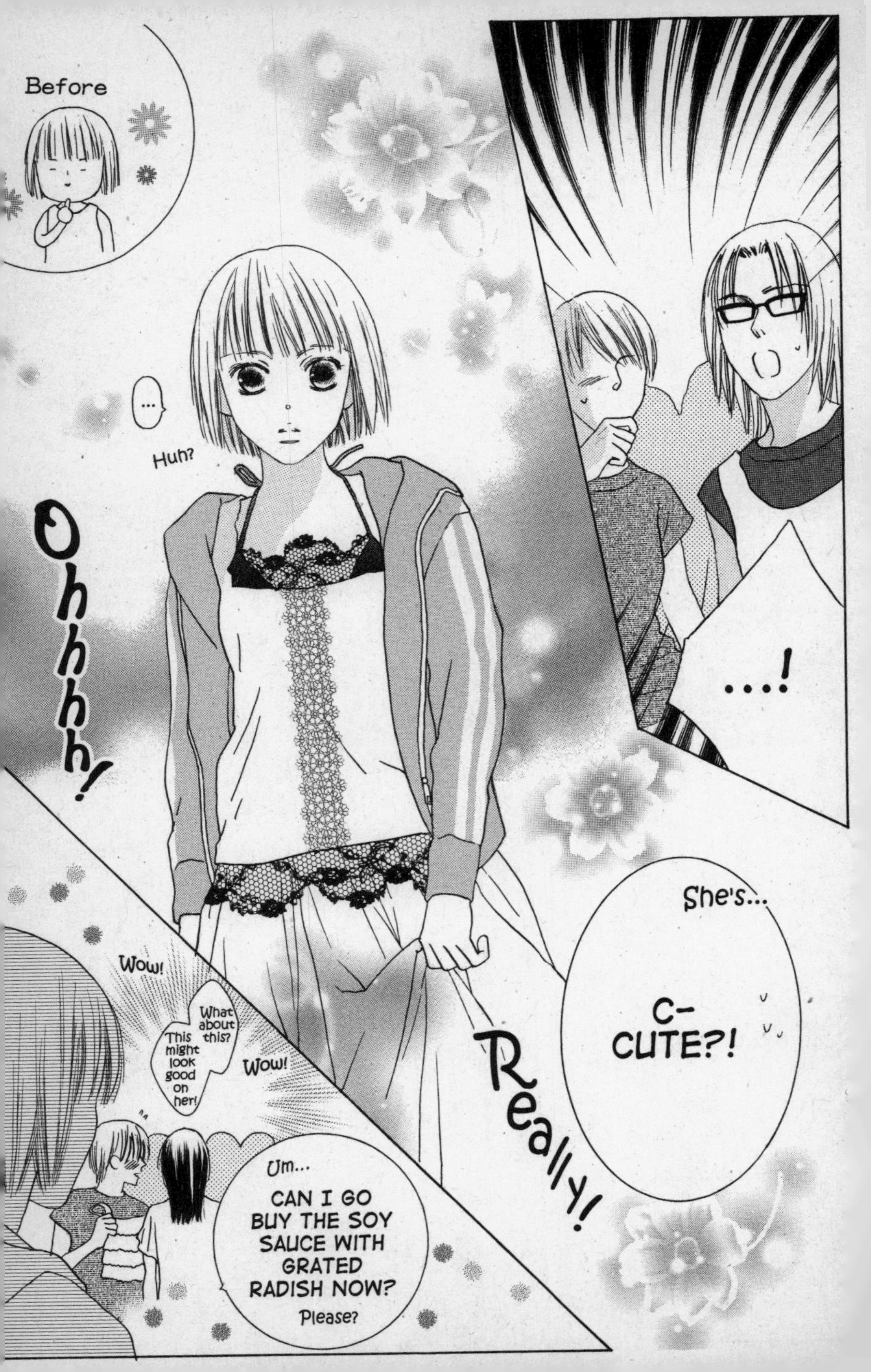

...!
Before
...
Huh?
She's... C-CUTE?!
Ohhhh!
Really!
Wow!
What about this? This might look good on her!
Wow!
Um... CAN I GO BUY THE SOY SAUCE WITH GRATED RADISH NOW? Please?

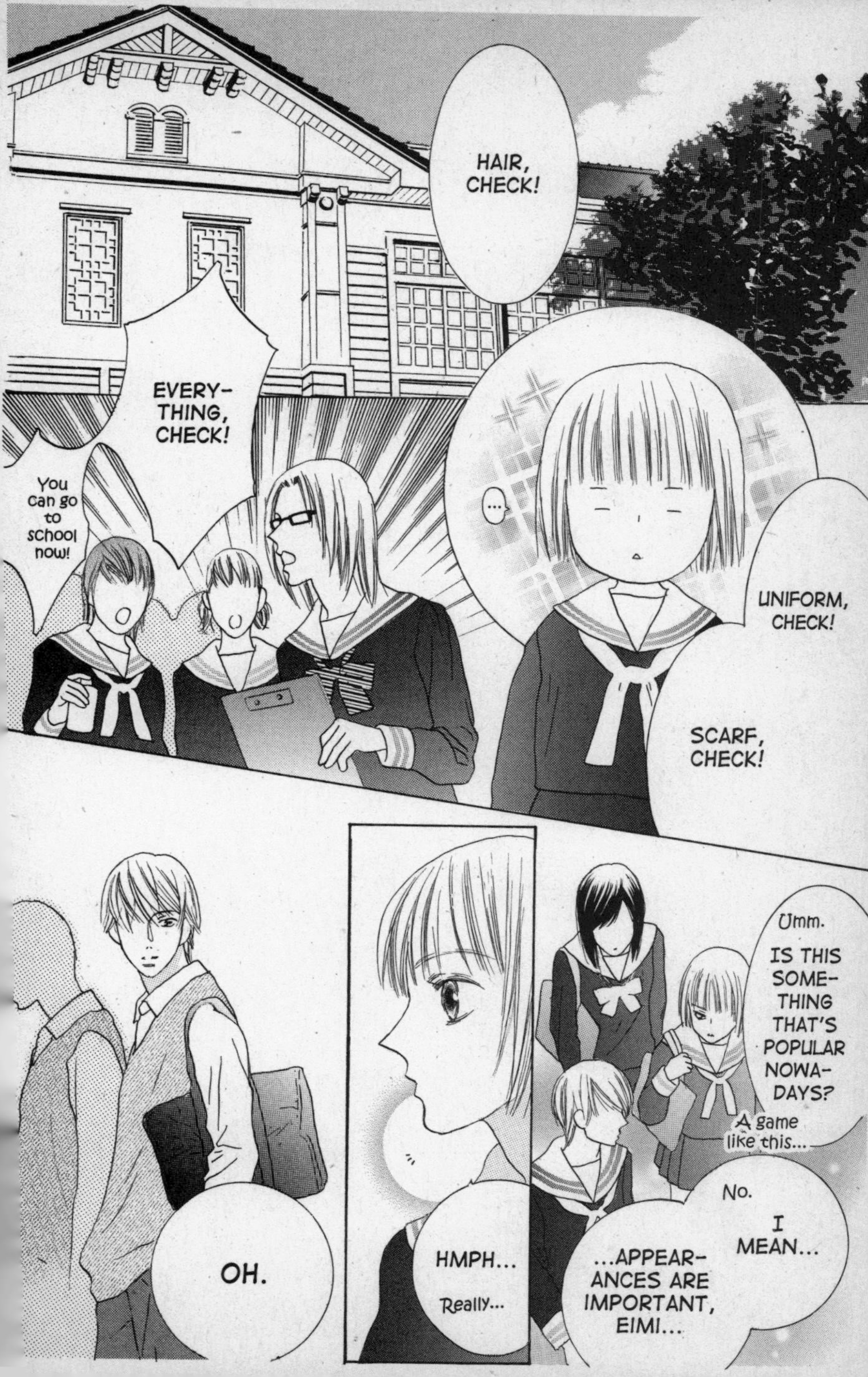
HAIR, CHECK!
UNIFORM, CHECK!
SCARF, CHECK!
...
EVERY-THING, CHECK!
You can go to school now!
Umm.
IS THIS SOME-THING THAT'S POPULAR NOWA-DAYS?
A game like this...
No.
I MEAN...
...APPEAR-ANCES ARE IMPORTANT, EIMI...
HMPH...
Really...
OH.

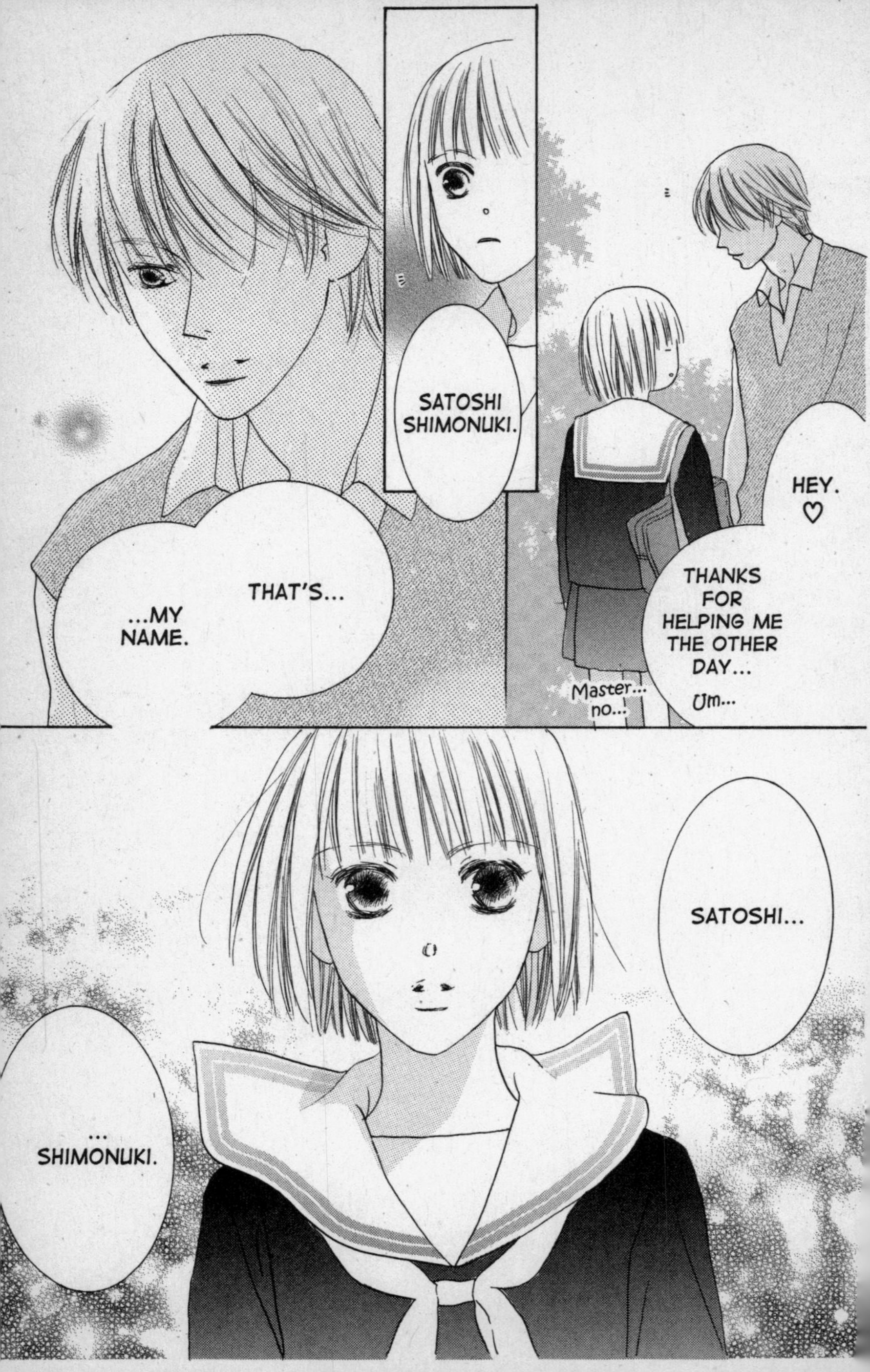
HEY. ♡
THANKS FOR HELPING ME THE OTHER DAY...
Um...
Master... no...
SATOSHI SHIMONUKI.
THAT'S...
...MY NAME.
SATOSHI...
...SHIMONUKI.

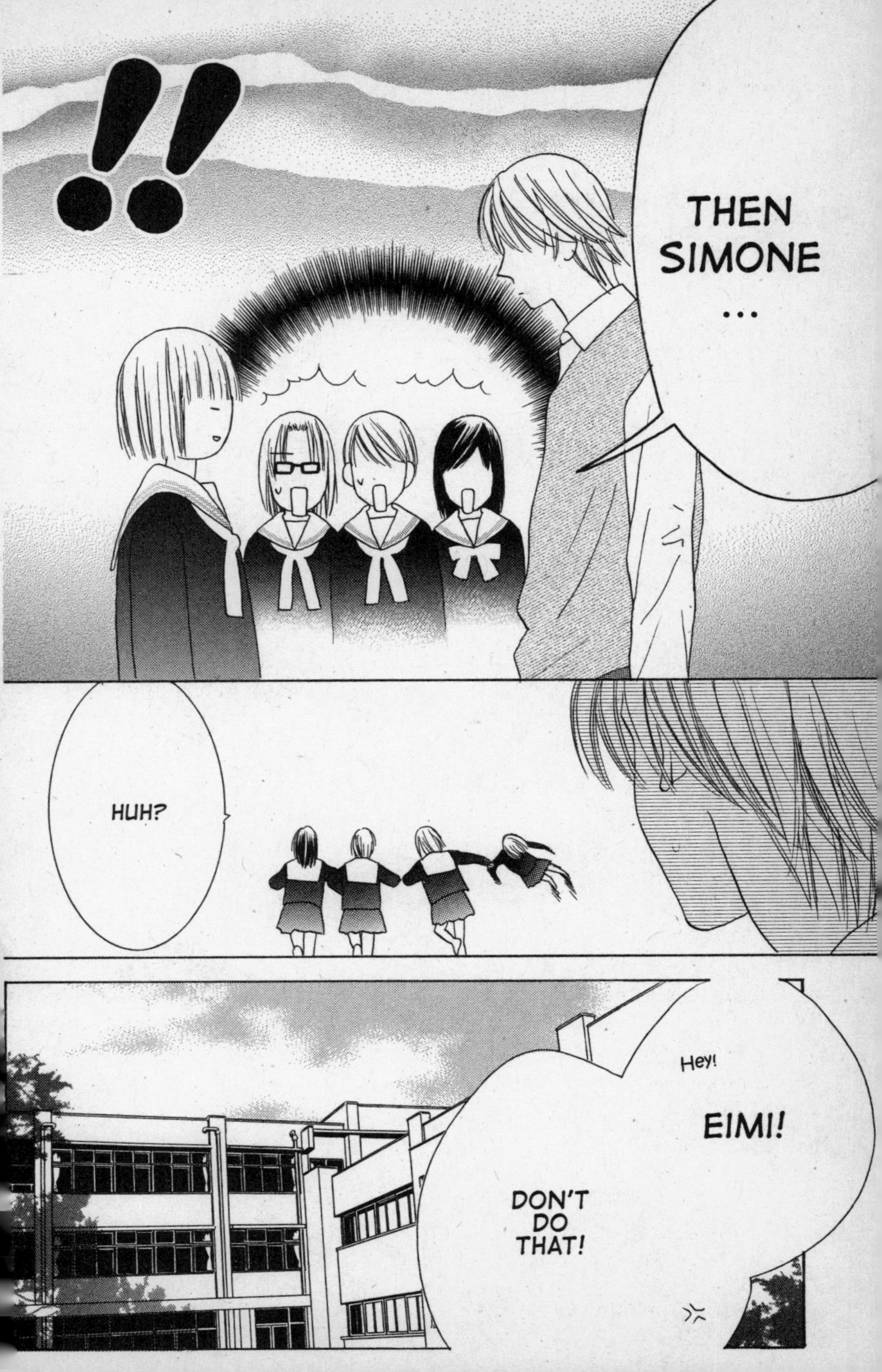
THEN SIMONE ...
!!
HUH?
Hey!
EIMI!
DON'T DO THAT!

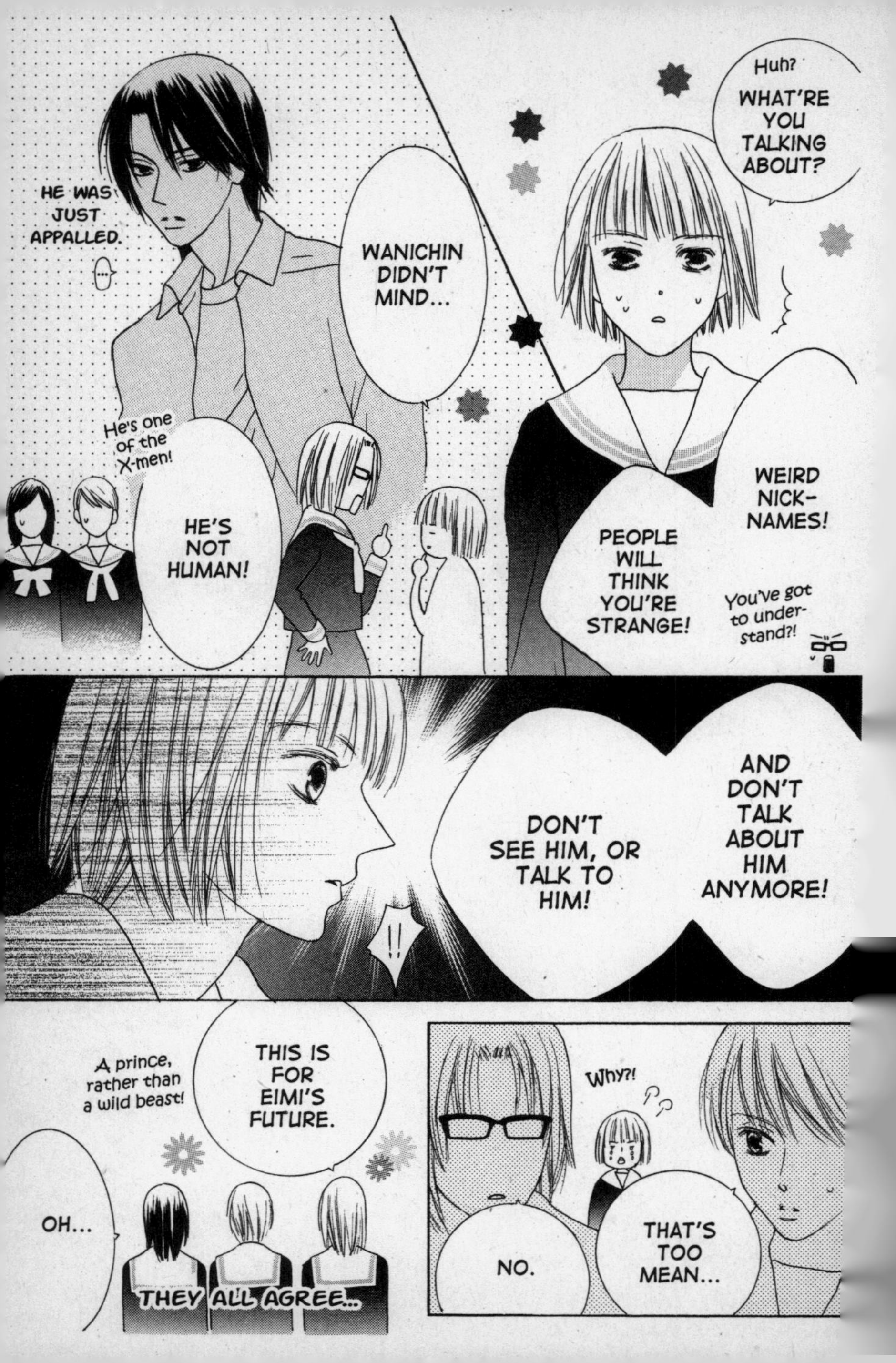
Huh?
WHAT'RE YOU TALKING ABOUT?
WEIRD NICK-NAMES!
PEOPLE WILL THINK YOU'RE STRANGE!
You've got to under-stand?!
WANICHIN DIDN'T MIND...
HE WAS JUST APPALLED.
...
He's one of the X-men!
HE'S NOT HUMAN!
DON'T SEE HIM, OR TALK TO HIM!
AND DON'T TALK ABOUT HIM ANYMORE!
!!
Why?!
THAT'S TOO MEAN...
NO.
THIS IS FOR EIMI'S FUTURE.
A prince, rather than a wild beast!
OH...
THEY ALL AGREE...

—CONTINUED TRAINING TO "GET" SHIMONUKI—

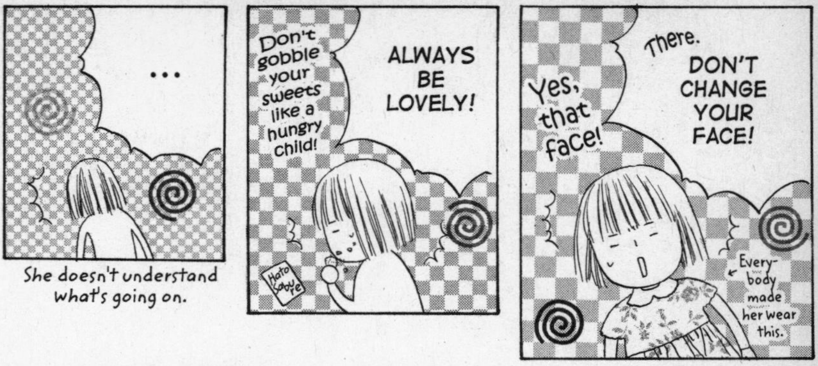
There.
DON'T CHANGE YOUR FACE!
Yes, that face!
Everybody made her wear this.
ALWAYS BE LOVELY!
Don't gobble your sweets like a hungry child!
Hato Sabure
...
She doesn't understand what's going on.

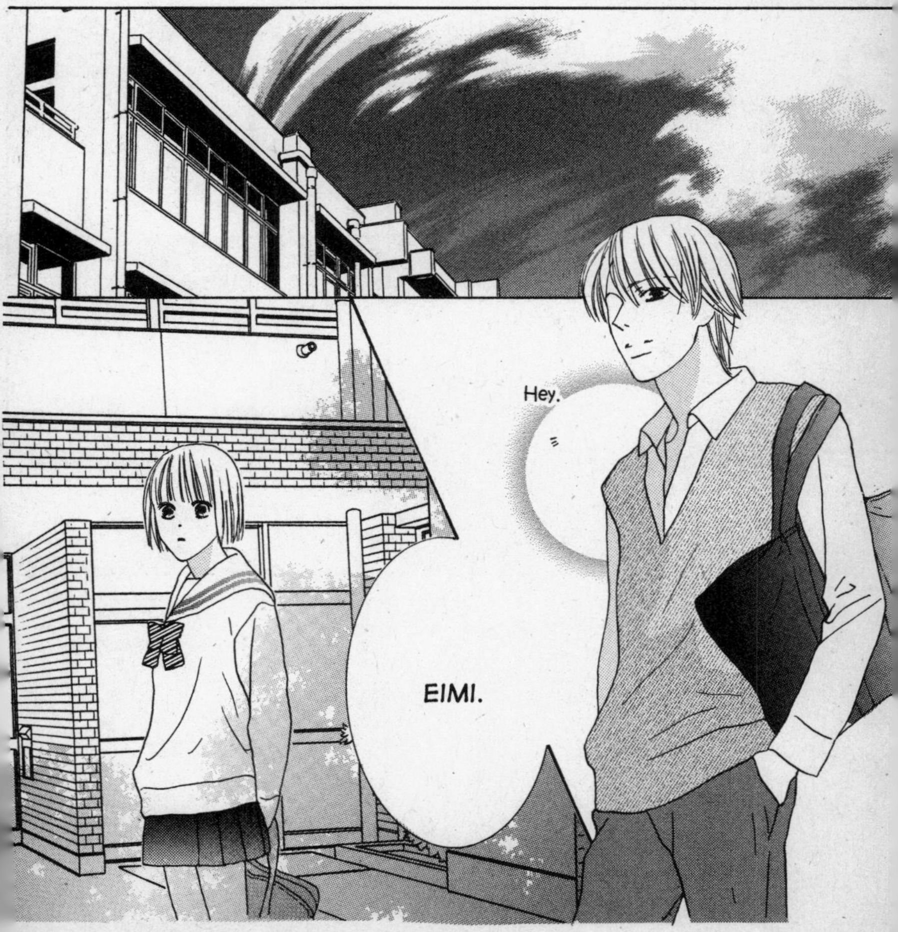
Hey.
EIMI.

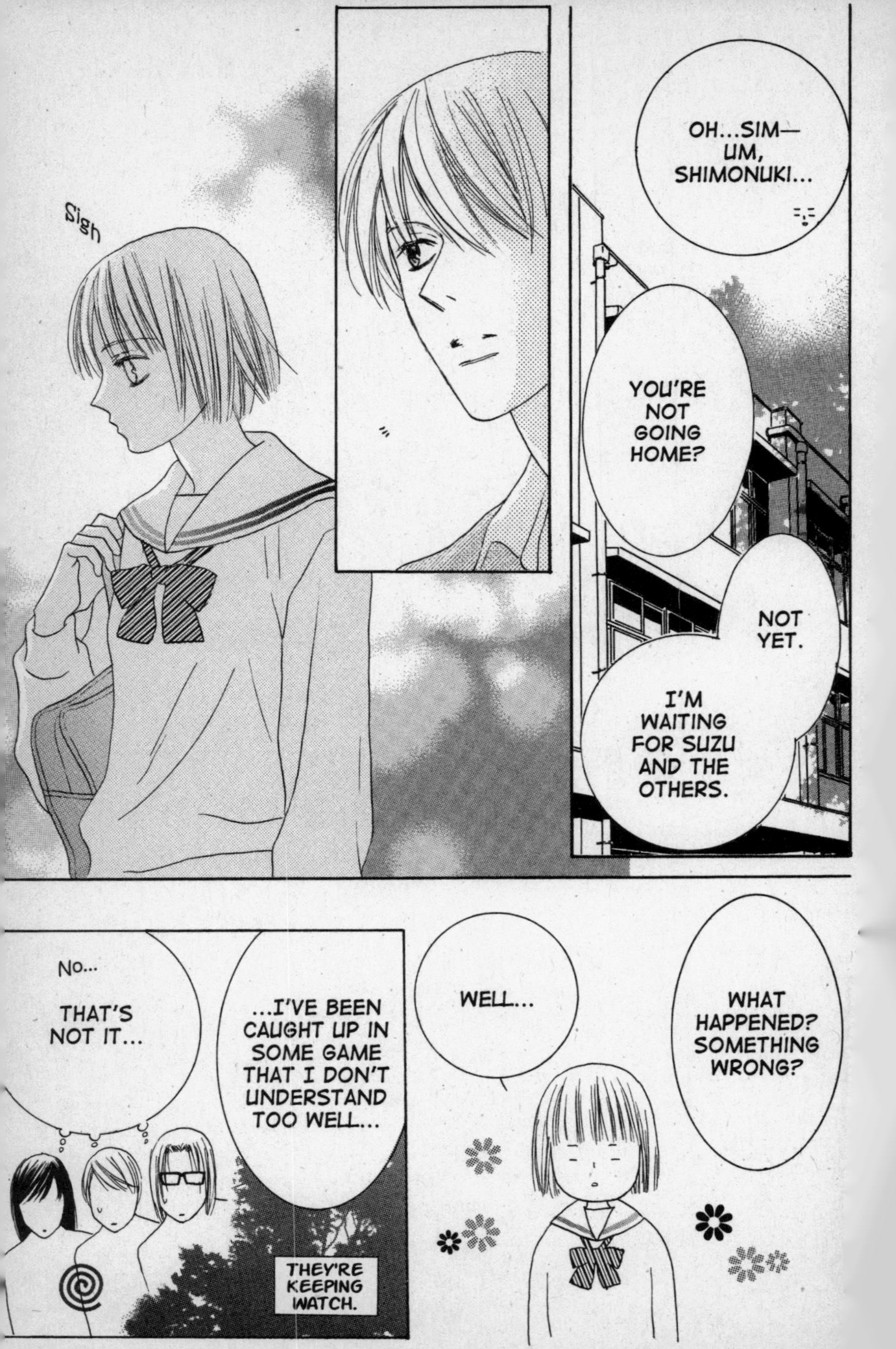
OH...SIM— UM, SHIMONUKI...
YOU'RE NOT GOING HOME?
NOT YET.
I'M WAITING FOR SUZU AND THE OTHERS.
Sigh
WHAT HAPPENED? SOMETHING WRONG?
WELL...
...I'VE BEEN CAUGHT UP IN SOME GAME THAT I DON'T UNDERSTAND TOO WELL...
No...
THAT'S NOT IT...
THEY'RE KEEPING WATCH.

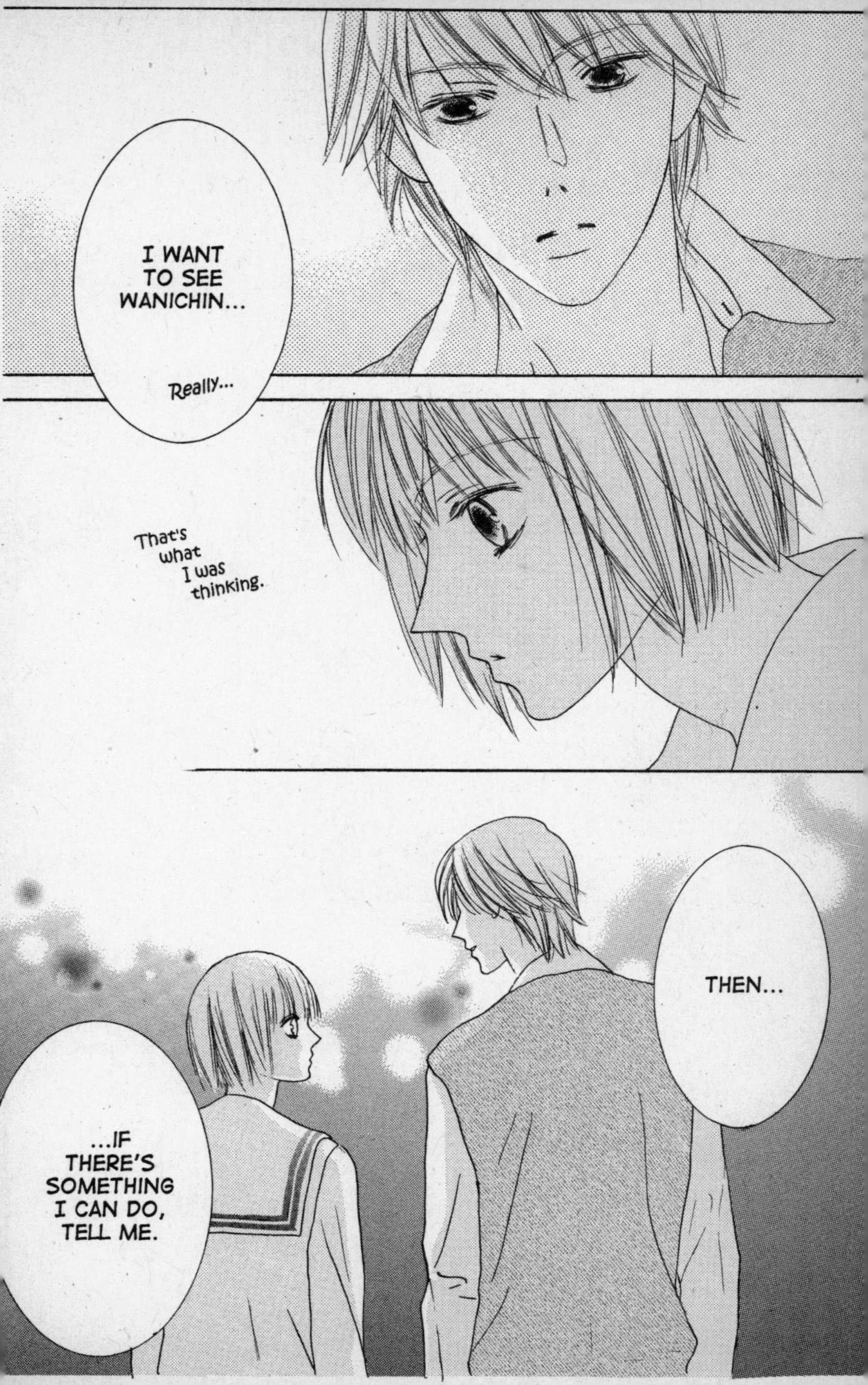
I WANT TO SEE WANICHIN...
Really...
That's what I was thinking.
THEN...
...IF THERE'S SOMETHING I CAN DO, TELL ME.

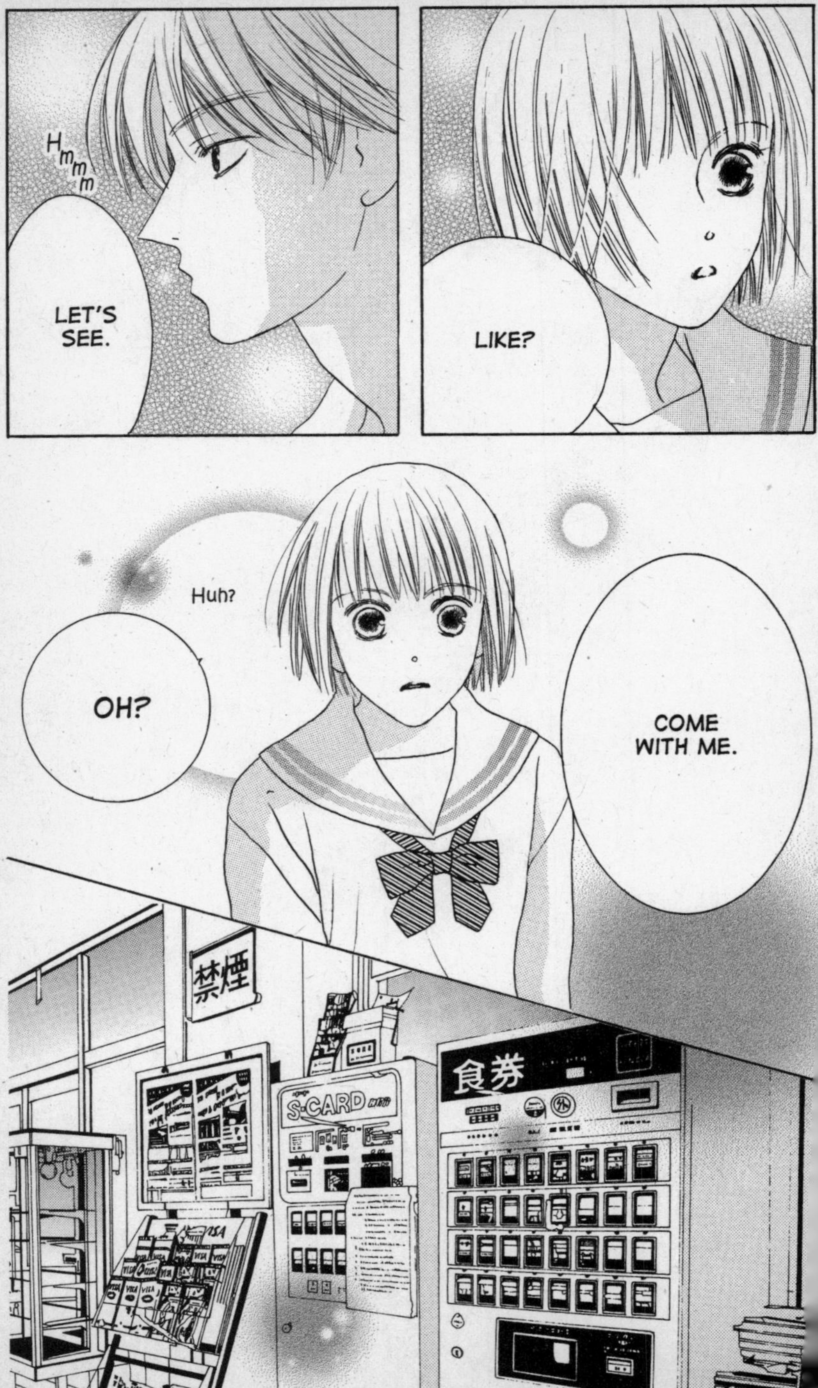
LIKE?
Hmmm
LET'S SEE.
COME WITH ME.
Huh?
OH?
禁煙
食券
S-CARD

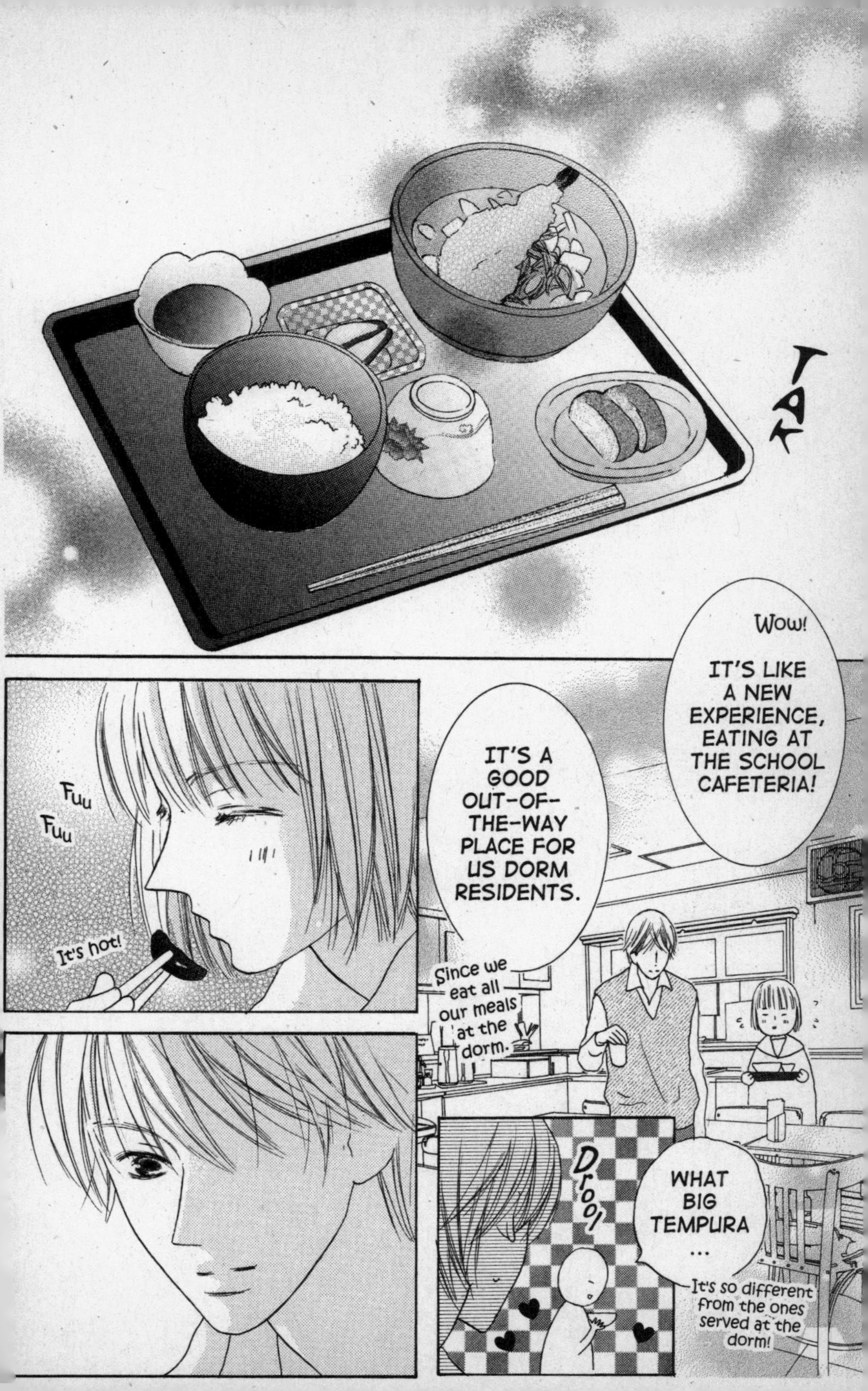
TAK
WOW!
IT'S LIKE A NEW EXPERIENCE, EATING AT THE SCHOOL CAFETERIA!
IT'S A GOOD OUT-OF-THE-WAY PLACE FOR US DORM RESIDENTS.
Since we eat all our meals at the dorm.
Drool
WHAT BIG TEMPURA ...
It's so different from the ones served at the dorm!
Fuu
Fuu
It's hot!

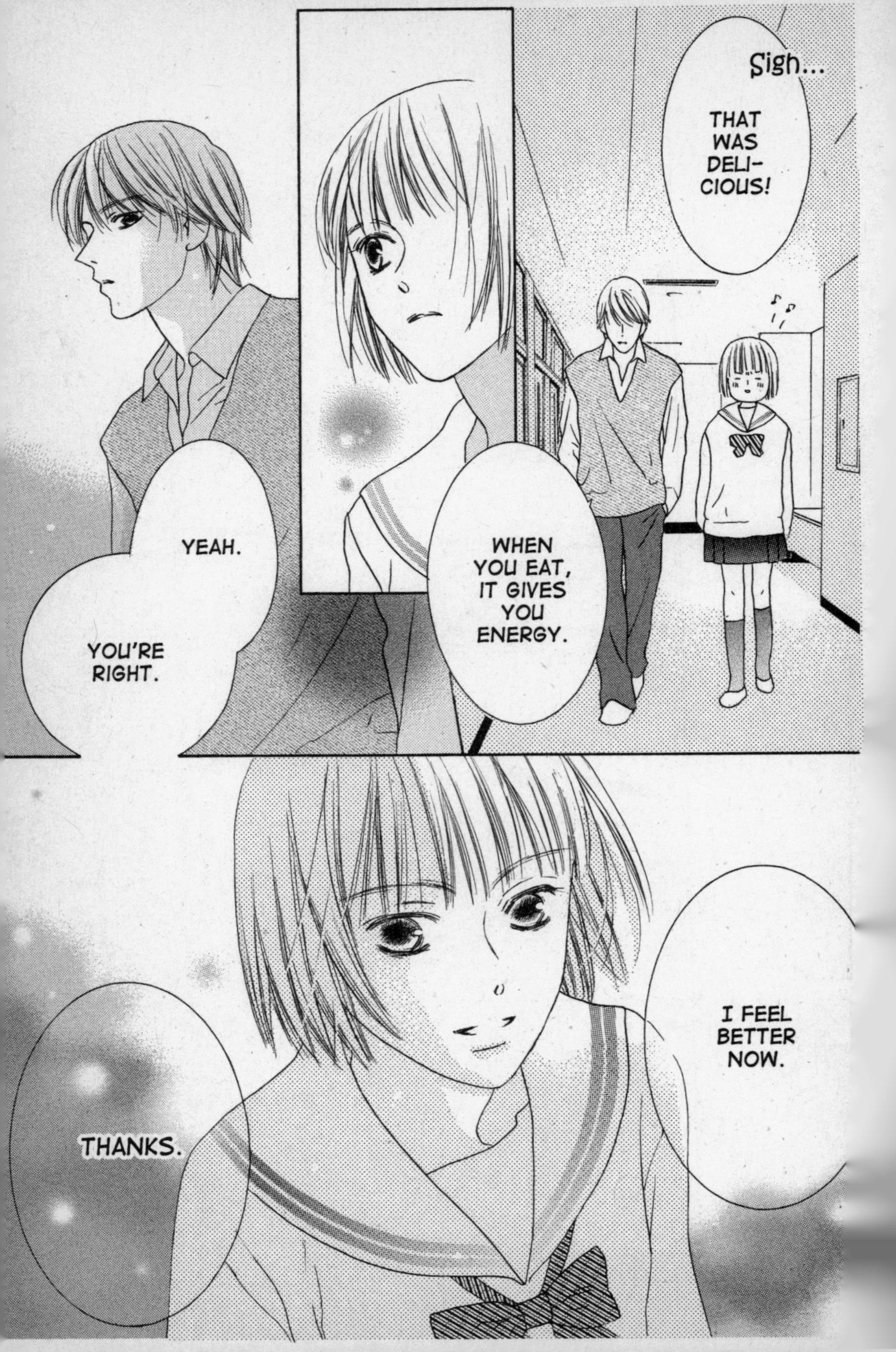
Sigh...
THAT WAS DELICIOUS!
WHEN YOU EAT, IT GIVES YOU ENERGY.
YEAH.
YOU'RE RIGHT.
I FEEL BETTER NOW.
THANKS.

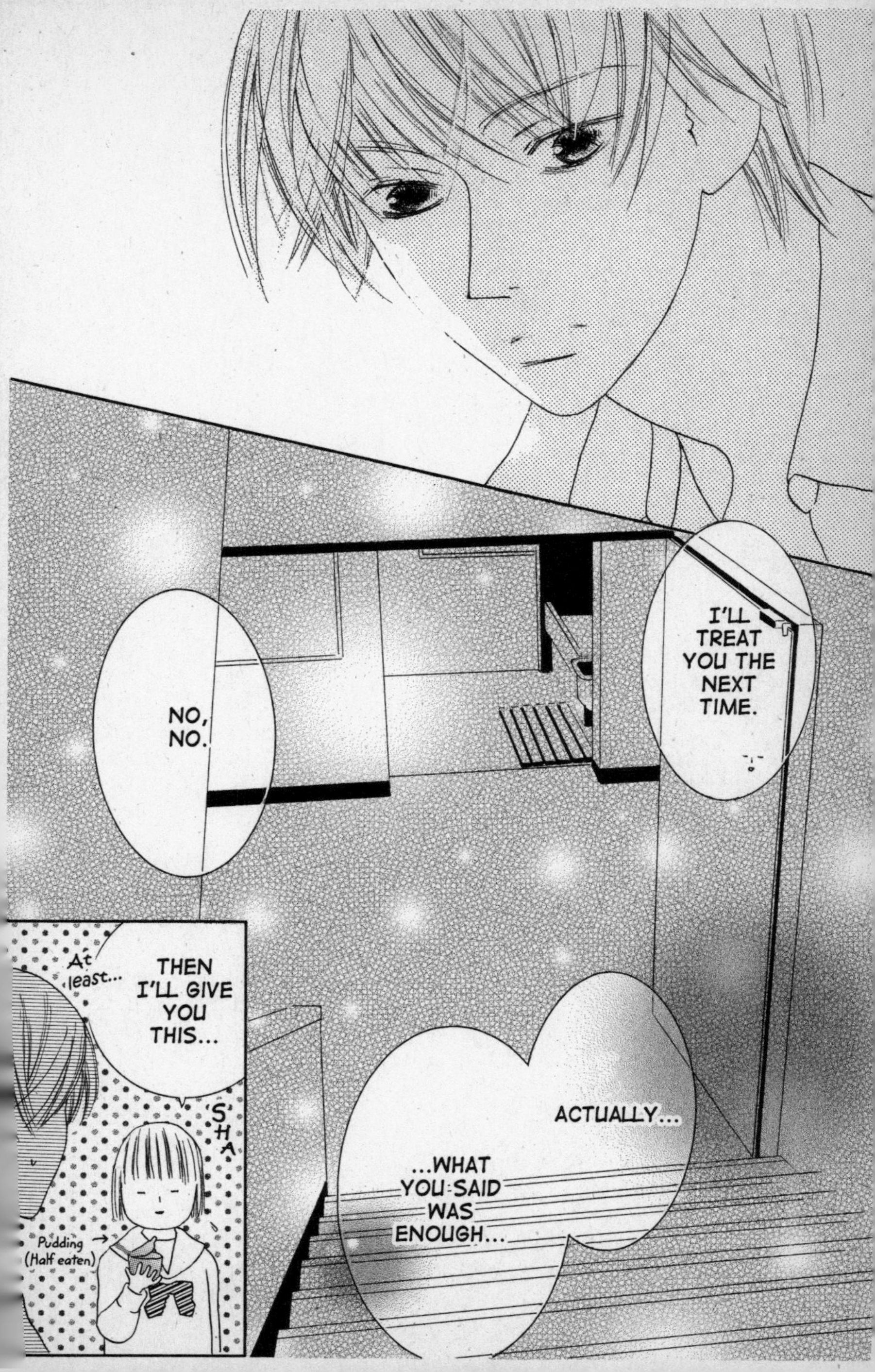
I'LL TREAT YOU THE NEXT TIME.
NO, NO.
ACTUALLY...
...WHAT YOU SAID WAS ENOUGH...
THEN I'LL GIVE YOU THIS...
At least...
SHA
Pudding (Half eaten)

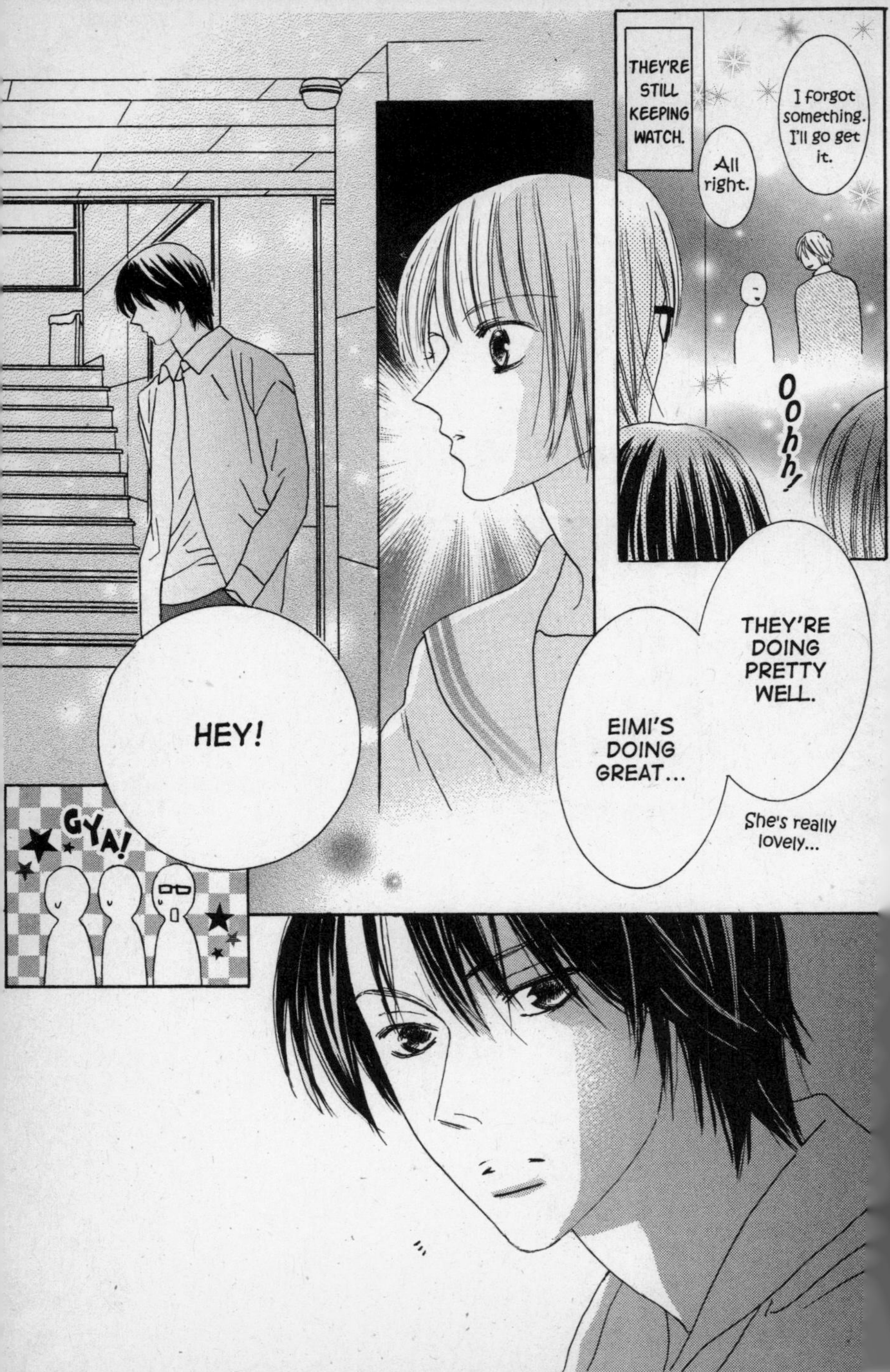
I forgot something. I'll go get it.
All right.
THEY'RE STILL KEEPING WATCH.
Oohh!
THEY'RE DOING PRETTY WELL.
EIMI'S DOING GREAT...
She's really lovely...
HEY!
GYA!

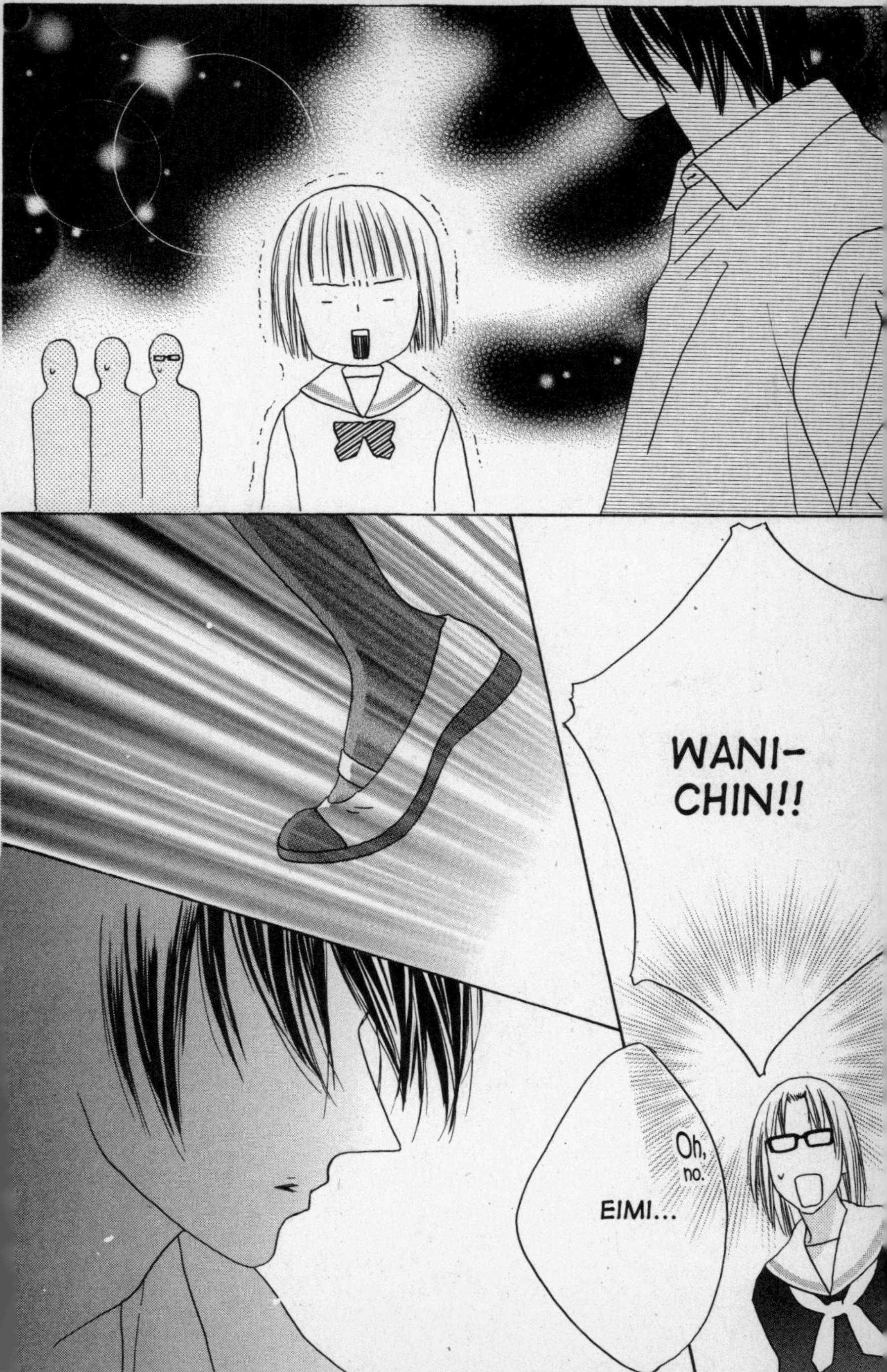
WANI-CHIN!!
Oh, no.
EIMI...

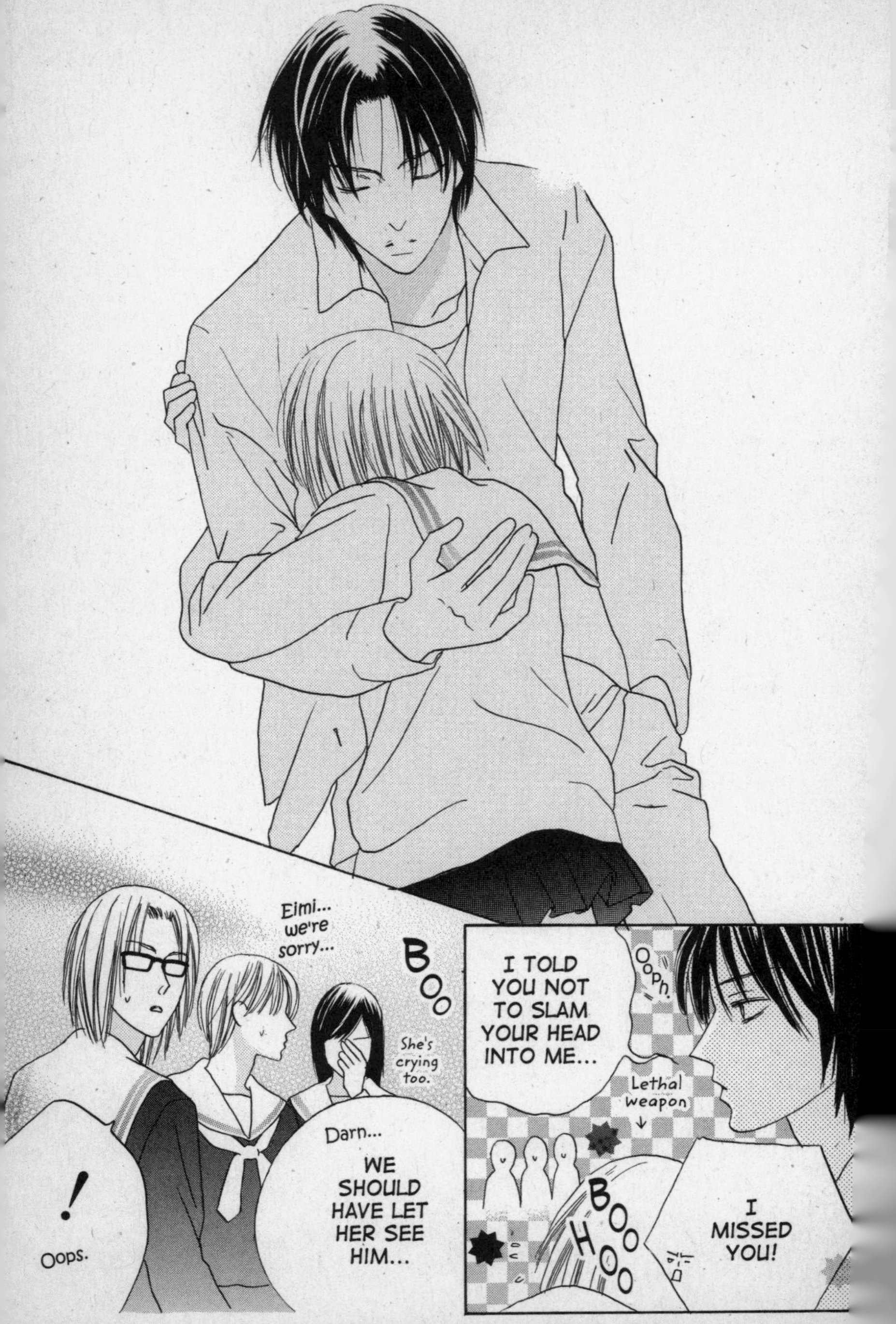
Ooph.
I TOLD YOU NOT TO SLAM YOUR HEAD INTO ME...
Lethal weapon
I MISSED YOU!
BOO HOO
BOO
Eimi... we're sorry...
She's crying too.
Darn... WE SHOULD HAVE LET HER SEE HIM...
!
Oops.

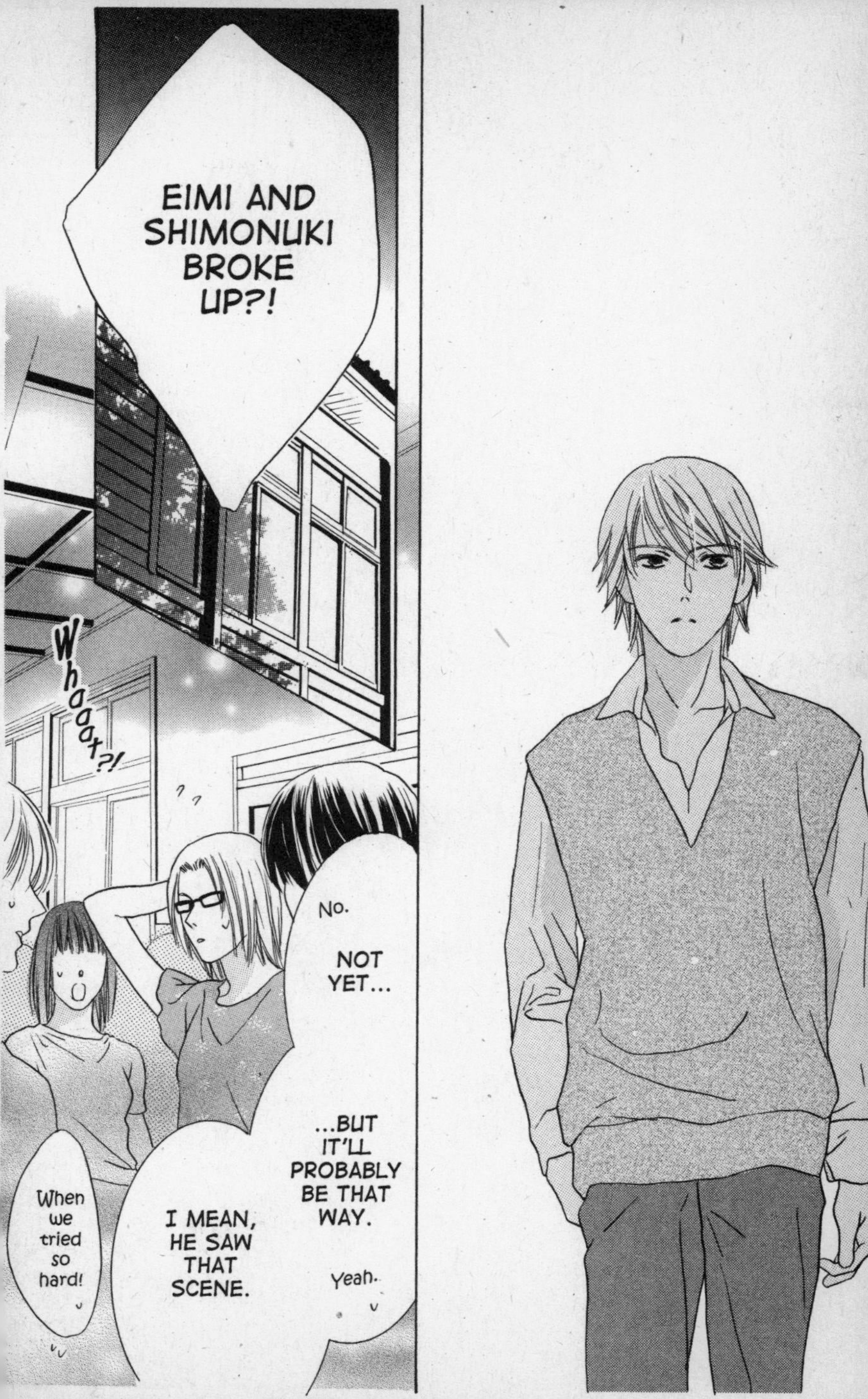
EIMI AND SHIMONUKI BROKE UP?!
Whaaat?!
No.
NOT YET...
...BUT IT'LL PROBABLY BE THAT WAY.
Yeah.
I MEAN, HE SAW THAT SCENE.
When we tried so hard!

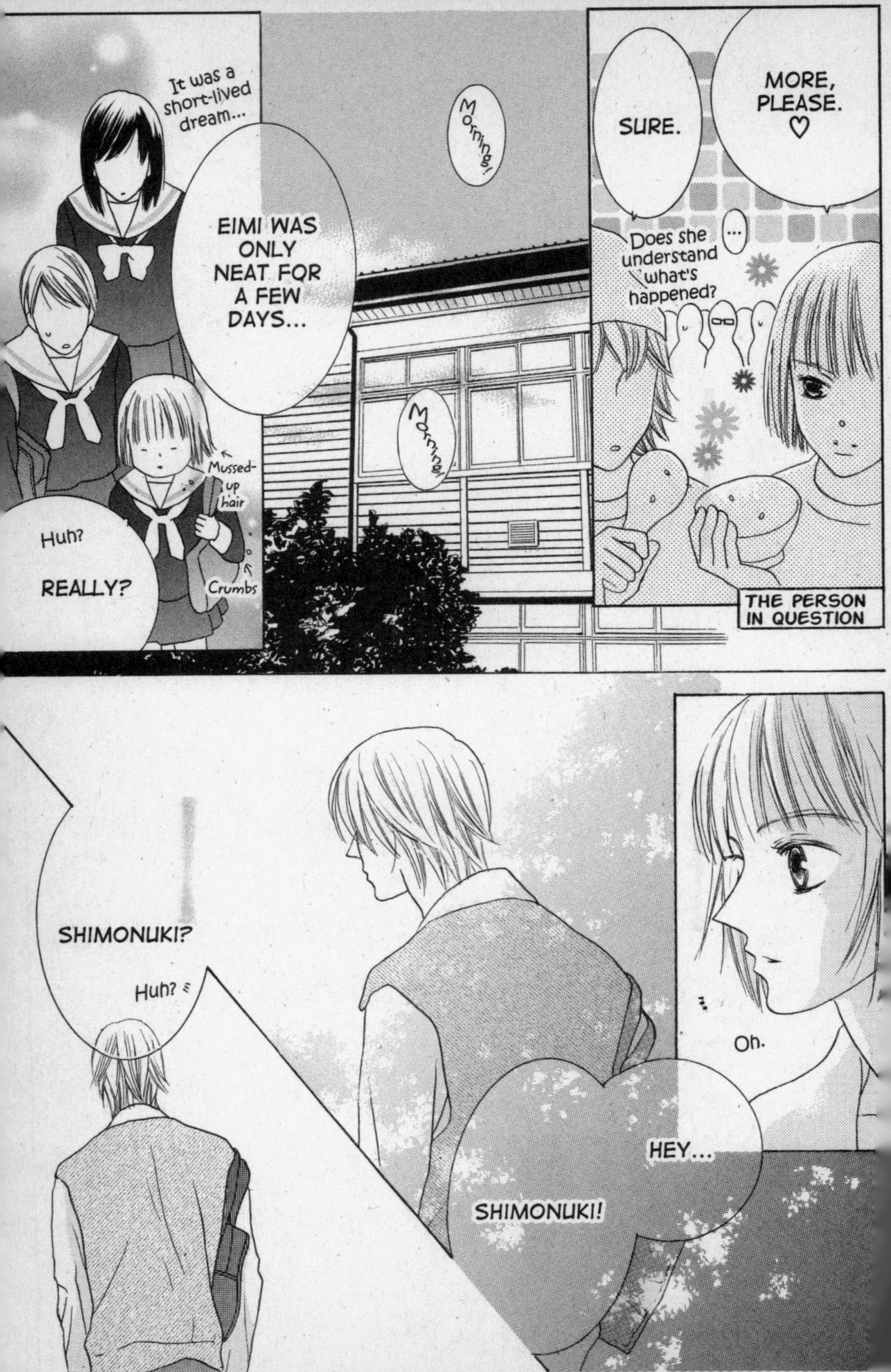
MORE, PLEASE. ♡
SURE.
...
Does she understand what's happened?
THE PERSON IN QUESTION
Morning!
Morning!
It was a short-lived dream...
EIMI WAS ONLY NEAT FOR A FEW DAYS...
Mussed-up hair
Crumbs
Huh?
REALLY?
Oh.
HEY...
SHIMONUKI!
SHIMONUKI?
Huh?

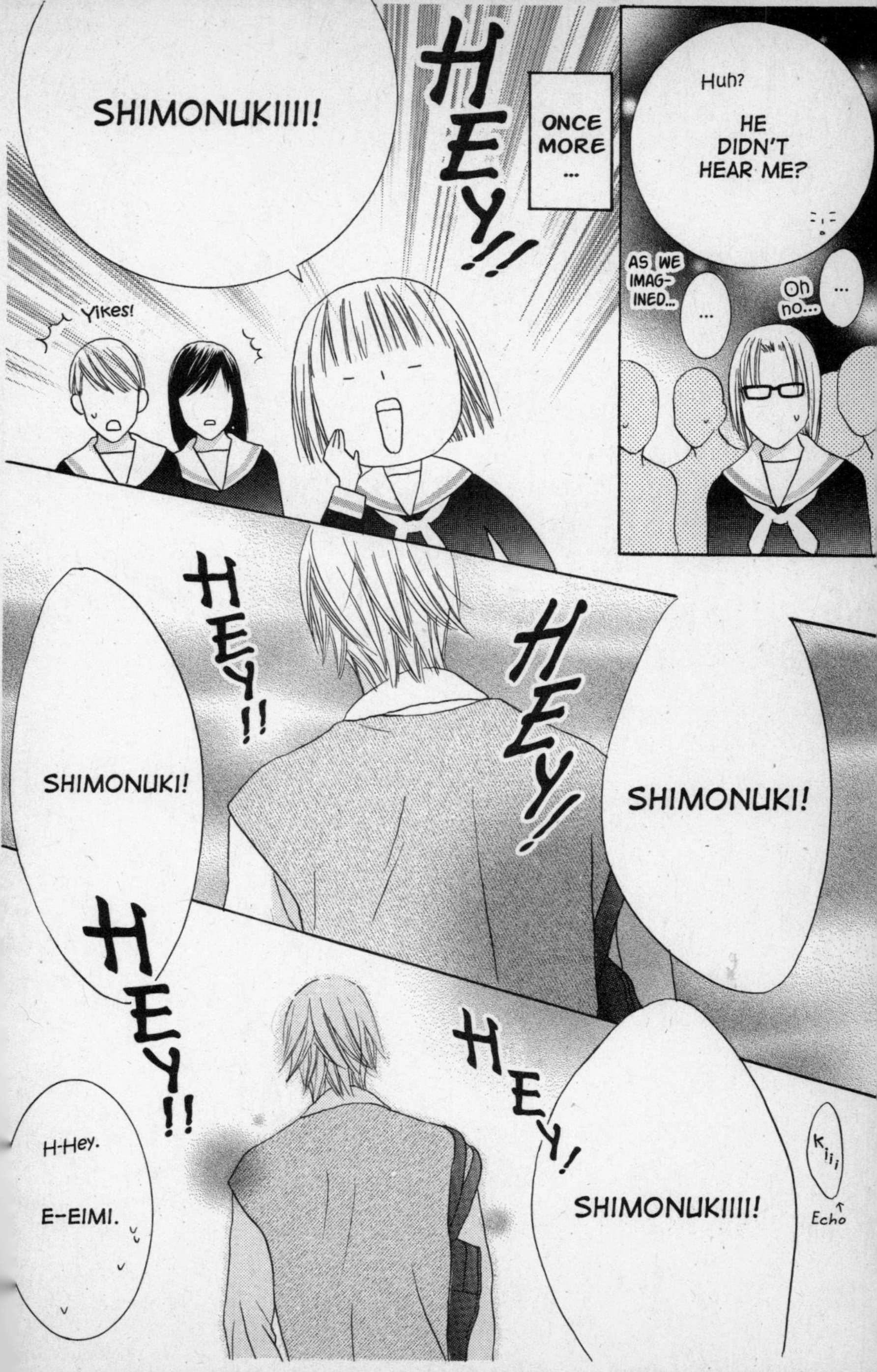

Huh?
HE DIDN'T HEAR ME?
...
Oh no...
...
AS WE IMAGINED...
ONCE MORE ...
HEY!!!
SHIMONUKIIIII!
Yikes!
SHIMONUKI!
HEY!
HEY!!
SHIMONUKI!
Kiii
Echo
SHIMONUKIIIII!
HEY!
HEY!!
H-Hey.
E-EIMI.

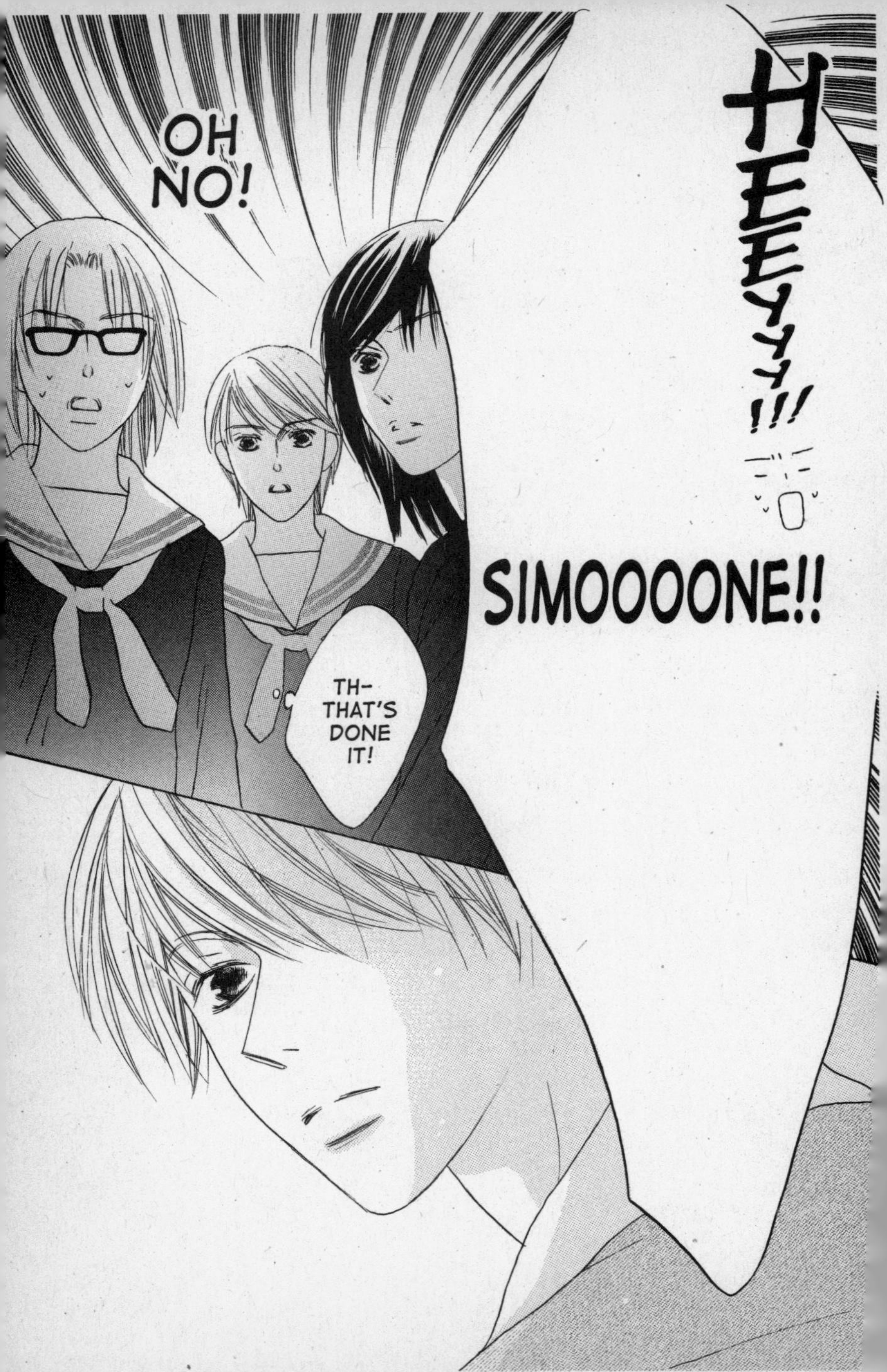
HEEEEEE!!
SIMOOOONE!!
OH NO!
TH- THAT'S DONE IT!

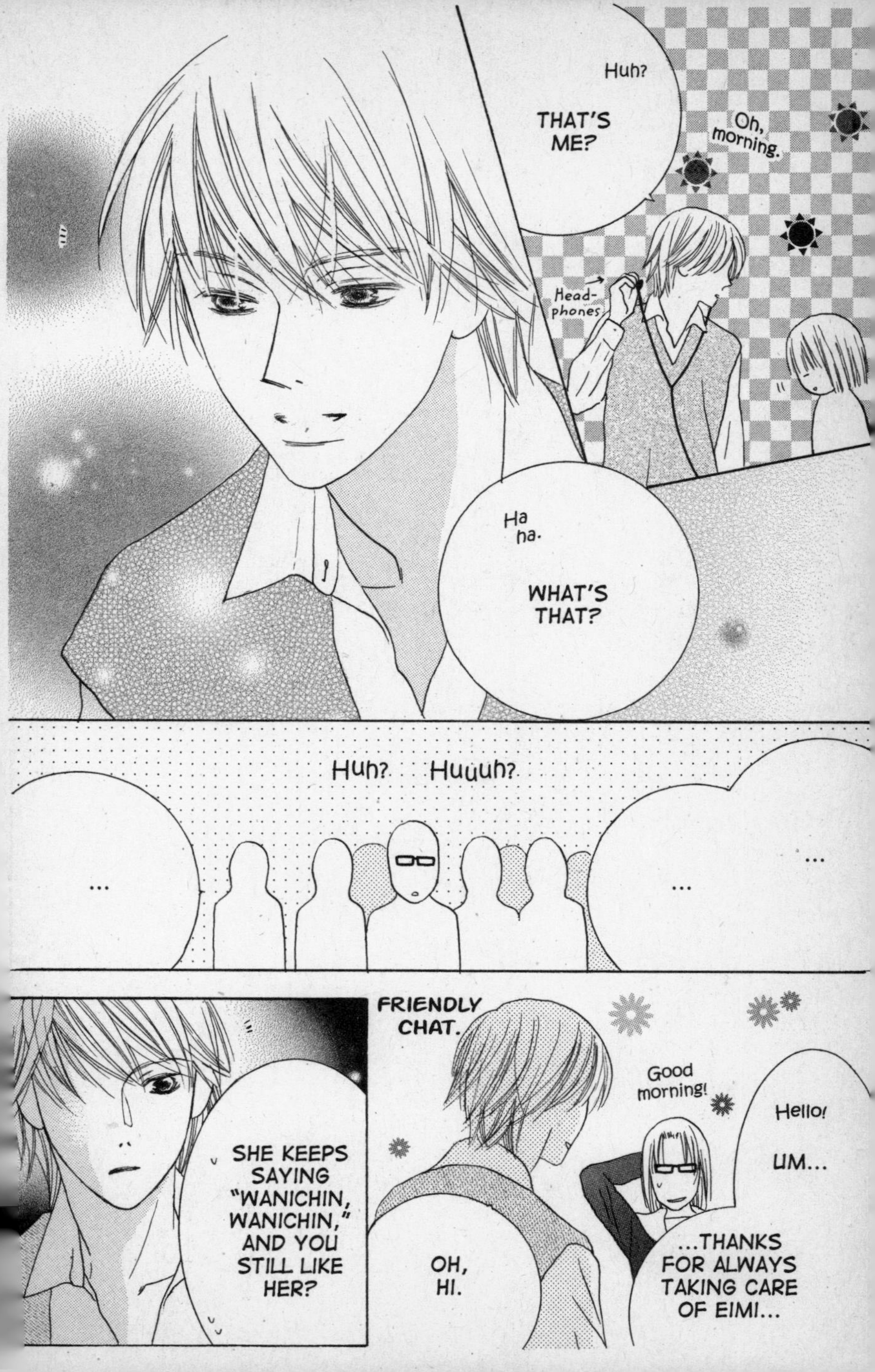

Oh, morning.
Headphones
Huh? THAT'S ME?
Ha ha. WHAT'S THAT?
Huh? Huuuh?
...
...
...
FRIENDLY CHAT.
Hello! UM... ...THANKS FOR ALWAYS TAKING CARE OF EIMI...
Good morning!
OH, HI.
SHE KEEPS SAYING "WANICHIN, WANICHIN," AND YOU STILL LIKE HER?

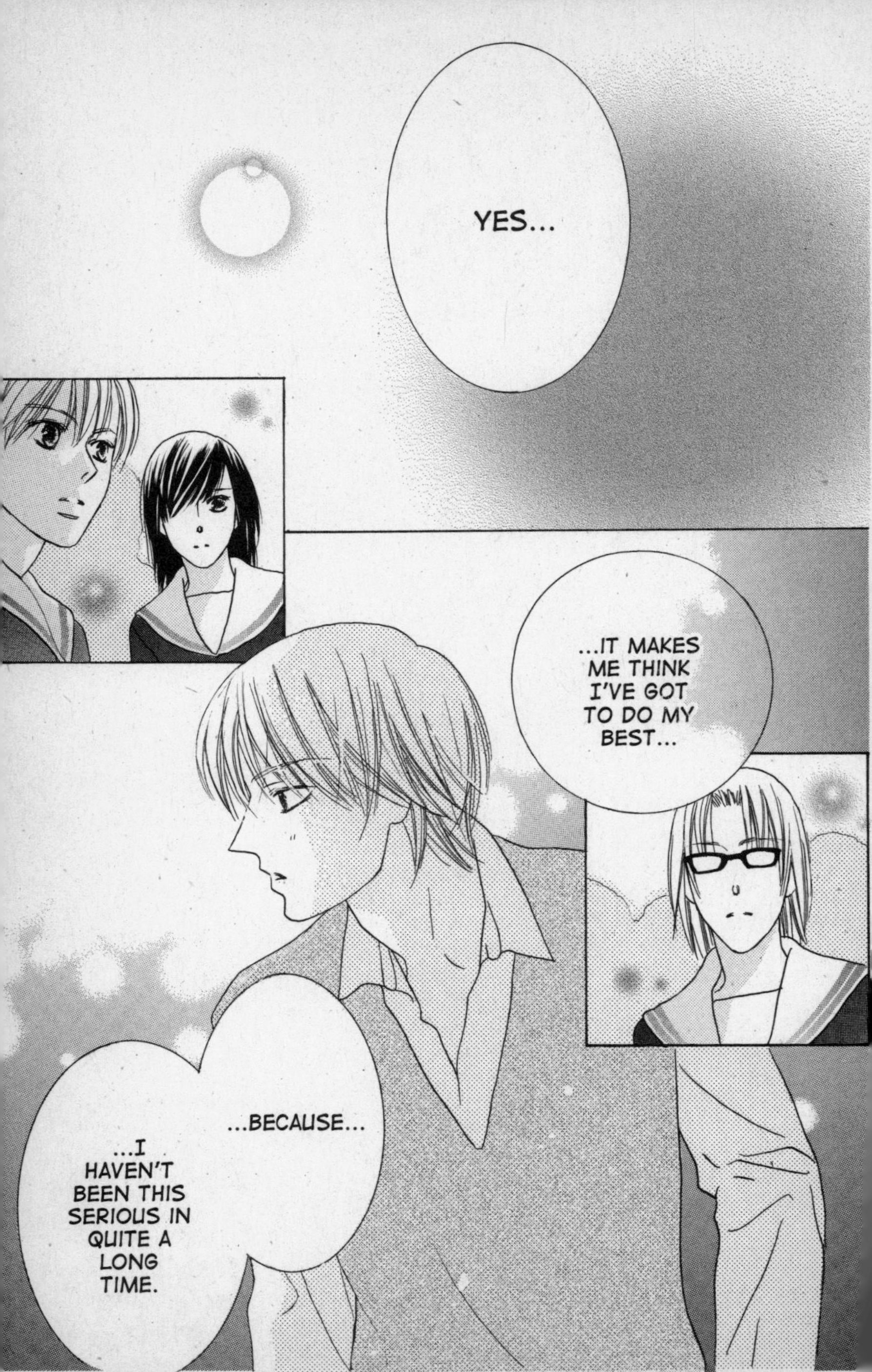
YES...
...IT MAKES ME THINK I'VE GOT TO DO MY BEST...
...BECAUSE...
...I HAVEN'T BEEN THIS SERIOUS IN QUITE A LONG TIME.

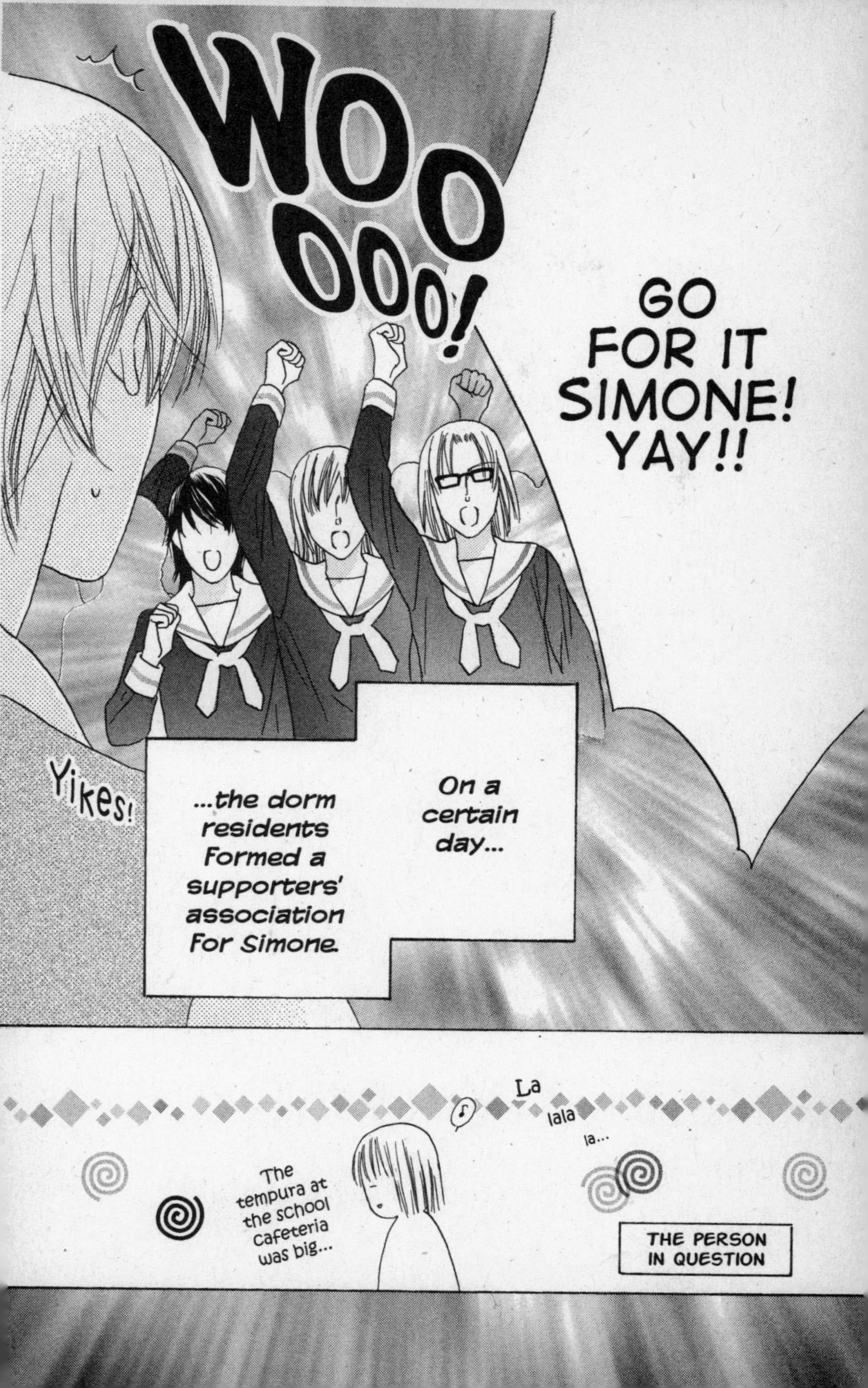
WOOOOOO!
GO FOR IT SIMONE! YAY!!
On a certain day...
...the dorm residents formed a supporters' association for Simone.
Yikes!
THE PERSON IN QUESTION
La lala la...
The tempura at the school cafeteria was big...

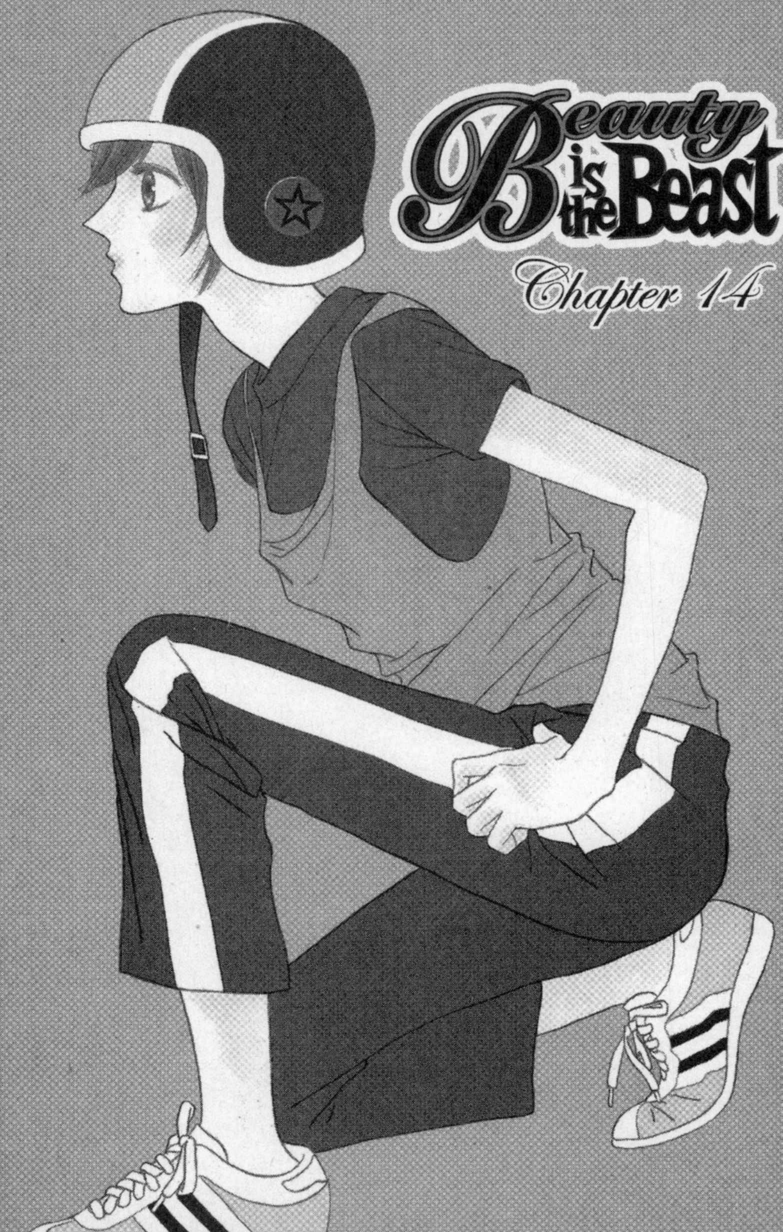
Beauty is the Beast
Chapter 14

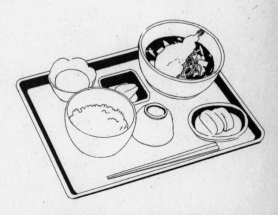

BEAUTY IS THE BEAST

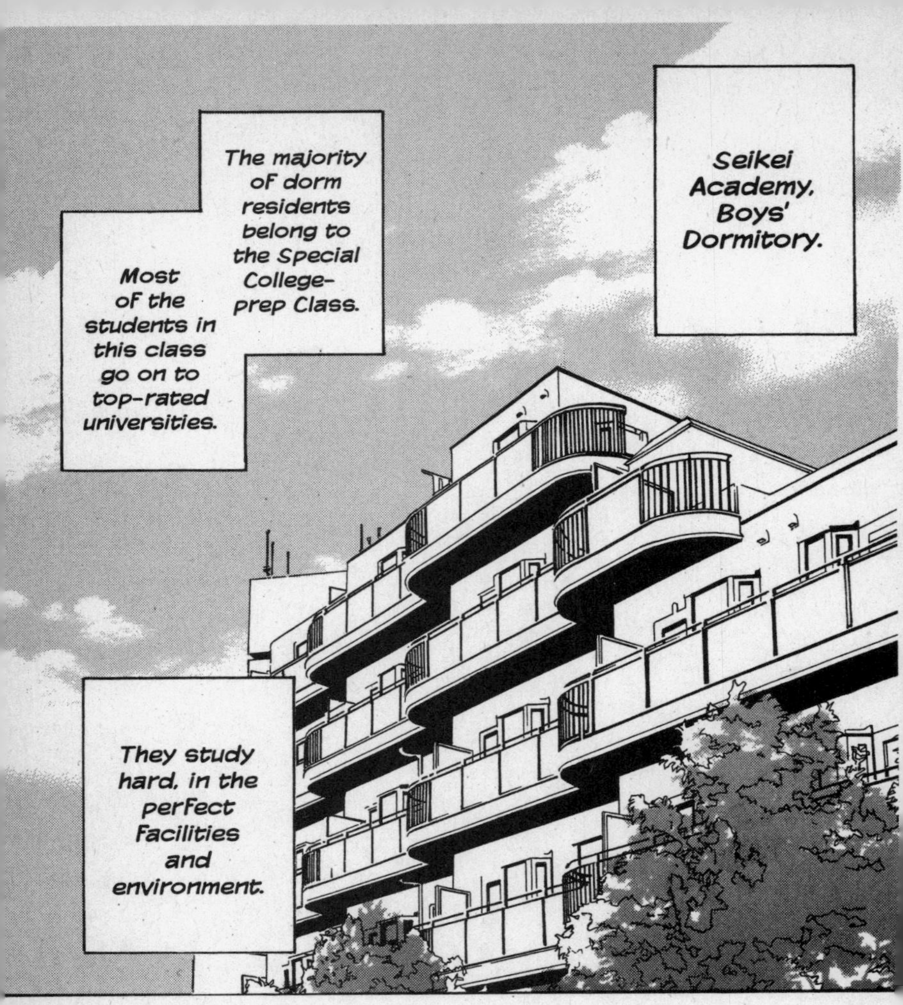
Seikei Academy, Boys' Dormitory.
The majority of dorm residents belong to the Special College-prep Class.
Most of the students in this class go on to top-rated universities.
They study hard, in the perfect facilities and environment.

Twill/Before I fall

This is Simone's theme. (☺)
The song is like a choking, heart-fluttering, spring breeze.
I can get in the mood when I'm drawing his wandering feelings of love. (☺)
I'm not too familiar with them, but Twill seems to be teen Japanese twins.

I like their innocent, cute voices.

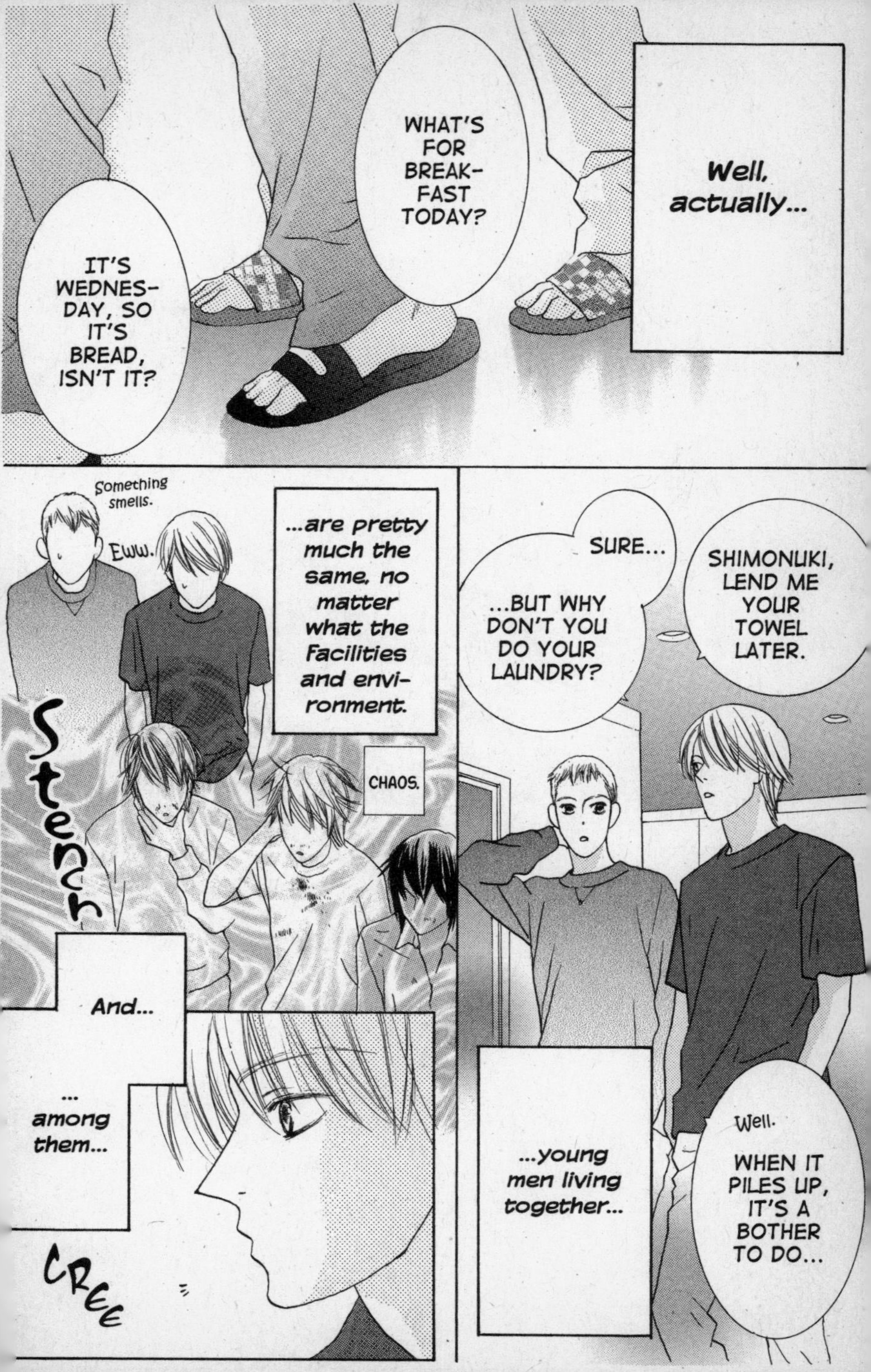
Well, actually...
WHAT'S FOR BREAK-FAST TODAY?
IT'S WEDNES-DAY, SO IT'S BREAD, ISN'T IT?
SHIMONUKI, LEND ME YOUR TOWEL LATER.
SURE...
...BUT WHY DON'T YOU DO YOUR LAUNDRY?
Well.
WHEN IT PILES UP, IT'S A BOTHER TO DO...
...young men living together...
...are pretty much the same, no matter what the facilities and envi-ronment.
CHAOS.
Something smells.
Eww.
Stench
And...
... among them...
CREE

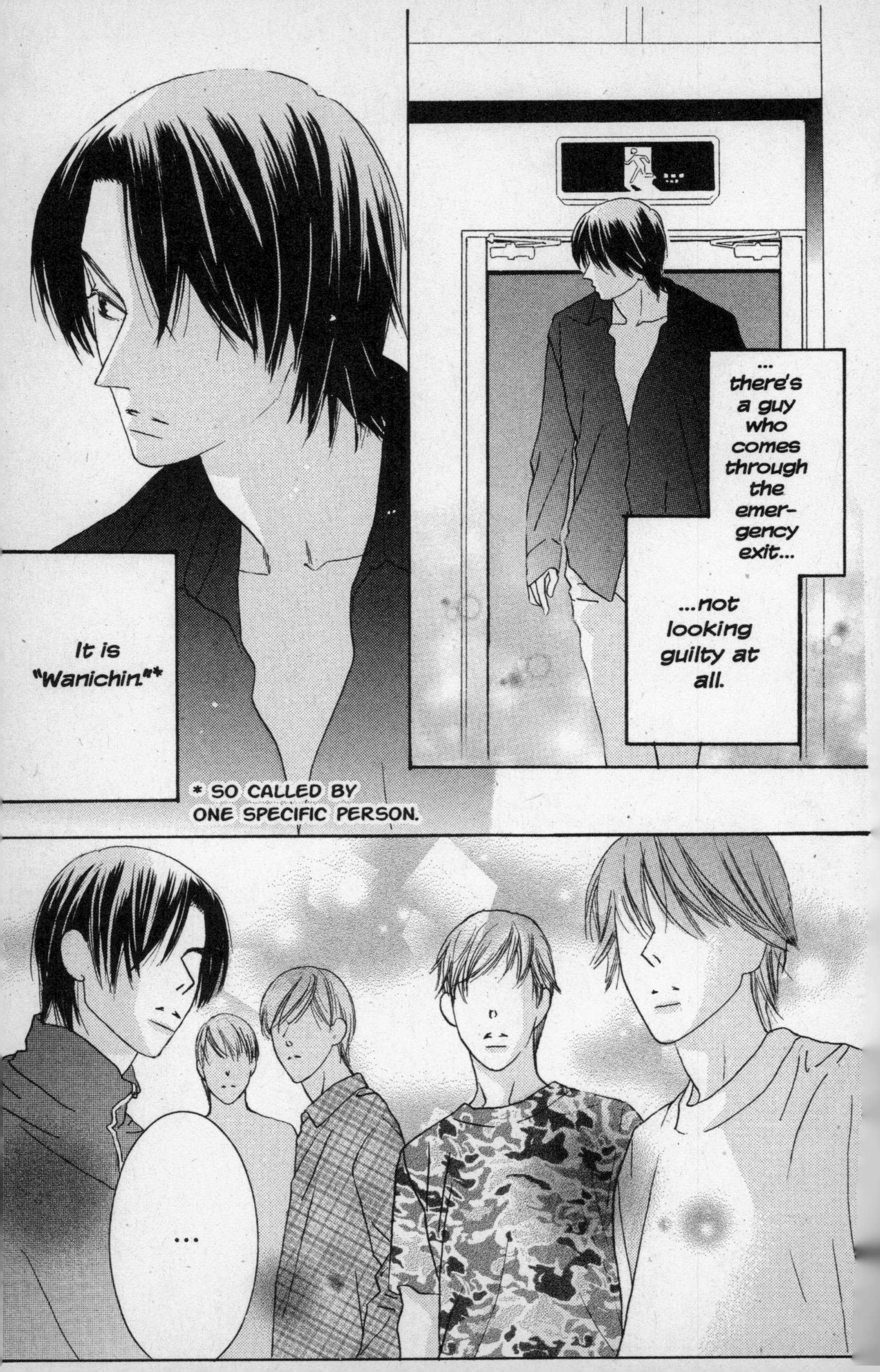
... there's a guy who comes through the emergency exit...
...not looking guilty at all.
It is "Wanichin."*
* SO CALLED BY ONE SPECIFIC PERSON.
...

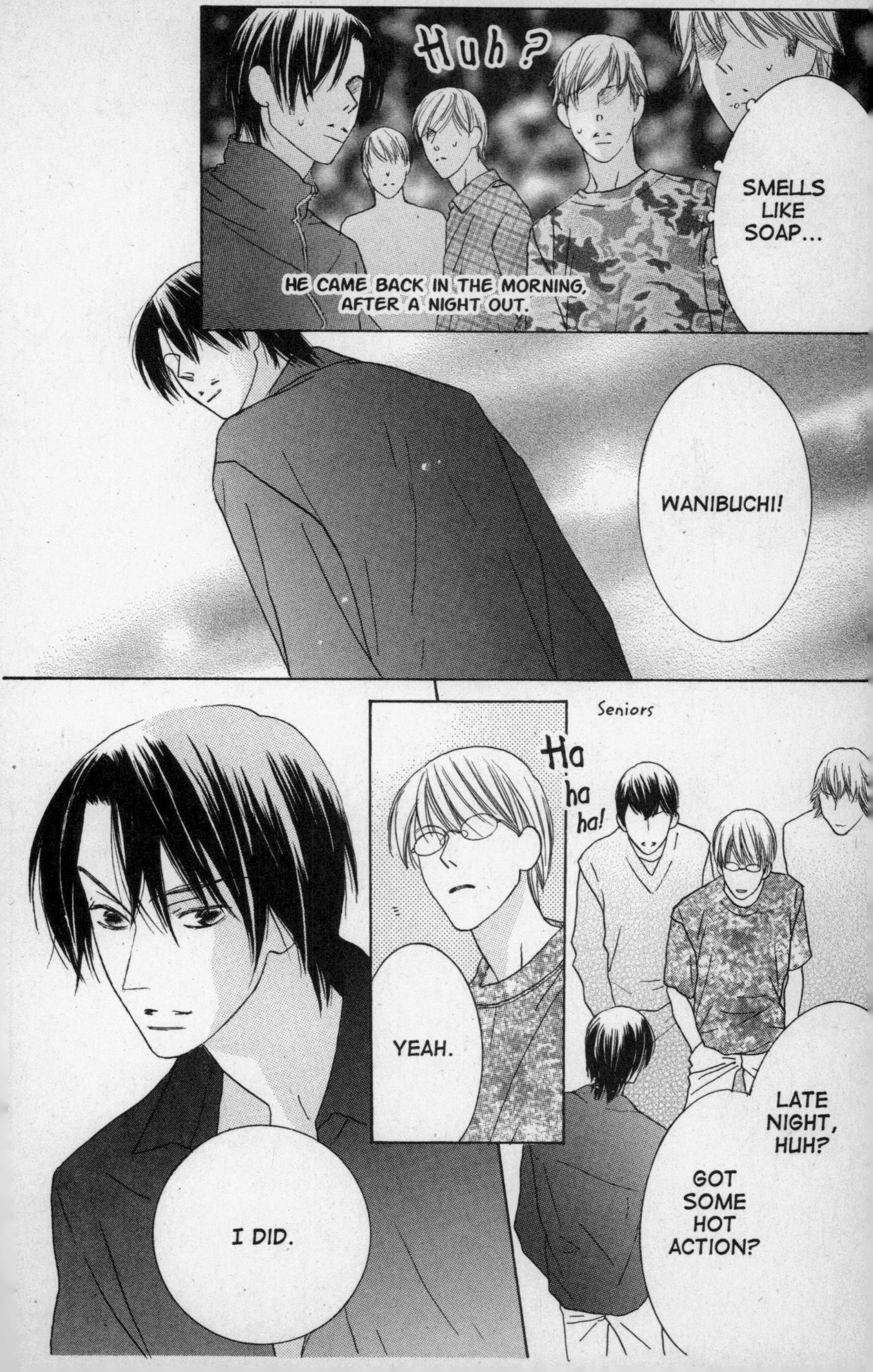
SMELLS LIKE SOAP...
Huh?
HE CAME BACK IN THE MORNING, AFTER A NIGHT OUT.
WANIBUCHI!
Seniors
Ha ha ha!
LATE NIGHT, HUH?
GOT SOME HOT ACTION?
YEAH.
I DID.

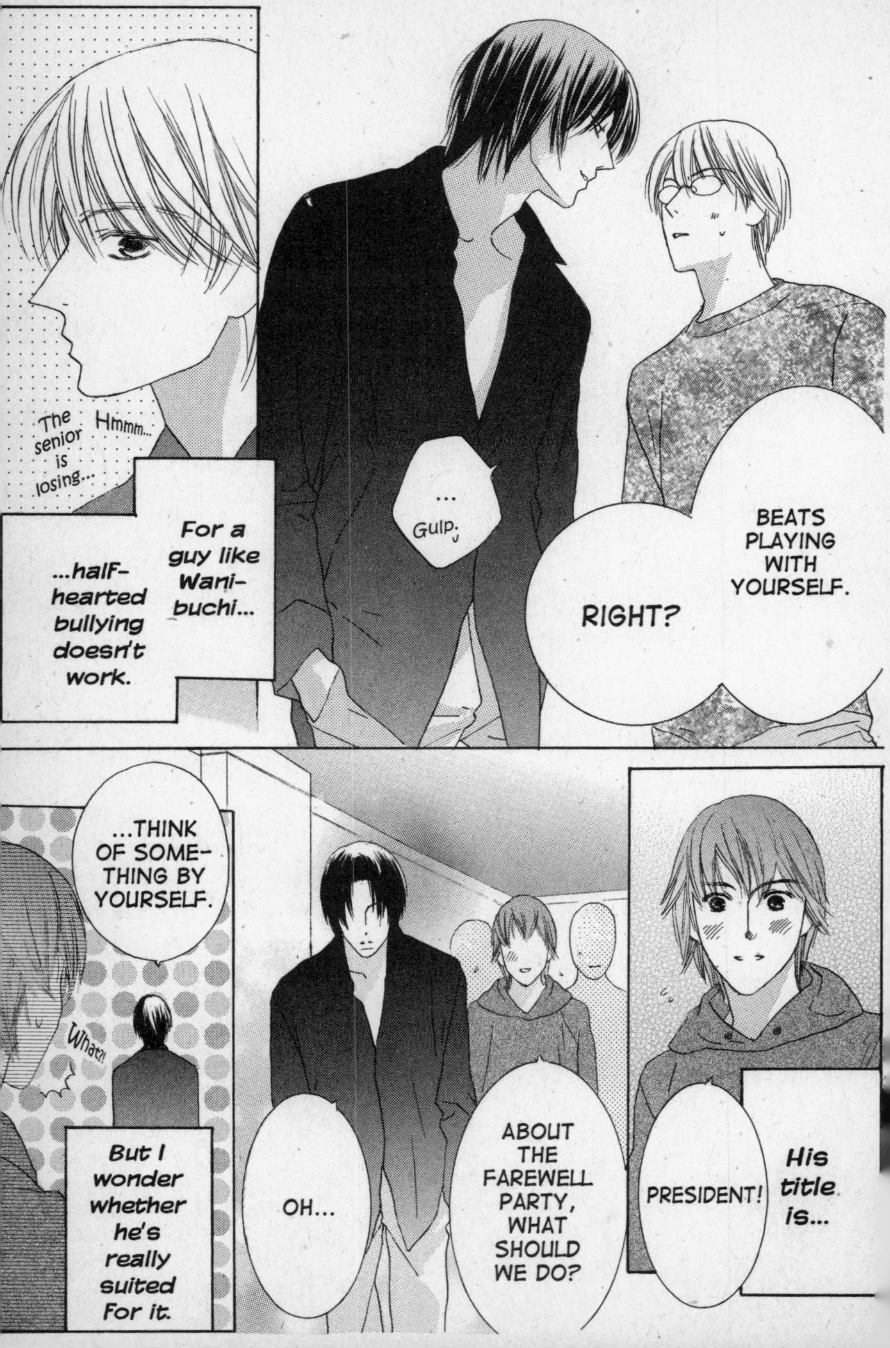
BEATS PLAYING WITH YOURSELF.
RIGHT?
... Gulp.
Hmmm...
The senior is losing...
For a guy like Wani-buchi...
...half-hearted bullying doesn't work.
His title is...
PRESIDENT!
ABOUT THE FAREWELL PARTY, WHAT SHOULD WE DO?
OH...
...THINK OF SOME-THING BY YOURSELF.
What?!
But I wonder whether he's really suited For it.

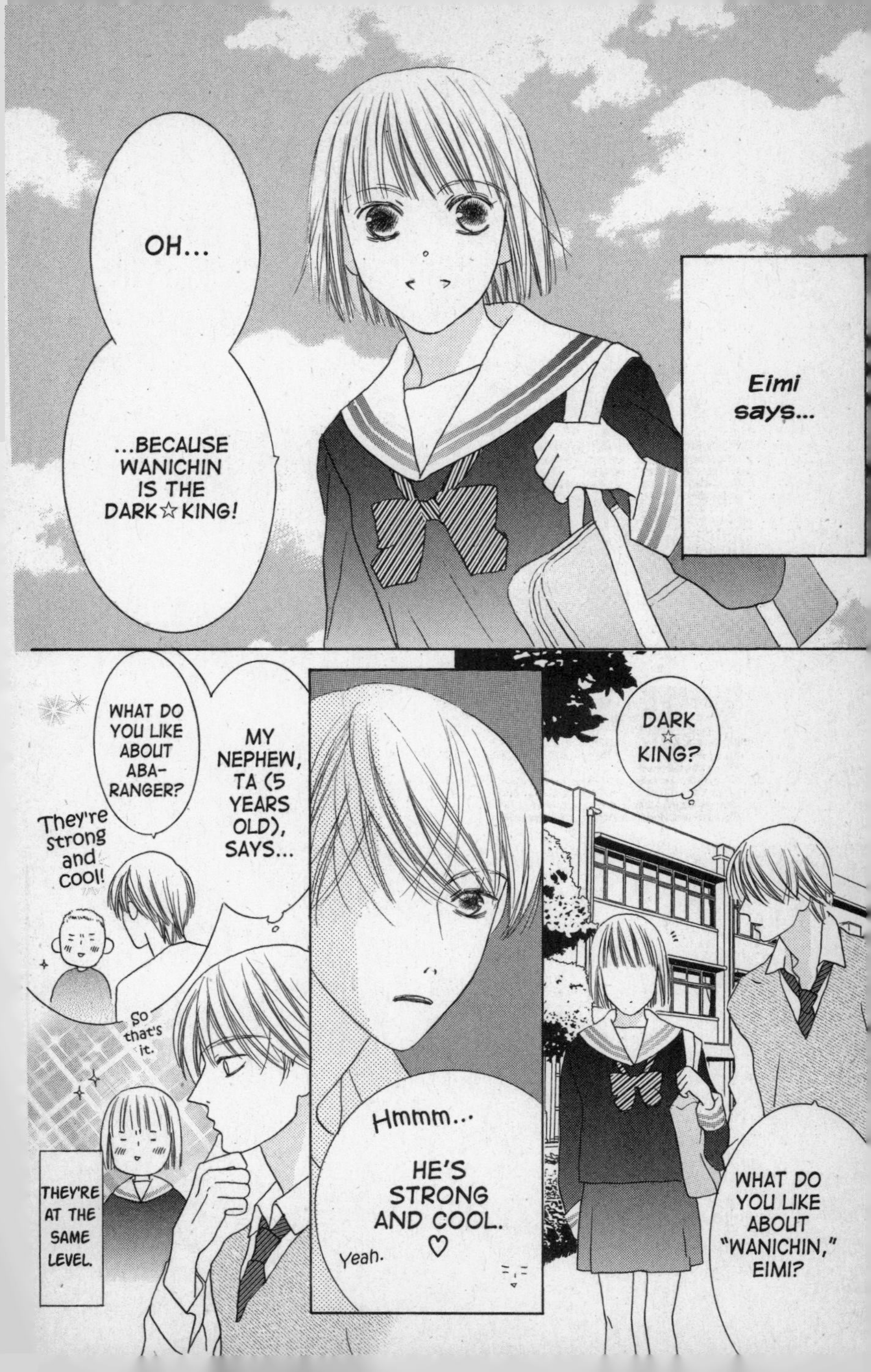

Eimi says...
OH... ...BECAUSE WANICHIN IS THE DARK☆KING!
DARK☆KING?
WHAT DO YOU LIKE ABOUT "WANICHIN," EIMI?
Hmmm...
HE'S STRONG AND COOL. ♡
Yeah.
MY NEPHEW, TA (5 YEARS OLD), SAYS...
WHAT DO YOU LIKE ABOUT ABA-RANGER?
They're strong and cool!
So that's it.
THEY'RE AT THE SAME LEVEL.

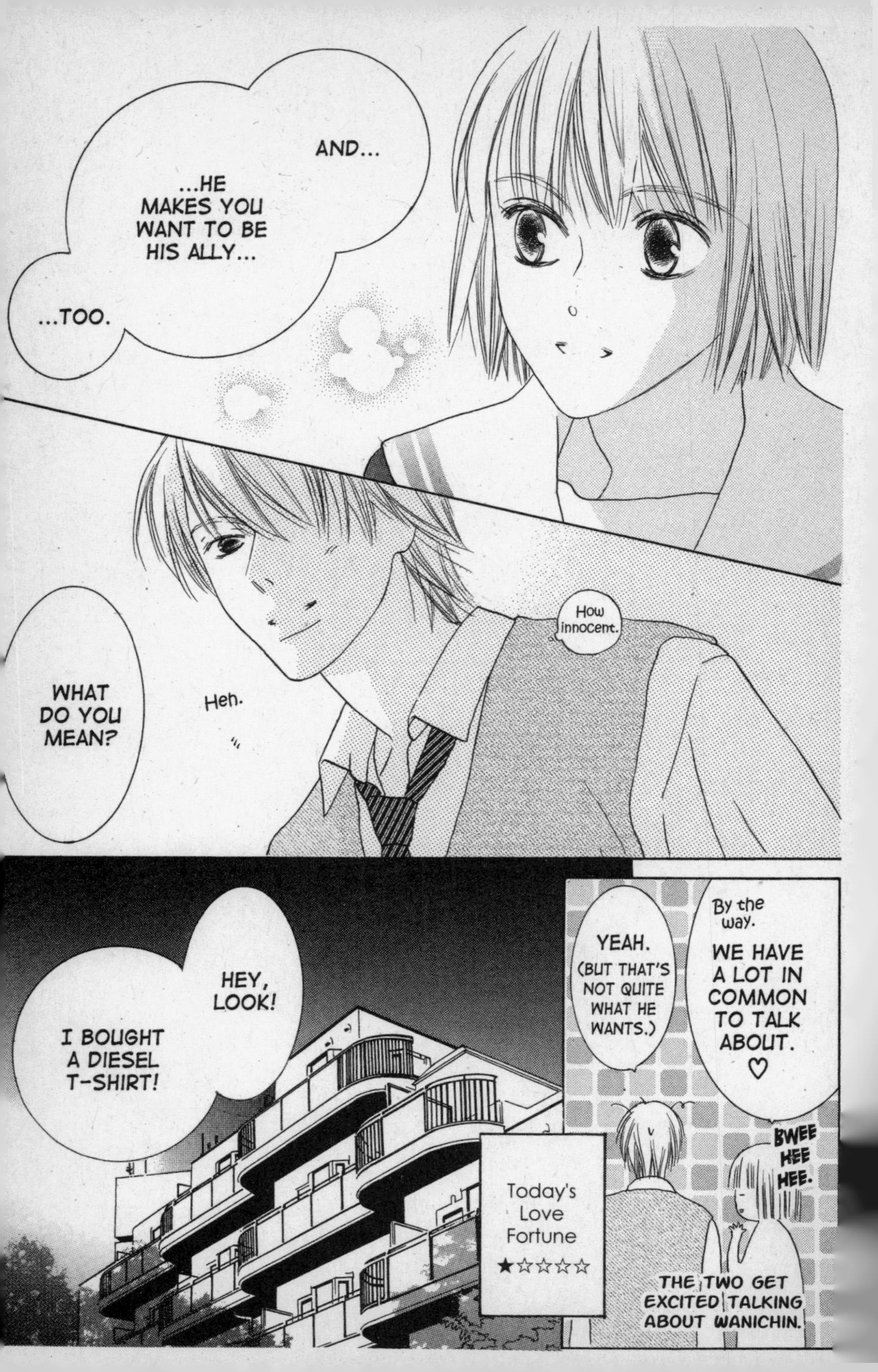
AND...
...HE MAKES YOU WANT TO BE HIS ALLY...
...TOO.
How innocent.
Heh.
WHAT DO YOU MEAN?
By the way.
WE HAVE A LOT IN COMMON TO TALK ABOUT. ♡
YEAH. (BUT THAT'S NOT QUITE WHAT HE WANTS.)
BWEE HEE HEE.
THE TWO GET EXCITED TALKING ABOUT WANICHIN.
Today's Love Fortune ★☆☆☆☆
HEY, LOOK!
I BOUGHT A DIESEL T-SHIRT!

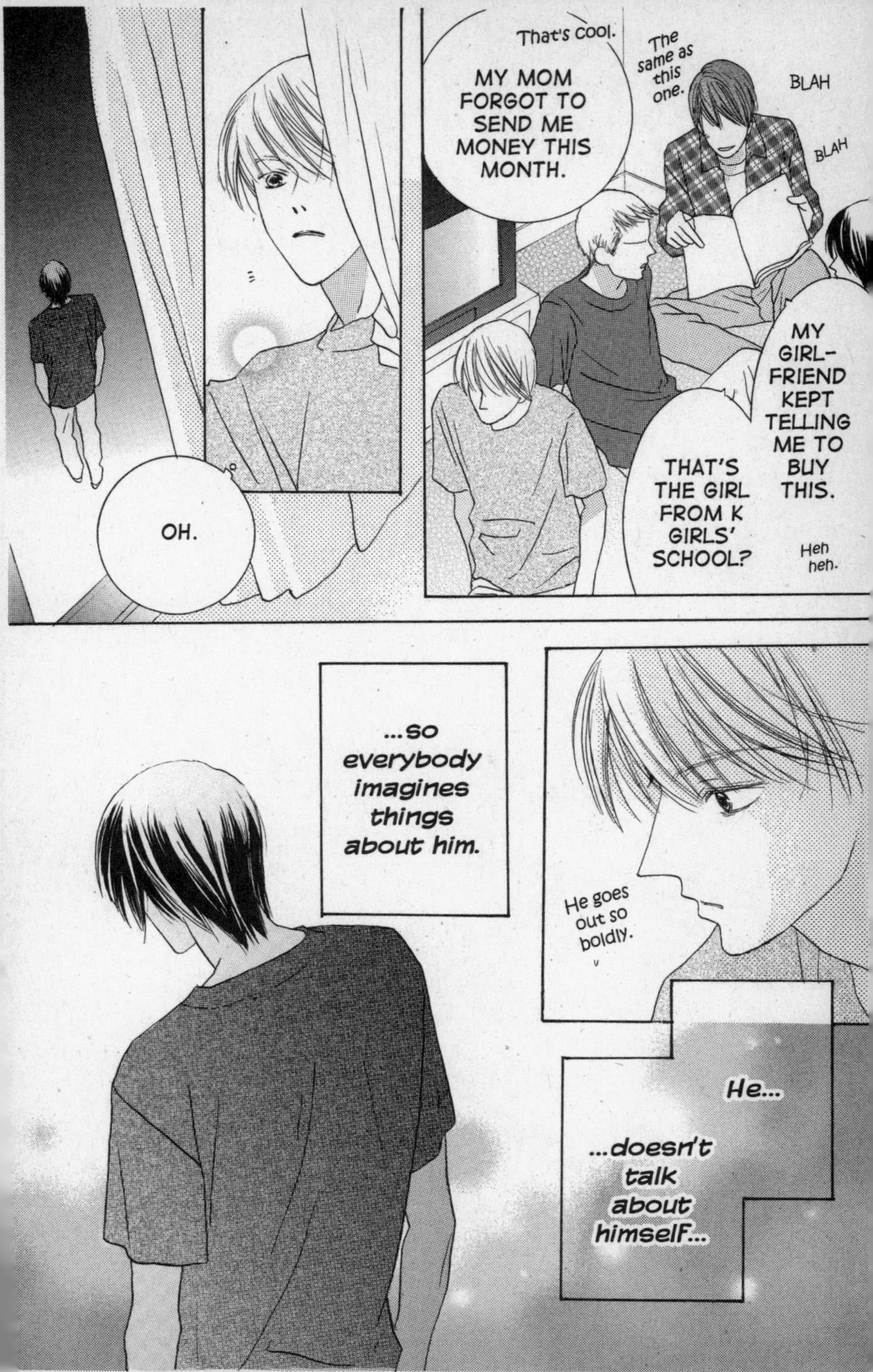
BLAH
BLAH
The same as this one.
That's cool.
MY MOM FORGOT TO SEND ME MONEY THIS MONTH.
MY GIRL-FRIEND KEPT TELLING ME TO BUY THIS.
Heh heh.
THAT'S THE GIRL FROM K GIRLS' SCHOOL?
OH.
He goes out so boldly.
He...
...doesn't talk about himself...
...so everybody imagines things about him.

I realized it now, but boys working at night appear a lot in my manga. I myself can't drink alcohol, and don't go to bars or clubs at all. It's a mystery. I like appetizers, and I eat at lot of cheeze tara and surume.
When I'm tired of working on my manga, I eat edamame, so I look like I can drink a lot. (☺)
...But I can't drink...
It's a mystery... what the heck...?
(oh dear)

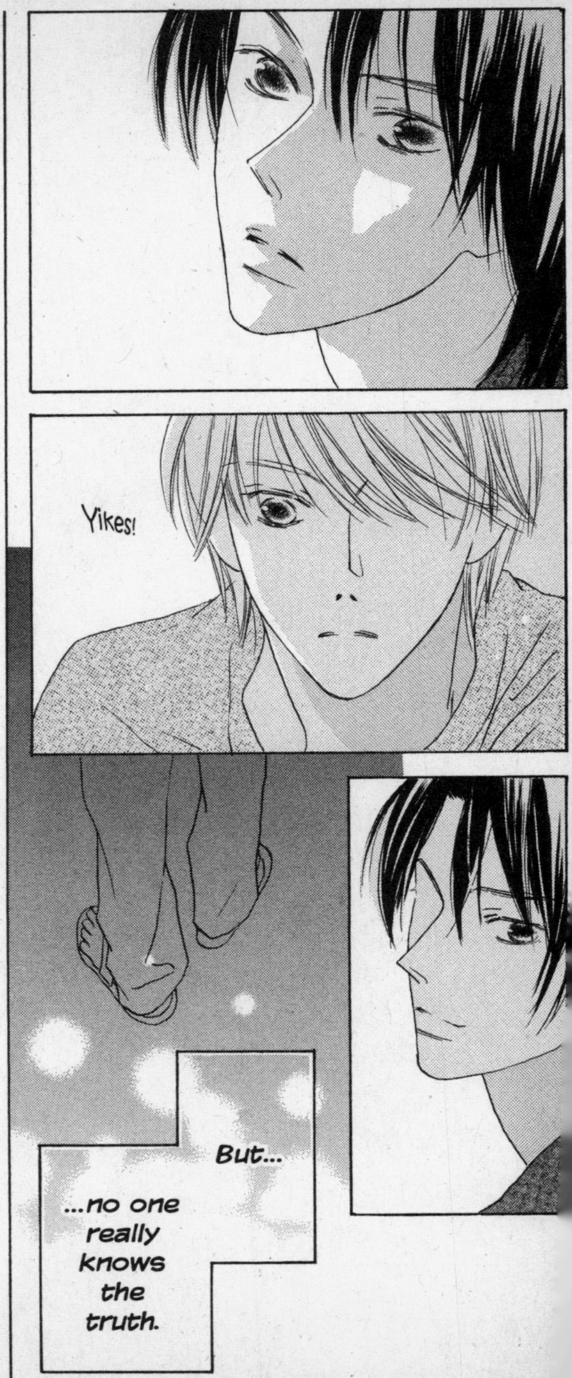
Yikes!
But...
...no one really knows the truth.

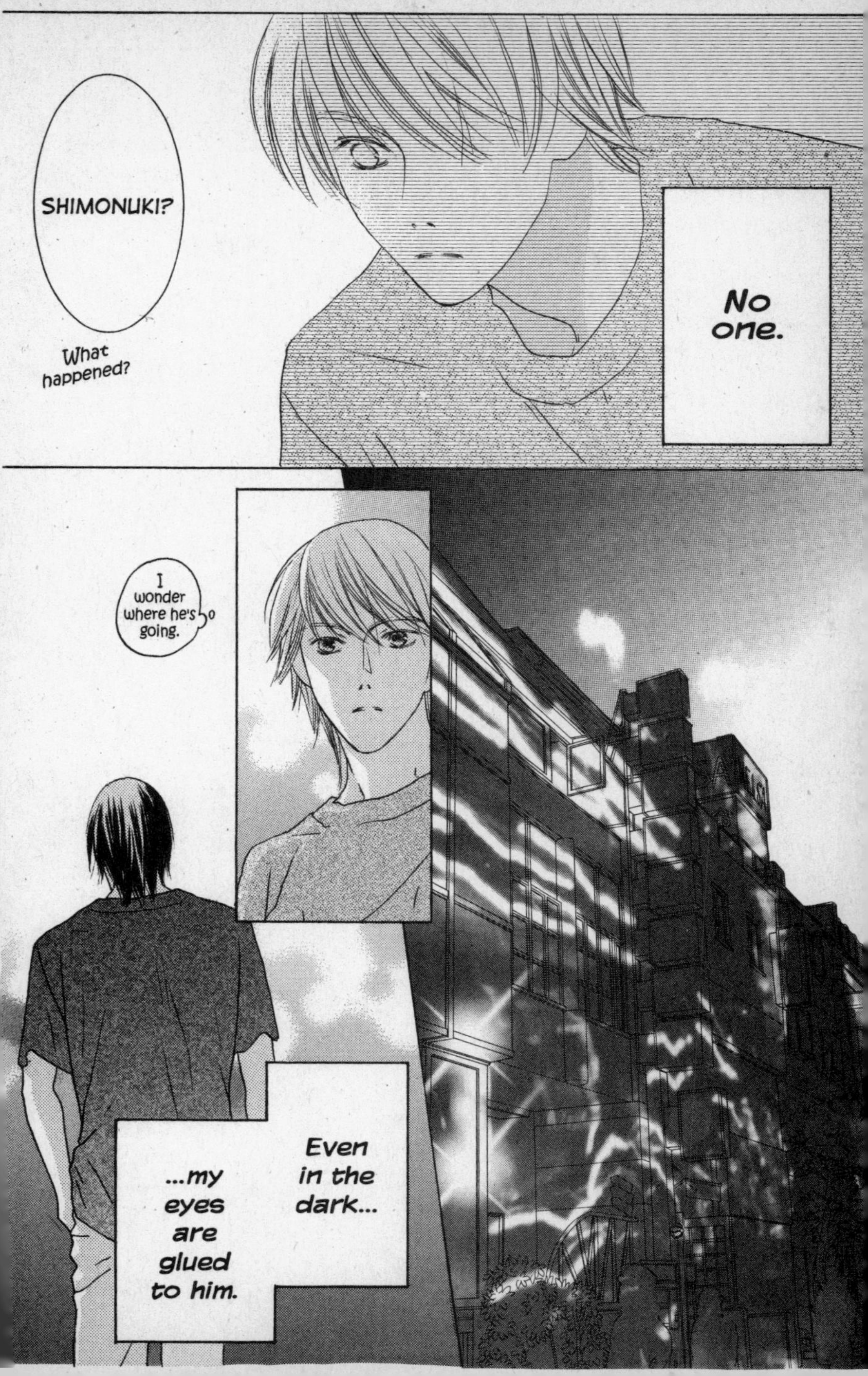
No one.
SHIMONUKI?
What happened?
I wonder where he's going.
Even in the dark...
...my eyes are glued to him.

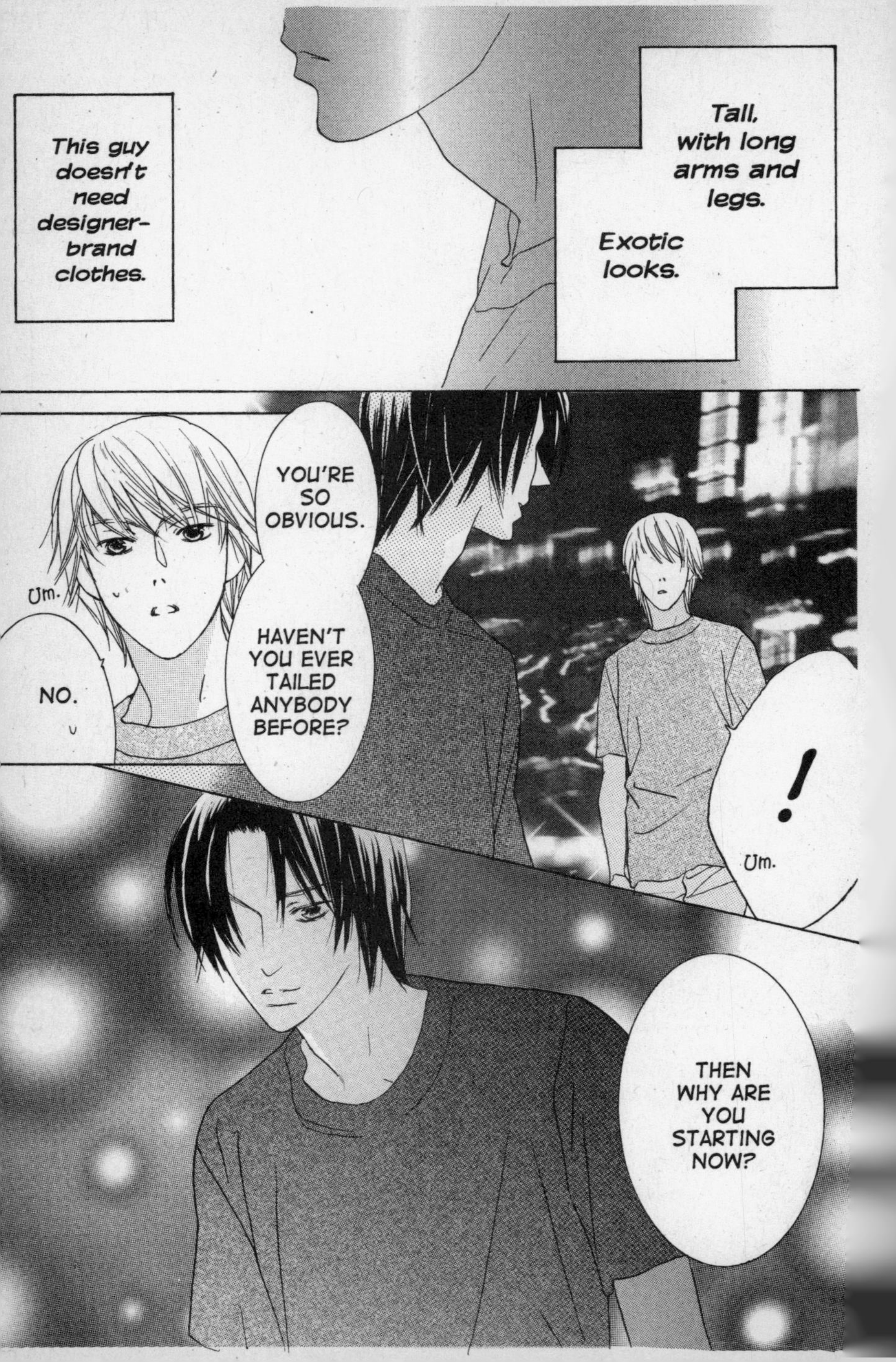
Tall, with long arms and legs.
Exotic looks.
This guy doesn't need designer-brand clothes.
!
Um.
YOU'RE SO OBVIOUS.
HAVEN'T YOU EVER TAILED ANYBODY BEFORE?
Um.
NO.
THEN WHY ARE YOU STARTING NOW?

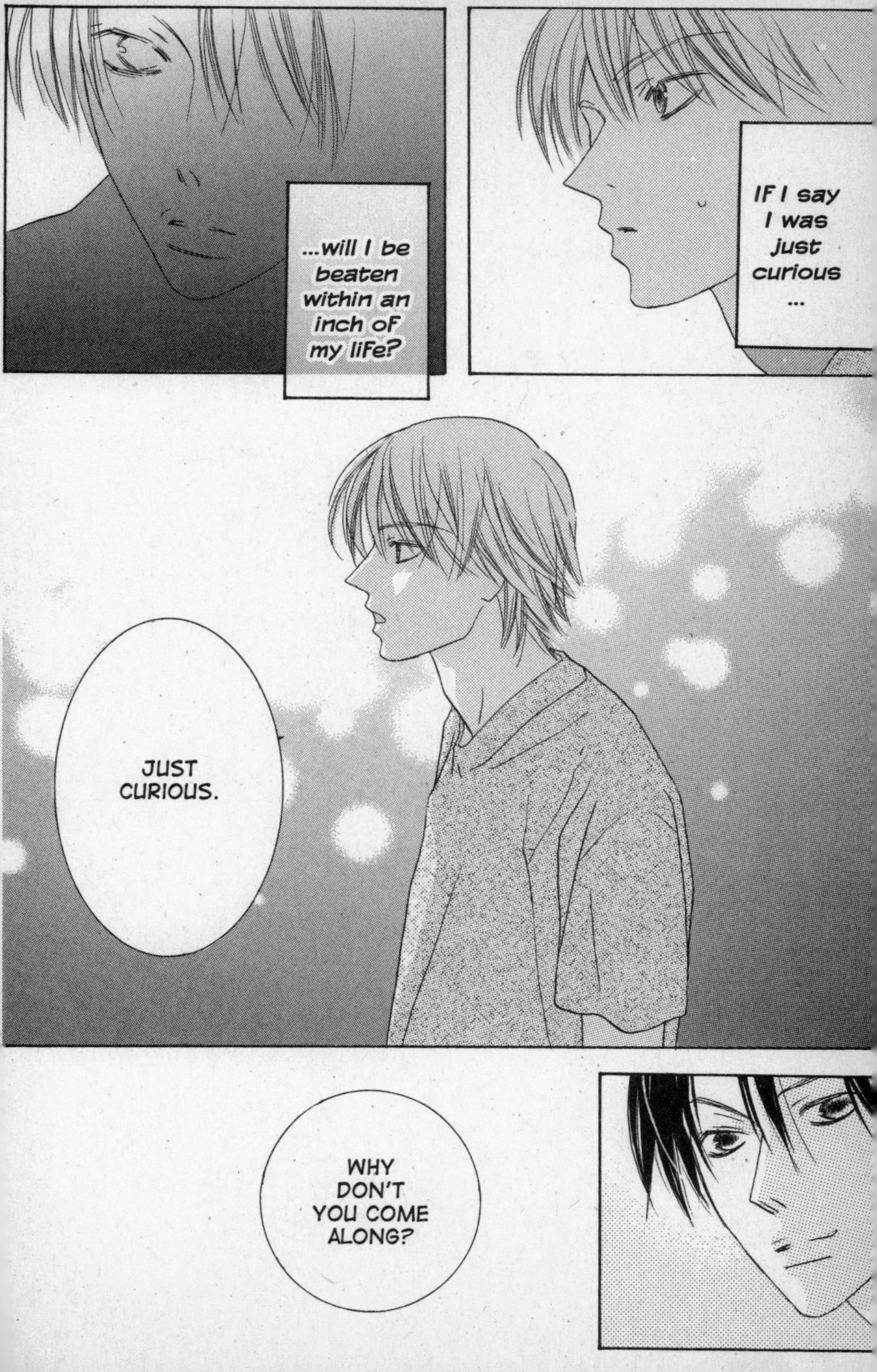
IF I say I was just curious ...
...will I be beaten within an inch of my life?
JUST CURIOUS.
WHY DON'T YOU COME ALONG?

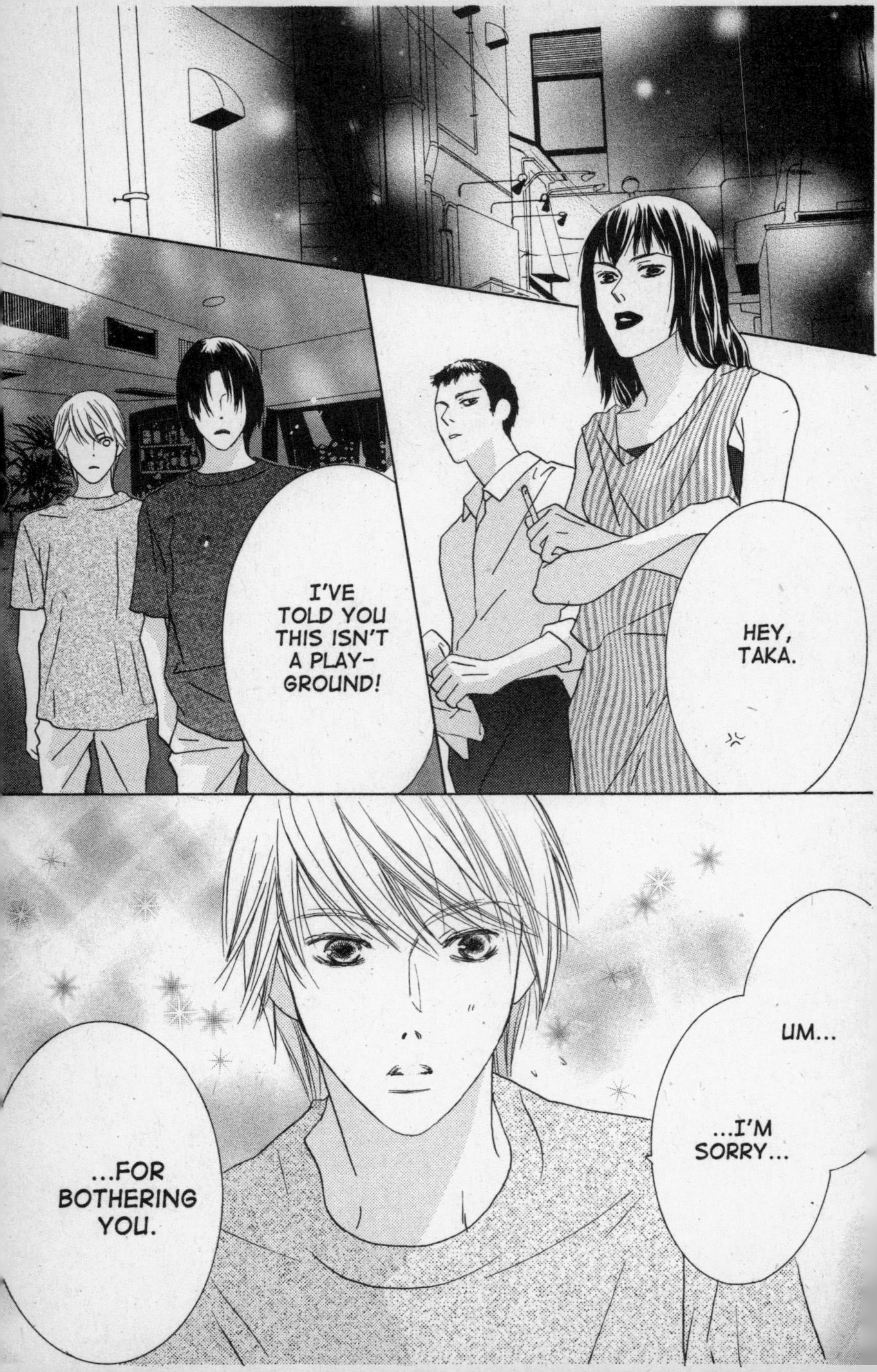
HEY, TAKA.
I'VE TOLD YOU THIS ISN'T A PLAY-GROUND!
UM...
...I'M SORRY...
...FOR BOTHERING YOU.

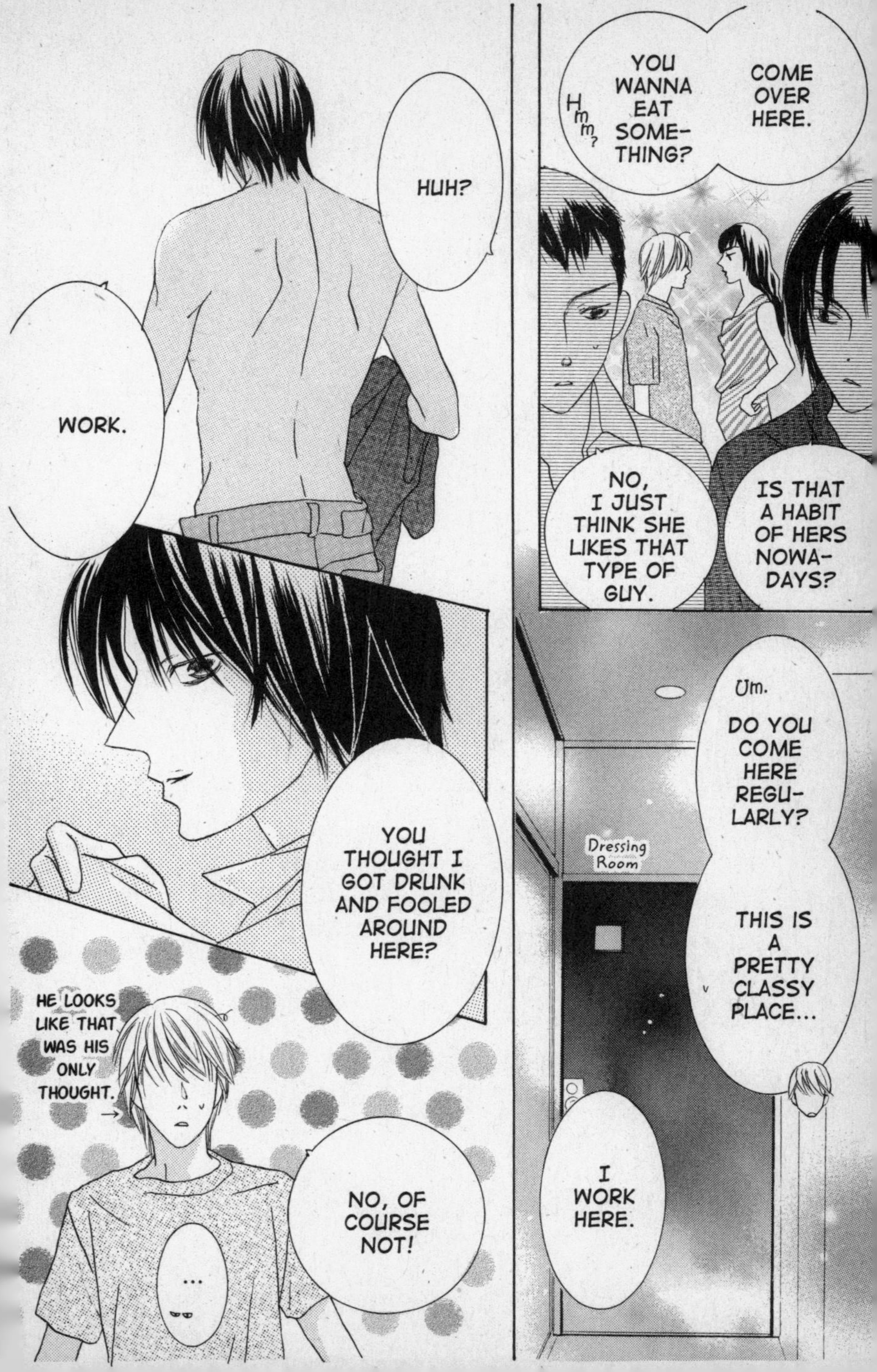
COME OVER HERE.
YOU WANNA EAT SOME-THING?
Hmm?
IS THAT A HABIT OF HERS NOWA-DAYS?
NO, I JUST THINK SHE LIKES THAT TYPE OF GUY.
Um.
DO YOU COME HERE REGU-LARLY?
THIS IS A PRETTY CLASSY PLACE...
Dressing Room
I WORK HERE.
HUH?
WORK.
YOU THOUGHT I GOT DRUNK AND FOOLED AROUND HERE?
NO, OF COURSE NOT!
HE LOOKS LIKE THAT WAS HIS ONLY THOUGHT.
...

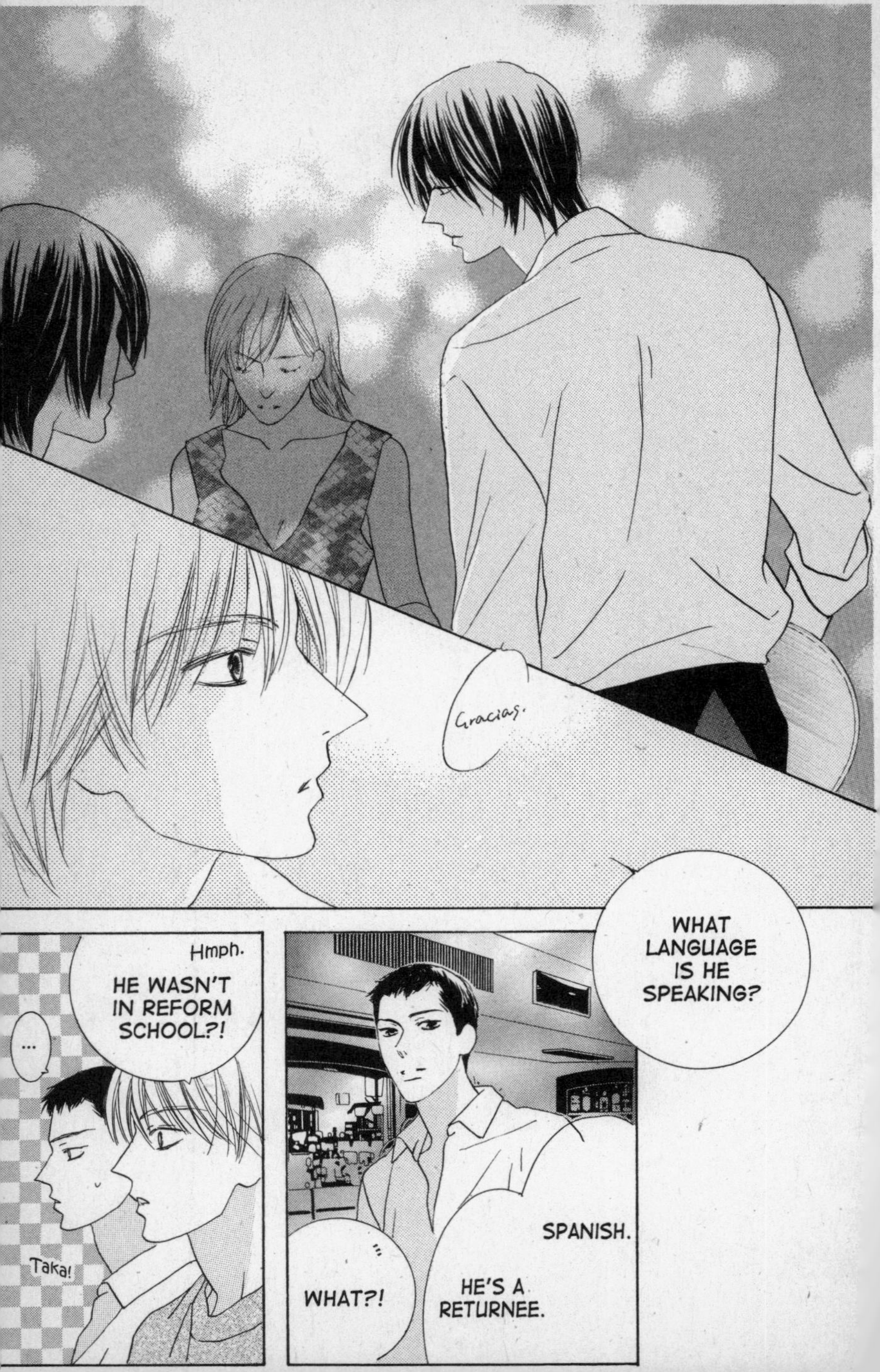
Gracias.
WHAT LANGUAGE IS HE SPEAKING?
SPANISH.
HE'S A RETURNEE.
WHAT?!
Hmph.
HE WASN'T IN REFORM SCHOOL?!
...
Taka!

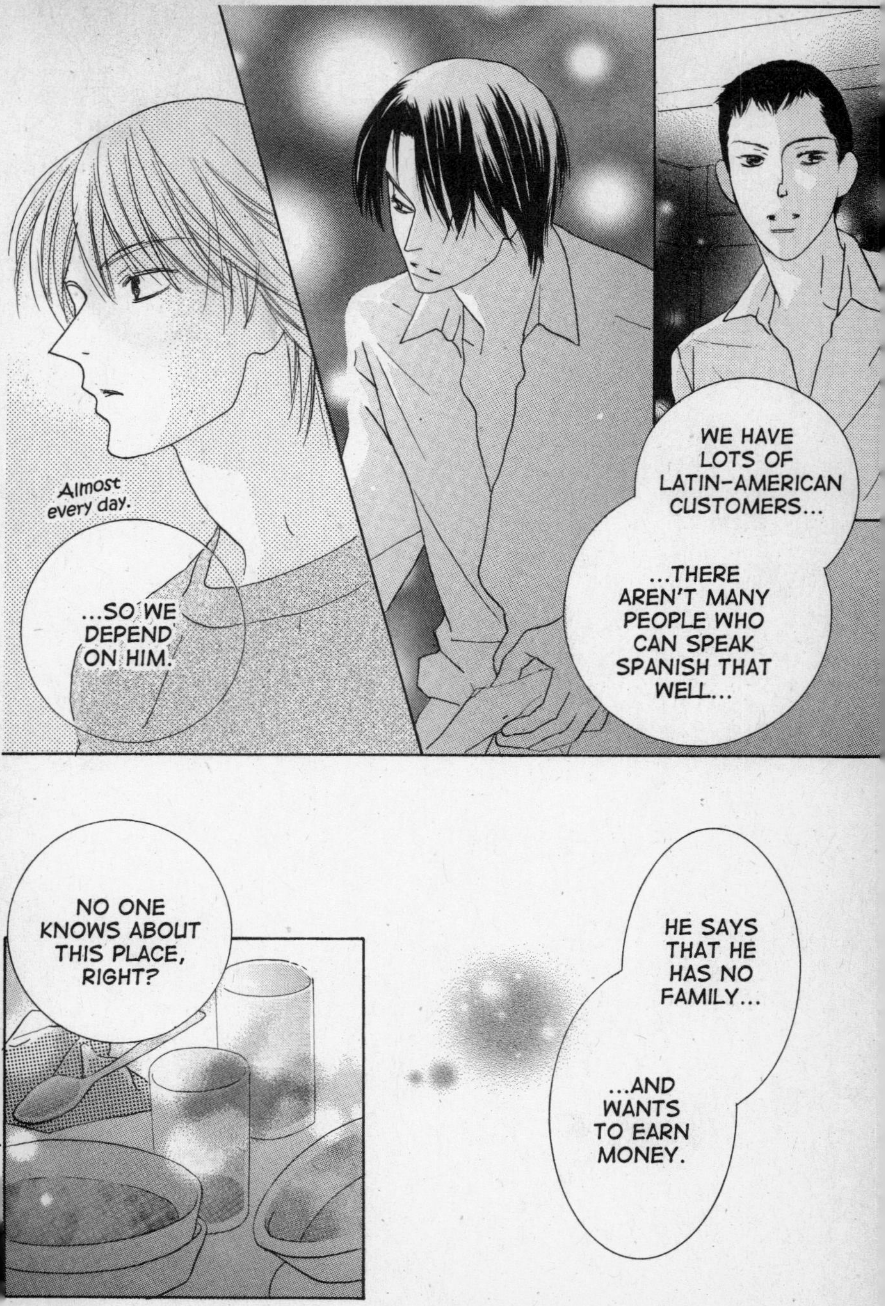
WE HAVE LOTS OF LATIN-AMERICAN CUSTOMERS...
...THERE AREN'T MANY PEOPLE WHO CAN SPEAK SPANISH THAT WELL...
Almost every day.
...SO WE DEPEND ON HIM.
HE SAYS THAT HE HAS NO FAMILY...
...AND WANTS TO EARN MONEY.
NO ONE KNOWS ABOUT THIS PLACE, RIGHT?

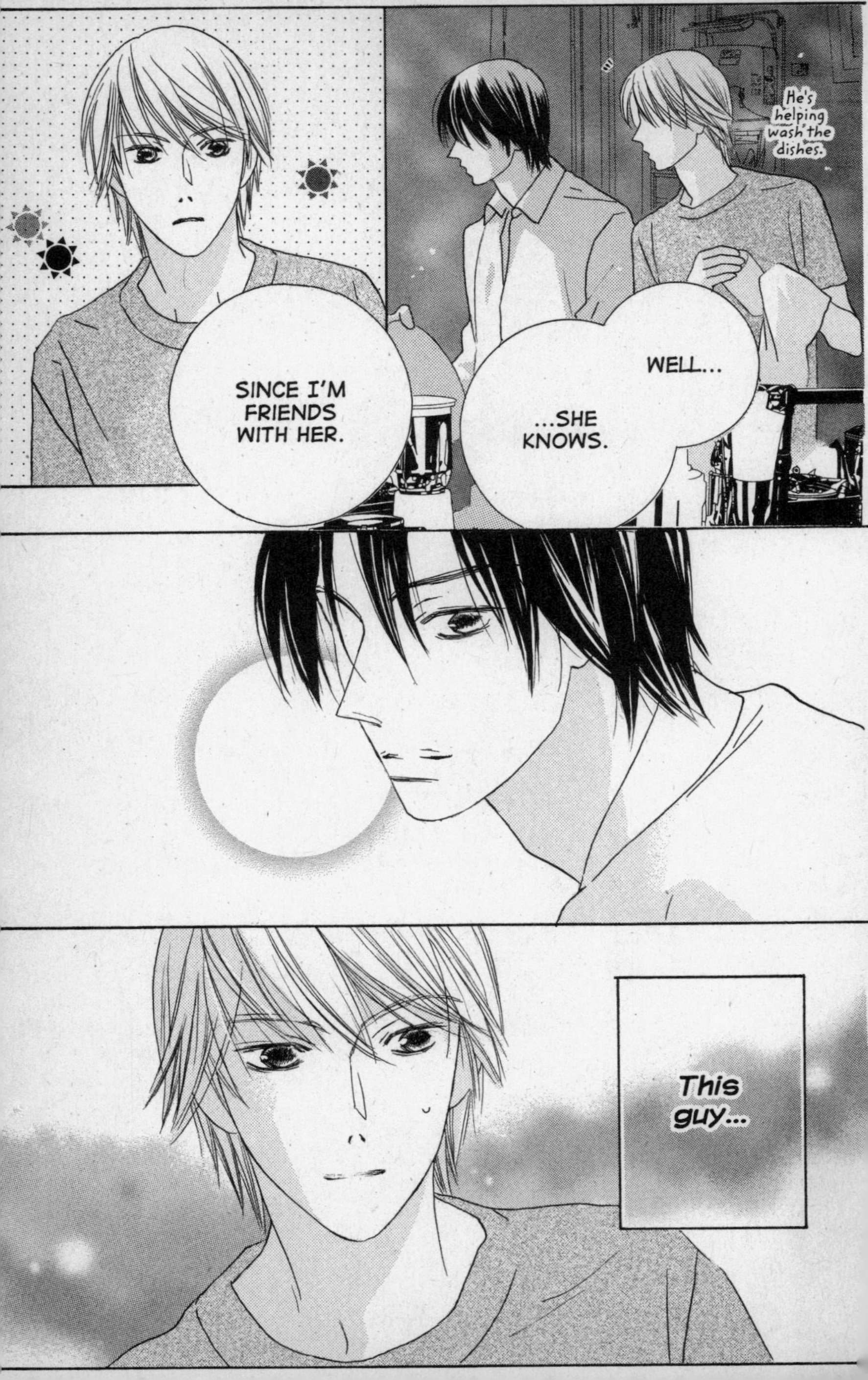
He's helping wash the dishes.
WELL...
...SHE KNOWS.
SINCE I'M FRIENDS WITH HER.
This guy...

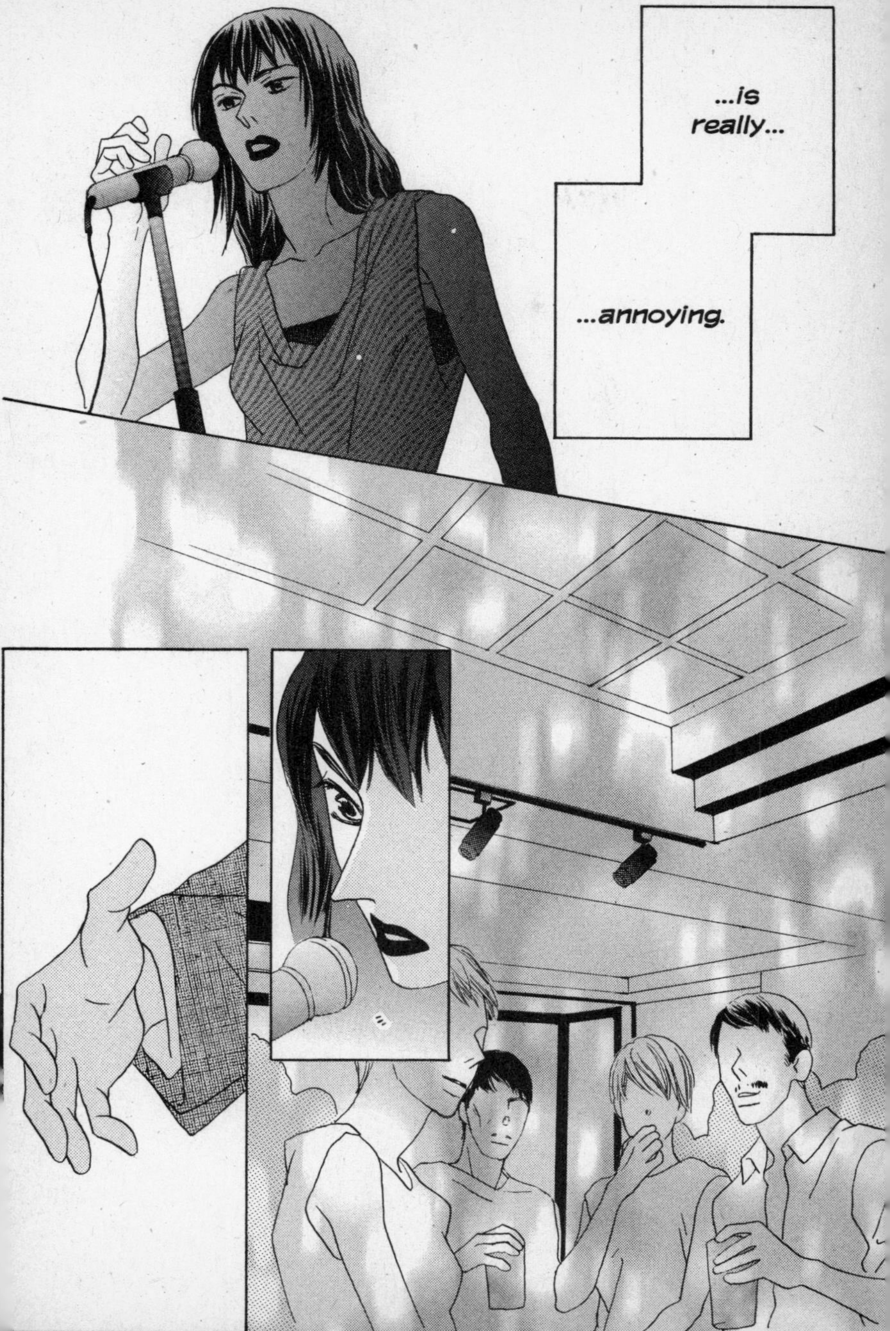

...is really...
...annoying.

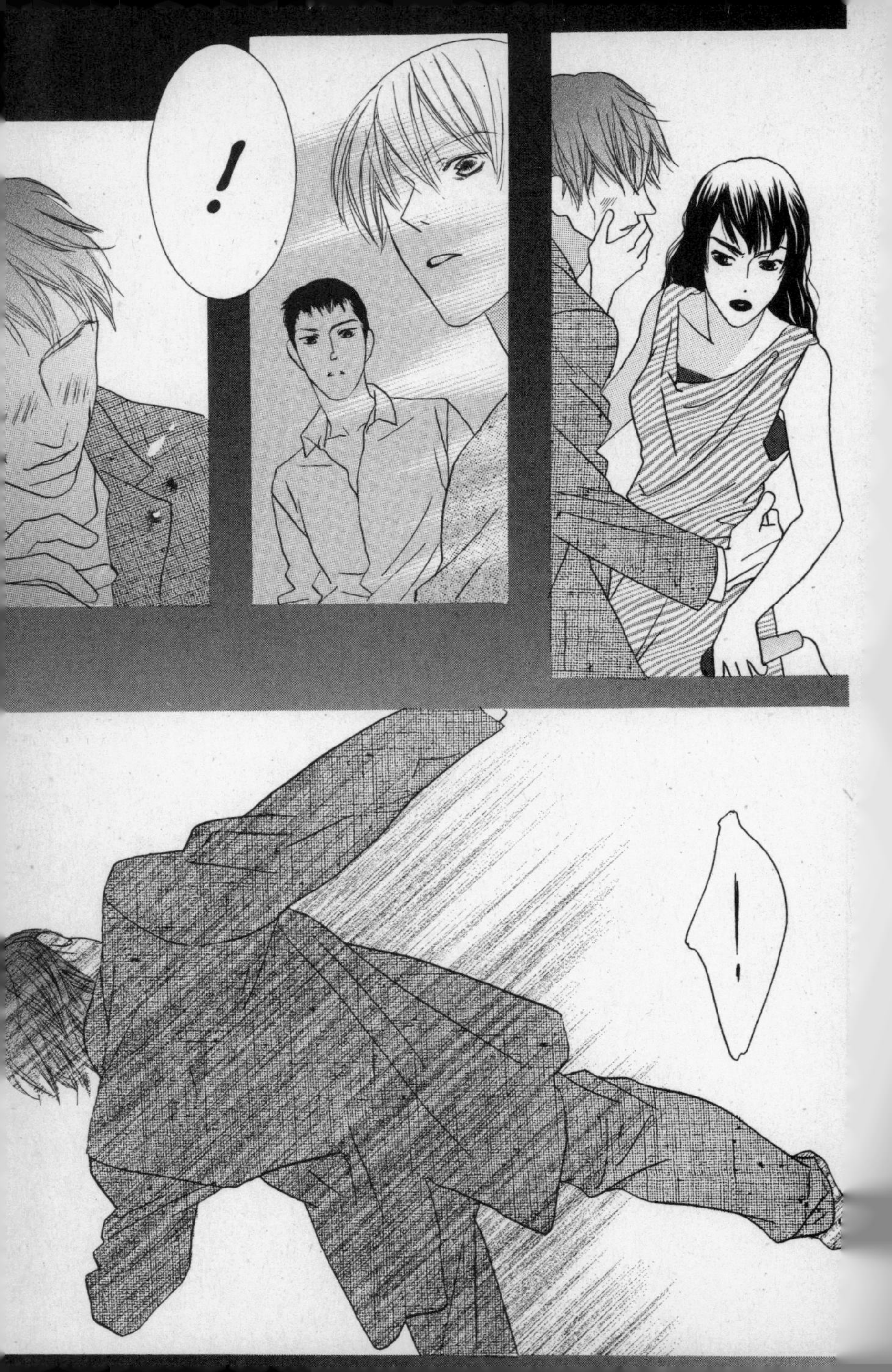
!
!

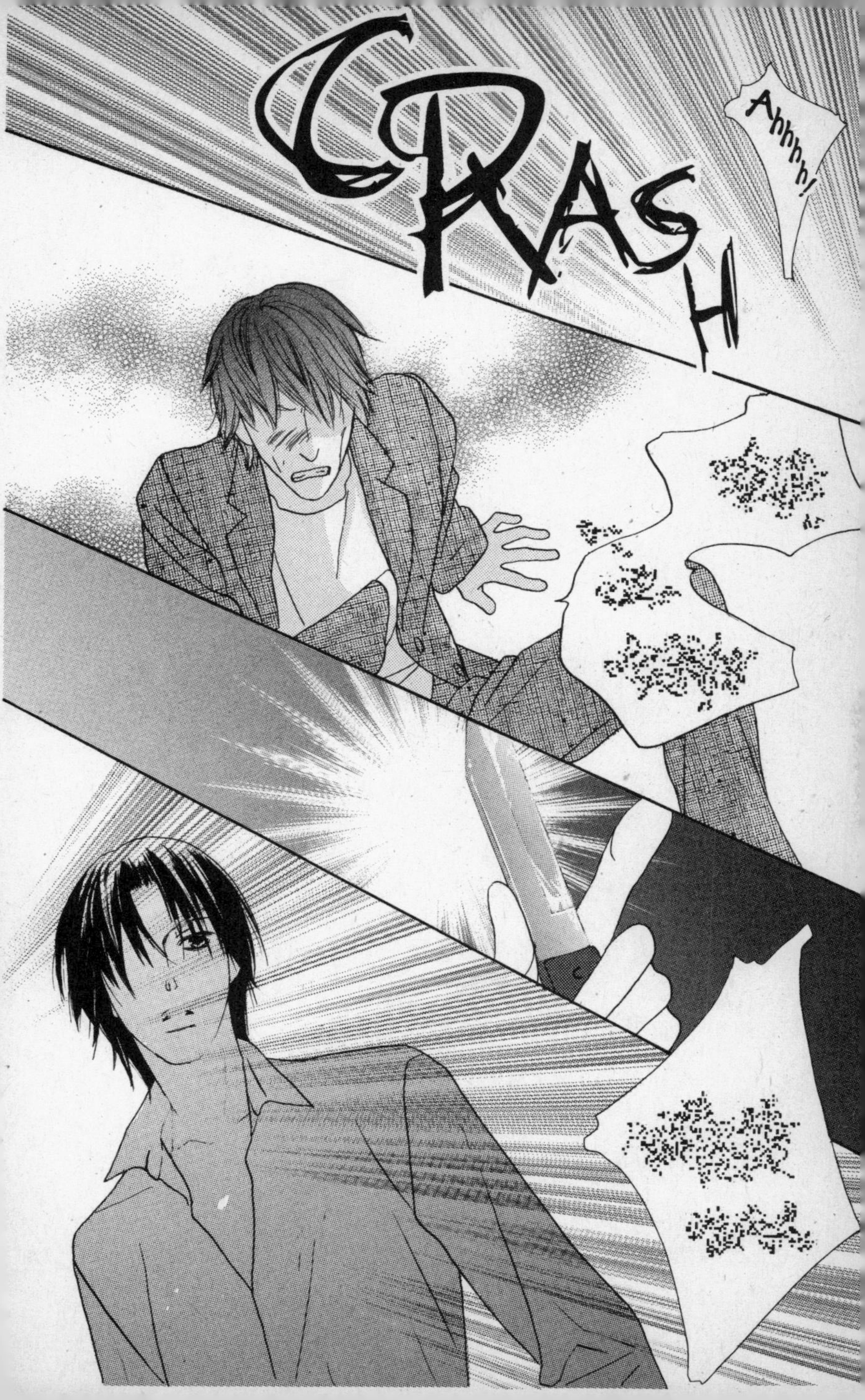
Ahhhh!
CRASH

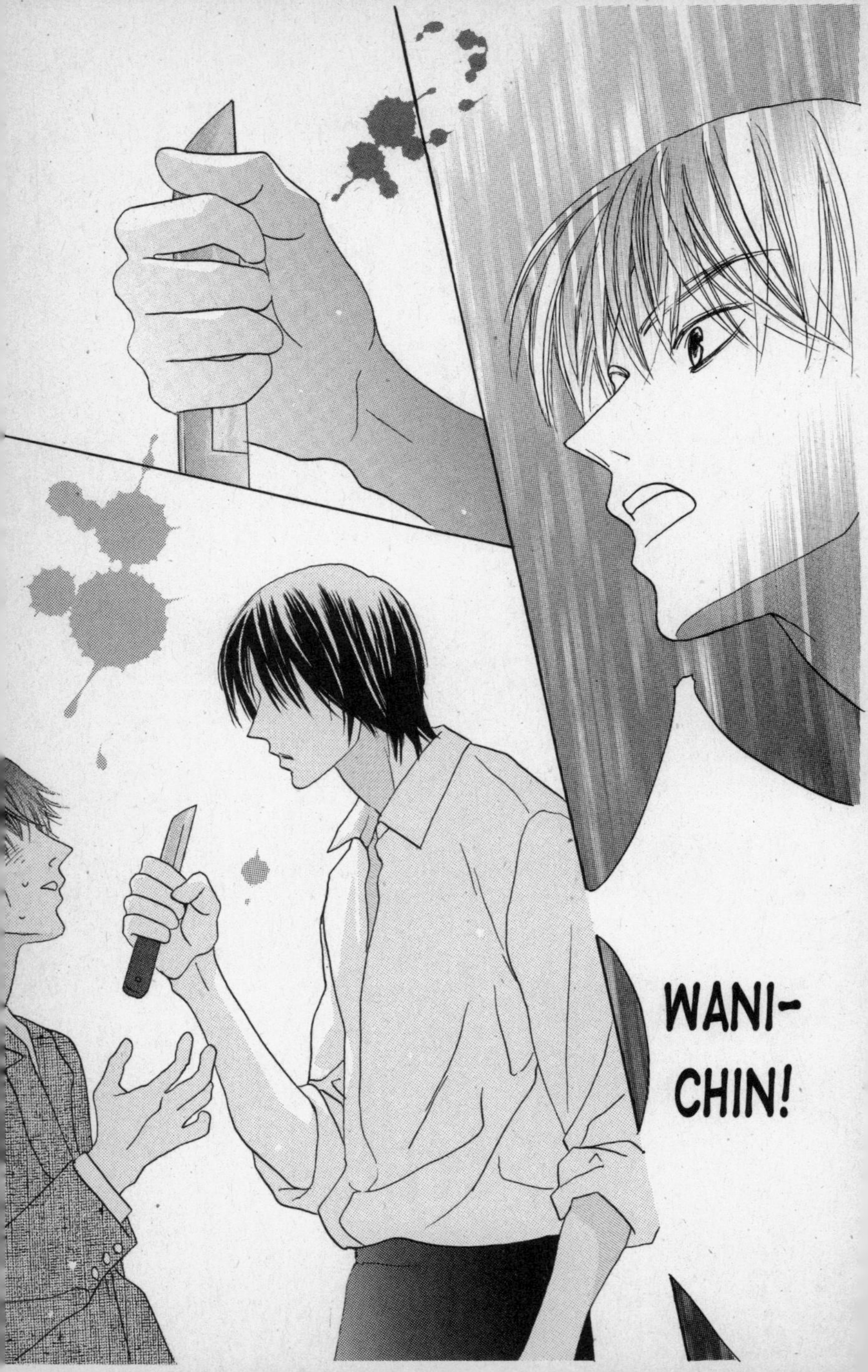
WANI-
CHIN!

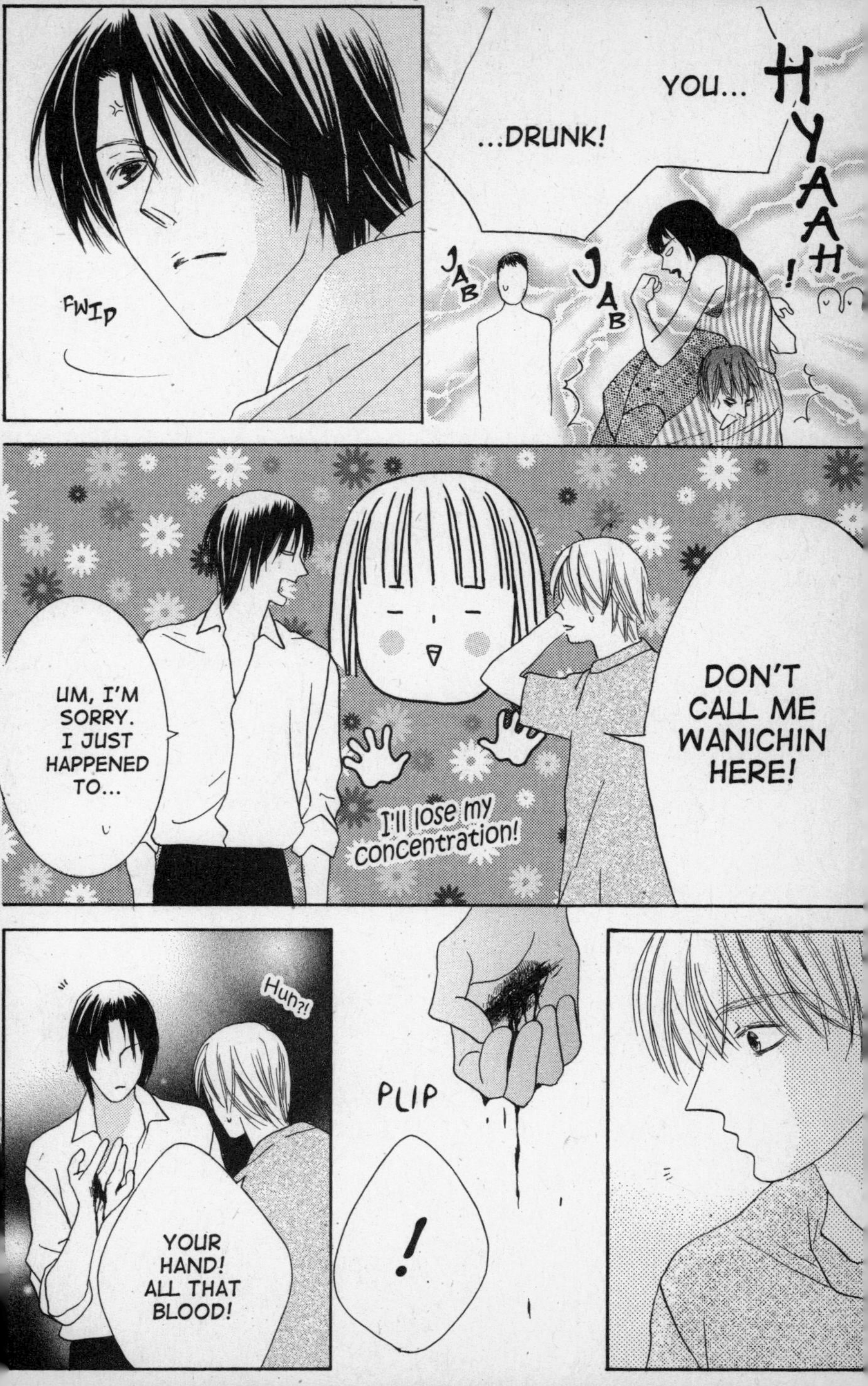

YOU...
HYAAAH!
...DRUNK!
JAB
JAB
FWIP
DON'T CALL ME WANICHIN HERE!
I'll lose my concentration!
UM, I'M SORRY. I JUST HAPPENED TO...
PLIP
!
Huh?!
YOUR HAND! ALL THAT BLOOD!

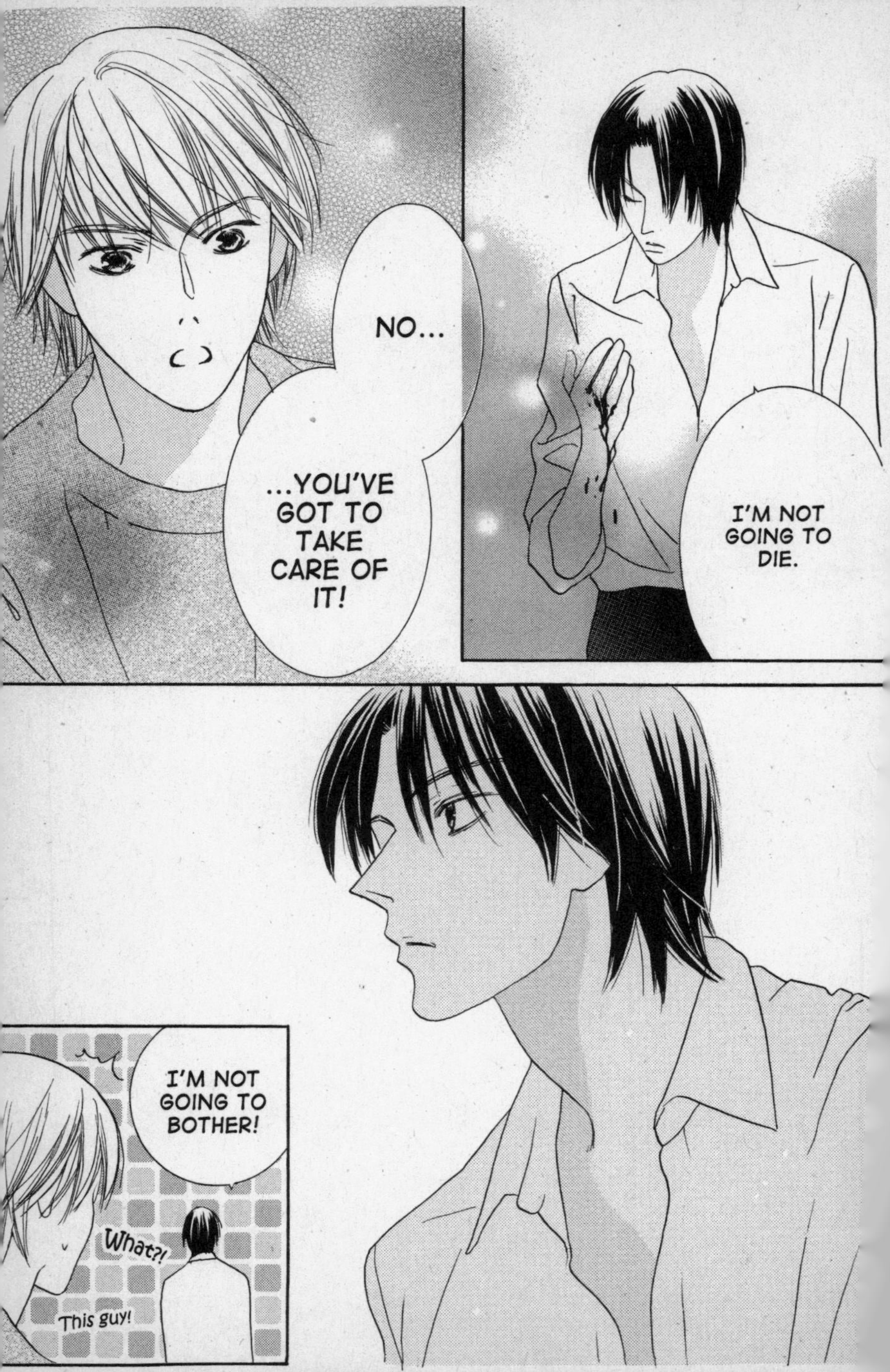
I'M NOT GOING TO DIE.
NO...
...YOU'VE GOT TO TAKE CARE OF IT!
I'M NOT GOING TO BOTHER!
What?!
This guy!

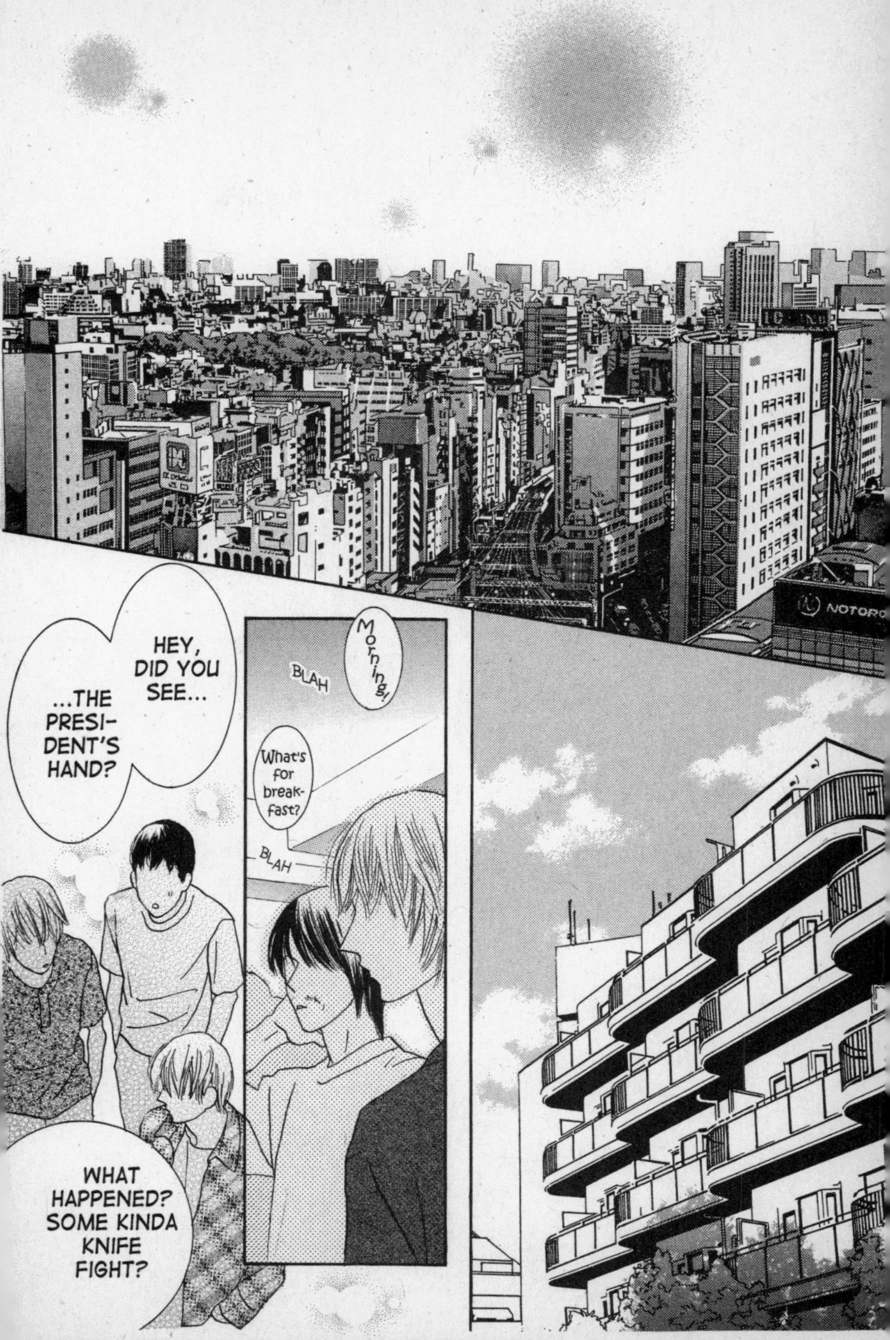
Morning!
BLAH
What's for breakfast?
BLAH
HEY, DID YOU SEE...
...THE PRESIDENT'S HAND?
WHAT HAPPENED? SOME KINDA KNIFE FIGHT?

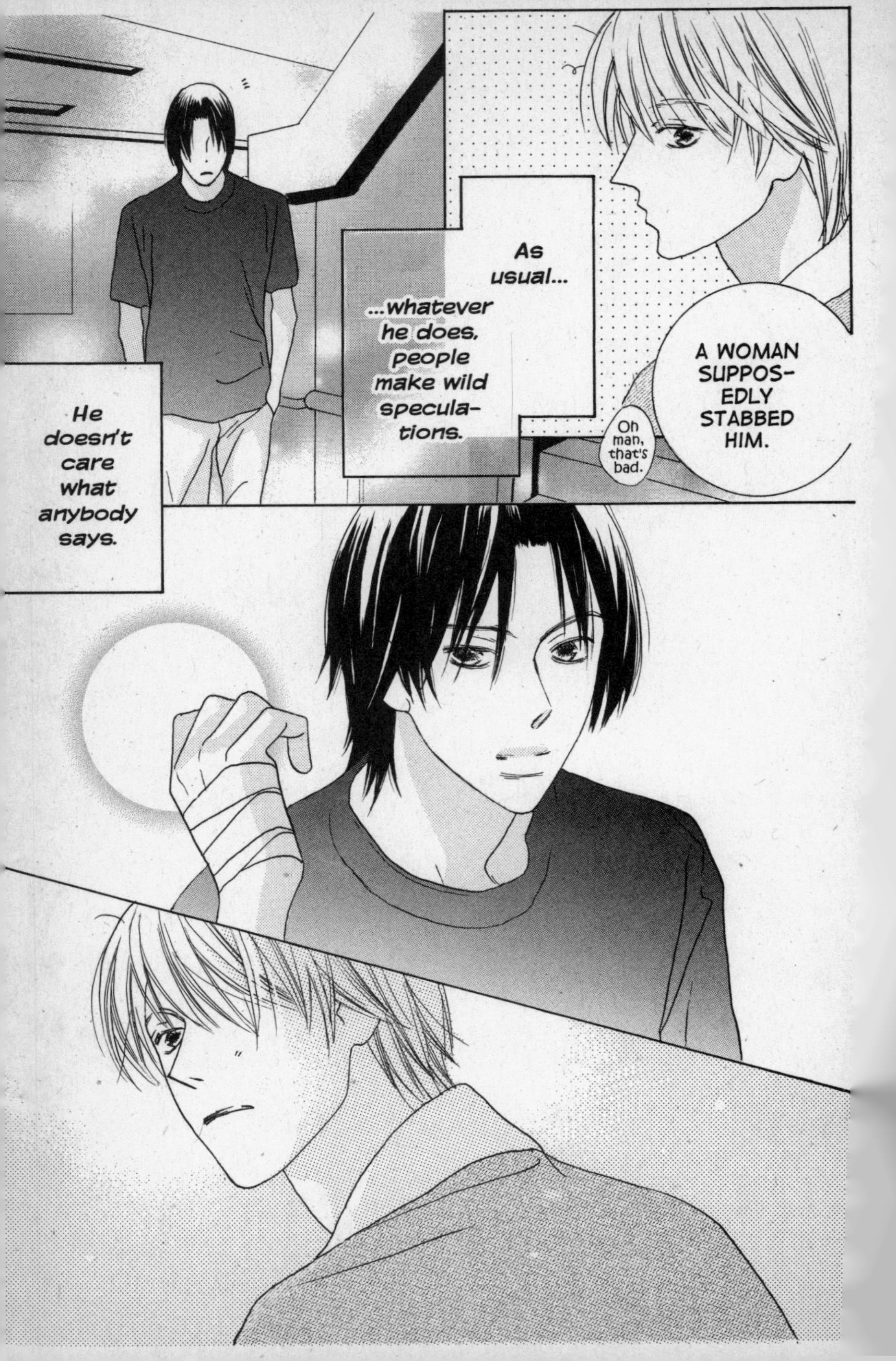
A WOMAN SUPPOSEDLY STABBED HIM.
Oh man, that's bad.
As usual...
...whatever he does, people make wild speculations.
He doesn't care what anybody says.

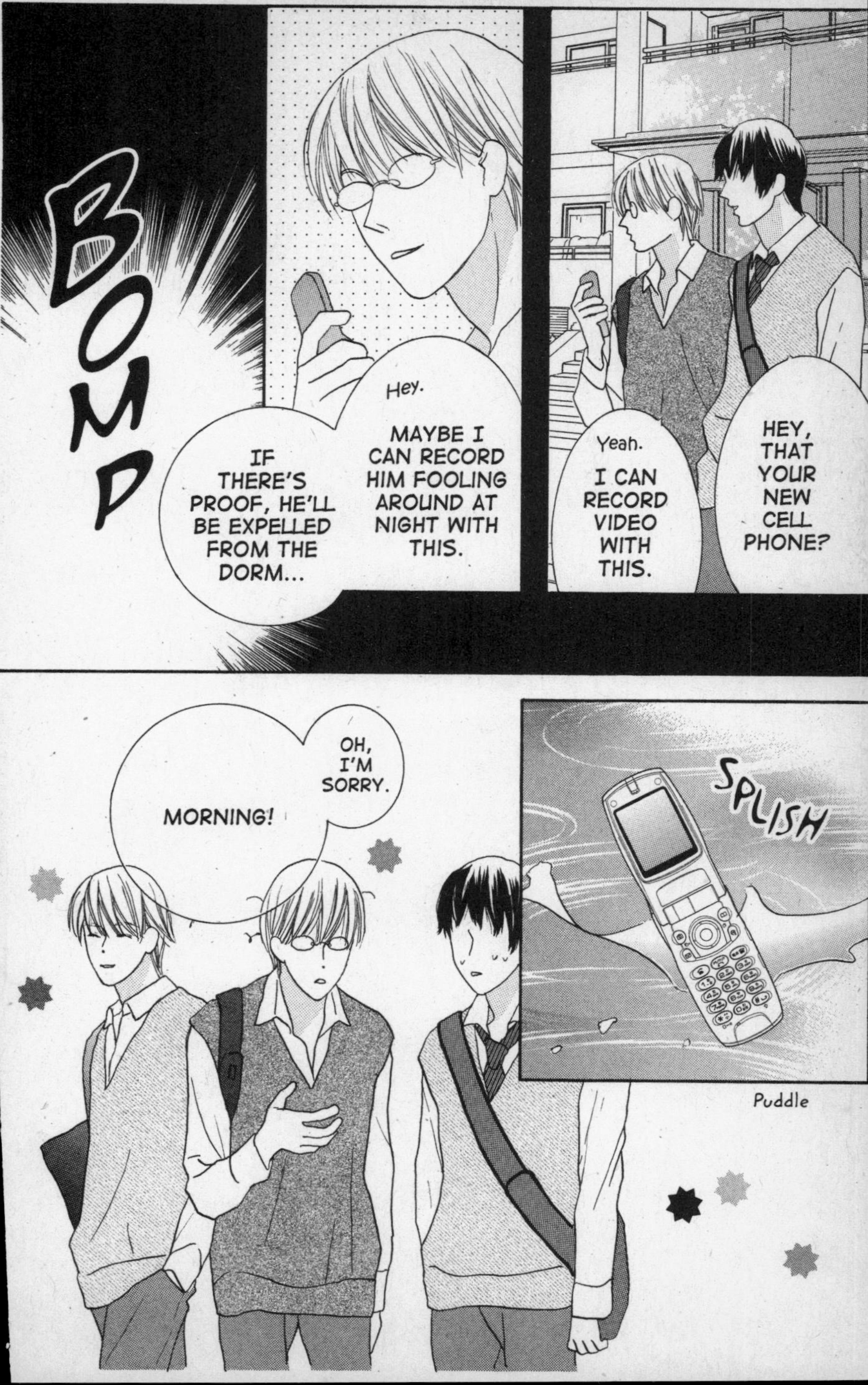
HEY, THAT YOUR NEW CELL PHONE?
Yeah.
I CAN RECORD VIDEO WITH THIS.
Hey.
MAYBE I CAN RECORD HIM FOOLING AROUND AT NIGHT WITH THIS.
IF THERE'S PROOF, HE'LL BE EXPELLED FROM THE DORM...
BOMP
SPLISH
Puddle
OH, I'M SORRY.
MORNING!

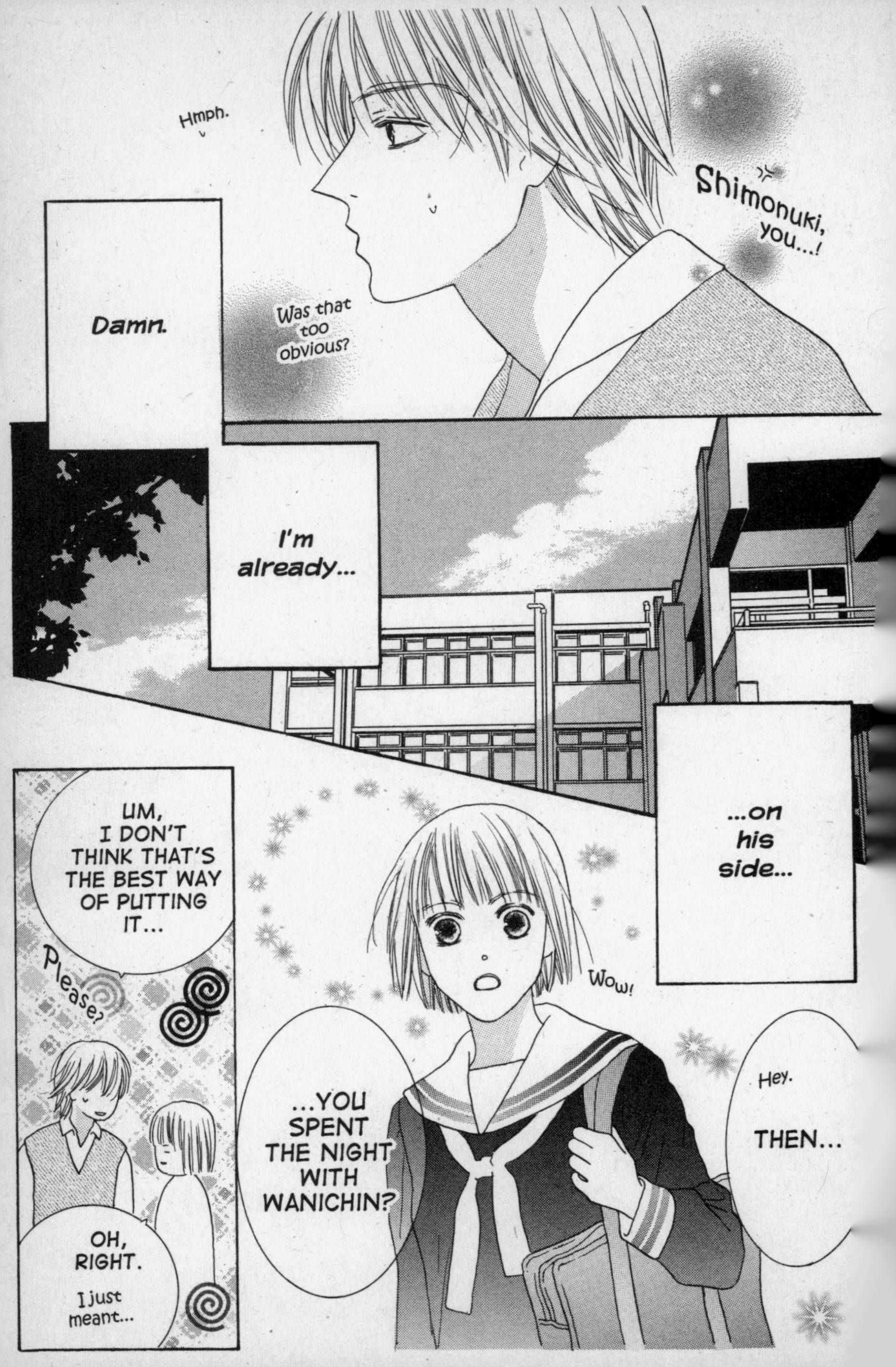
Shimonuki, you...!
Hmph.
Was that too obvious?
Damn.
I'm already...
...on his side...
Hey.
THEN...
Wow!
...YOU SPENT THE NIGHT WITH WANICHIN?
UM, I DON'T THINK THAT'S THE BEST WAY OF PUTTING IT...
Please?
OH, RIGHT.
I just meant...

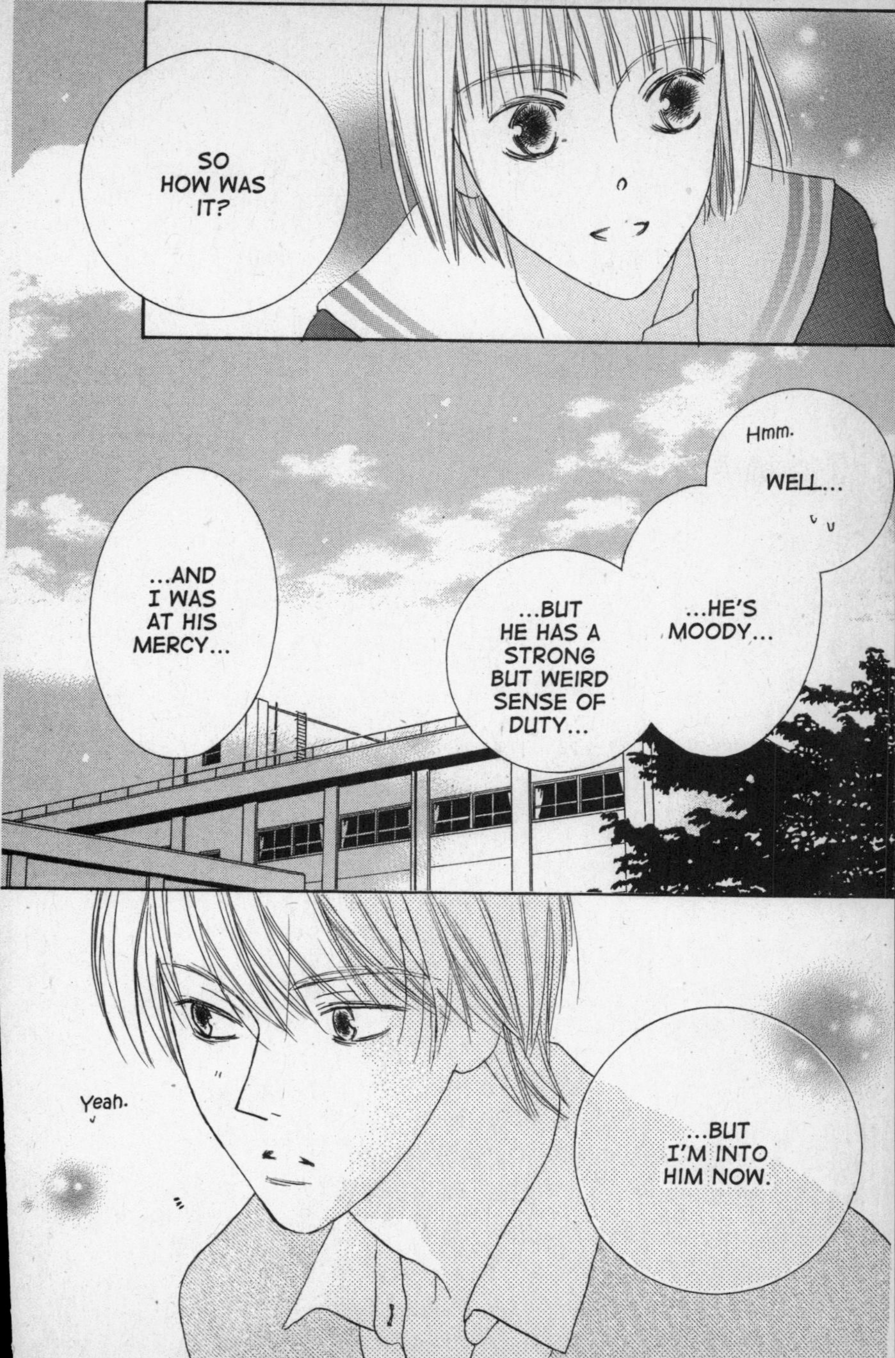
SO HOW WAS IT?
Hmm.
WELL...
...HE'S MOODY...
...BUT HE HAS A STRONG BUT WEIRD SENSE OF DUTY...
...AND I WAS AT HIS MERCY...
...BUT I'M INTO HIM NOW.
Yeah.

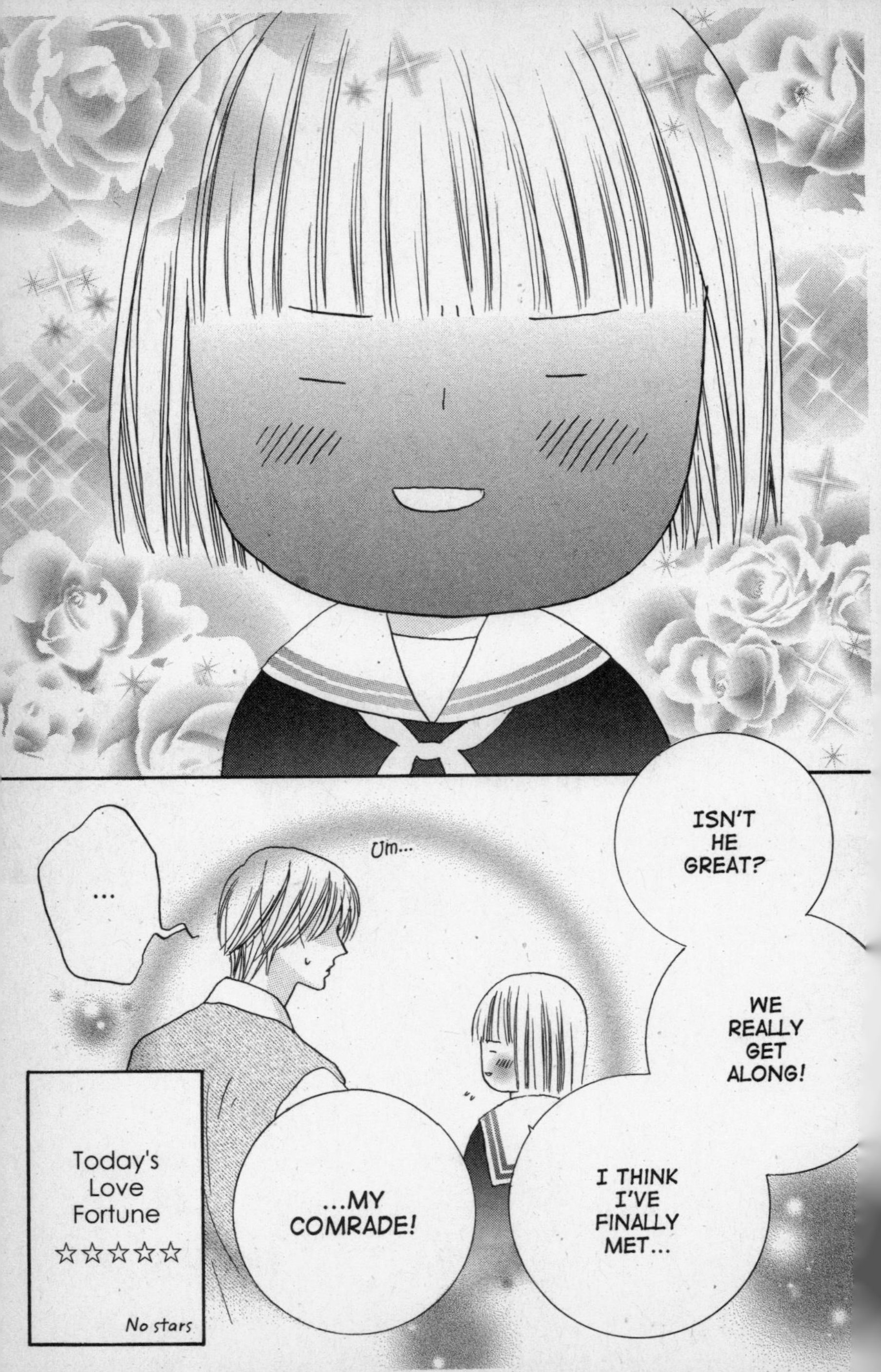
ISN'T HE GREAT?
WE REALLY GET ALONG!
I THINK I'VE FINALLY MET...
...MY COMRADE!
Um...
...
Today's Love Fortune
☆☆☆☆☆
No stars

BEAUTY IS THE BEAST

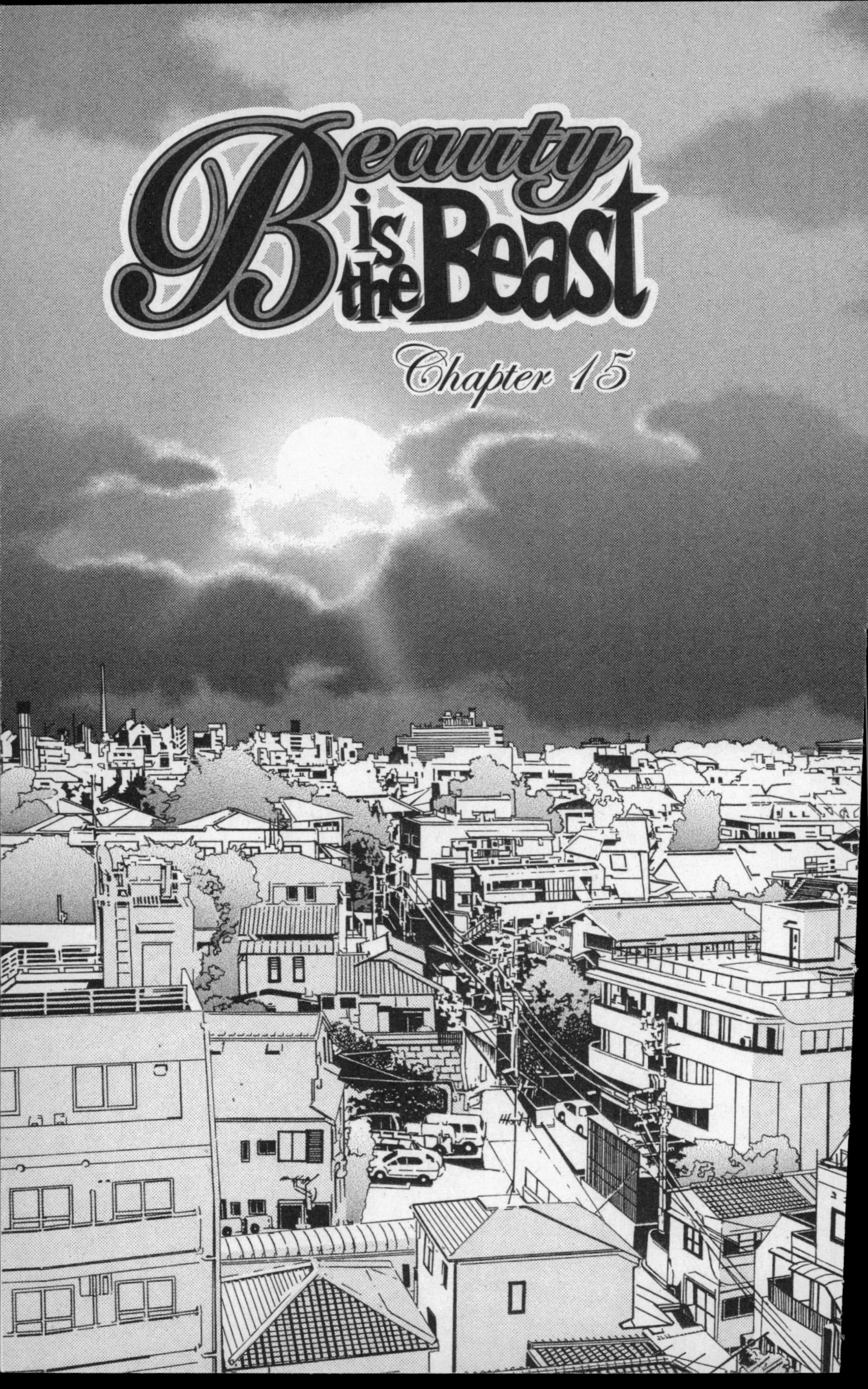
Beauty is the Beast
Chapter 15

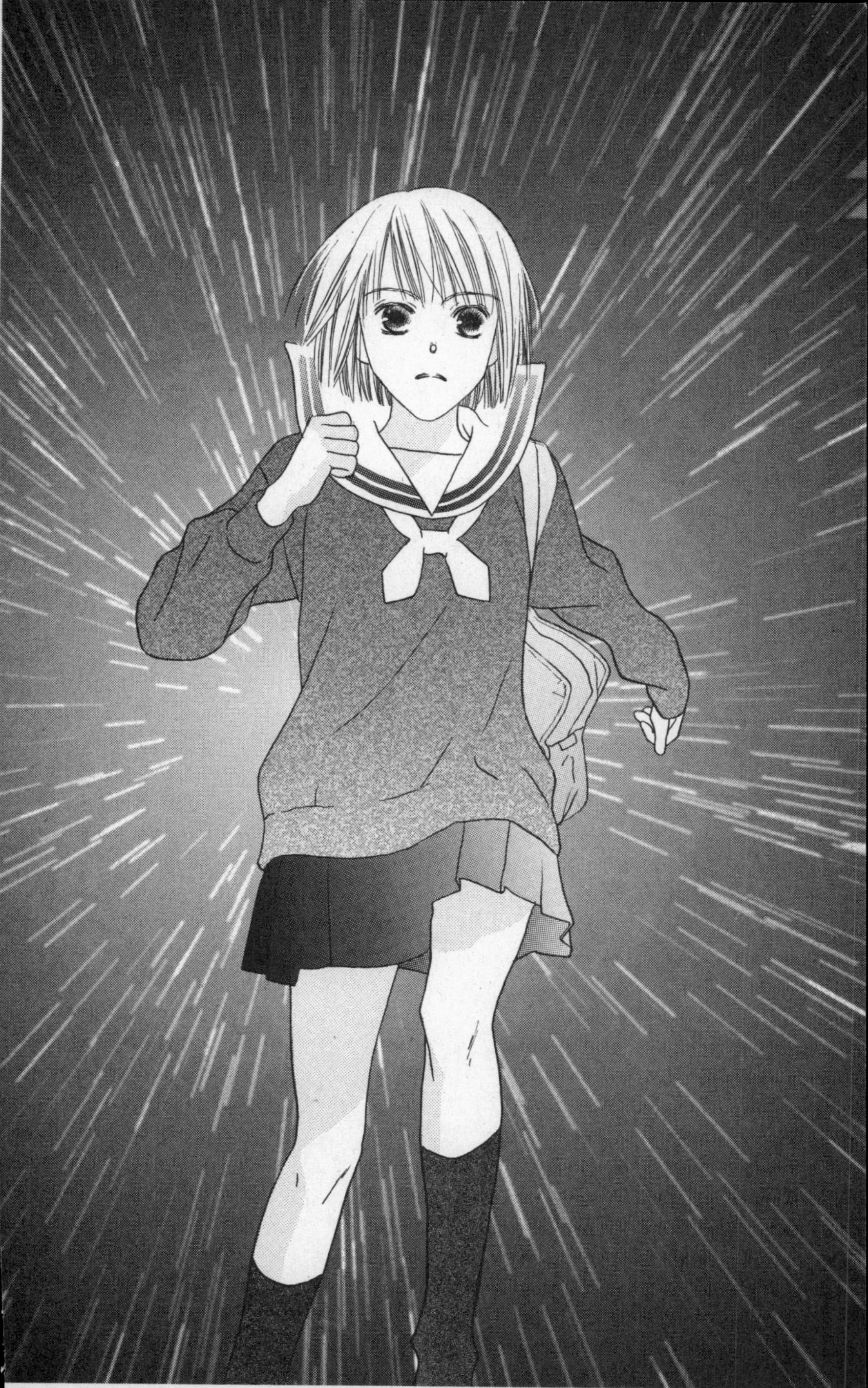

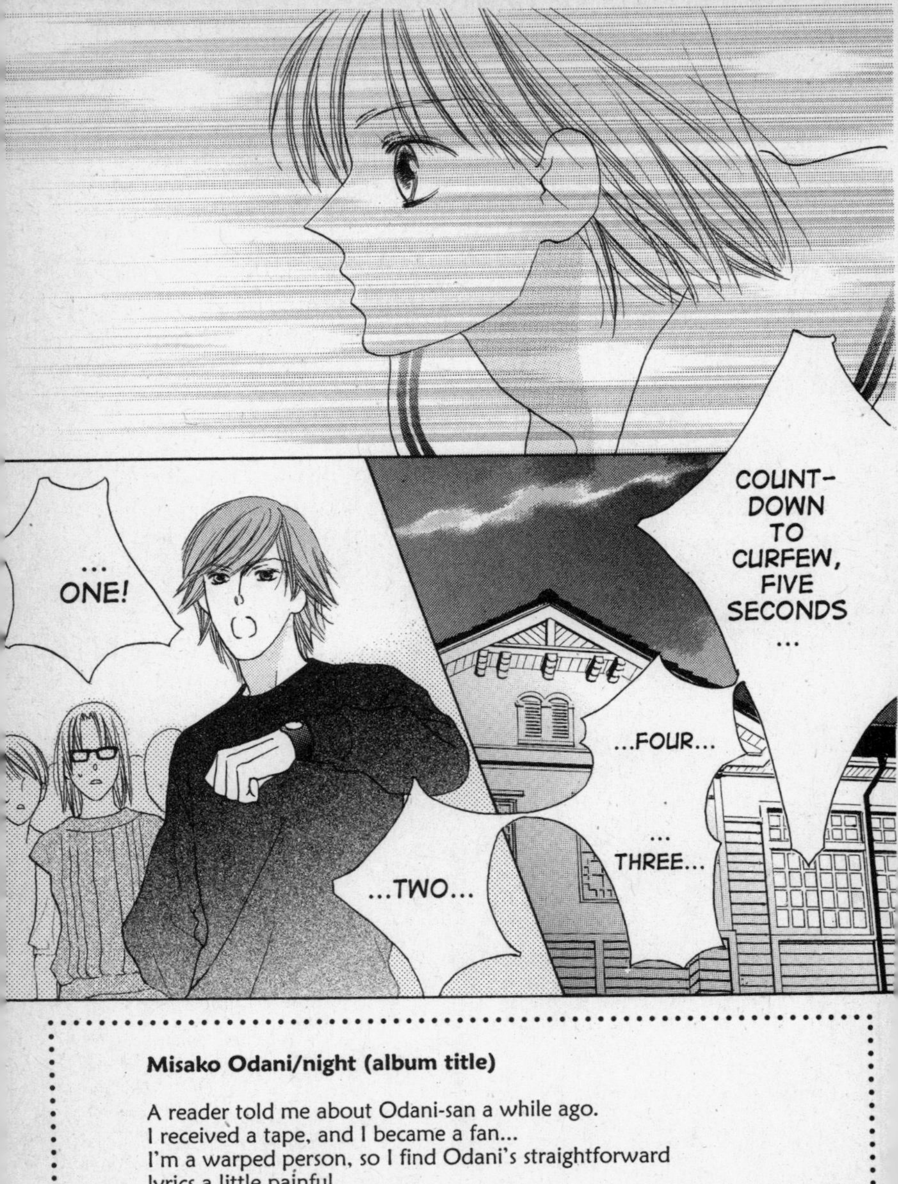
COUNT-DOWN TO CURFEW, FIVE SECONDS ...
...FOUR...
... THREE...
...TWO...
... ONE!

Misako Odani/night (album title)

A reader told me about Odani-san a while ago.
I received a tape, and I became a fan...
I'm a warped person, so I find Odani's straightforward lyrics a little painful.
But...she's, um...a person who plays the piano so her soul shows through... No, I've never met her, so it might be different (☺). Anyway, I listen to her. A lot.
Recently, she's doing guitar pieces too, and I grew to like guitars, too.

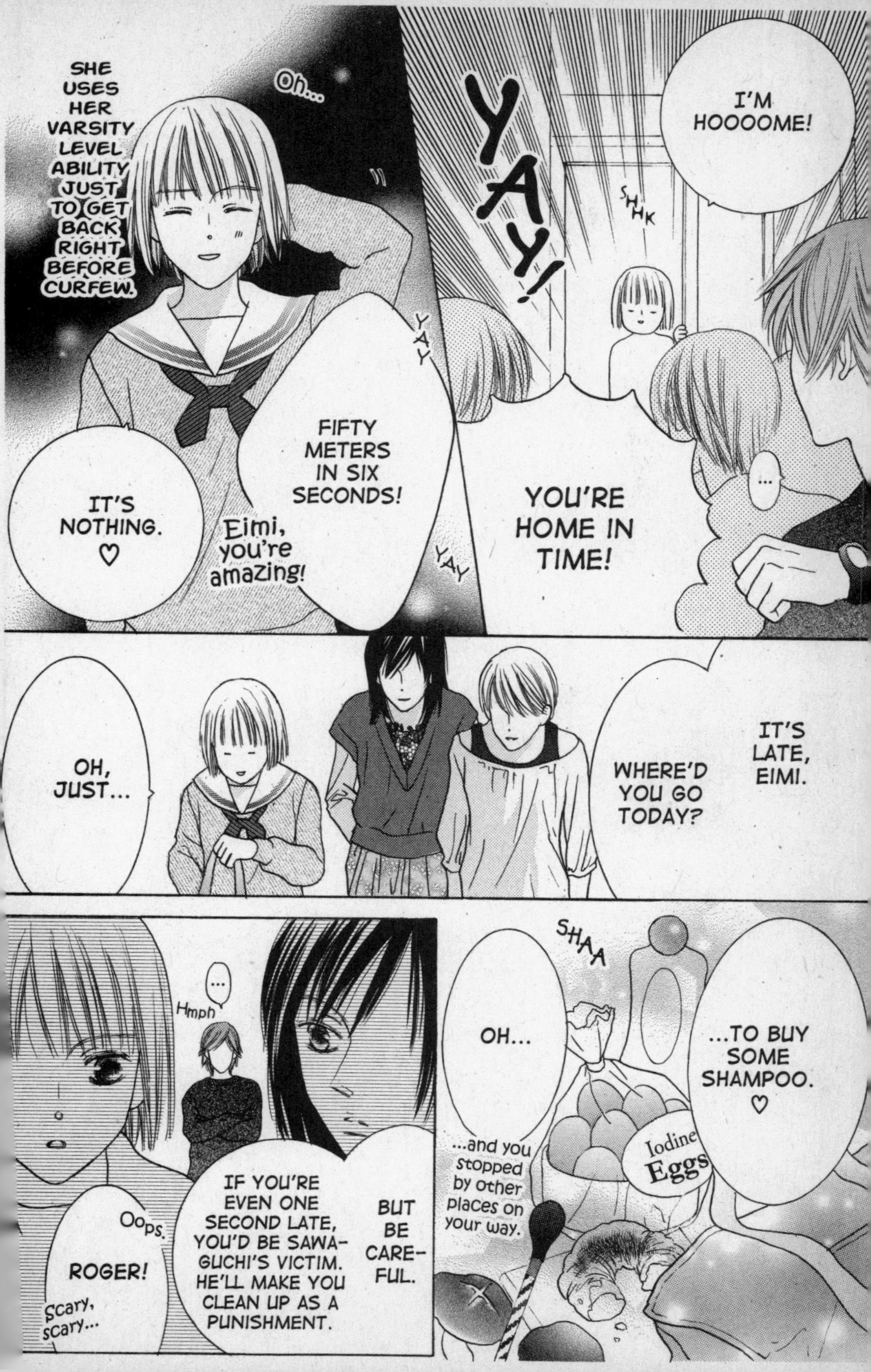
I'M HOOOOME!
YAY!
SHHK
...
YOU'RE HOME IN TIME!
YAY
YAY
Oh...
SHE USES HER VARSITY LEVEL ABILITY JUST TO GET BACK RIGHT BEFORE CURFEW.
FIFTY METERS IN SIX SECONDS!
Eimi, you're amazing!
IT'S NOTHING. ♡
IT'S LATE, EIMI.
WHERE'D YOU GO TODAY?
OH, JUST...
...TO BUY SOME SHAMPOO. ♡
SHAA
OH...
Iodine Eggs
...and you stopped by other places on your way.
BUT BE CARE-FUL.
IF YOU'RE EVEN ONE SECOND LATE, YOU'D BE SAWA-GUCHI'S VICTIM. HE'LL MAKE YOU CLEAN UP AS A PUNISHMENT.
...
Hmph
Oops.
ROGER!
Scary, scary...

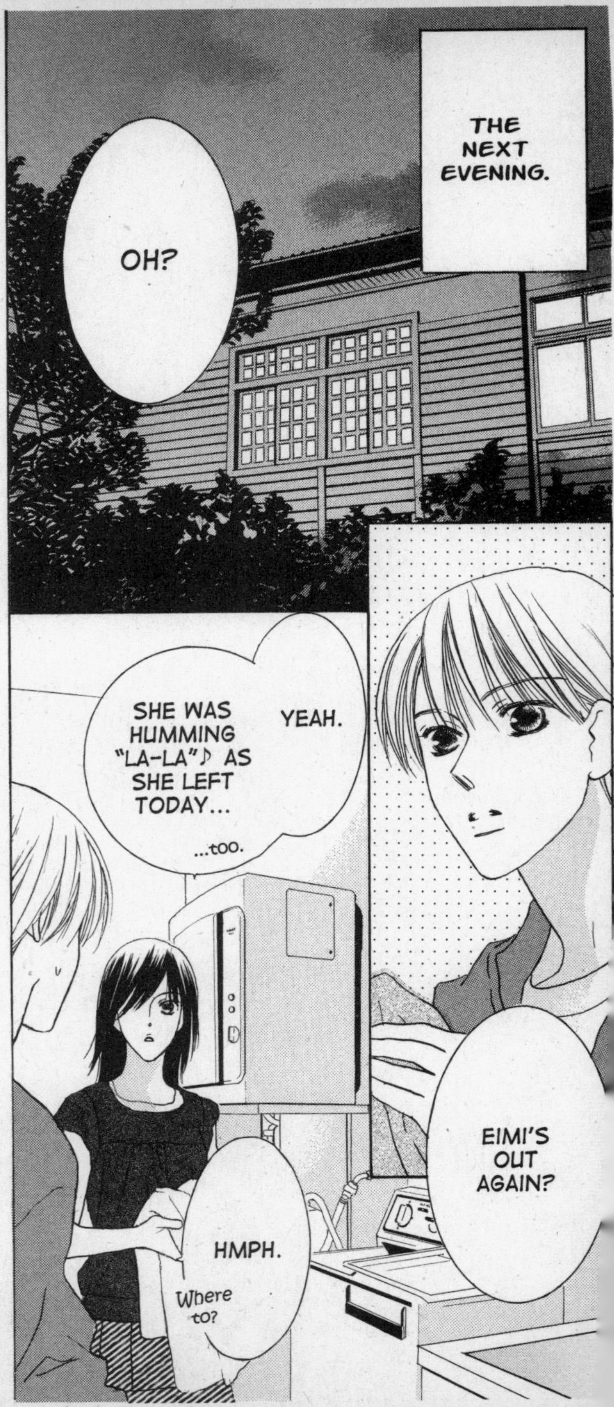
THE NEXT EVENING.
OH?
EIMI'S OUT AGAIN?
HMPH.
Where to?
SHE WAS HUMMING "LA-LA"♪ AS SHE LEFT TODAY...
...too.
YEAH.

I went to South Korea for work. I was very nervous, but the people there were all kind, cute, and easy to talk, and it was really lovely.☆ People had read in my comics that I'm always eating sweets (☺), and many people gave me lots of sweets and juice. I also received CDs of Korean artists that people wanted me to listen to, books, small items, etc. Thanks to everyone who came, my brain instantaneously turned into Korean colors!!
I may never have been able to meet these people if I hadn't had this opportunity. It's enough just to have people read my works, but to have people come to see me... there's nothing but thanks.
I'm worried that because I don't know the language, people might not have understood that I was very happy... since I'm not too sociable... I want to really say thank you from the bottom of my heart.

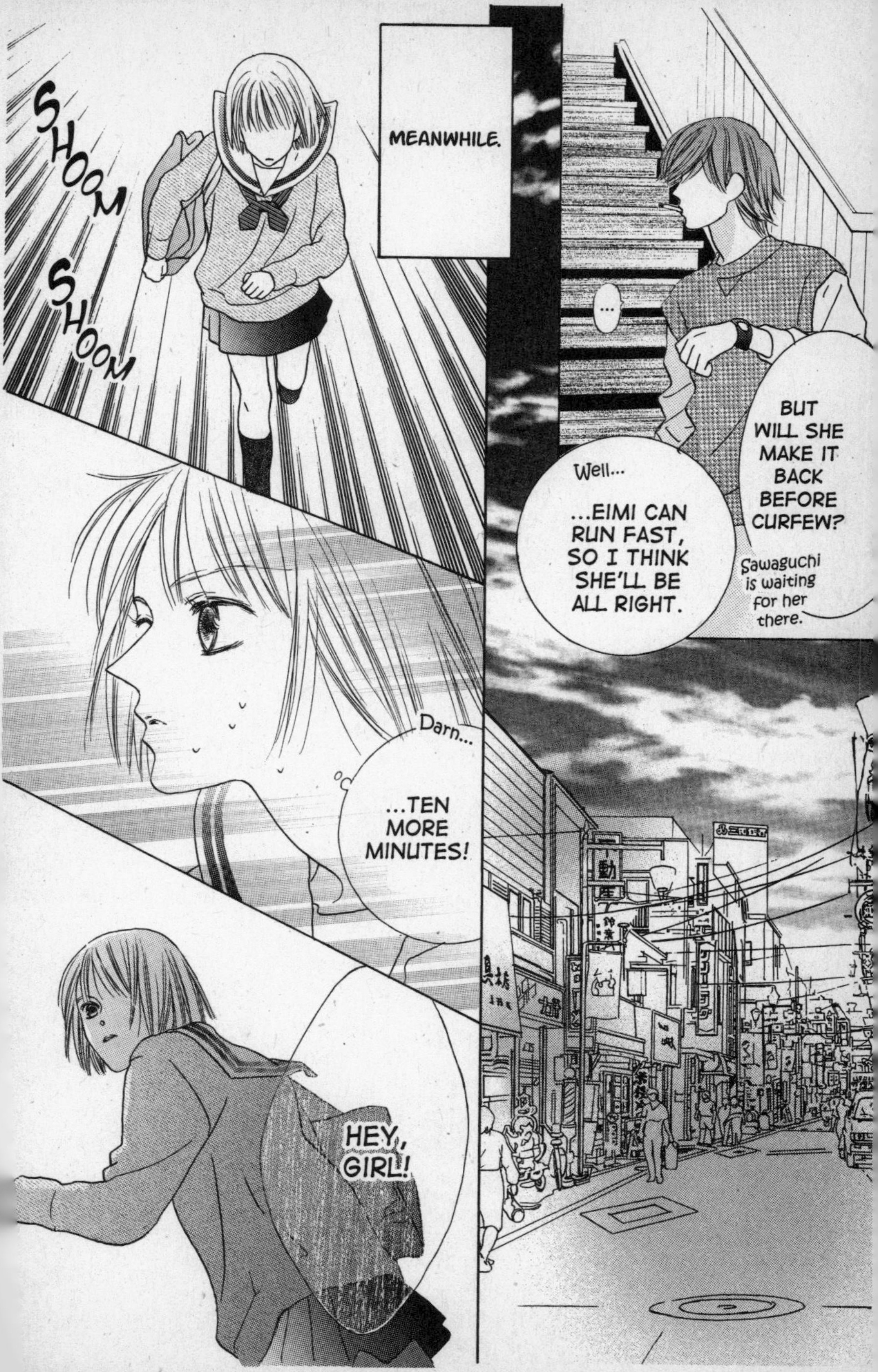
...
BUT WILL SHE MAKE IT BACK BEFORE CURFEW?
Sawaguchi is waiting for her there.
Well...
...EIMI CAN RUN FAST, SO I THINK SHE'LL BE ALL RIGHT.
MEANWHILE.
SHOOM SHOOM SHOOM
Darn...
...TEN MORE MINUTES!
HEY, GIRL!

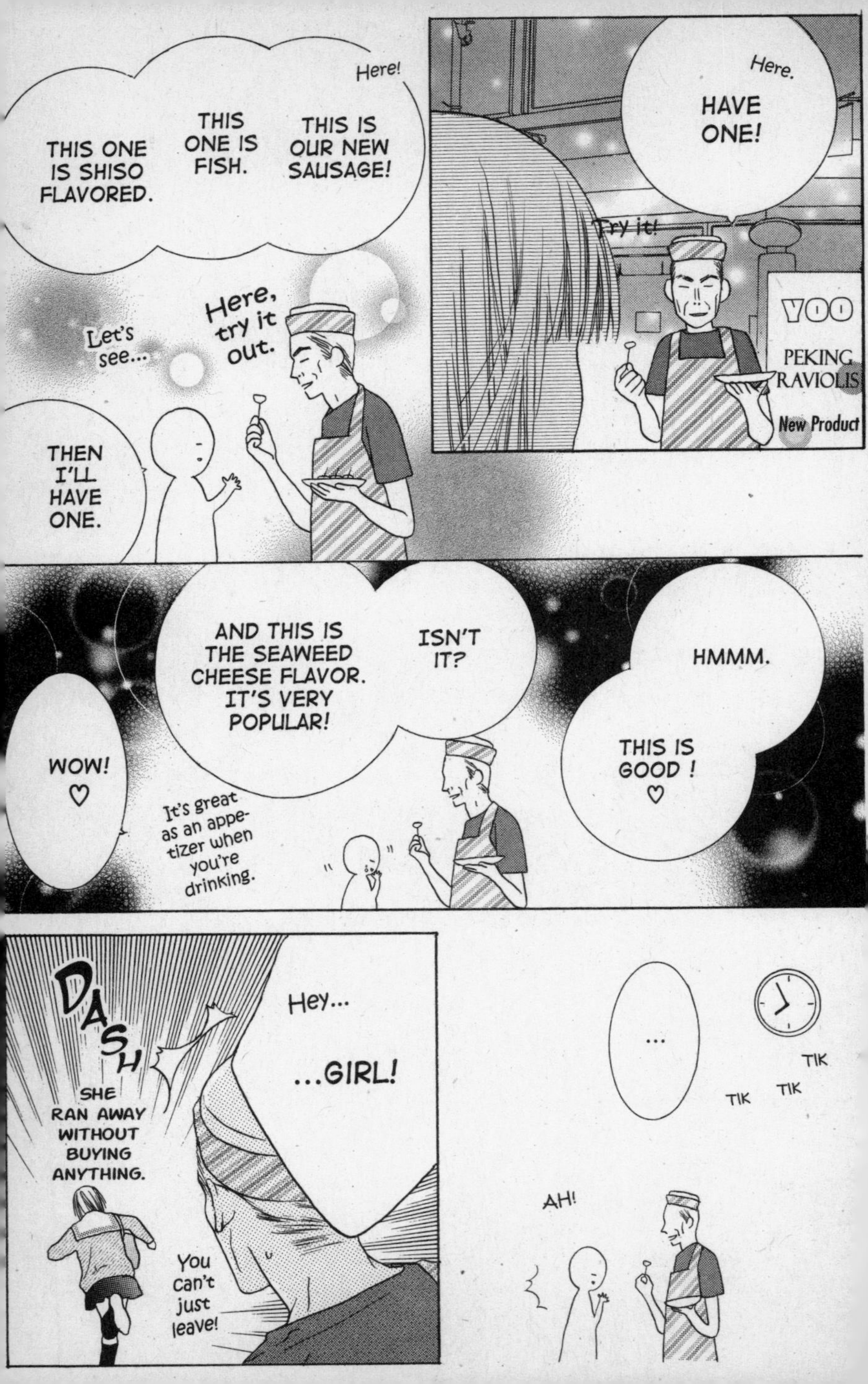
Here.
HAVE ONE!
Try it!
YOO
PEKING RAVIOLIS
New Product
Here!
THIS IS OUR NEW SAUSAGE!
THIS ONE IS FISH.
THIS ONE IS SHISO FLAVORED.
Here, try it out.
Let's see...
THEN I'LL HAVE ONE.
HMMM.
THIS IS GOOD! ♡
ISN'T IT?
AND THIS IS THE SEAWEED CHEESE FLAVOR. IT'S VERY POPULAR!
It's great as an appetizer when you're drinking.
WOW! ♡
...
TIK
TIK
TIK
AH!
Hey...
...GIRL!
DASH
SHE RAN AWAY WITHOUT BUYING ANYTHING.
You can't just leave!

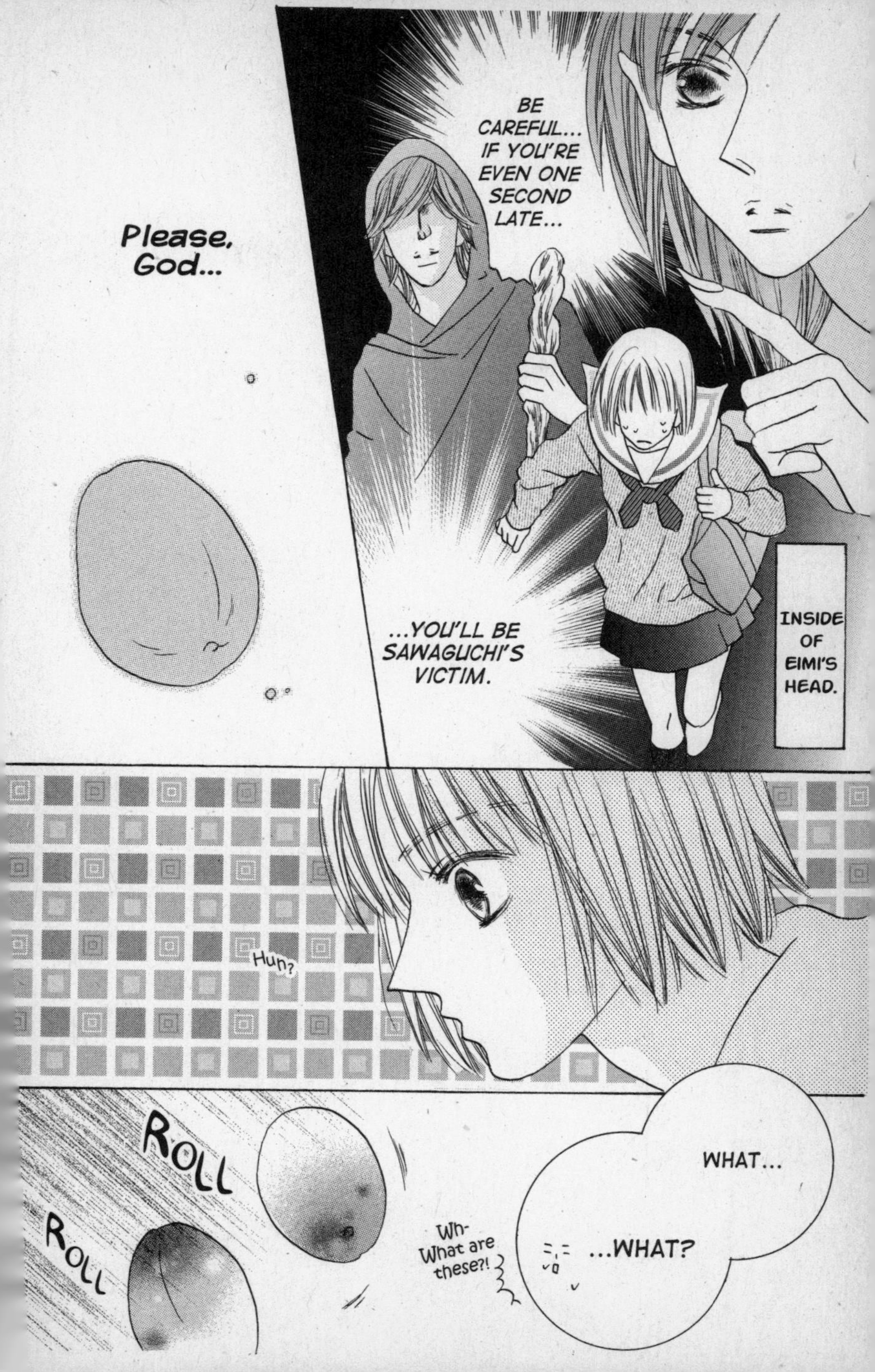
BE CAREFUL... IF YOU'RE EVEN ONE SECOND LATE...
...YOU'LL BE SAWAGUCHI'S VICTIM.
INSIDE OF EIMI'S HEAD.
Please, God...
Hun?
WHAT... ...WHAT?
Wh- What are these?!
ROLL
ROLL

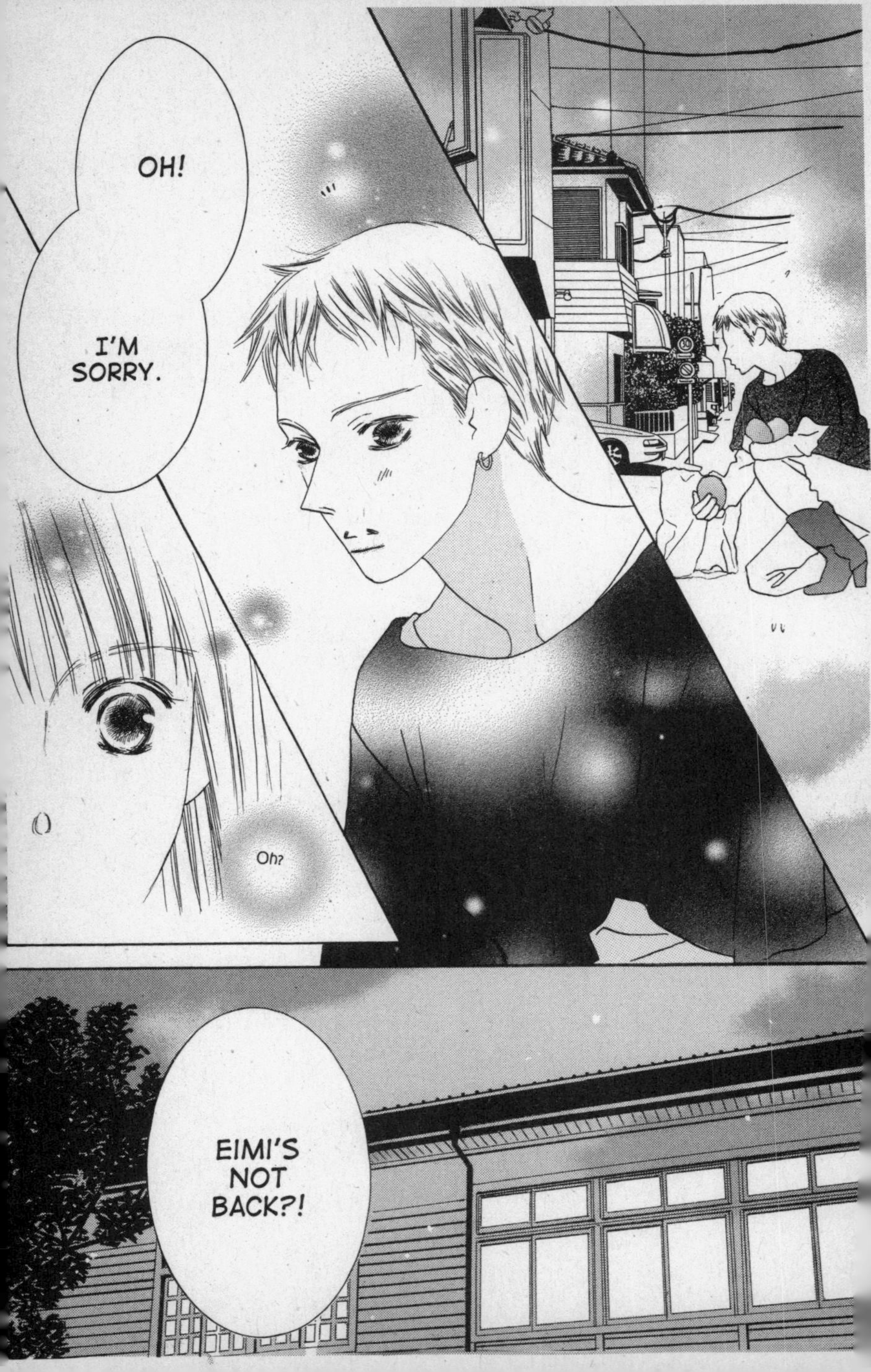
OH!
I'M SORRY.
Oh?
EIMI'S NOT BACK?!

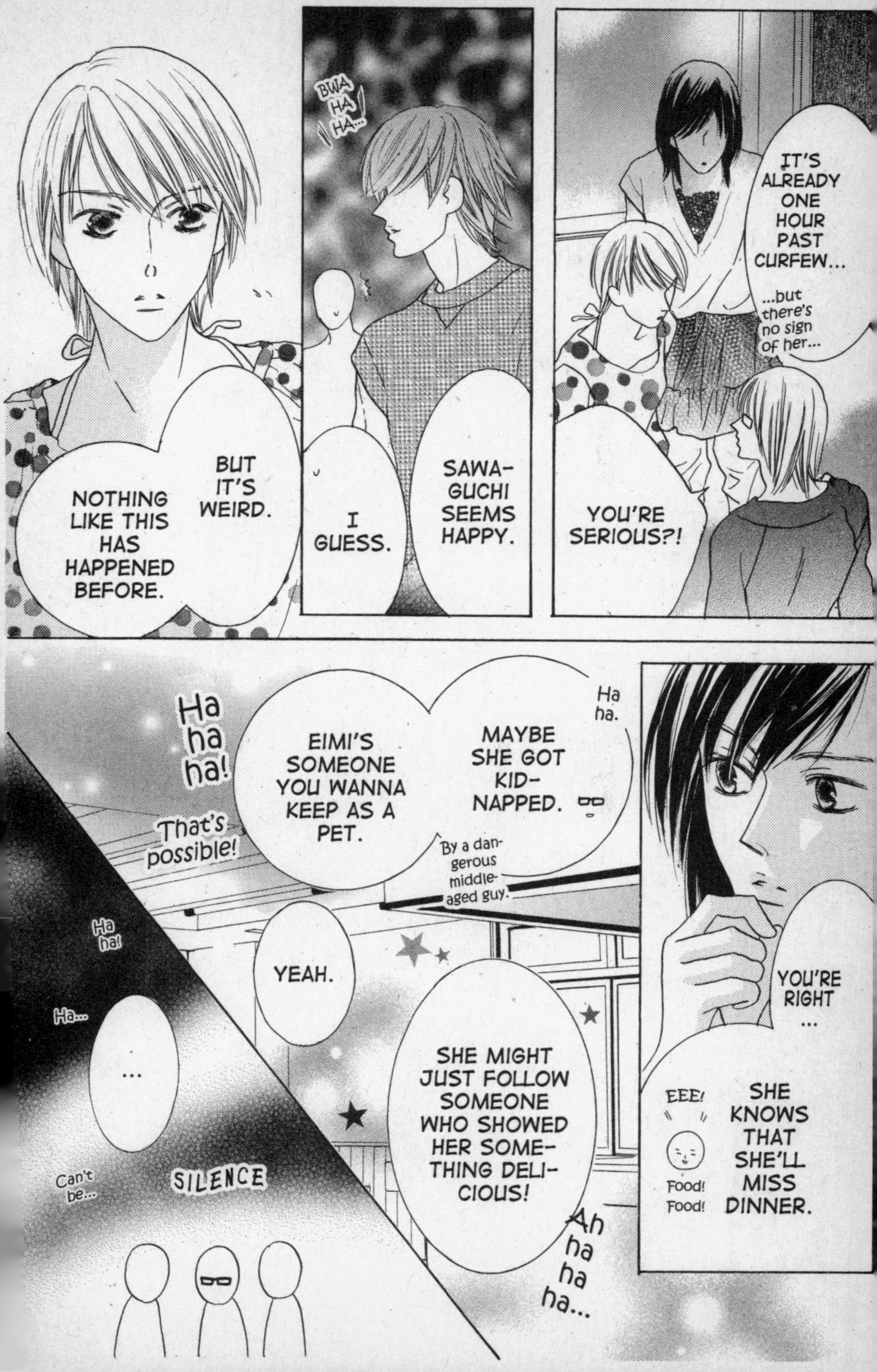
IT'S ALREADY ONE HOUR PAST CURFEW...
...but there's no sign of her...
YOU'RE SERIOUS?!
BWA HA HA...
SAWAGUCHI SEEMS HAPPY.
I GUESS.
BUT IT'S WEIRD.
NOTHING LIKE THIS HAS HAPPENED BEFORE.
YOU'RE RIGHT...
SHE KNOWS THAT SHE'LL MISS DINNER.
EEE!
Food! Food!
Ha ha.
MAYBE SHE GOT KIDNAPPED.
By a dangerous middle-aged guy.
EIMI'S SOMEONE YOU WANNA KEEP AS A PET.
Ha ha ha!
That's possible!
SHE MIGHT JUST FOLLOW SOMEONE WHO SHOWED HER SOMETHING DELICIOUS!
YEAH.
Ah ha ha ha...
Ha ha!
Ha...
...
Can't be...
SILENCE

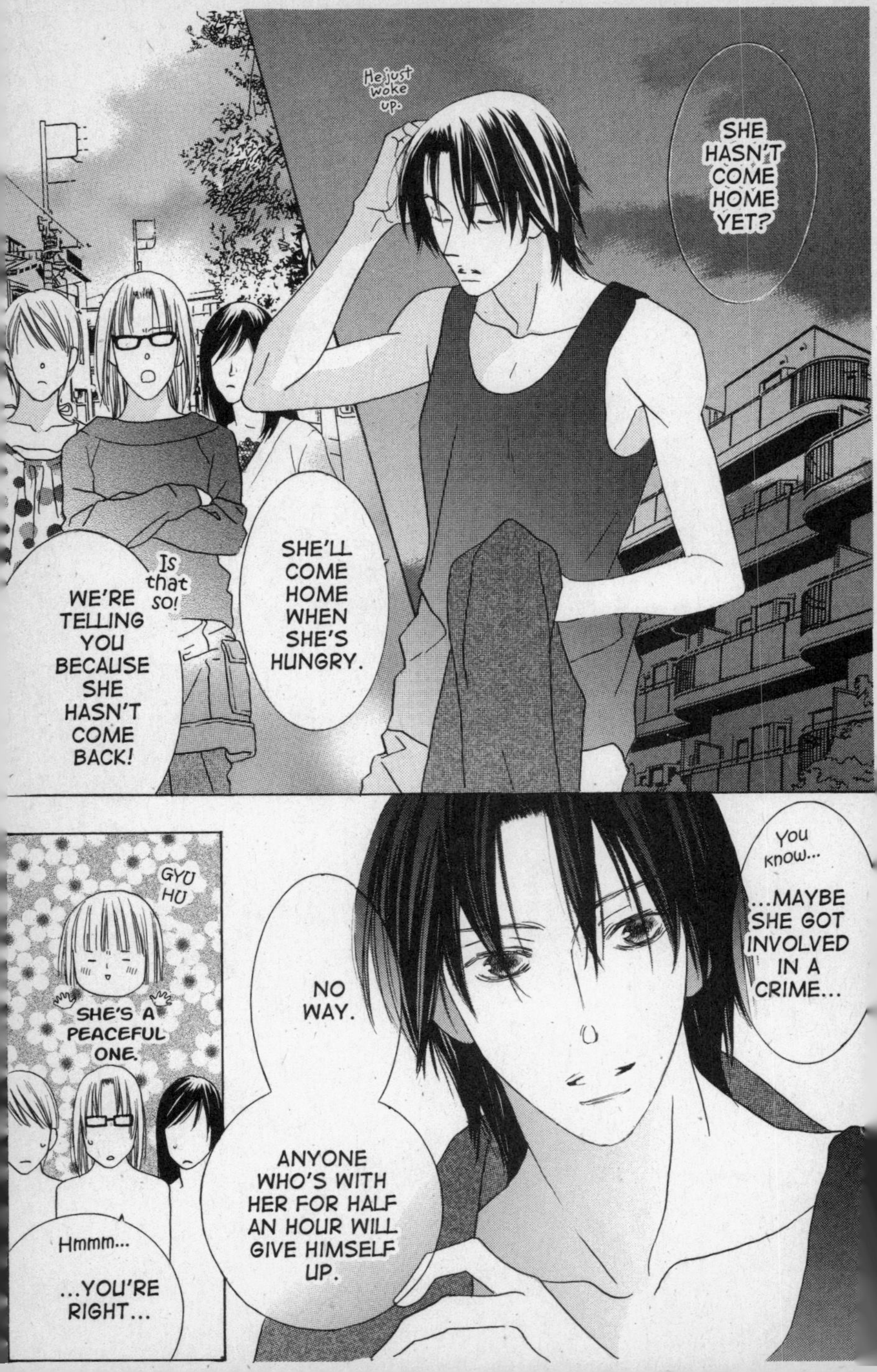
SHE HASN'T COME HOME YET?
He just woke up.
SHE'LL COME HOME WHEN SHE'S HUNGRY.
Is that so!
WE'RE TELLING YOU BECAUSE SHE HASN'T COME BACK!
You know...
...MAYBE SHE GOT INVOLVED IN A CRIME...
NO WAY.
ANYONE WHO'S WITH HER FOR HALF AN HOUR WILL GIVE HIMSELF UP.
GYU HU
SHE'S A PEACEFUL ONE.
Hmmm...
...YOU'RE RIGHT...

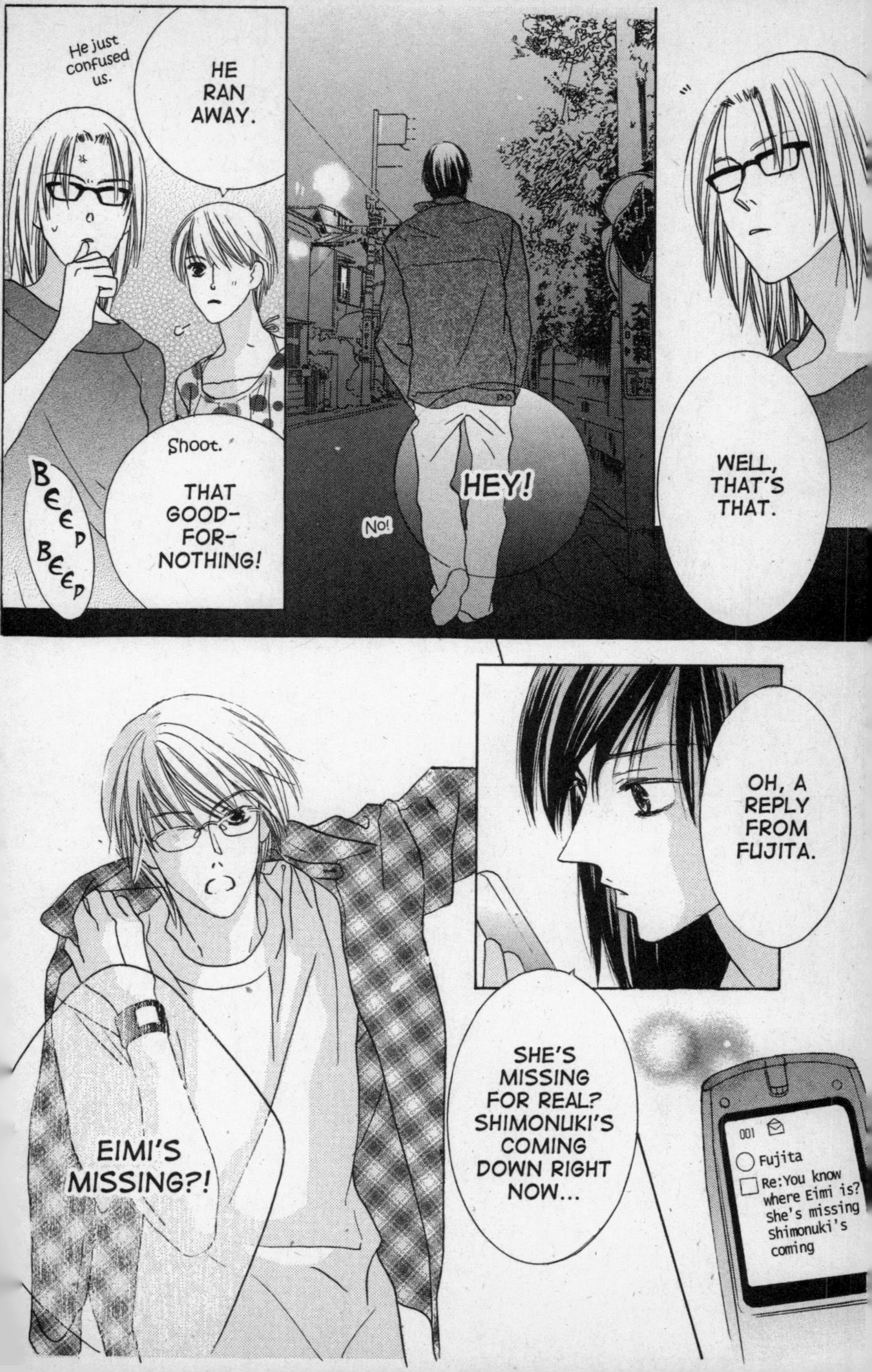
WELL, THAT'S THAT.
HEY!
No!
HE RAN AWAY.
He just confused us.
Shoot.
THAT GOOD-FOR-NOTHING!
BEEP BEEP
OH, A REPLY FROM FUJITA.
001
Fujita
Re:You know where Eimi is? She's missing Shimonuki's coming
SHE'S MISSING FOR REAL? SHIMONUKI'S COMING DOWN RIGHT NOW...
EIMI'S MISSING?!

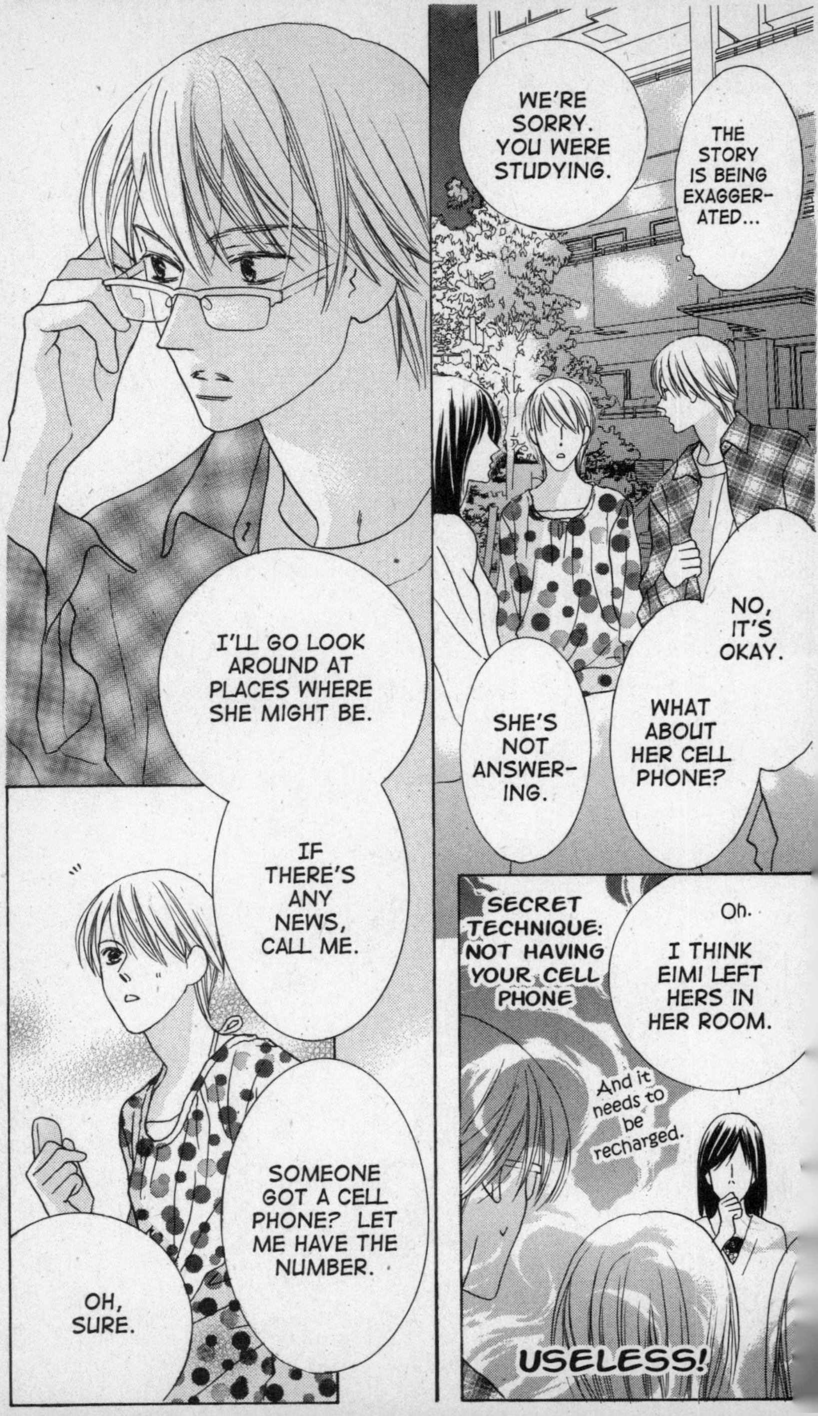
THE STORY IS BEING EXAGGERATED...
WE'RE SORRY. YOU WERE STUDYING.
NO, IT'S OKAY.
WHAT ABOUT HER CELL PHONE?
SHE'S NOT ANSWERING.
Oh.
I THINK EIMI LEFT HERS IN HER ROOM.
SECRET TECHNIQUE: NOT HAVING YOUR CELL PHONE
And it needs to be recharged.
USELESS!
I'LL GO LOOK AROUND AT PLACES WHERE SHE MIGHT BE.
IF THERE'S ANY NEWS, CALL ME.
SOMEONE GOT A CELL PHONE? LET ME HAVE THE NUMBER.
OH, SURE.

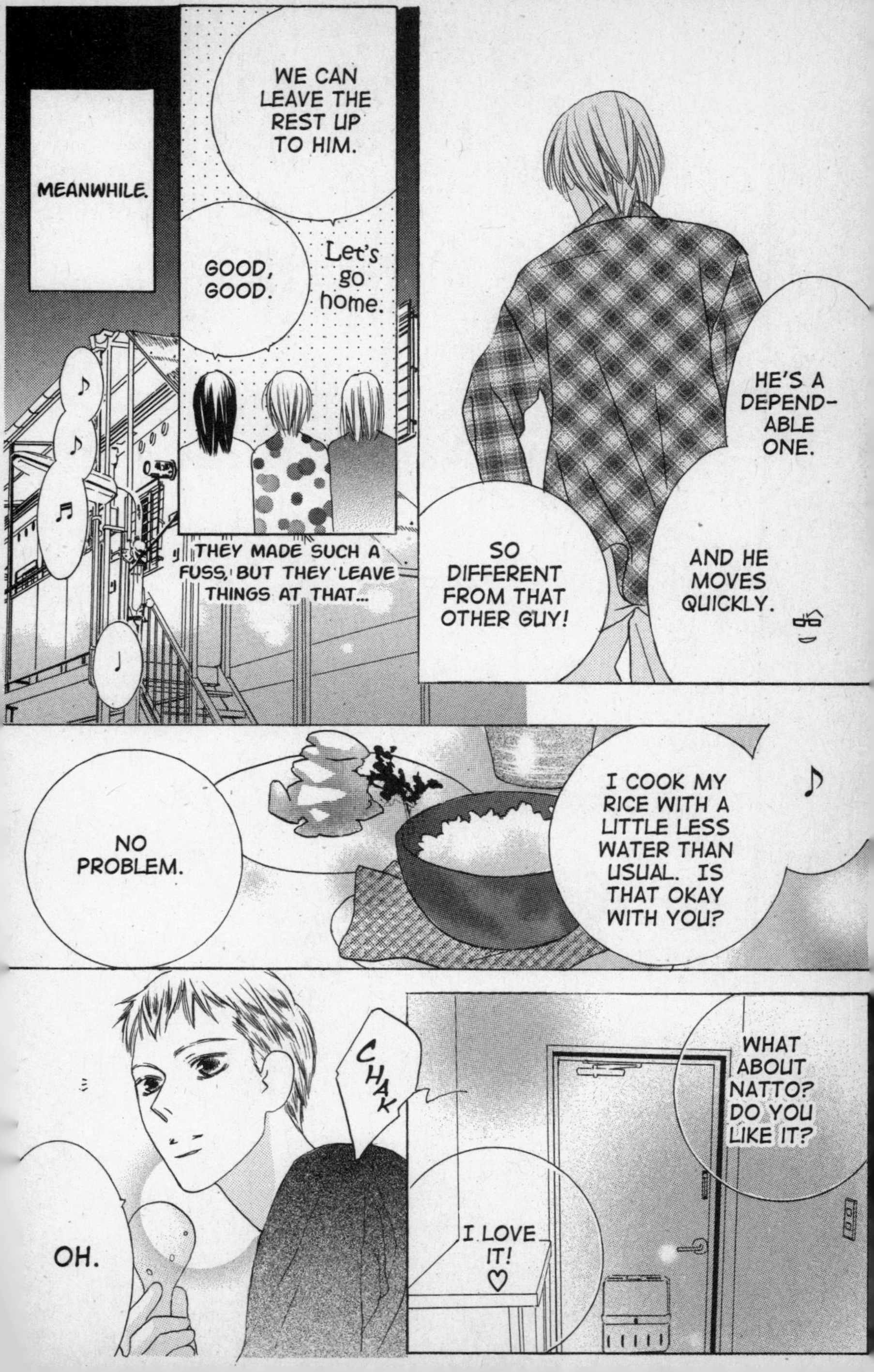
HE'S A DEPENDABLE ONE.
AND HE MOVES QUICKLY.
SO DIFFERENT FROM THAT OTHER GUY!
WE CAN LEAVE THE REST UP TO HIM.
Let's go home.
GOOD, GOOD.
THEY MADE SUCH A FUSS, BUT THEY LEAVE THINGS AT THAT...
MEANWHILE.
♪
♪
♬
♩
♪
I COOK MY RICE WITH A LITTLE LESS WATER THAN USUAL. IS THAT OKAY WITH YOU?
NO PROBLEM.
WHAT ABOUT NATTO? DO YOU LIKE IT?
I LOVE IT! ♡
CHAK
OH.

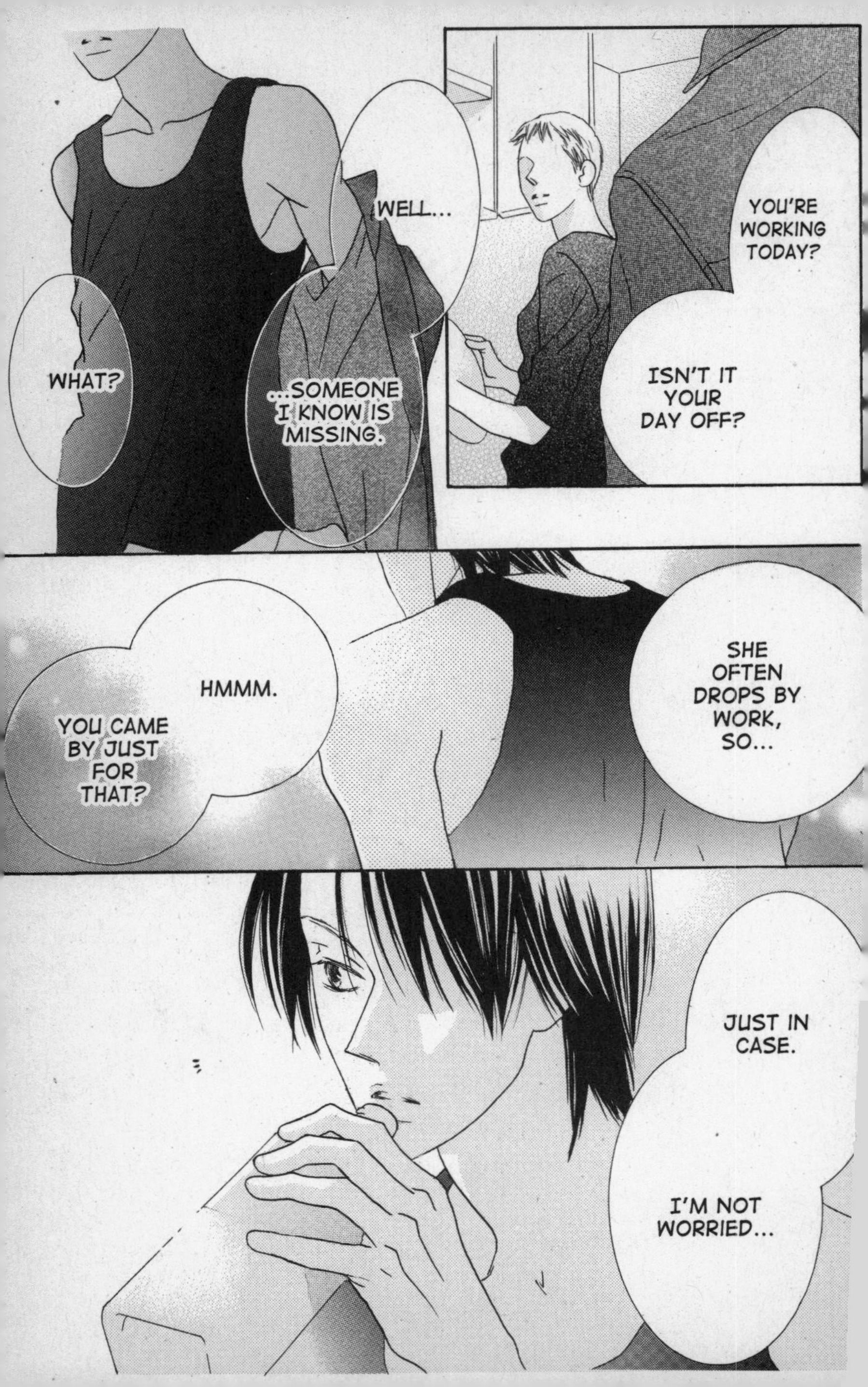
YOU'RE WORKING TODAY?
ISN'T IT YOUR DAY OFF?
WELL...
...SOMEONE I KNOW IS MISSING.
WHAT?
SHE OFTEN DROPS BY WORK, SO...
HMMM.
YOU CAME BY JUST FOR THAT?
JUST IN CASE.
I'M NOT WORRIED...

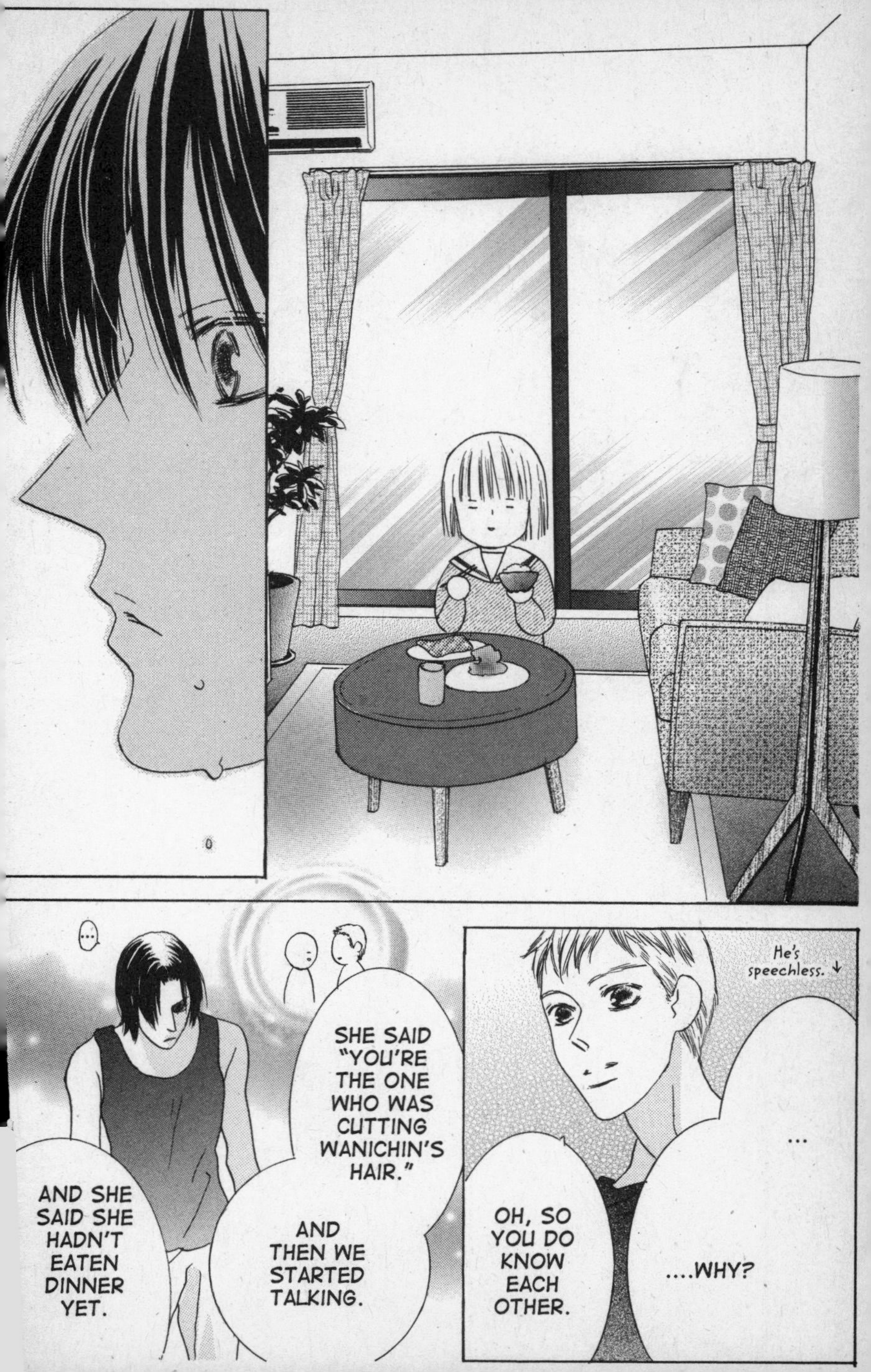
He's speechless.
...
....WHY?
OH, SO YOU DO KNOW EACH OTHER.
SHE SAID "YOU'RE THE ONE WHO WAS CUTTING WANICHIN'S HAIR."
AND THEN WE STARTED TALKING.
AND SHE SAID SHE HADN'T EATEN DINNER YET.
...

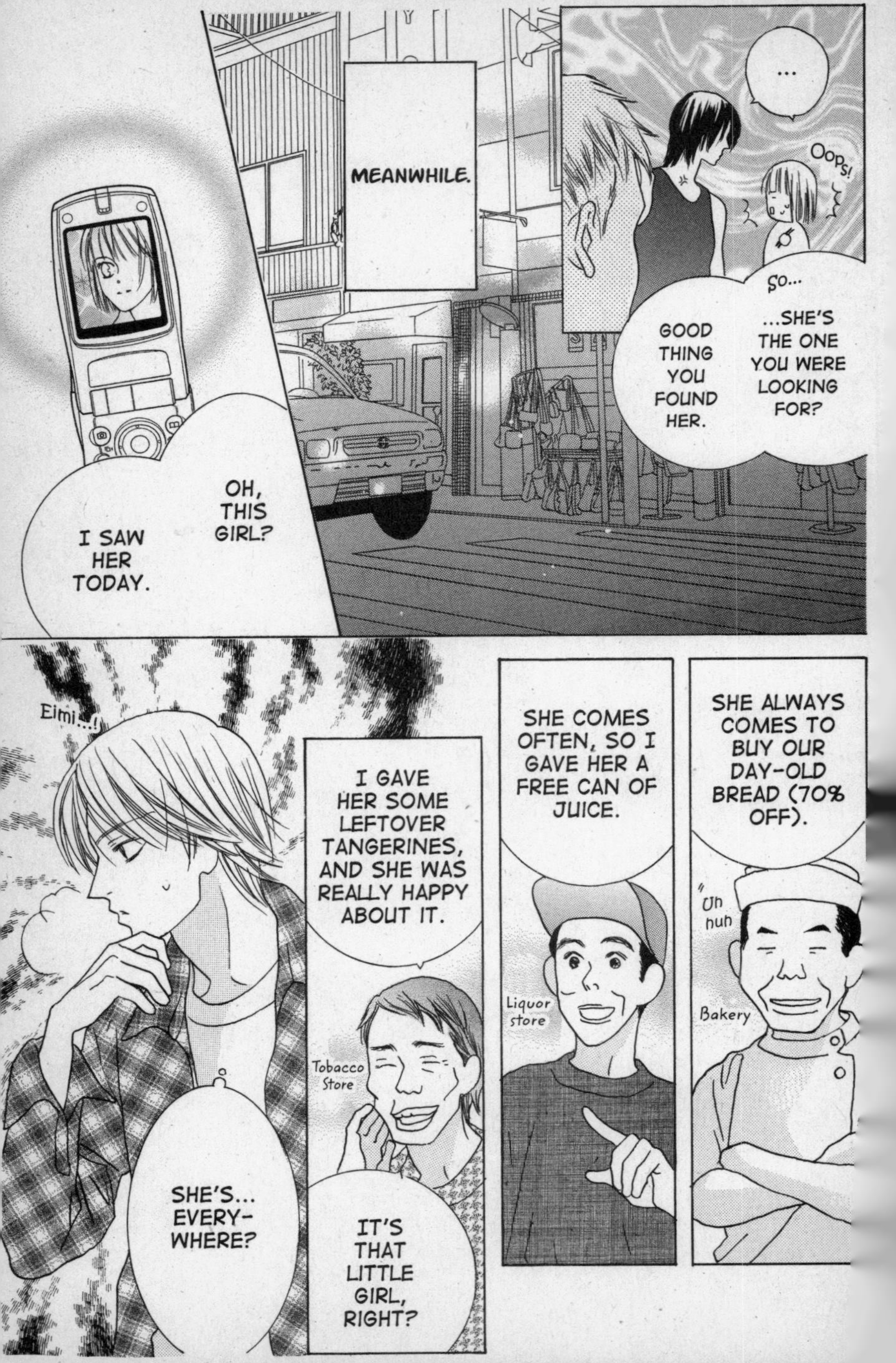
...
Oops!
So...
...SHE'S THE ONE YOU WERE LOOKING FOR?
GOOD THING YOU FOUND HER.
MEANWHILE.
OH, THIS GIRL?
I SAW HER TODAY.
SHE ALWAYS COMES TO BUY OUR DAY-OLD BREAD (70% OFF).
Uh huh
Bakery
SHE COMES OFTEN, SO I GAVE HER A FREE CAN OF JUICE.
Liquor store
I GAVE HER SOME LEFTOVER TANGERINES, AND SHE WAS REALLY HAPPY ABOUT IT.
Tobacco Store
IT'S THAT LITTLE GIRL, RIGHT?
Eimi...!
SHE'S... EVERY-WHERE?

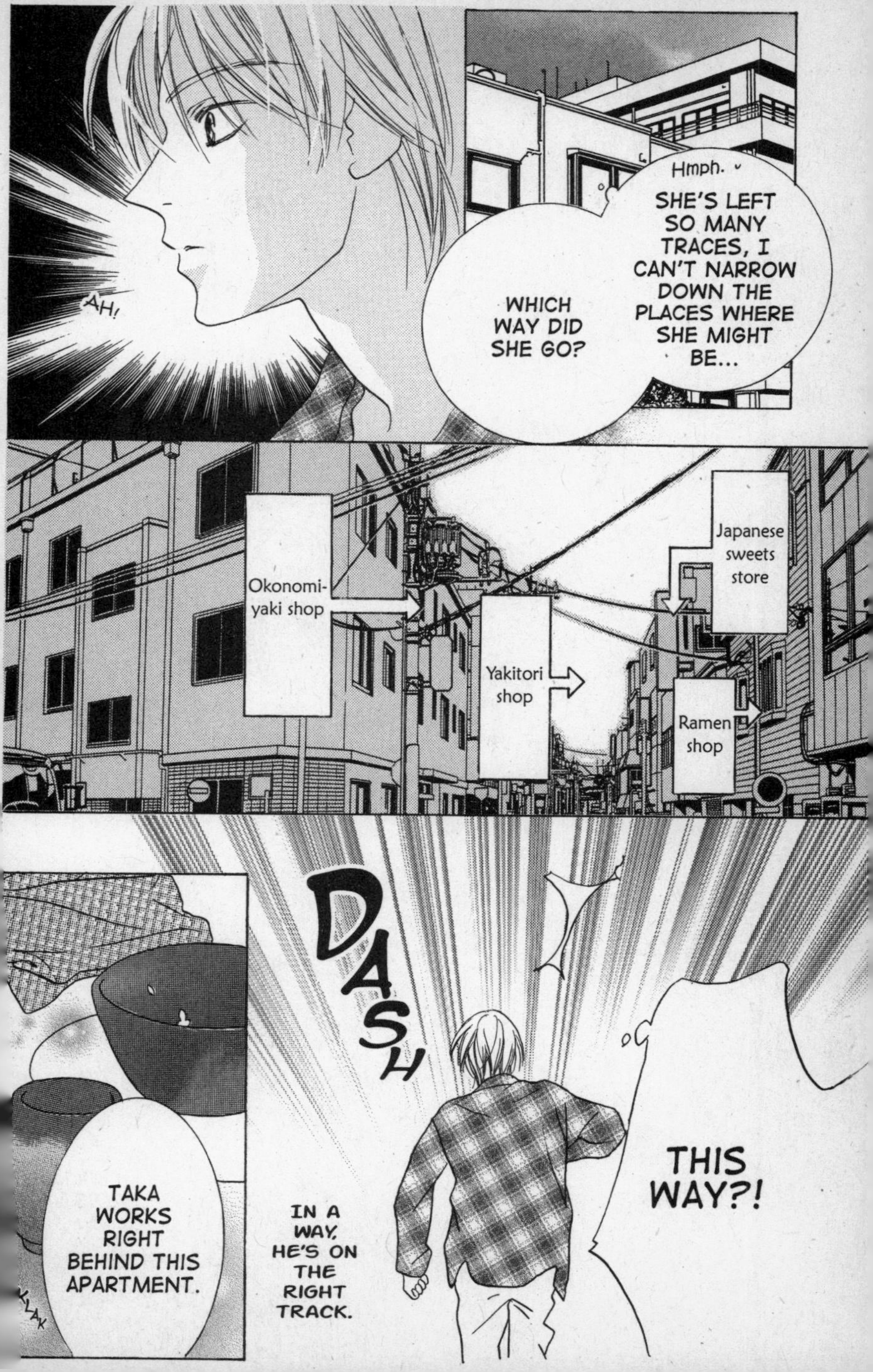
Hmph.
SHE'S LEFT SO MANY TRACES, I CAN'T NARROW DOWN THE PLACES WHERE SHE MIGHT BE...
WHICH WAY DID SHE GO?
AH!
Japanese sweets store
Ramen shop
Yakitori shop
Okonomi-yaki shop
DASH
THIS WAY?!
IN A WAY, HE'S ON THE RIGHT TRACK.
TAKA WORKS RIGHT BEHIND THIS APARTMENT.
KLAK

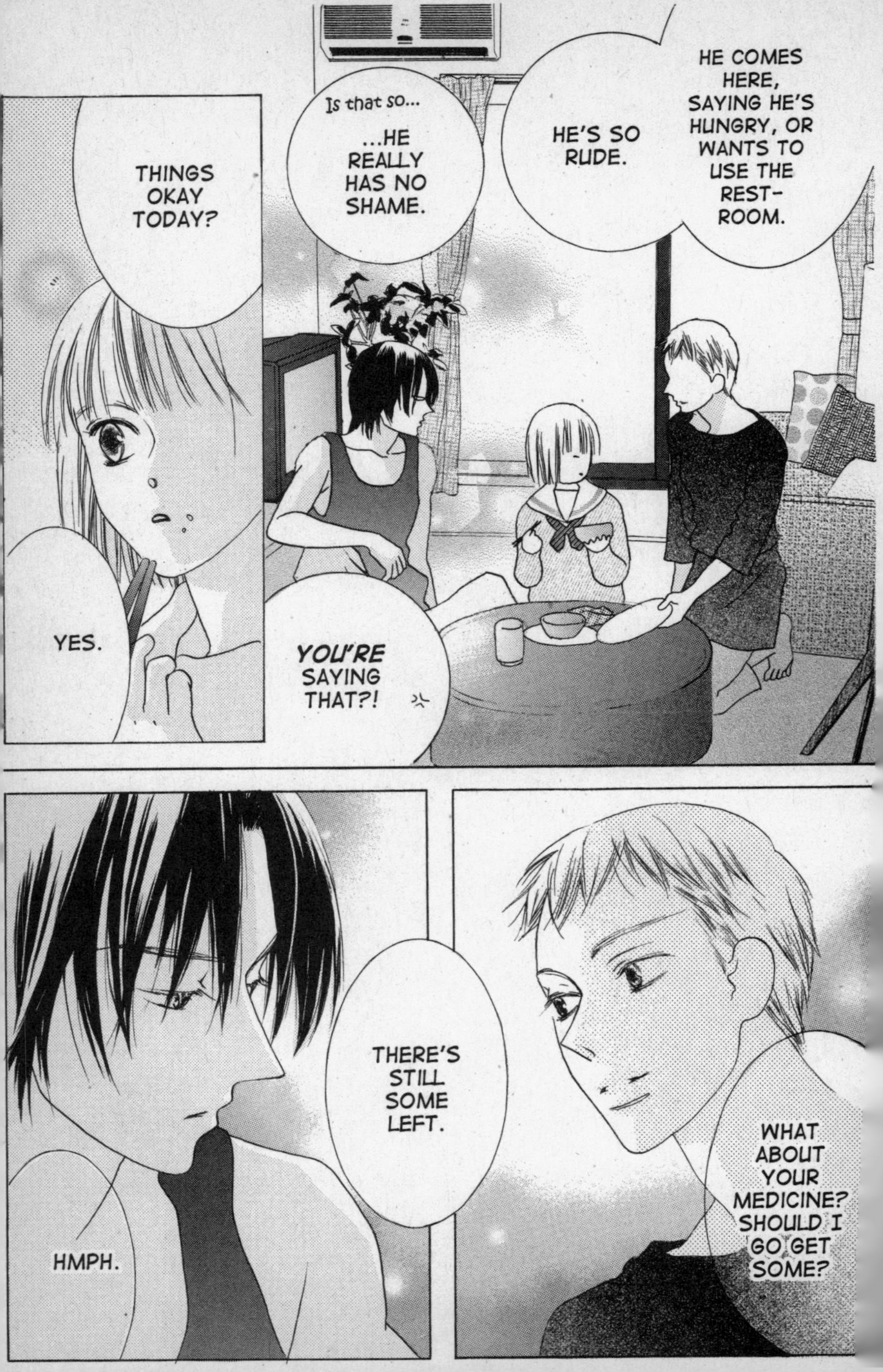
HE COMES HERE, SAYING HE'S HUNGRY, OR WANTS TO USE THE REST-ROOM.
HE'S SO RUDE.
Is that so... ...HE REALLY HAS NO SHAME.
YOU'RE SAYING THAT?!
THINGS OKAY TODAY?
YES.
WHAT ABOUT YOUR MEDICINE? SHOULD I GO GET SOME?
THERE'S STILL SOME LEFT.
HMPH.

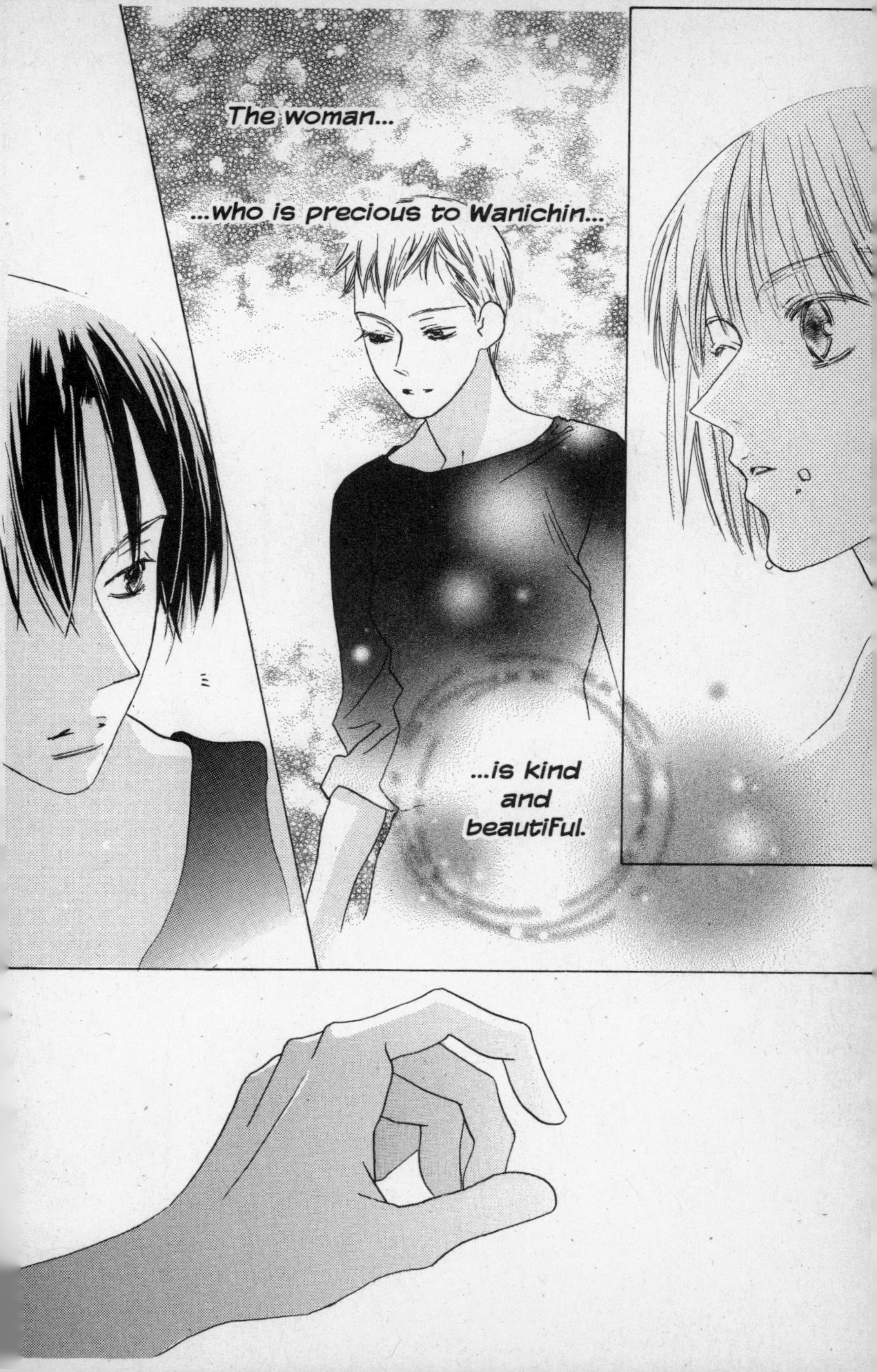
The woman...
...who is precious to Wanichin...
...is kind and beautiful.

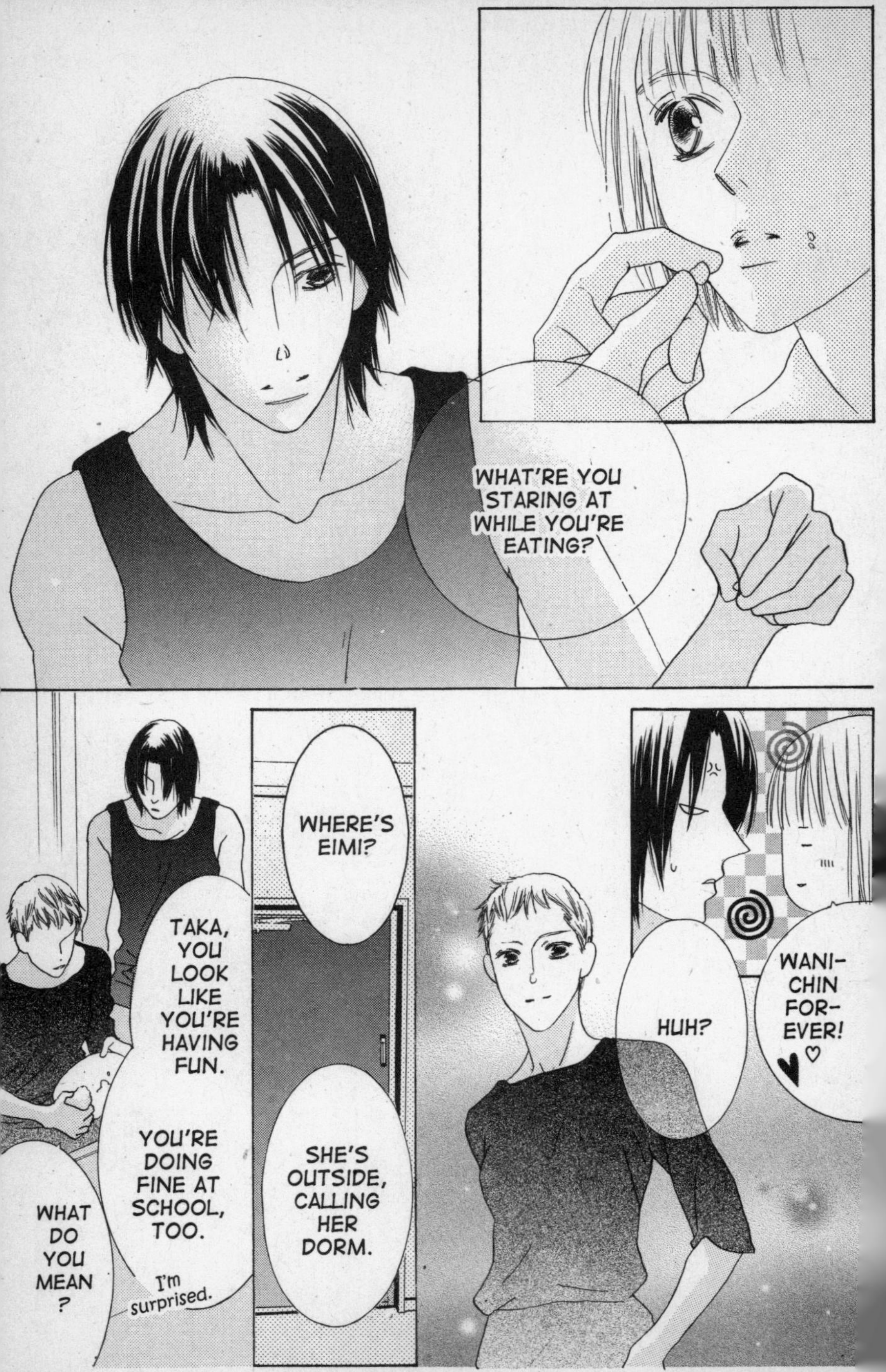
WHAT'RE YOU STARING AT WHILE YOU'RE EATING?
WANI-CHIN FOR-EVER! ♥♡
HUH?
WHERE'S EIMI?
SHE'S OUTSIDE, CALLING HER DORM.
TAKA, YOU LOOK LIKE YOU'RE HAVING FUN.
YOU'RE DOING FINE AT SCHOOL, TOO.
I'm surprised.
WHAT DO YOU MEAN?

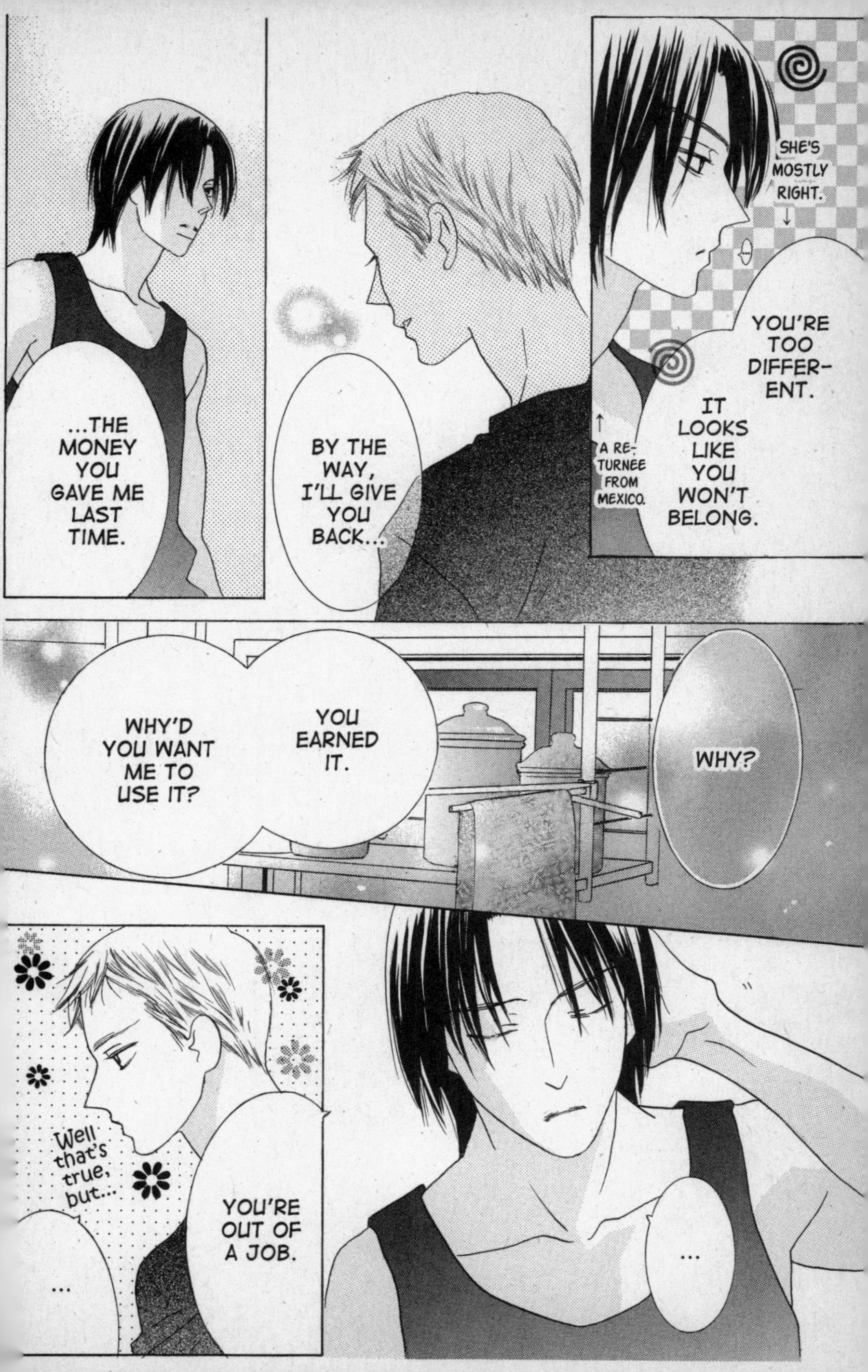
SHE'S MOSTLY RIGHT.
YOU'RE TOO DIFFER-ENT.
IT LOOKS LIKE YOU WON'T BELONG.
A RE-TURNEE FROM MEXICO.
BY THE WAY, I'LL GIVE YOU BACK...
...THE MONEY YOU GAVE ME LAST TIME.
WHY?
YOU EARNED IT.
WHY'D YOU WANT ME TO USE IT?
...
YOU'RE OUT OF A JOB.
Well that's true, but...
...

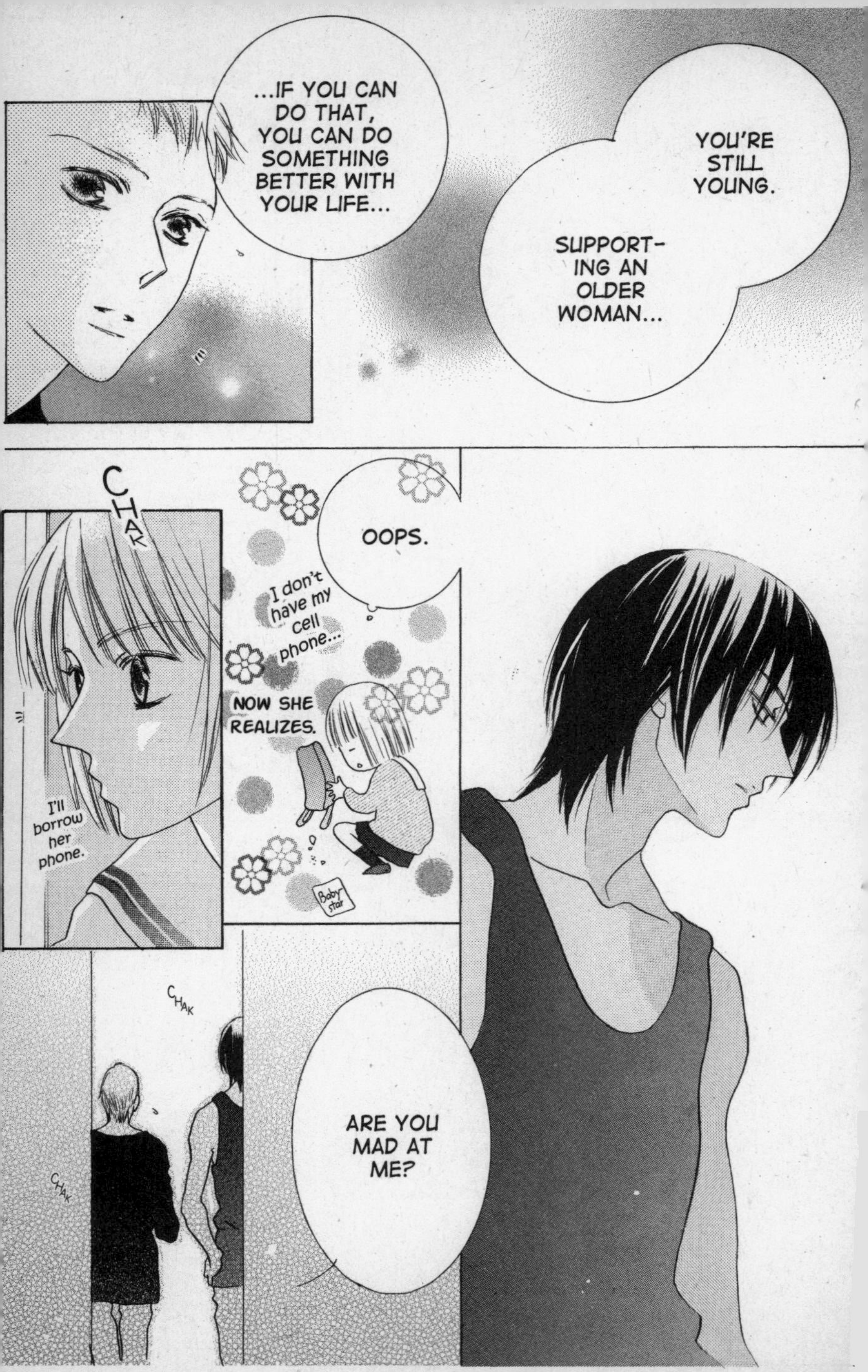
YOU'RE STILL YOUNG.
SUPPORT-ING AN OLDER WOMAN...
...IF YOU CAN DO THAT, YOU CAN DO SOMETHING BETTER WITH YOUR LIFE...
ARE YOU MAD AT ME?
OOPS.
I don't have my cell phone...
NOW SHE REALIZES.
Baby-star
CHAK
I'll borrow her phone.
CHAK
CHAK

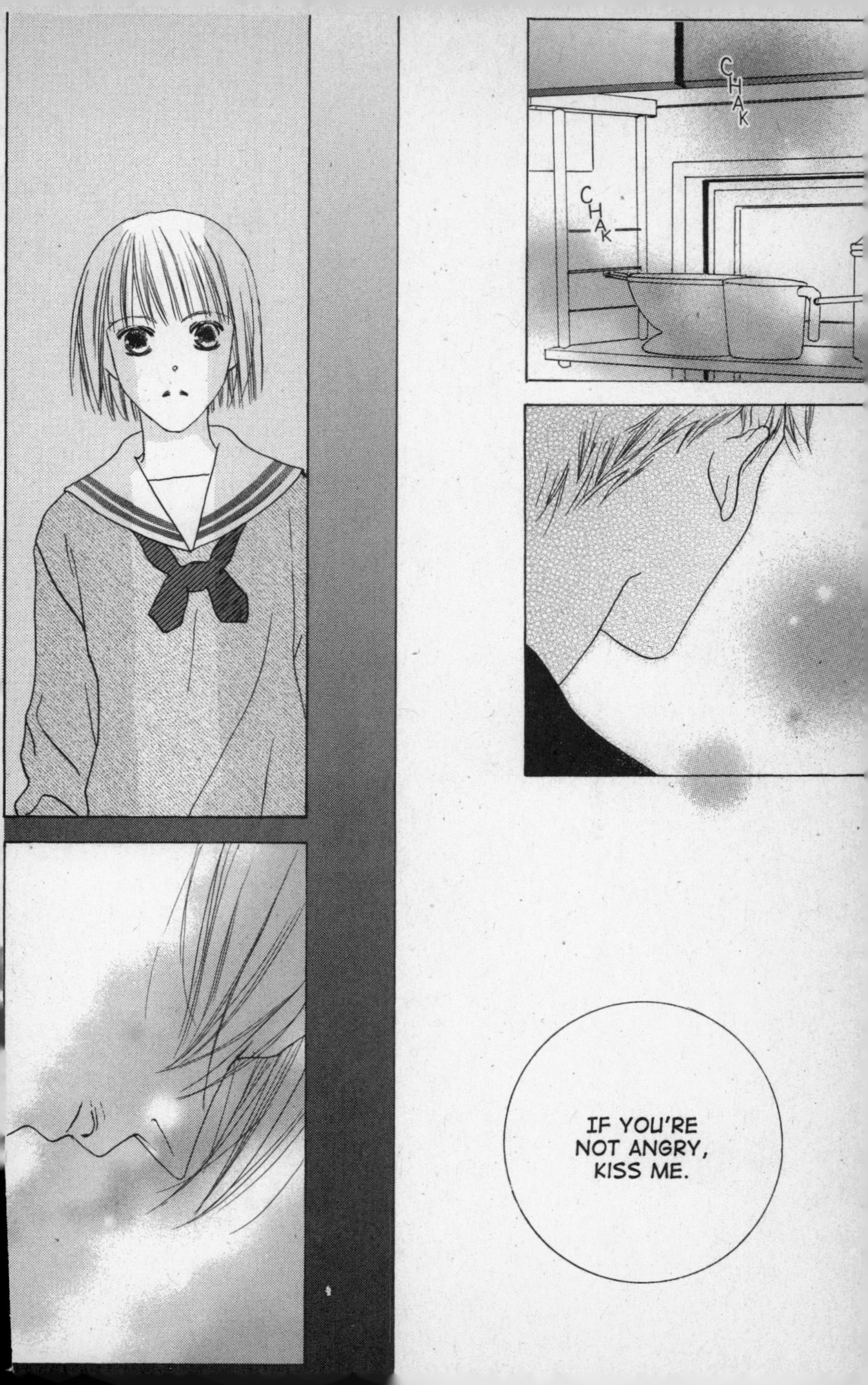
CHAK
CHAK
IF YOU'RE NOT ANGRY, KISS ME.

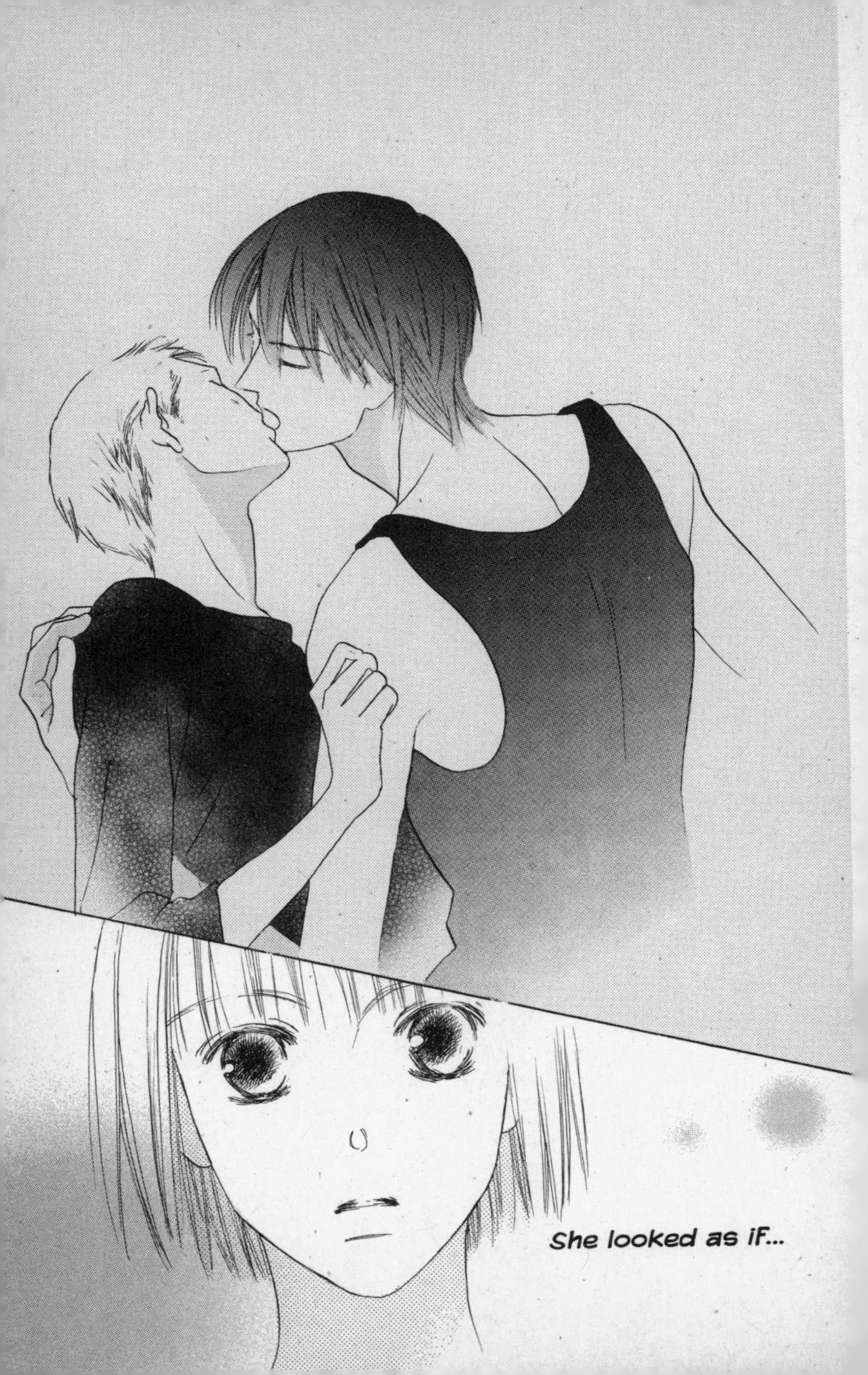
She looked as if...

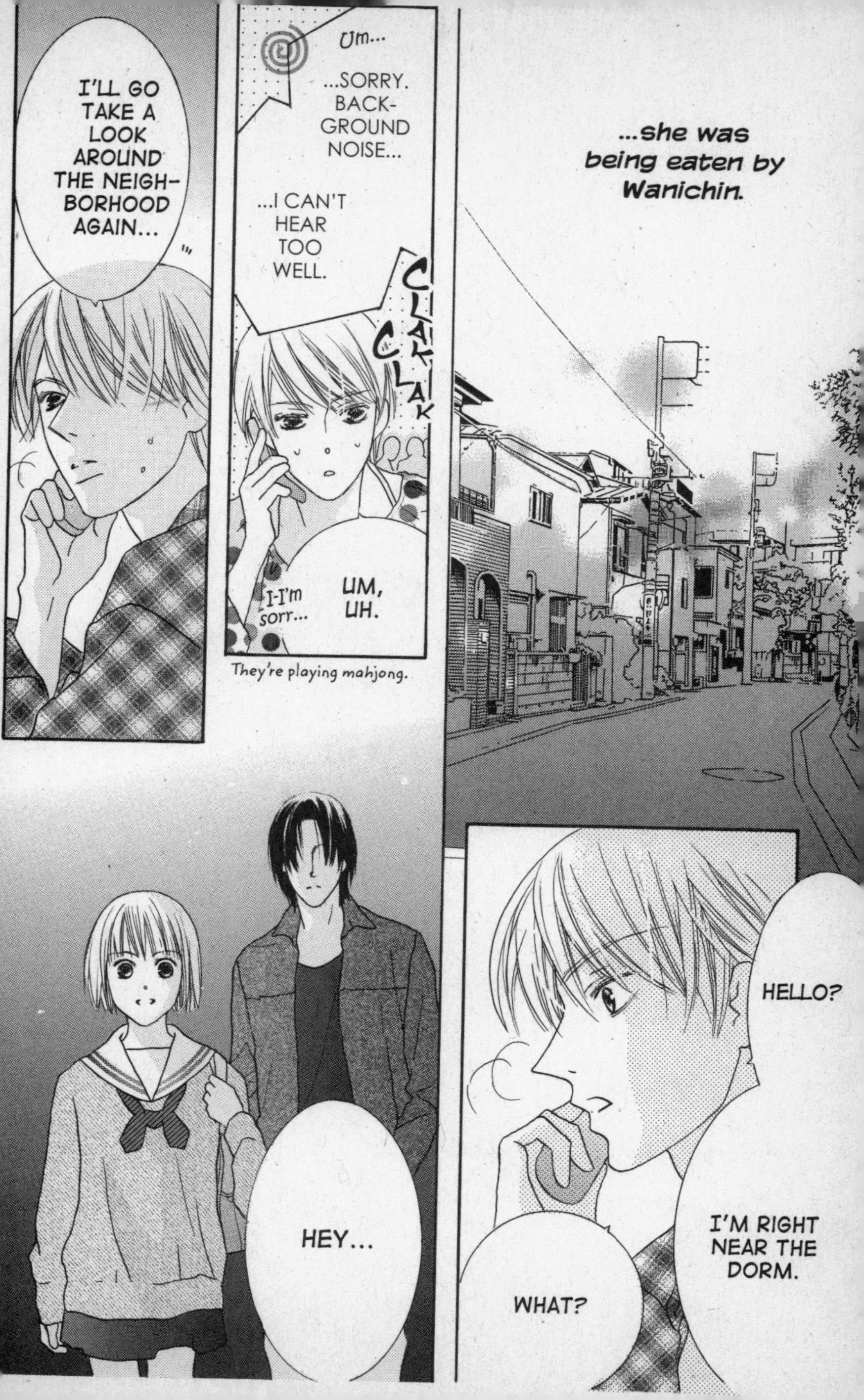
...she was being eaten by Wanichin.
Um...
...SORRY. BACKGROUND NOISE...
...I CAN'T HEAR TOO WELL.
CLAK CLAK
UM, UH.
I-I'm sorr...
They're playing mahjong.
I'LL GO TAKE A LOOK AROUND THE NEIGHBORHOOD AGAIN...
HELLO?
I'M RIGHT NEAR THE DORM.
WHAT?
HEY...

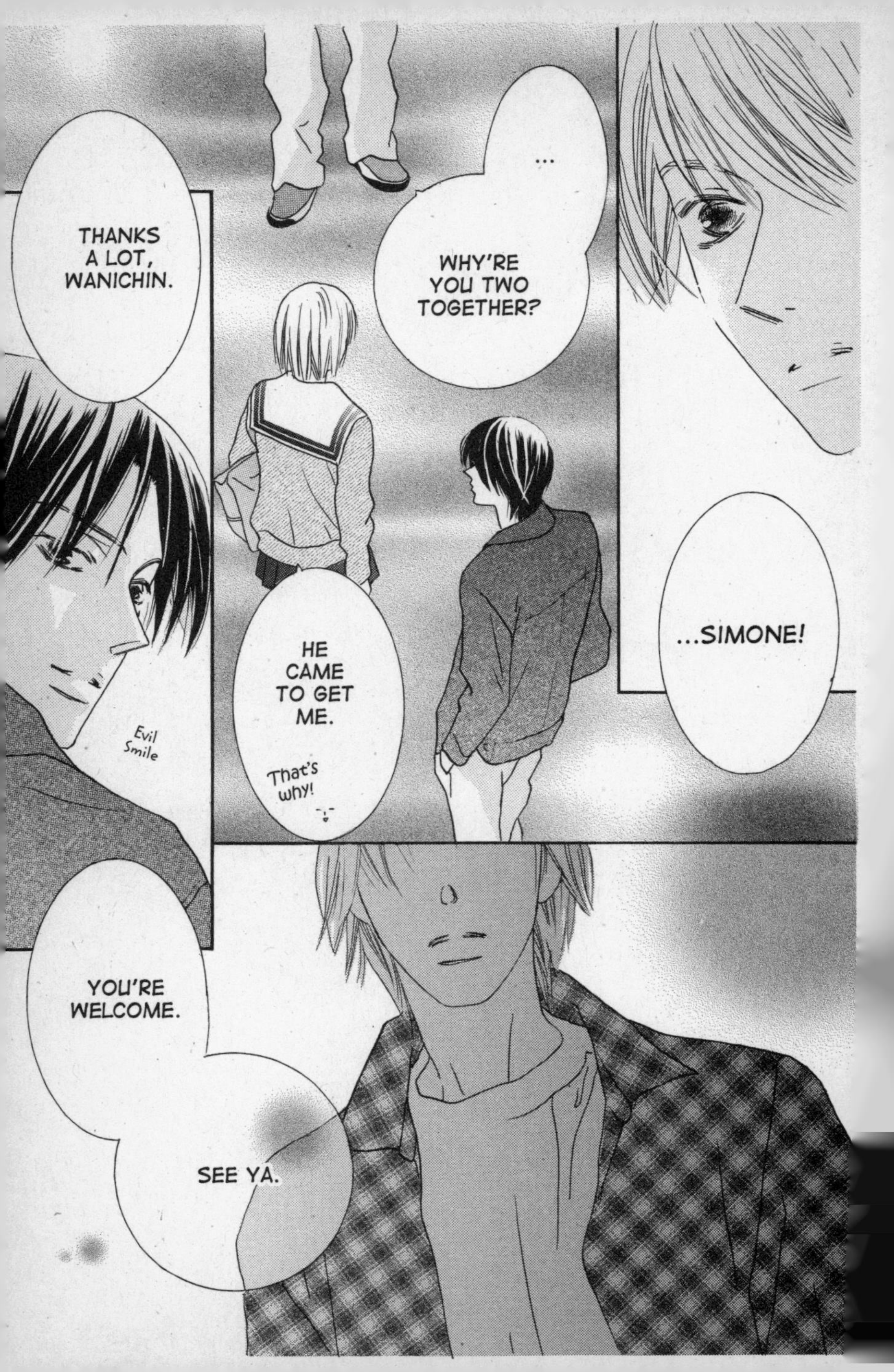
...SIMONE!
...
WHY'RE YOU TWO TOGETHER?
HE CAME TO GET ME.
That's why!
THANKS A LOT, WANICHIN.
Evil Smile
YOU'RE WELCOME.
SEE YA.

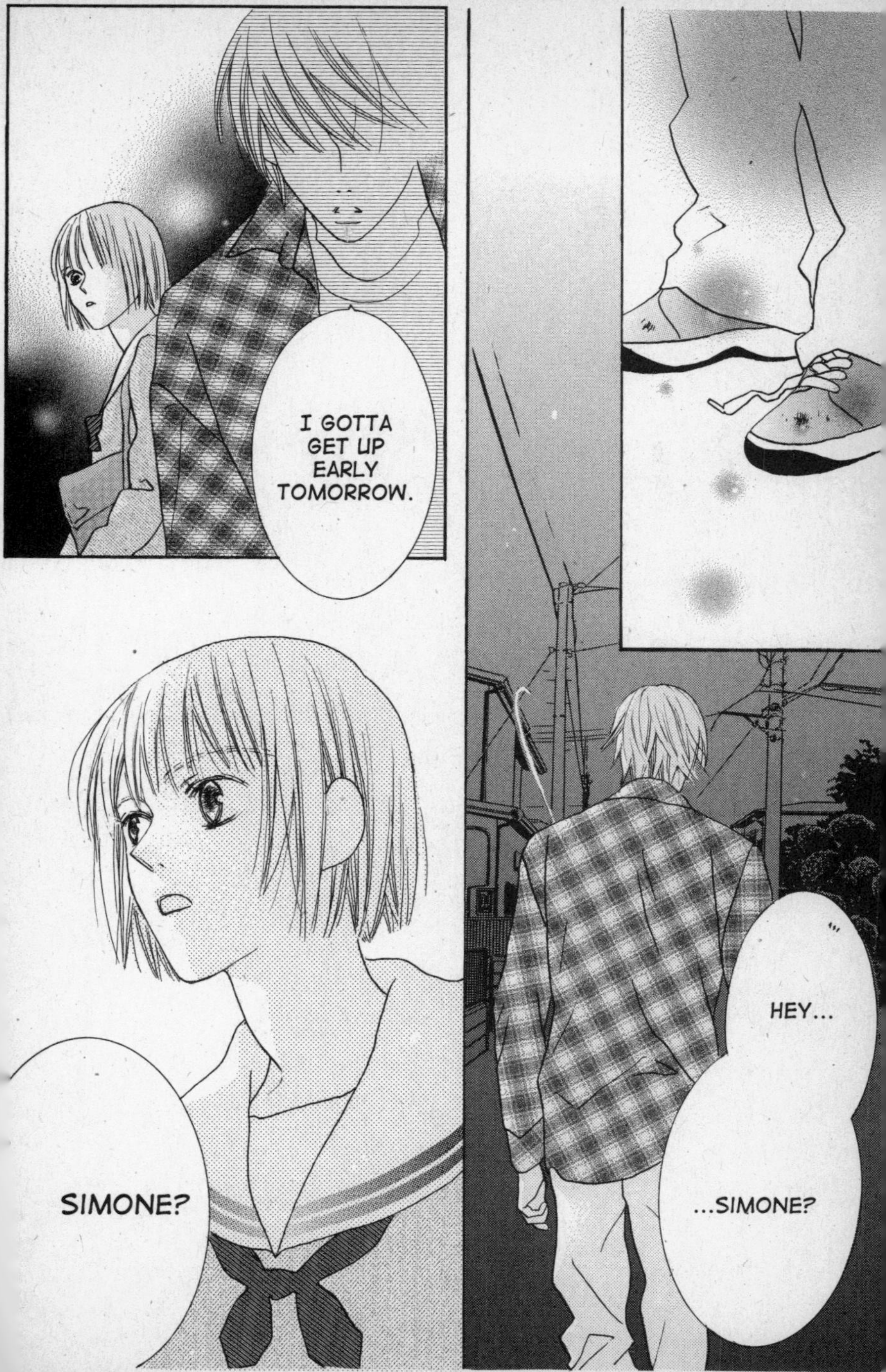
HEY...
...SIMONE?
I GOTTA GET UP EARLY TOMORROW.
SIMONE?

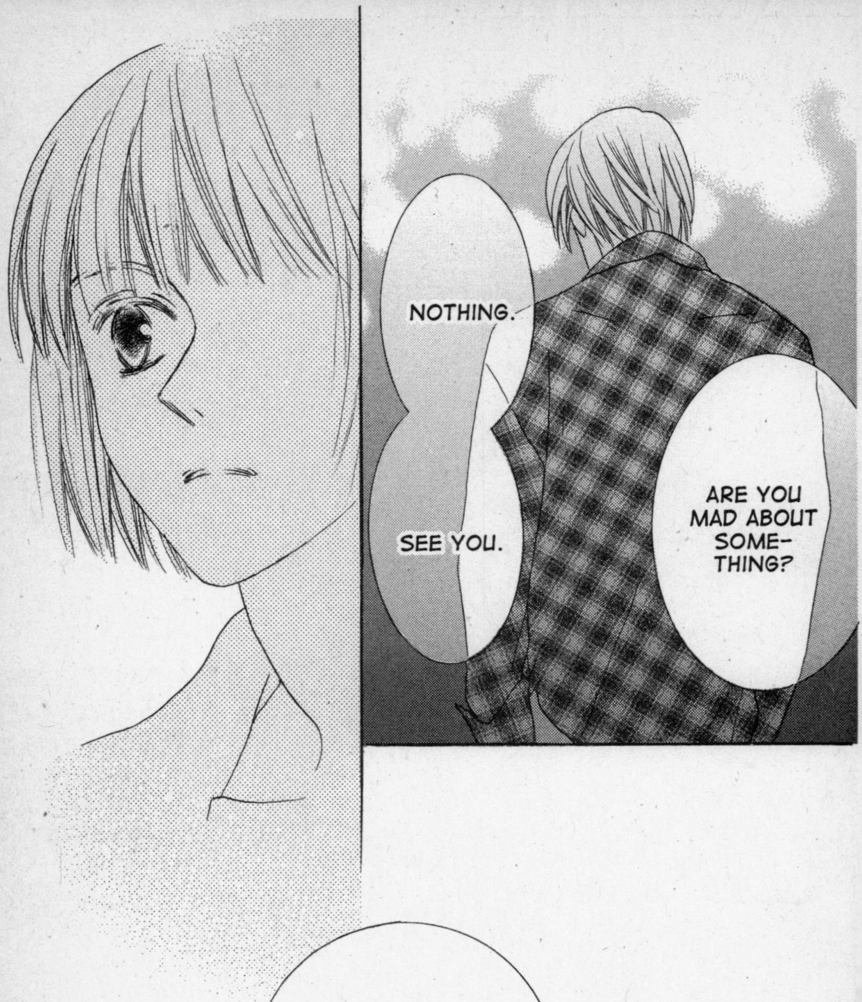
ARE YOU MAD ABOUT SOME-THING?
NOTHING.
SEE YOU.
IF YOU'RE NOT ANGRY, KISS ME.

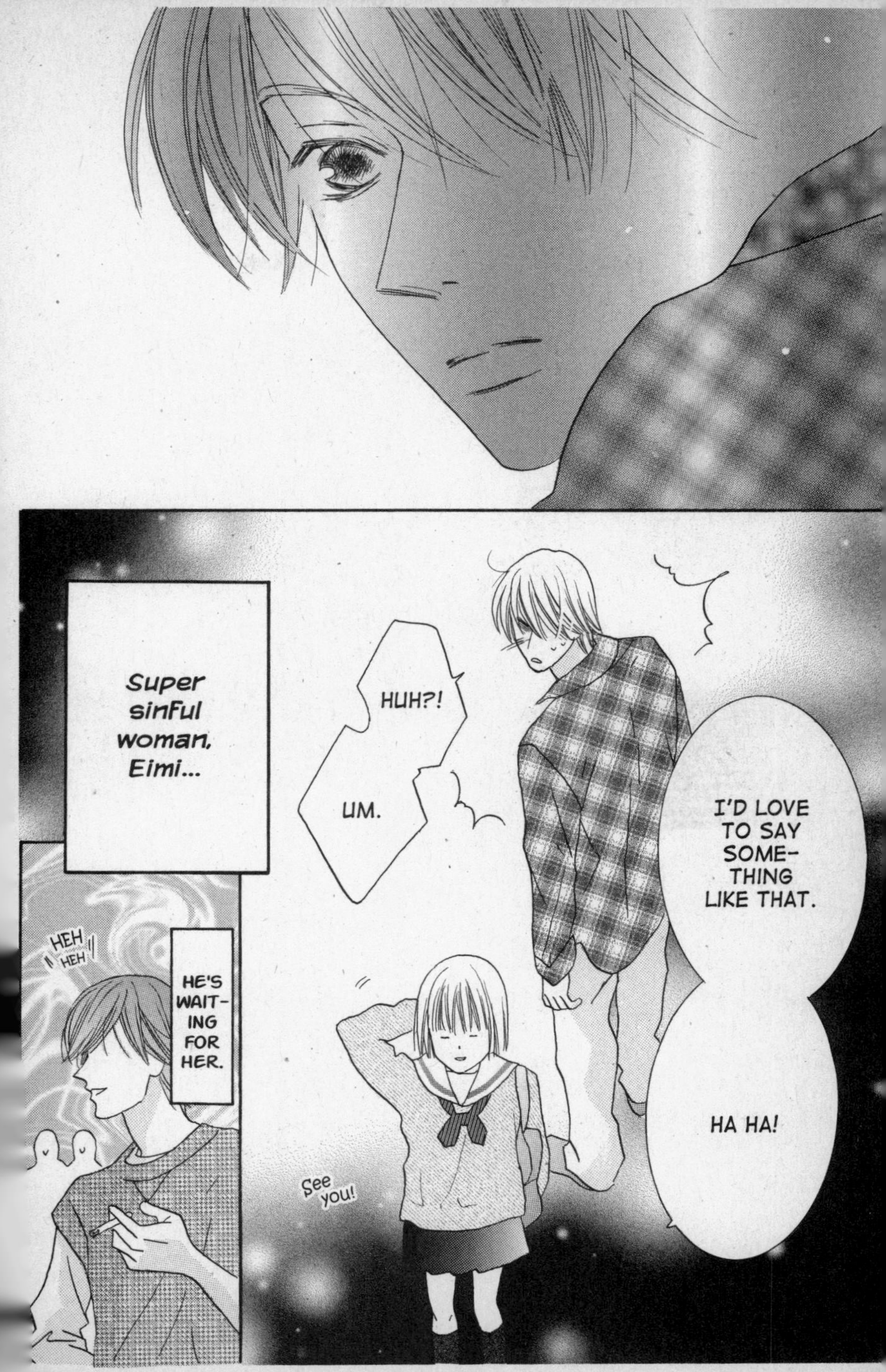
I'D LOVE TO SAY SOME-THING LIKE THAT.
HA HA!
HUH?!
UM.
Super sinful woman, Eimi...
See you!
HE'S WAIT-ING FOR HER.
HEH HEH

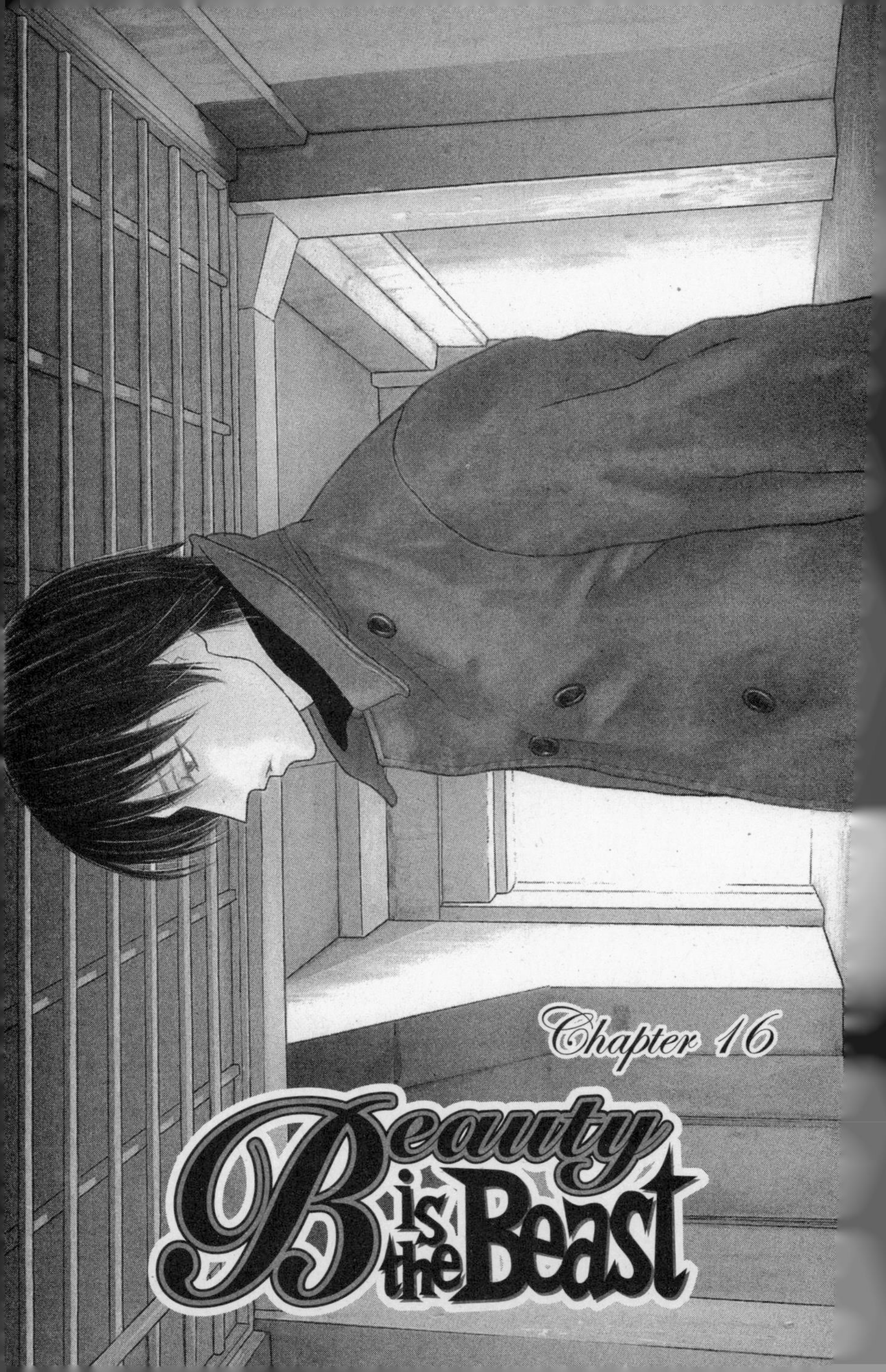
Chapter 16
Beauty is the Beast

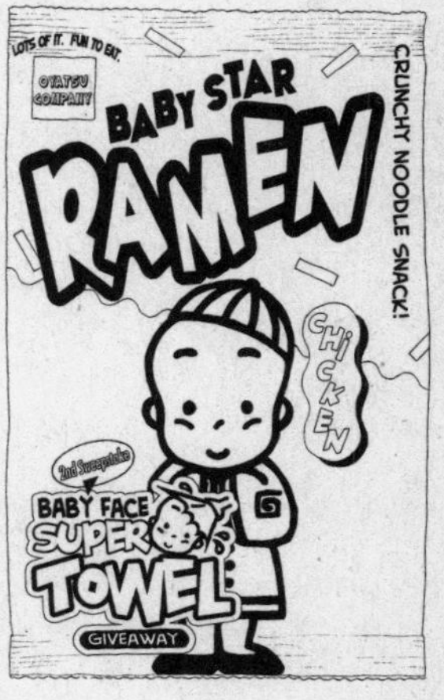
LOTS OF IT. FUN TO EAT.
OYATSU COMPANY
BABY STAR
RAMEN
CRUNCHY NOODLE SNACK!
CHICKEN
2nd Sweepstake
BABY FACE
SUPER
TOWEL
GIVEAWAY

BEAUTY IS THE BEAST

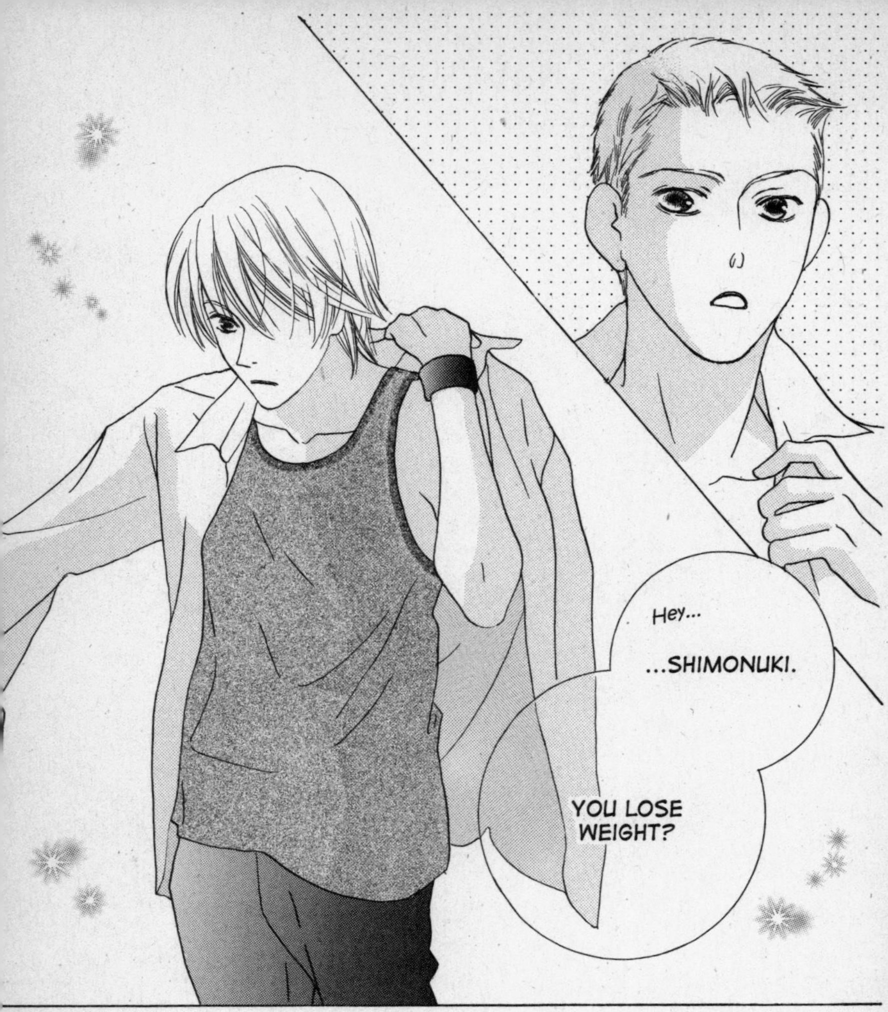

Hey...
...SHIMONUKI.
YOU LOSE WEIGHT?

Bruce Hornsby & The Range/The Way it is

I was looking for this song for about eight years.
The other day I finally found it, so I'll write it here since I'm happy (☺).
To put it simply, it's a song where the piano runs off.
When I listen to it, I get wide-awake, and my senses become really alert.
It's not soothing at all!

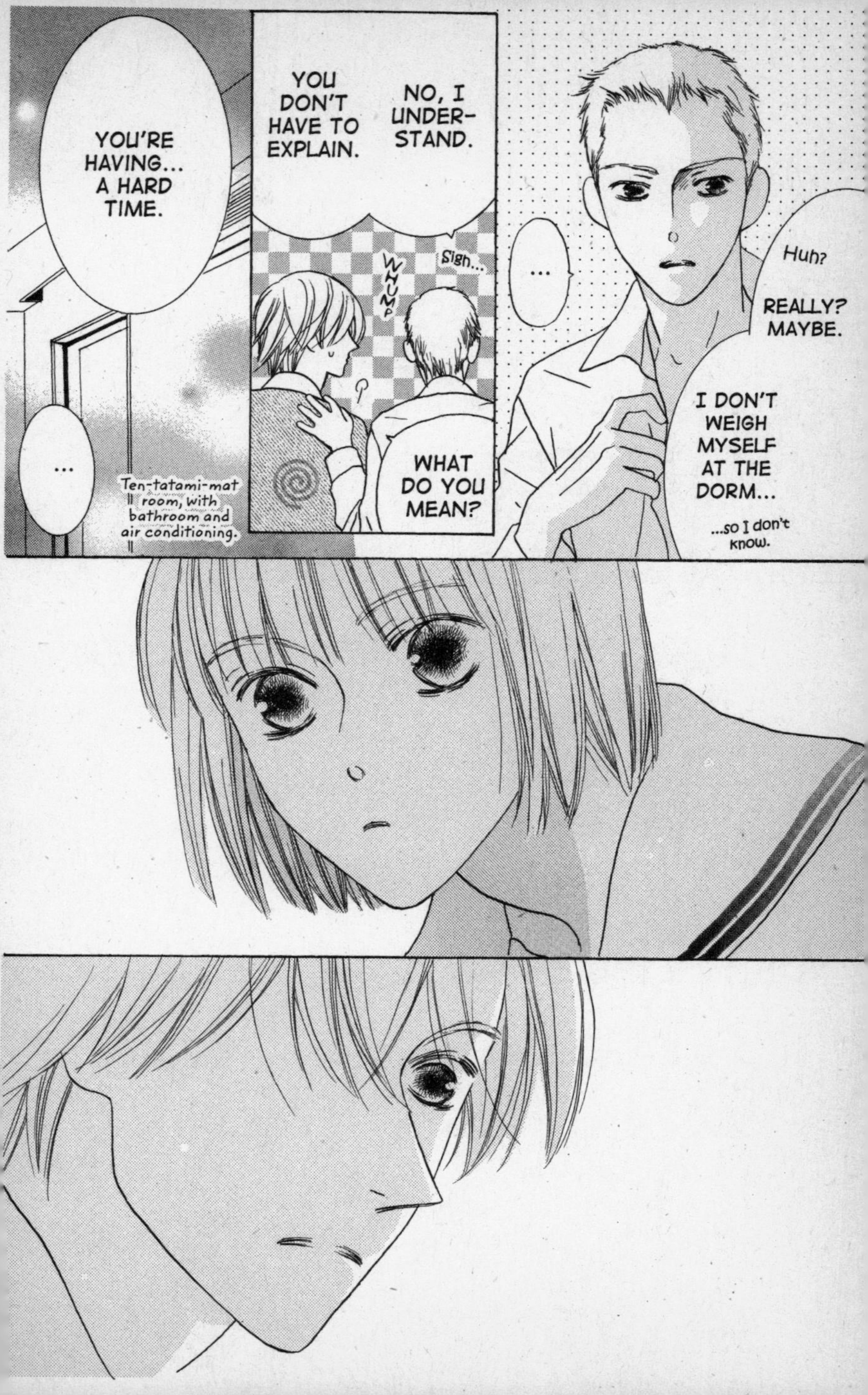
Huh?
REALLY? MAYBE.
I DON'T WEIGH MYSELF AT THE DORM...
...so I don't know.
...
NO, I UNDERSTAND.
YOU DON'T HAVE TO EXPLAIN.
Sigh...
WHUMP
WHAT DO YOU MEAN?
YOU'RE HAVING... A HARD TIME.
...
Ten-tatami-mat room, with bathroom and air conditioning.

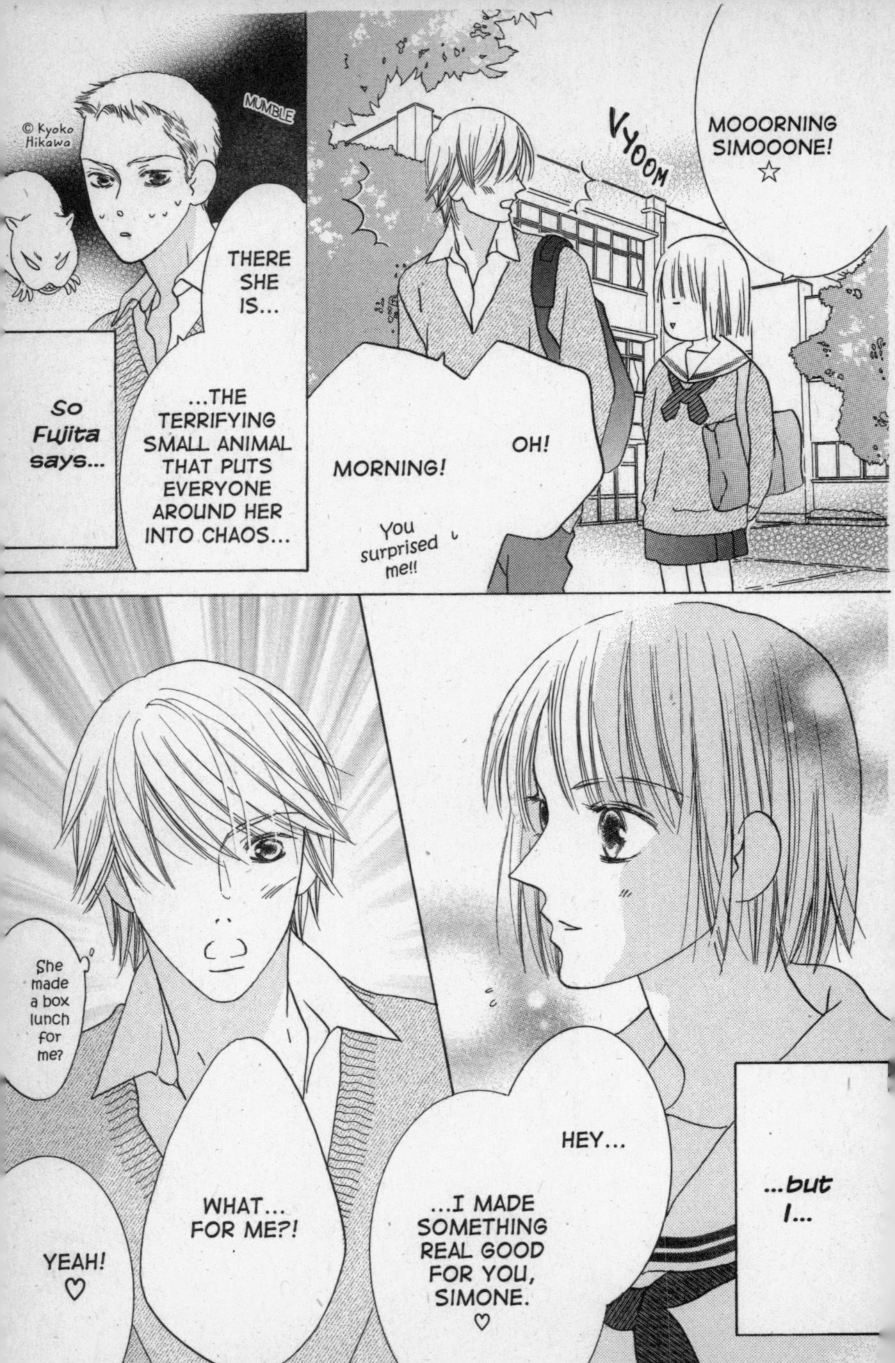
MOOORNING SIMOOONE! ☆
VYOOM
OH!
MORNING!
You surprised me!!
MUMBLE
© Kyoko Hikawa
THERE SHE IS...
...THE TERRIFYING SMALL ANIMAL THAT PUTS EVERYONE AROUND HER INTO CHAOS...
So Fujita says...
...but I...
HEY...
...I MADE SOMETHING REAL GOOD FOR YOU, SIMONE. ♡
WHAT... FOR ME?!
YEAH! ♡
She made a box lunch for me?

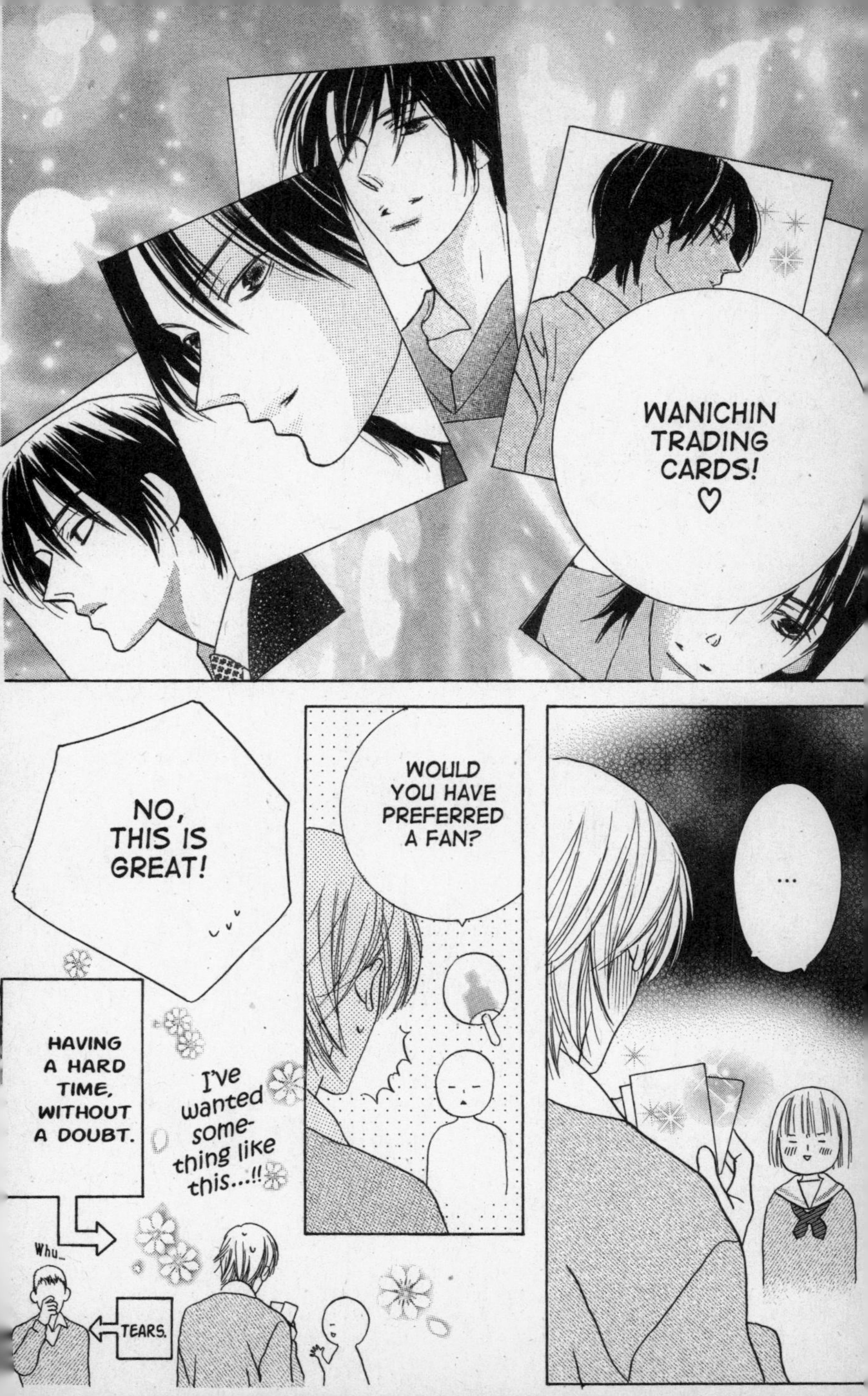
WANICHIN TRADING CARDS! ♡
...
WOULD YOU HAVE PREFERRED A FAN?
NO, THIS IS GREAT!
I've wanted something like this...!!
HAVING A HARD TIME, WITHOUT A DOUBT.
TEARS.
Whu...

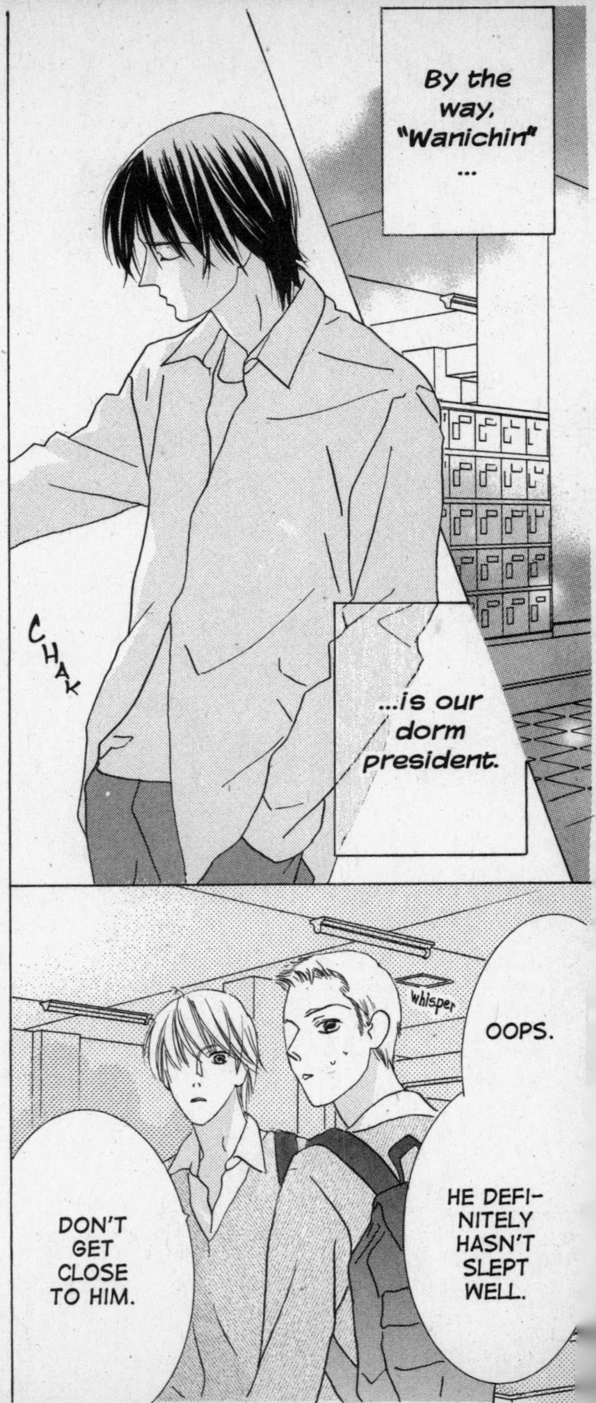
By the way, "Wanichin" ...
CHAK
...is our dorm president.
whisper
OOPS.
HE DEFI-NITELY HASN'T SLEPT WELL.
DON'T GET CLOSE TO HIM.

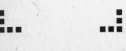

I've received questions about this before; Wanibuchi-kun, is called Taka, but his first name is really Takami. I decided on that recently.
(↑ Hey!)
When I was in high school, there was a girl in my class who was reaaaally beautiful called Takami. We didn't have much of a chance to speak before she quit school, but she really left an impression on me, so I borrowed it without permission.

By the way, the name of the piano teacher in a previous work was taken from the name of a boy I went to grade school and junior high with (without permission, too), because he was a very smart kid. He became a teacher, and I was very surprised when I received a letter from one of his students. (☺)
I keep using names of people I went to school with. I hope no one will get angry...

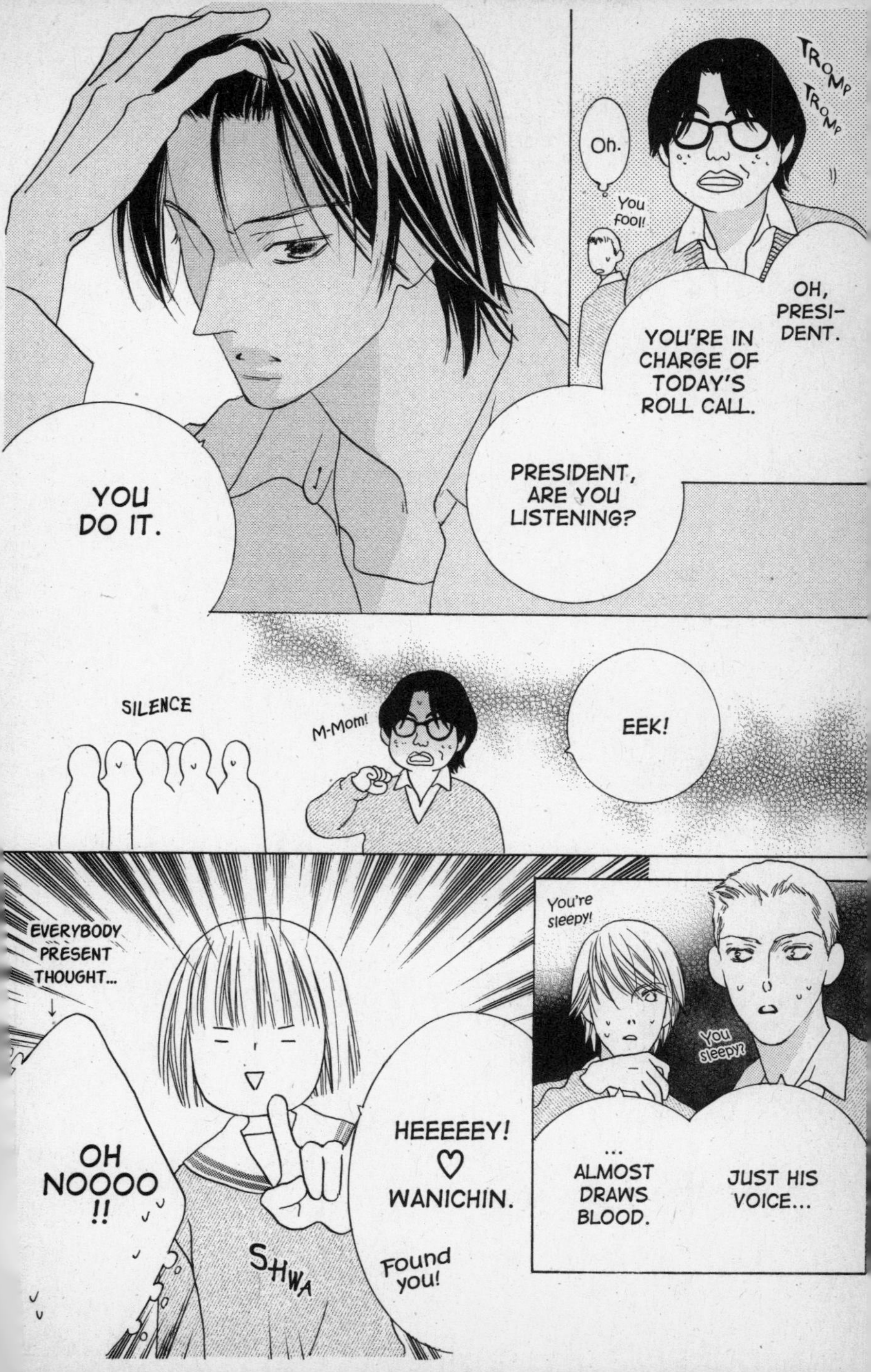
TROMP TROMP
Oh.
You fool!
OH, PRESIDENT.
YOU'RE IN CHARGE OF TODAY'S ROLL CALL.
PRESIDENT, ARE YOU LISTENING?
YOU DO IT.
EEK!
M-Mom!
SILENCE
You're sleepy!
You sleepy?
JUST HIS VOICE...
...ALMOST DRAWS BLOOD.
HEEEEEY! ♡ WANICHIN.
Found you!
SHWA
EVERYBODY PRESENT THOUGHT...
OH NOOOO!!

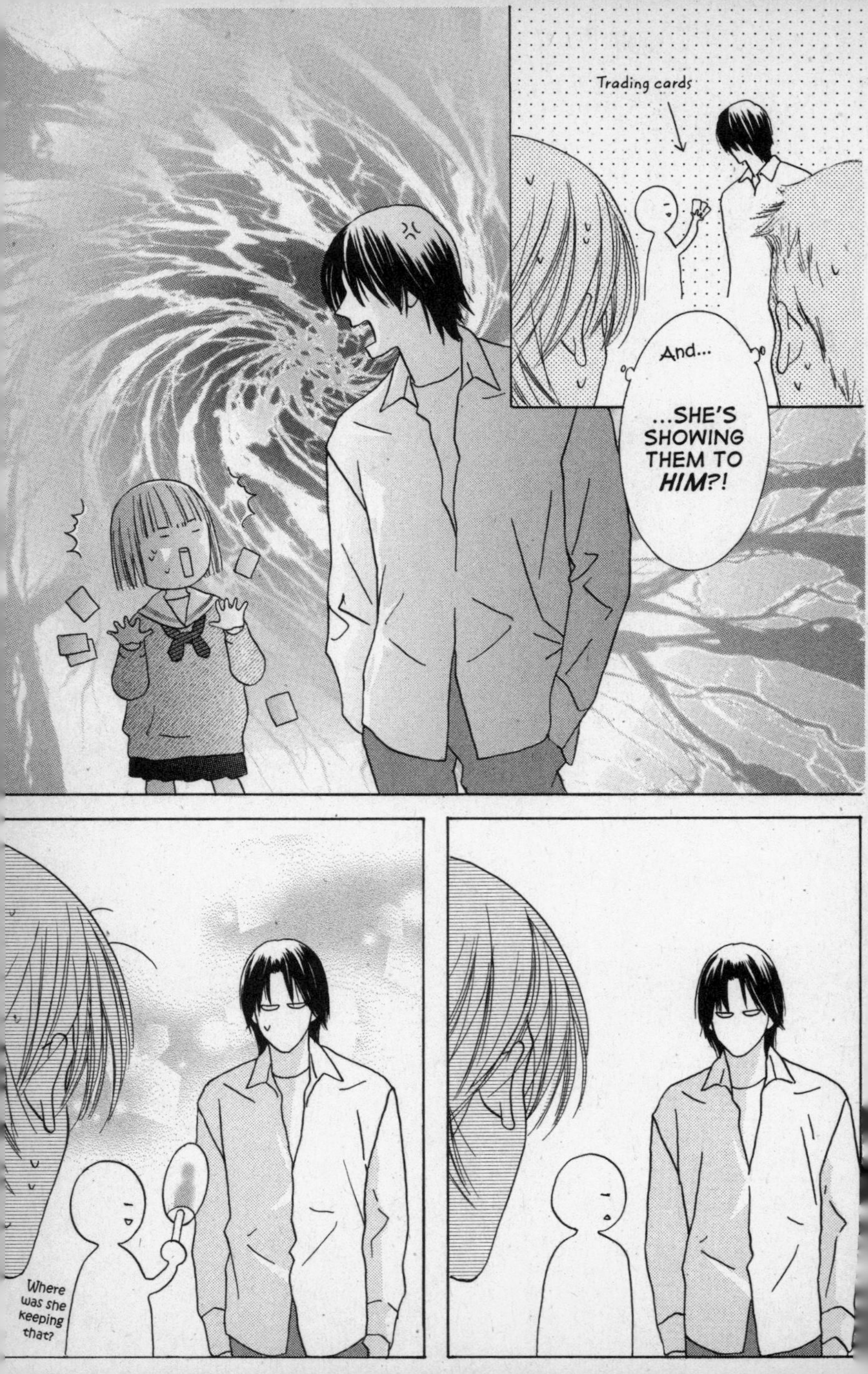
Trading cards
And...
...SHE'S SHOWING THEM TO *HIM*?!
Where was she keeping that?

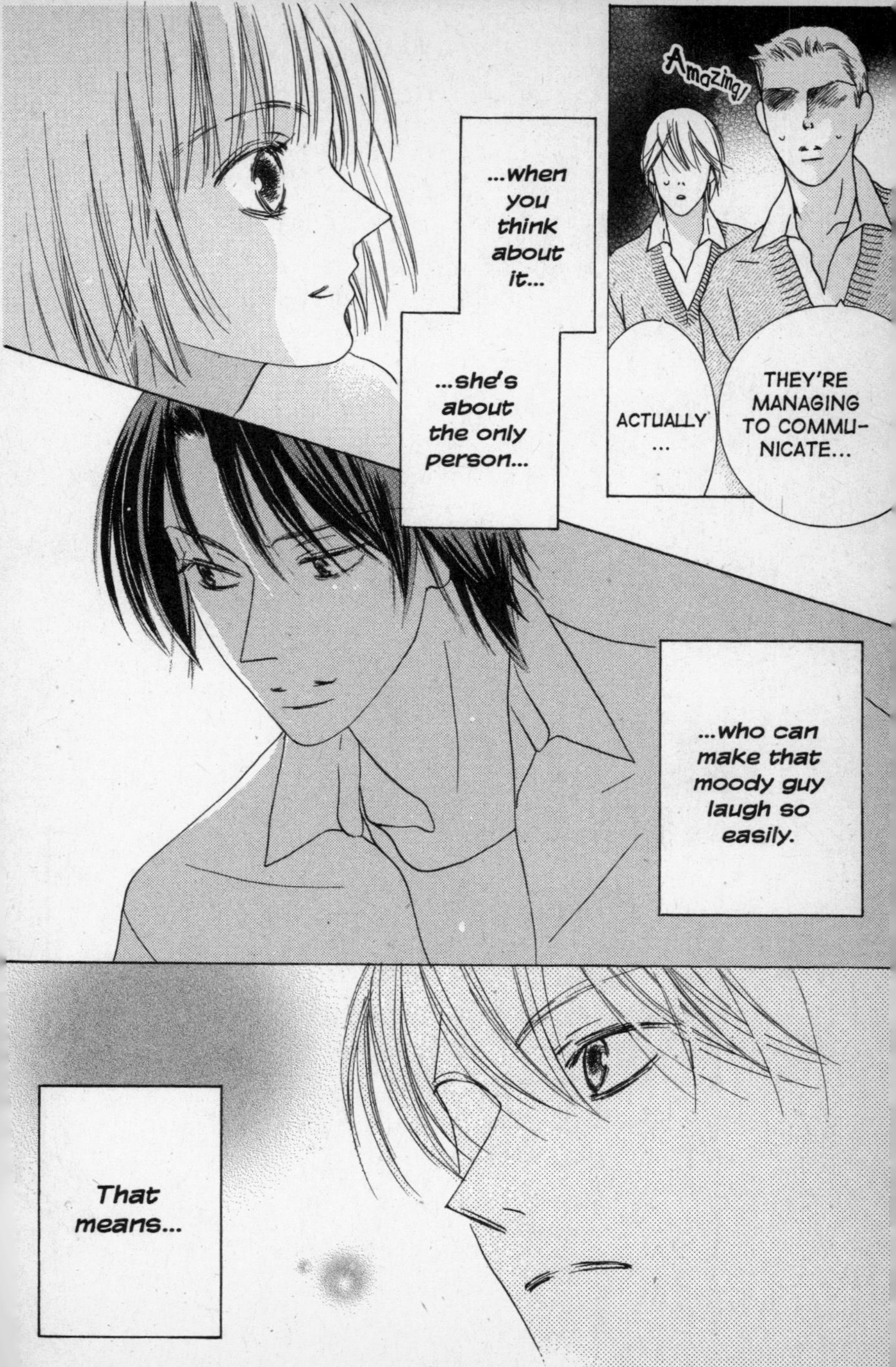
Amazing!
THEY'RE MANAGING TO COMMUNICATE...
ACTUALLY ...
...when you think about it...
...she's about the only person...
...who can make that moody guy laugh so easily.
That means...

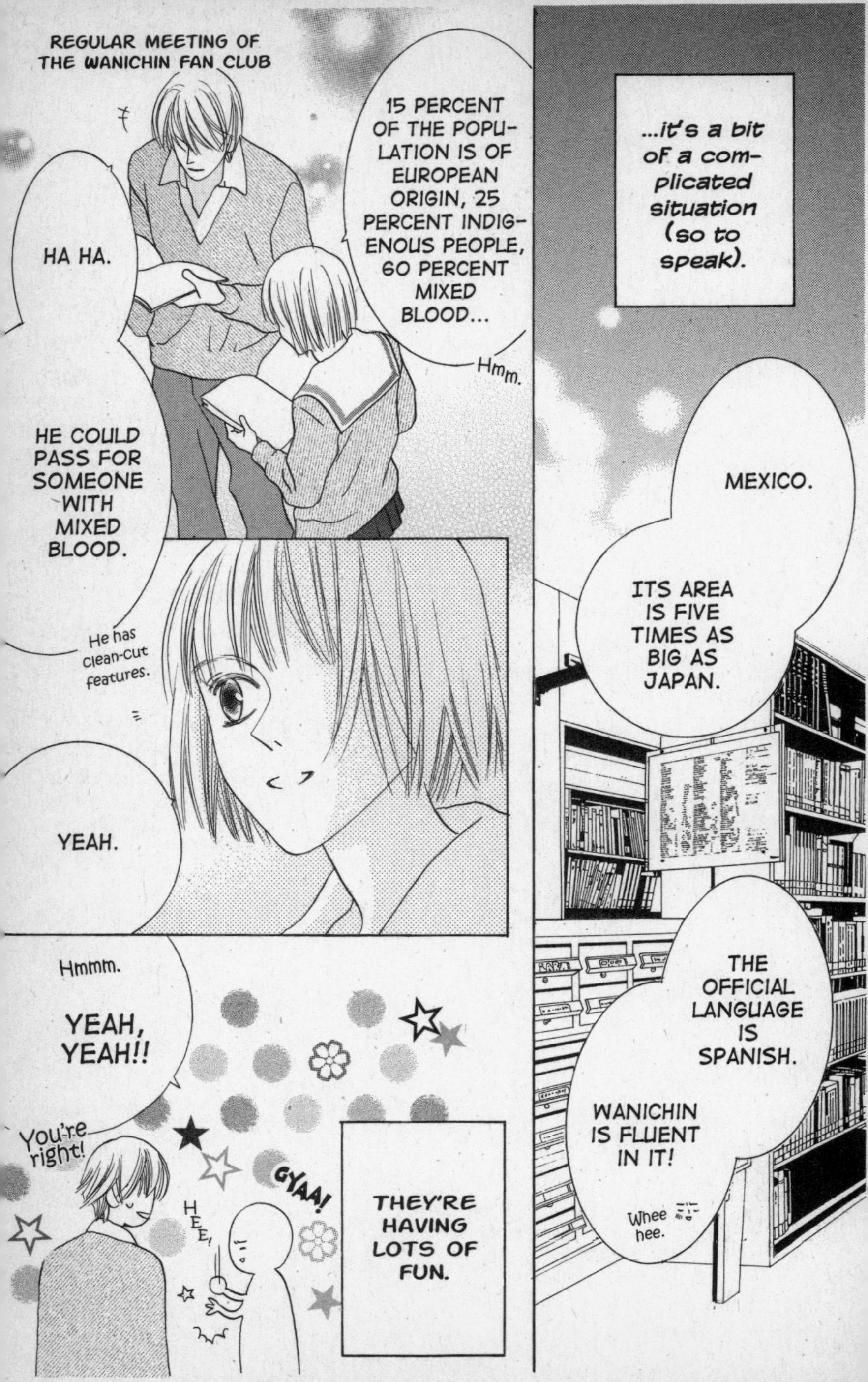
...it's a bit of a complicated situation (so to speak).
MEXICO.
ITS AREA IS FIVE TIMES AS BIG AS JAPAN.
THE OFFICIAL LANGUAGE IS SPANISH.
WANICHIN IS FLUENT IN IT!
Whee hee.
REGULAR MEETING OF THE WANICHIN FAN CLUB
15 PERCENT OF THE POPULATION IS OF EUROPEAN ORIGIN, 25 PERCENT INDIGENOUS PEOPLE, 60 PERCENT MIXED BLOOD...
Hmm.
HA HA.
HE COULD PASS FOR SOMEONE WITH MIXED BLOOD.
He has clean-cut features.
YEAH.
THEY'RE HAVING LOTS OF FUN.
GYAA!
HEE
Hmmm.
YEAH, YEAH!!
You're right!

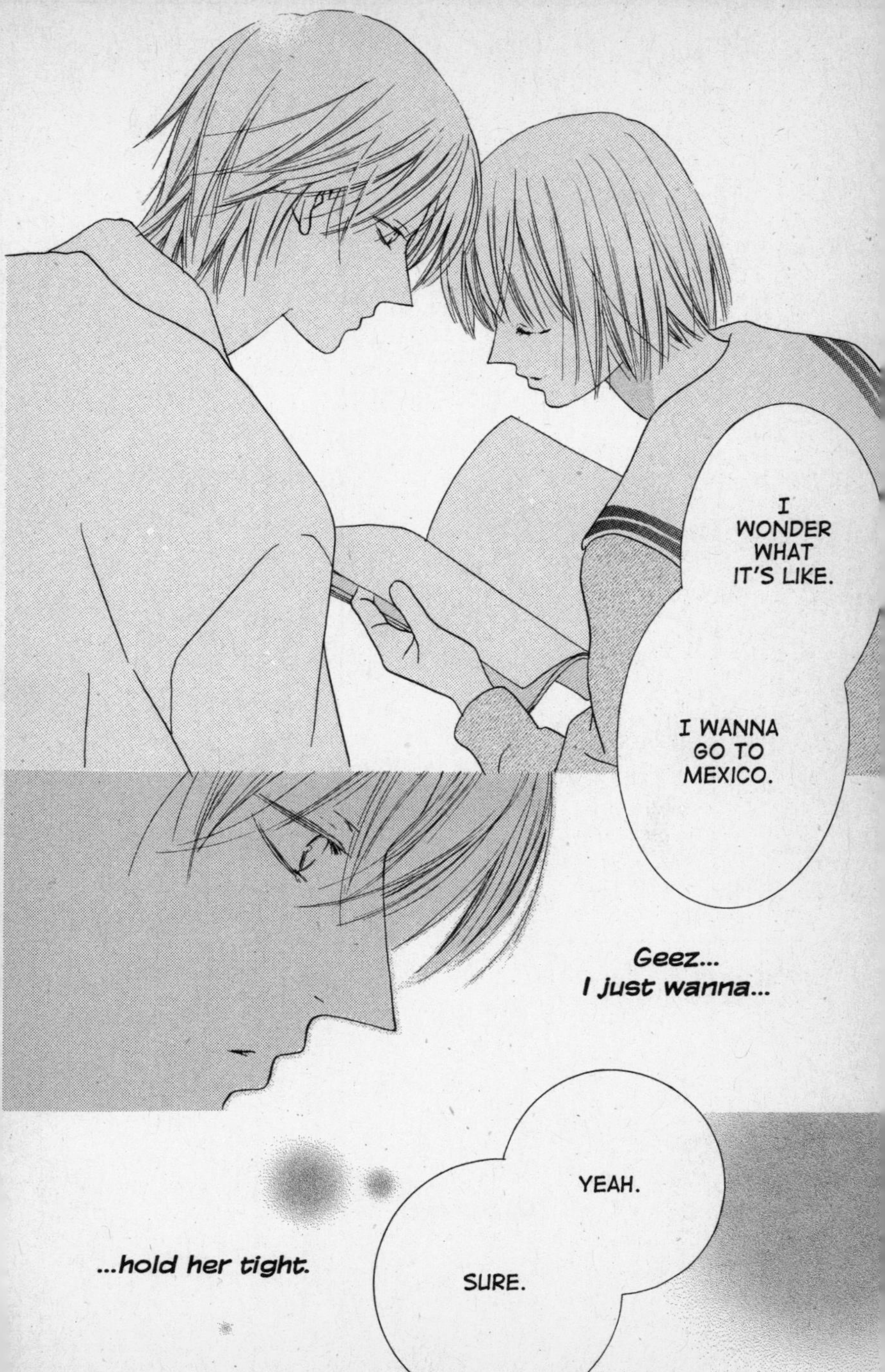
I WONDER WHAT IT'S LIKE.
I WANNA GO TO MEXICO.
Geez... I just wanna...
YEAH.
SURE.
...hold her tight.

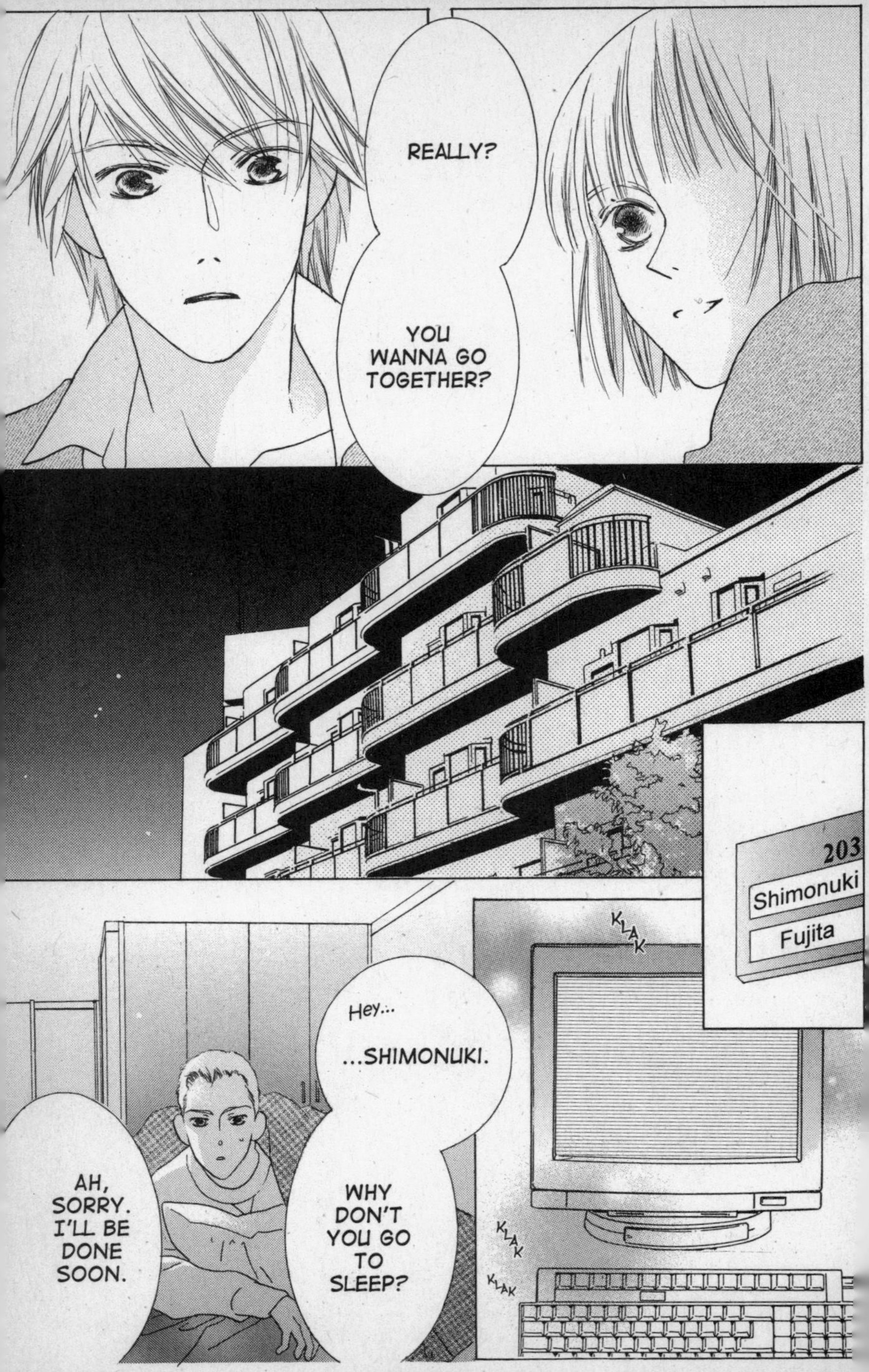
REALLY?
YOU WANNA GO TOGETHER?
203
Shimonuki
Fujita
KLAK
KLAK
KLAK
Hey...
...SHIMONUKI.
WHY DON'T YOU GO TO SLEEP?
AH, SORRY. I'LL BE DONE SOON.

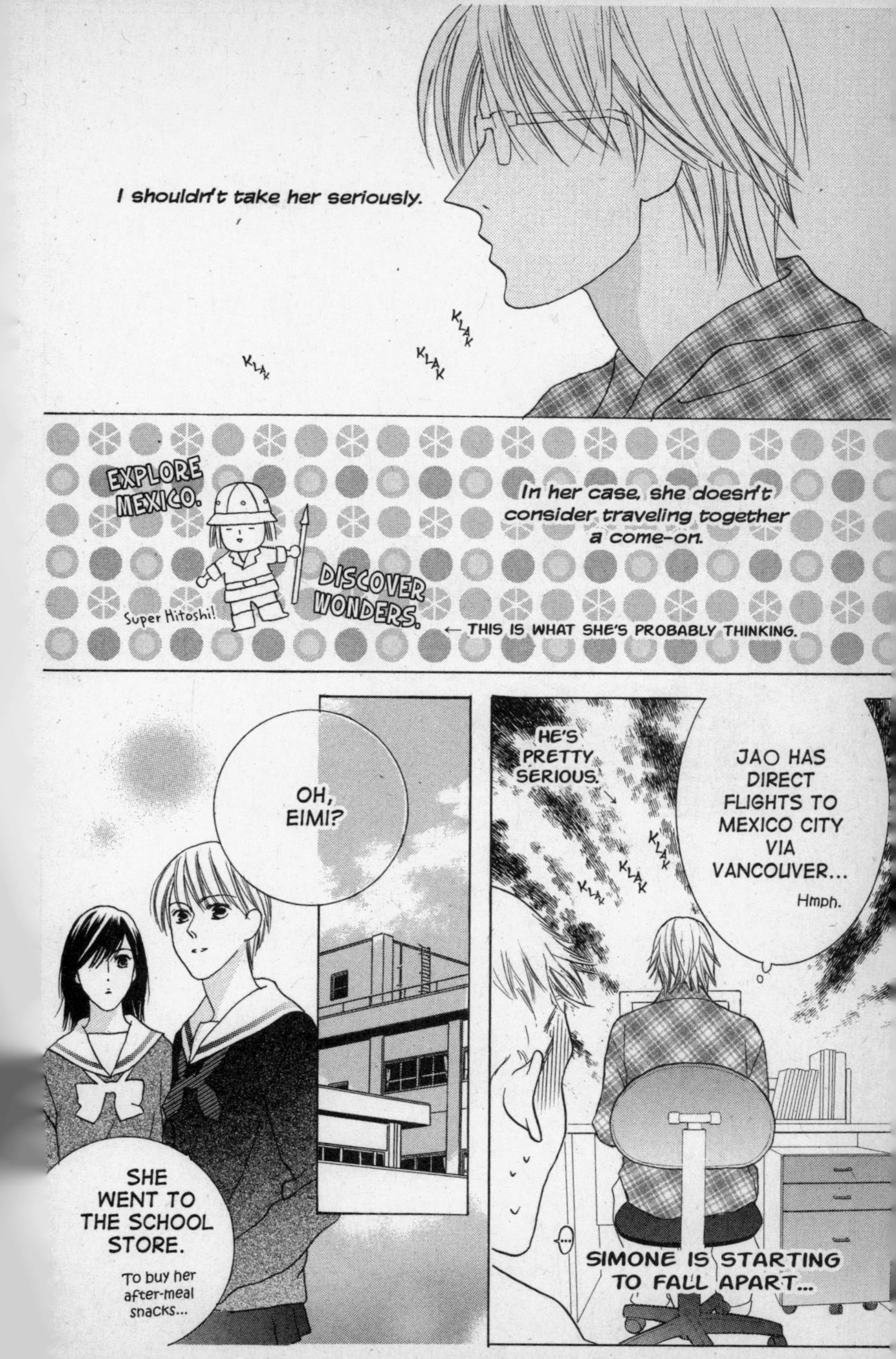

I shouldn't take her seriously.
KLAK
KLAK
KLAK
In her case, she doesn't consider traveling together a come-on.
EXPLORE MEXICO.
DISCOVER WONDERS.
Super Hitoshi!
← THIS IS WHAT SHE'S PROBABLY THINKING.
JAO HAS DIRECT FLIGHTS TO MEXICO CITY VIA VANCOUVER...
Hmph.
HE'S PRETTY SERIOUS.
KLAK
KLAK
KLAK
...
SIMONE IS STARTING TO FALL APART...
OH, EIMI?
SHE WENT TO THE SCHOOL STORE.
To buy her after-meal snacks...

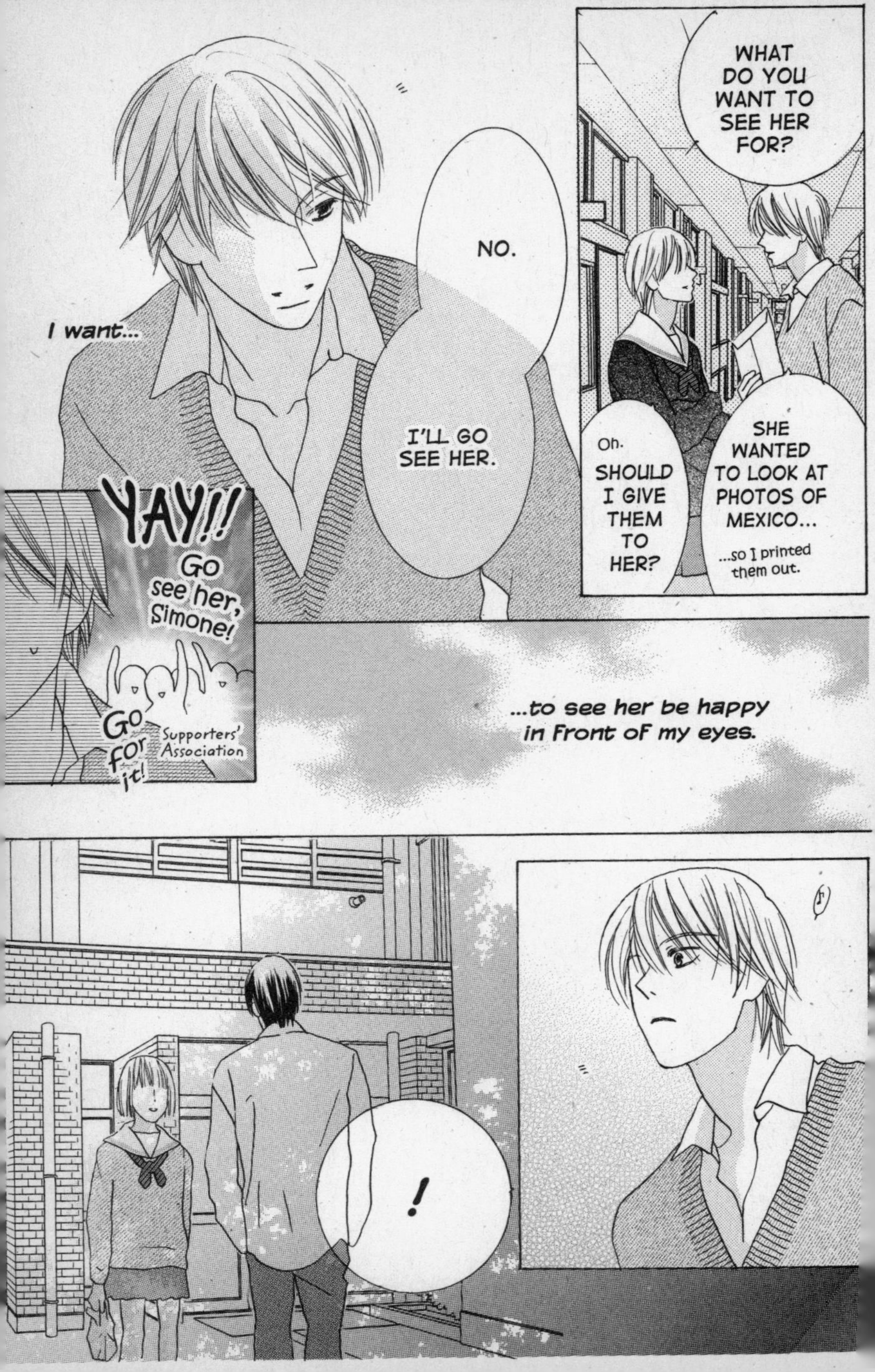
WHAT DO YOU WANT TO SEE HER FOR?
SHE WANTED TO LOOK AT PHOTOS OF MEXICO...
...so I printed them out.
Oh.
SHOULD I GIVE THEM TO HER?
NO.
I'LL GO SEE HER.
I want...
...to see her be happy in front of my eyes.
YAY!!
Go see her, Simone!
Go for it!
Supporters' Association
!

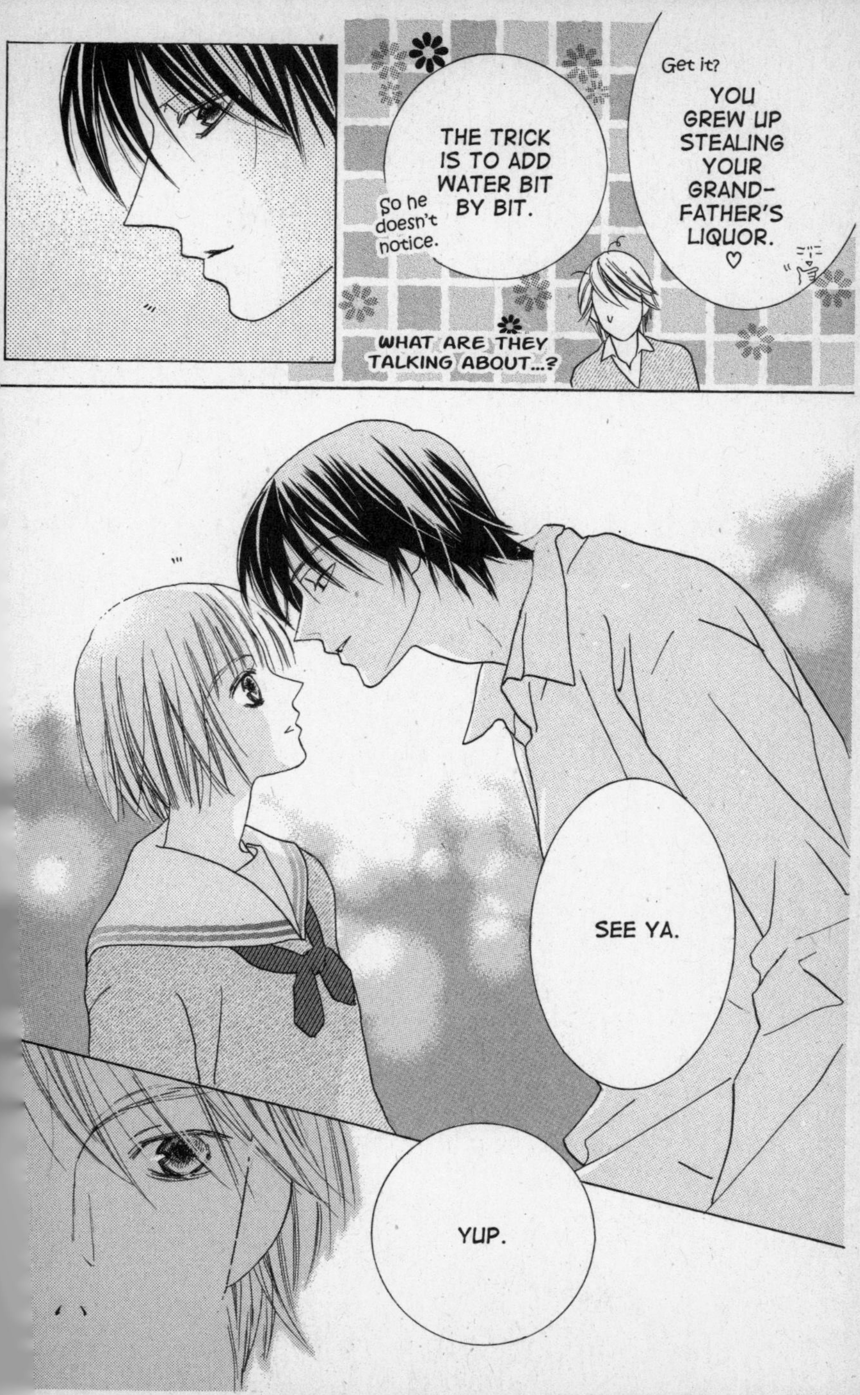
Get it?
YOU GREW UP STEALING YOUR GRAND-FATHER'S LIQUOR. ♡
THE TRICK IS TO ADD WATER BIT BY BIT.
So he doesn't notice.
WHAT ARE THEY TALKING ABOUT...?
SEE YA.
YUP.

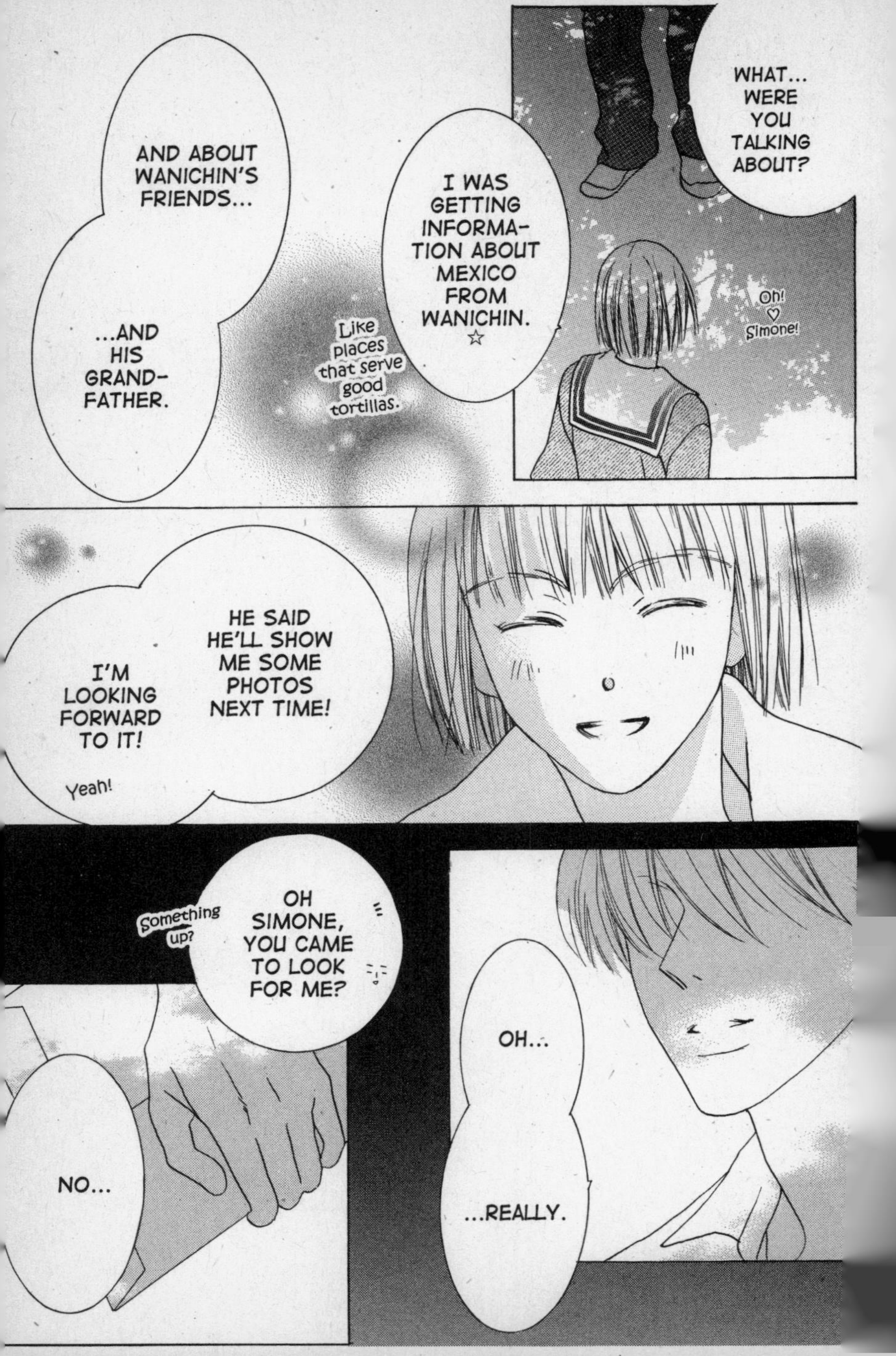
WHAT... WERE YOU TALKING ABOUT?
Oh! ♡ Simone!
I WAS GETTING INFORMA-TION ABOUT MEXICO FROM WANICHIN. ☆
Like places that serve good tortillas.
AND ABOUT WANICHIN'S FRIENDS...
...AND HIS GRAND-FATHER.
HE SAID HE'LL SHOW ME SOME PHOTOS NEXT TIME!
I'M LOOKING FORWARD TO IT!
Yeah!
OH...
...REALLY.
OH SIMONE, YOU CAME TO LOOK FOR ME?
Something up?
NO...

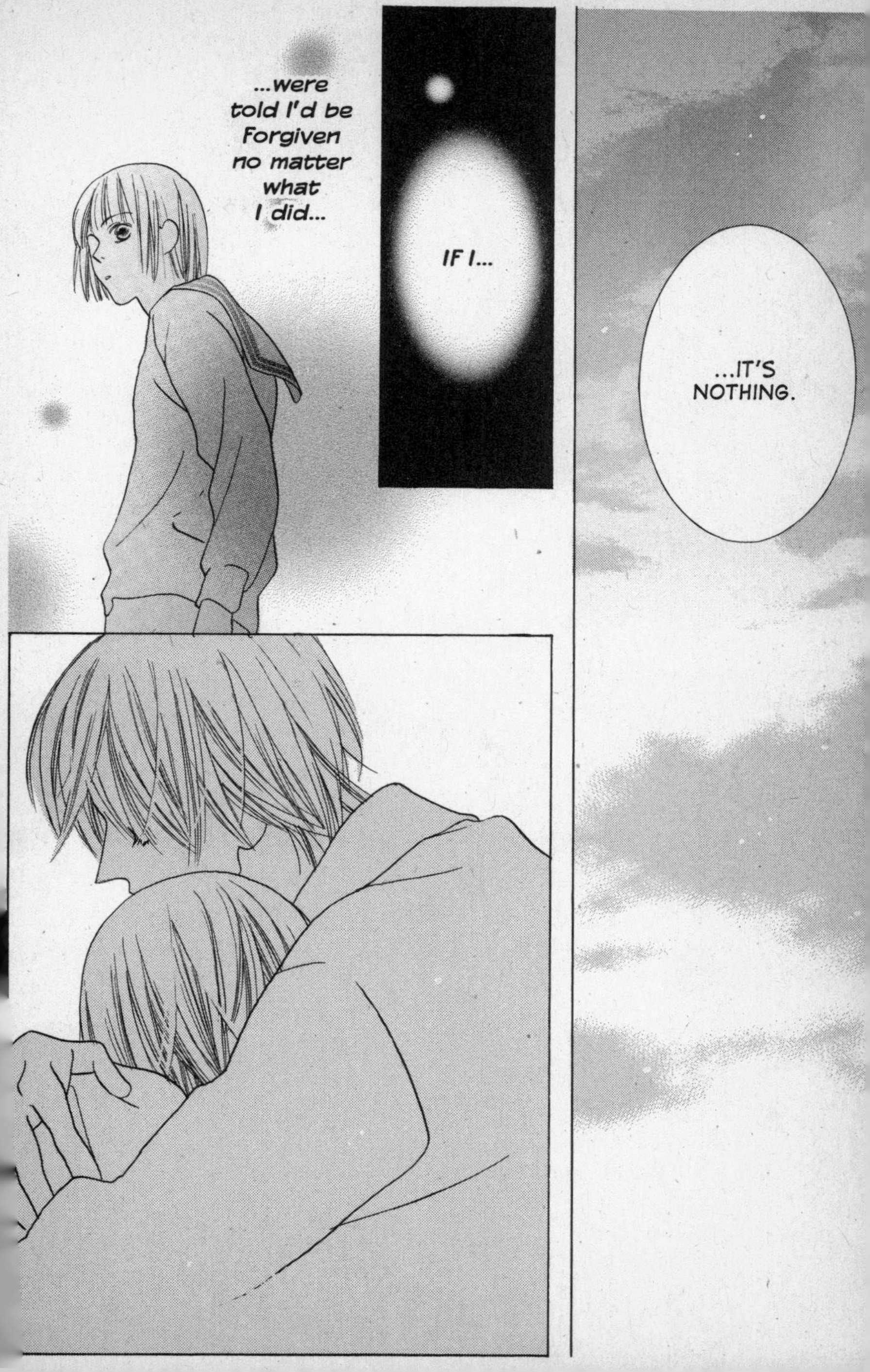
...IT'S NOTHING.
IF I...
...were told I'd be forgiven no matter what I did...

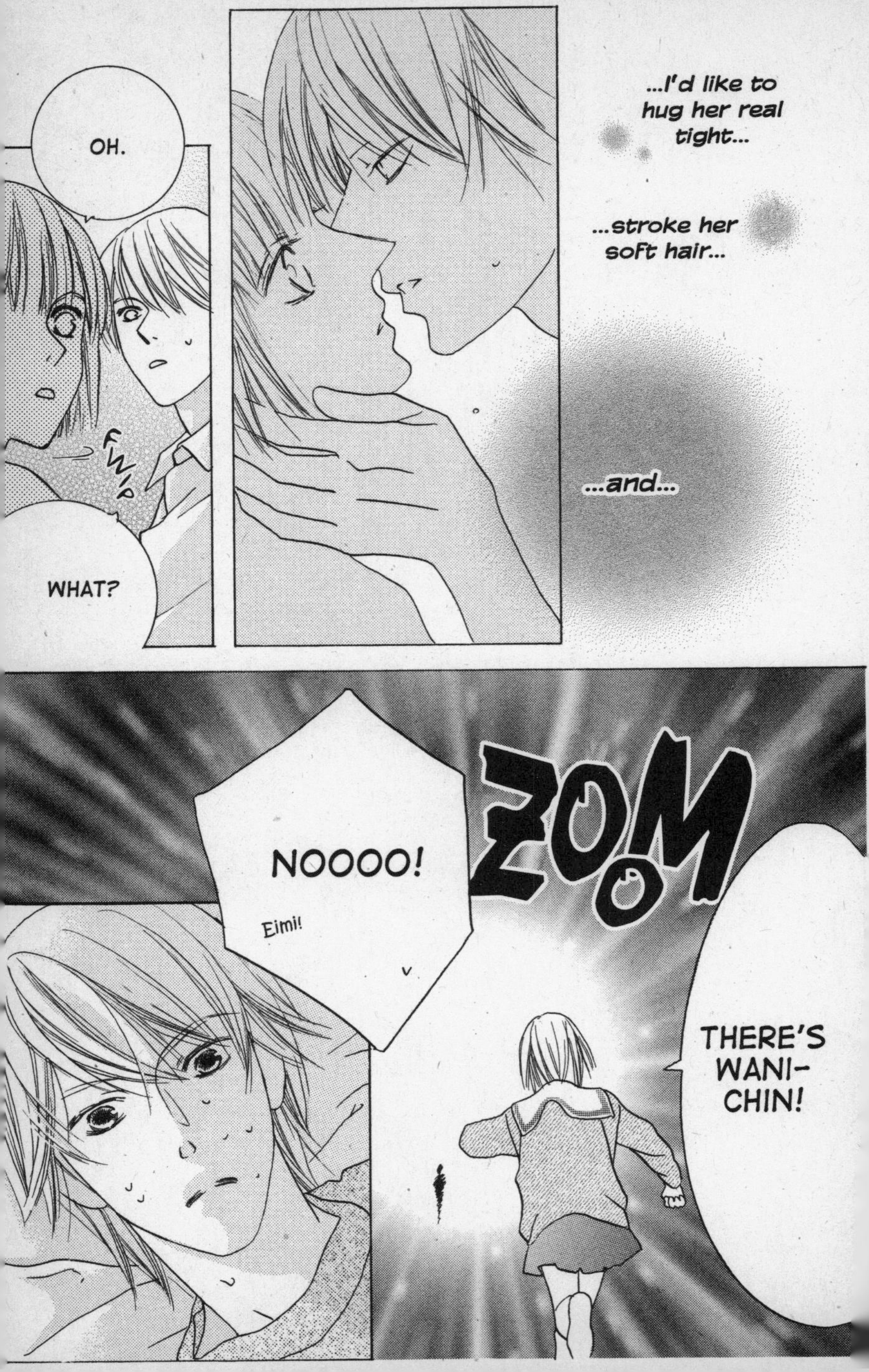
...I'd like to hug her real tight...
...stroke her soft hair...
...and...
OH.
FWIP
WHAT?
ZOOM
THERE'S WANI-CHIN!
NOOOO!
Eimi!

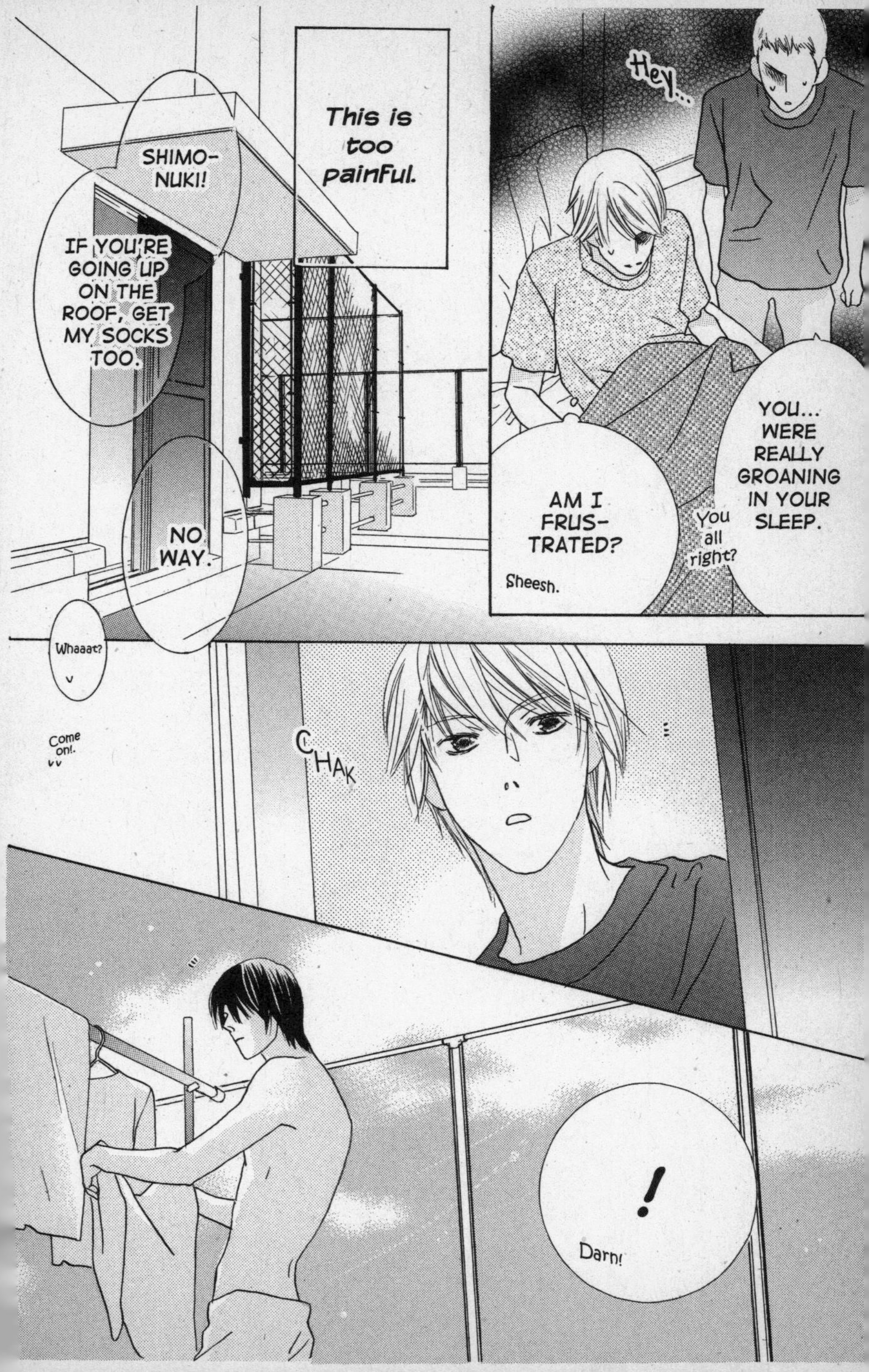
Hey...
YOU... WERE REALLY GROANING IN YOUR SLEEP.
You all right?
AM I FRUS-TRATED?
Sheesh.
This is too painful.
SHIMO-NUKI!
IF YOU'RE GOING UP ON THE ROOF, GET MY SOCKS TOO.
NO WAY.
Whaaat?
Come on!.
CHAK
!
Darn!

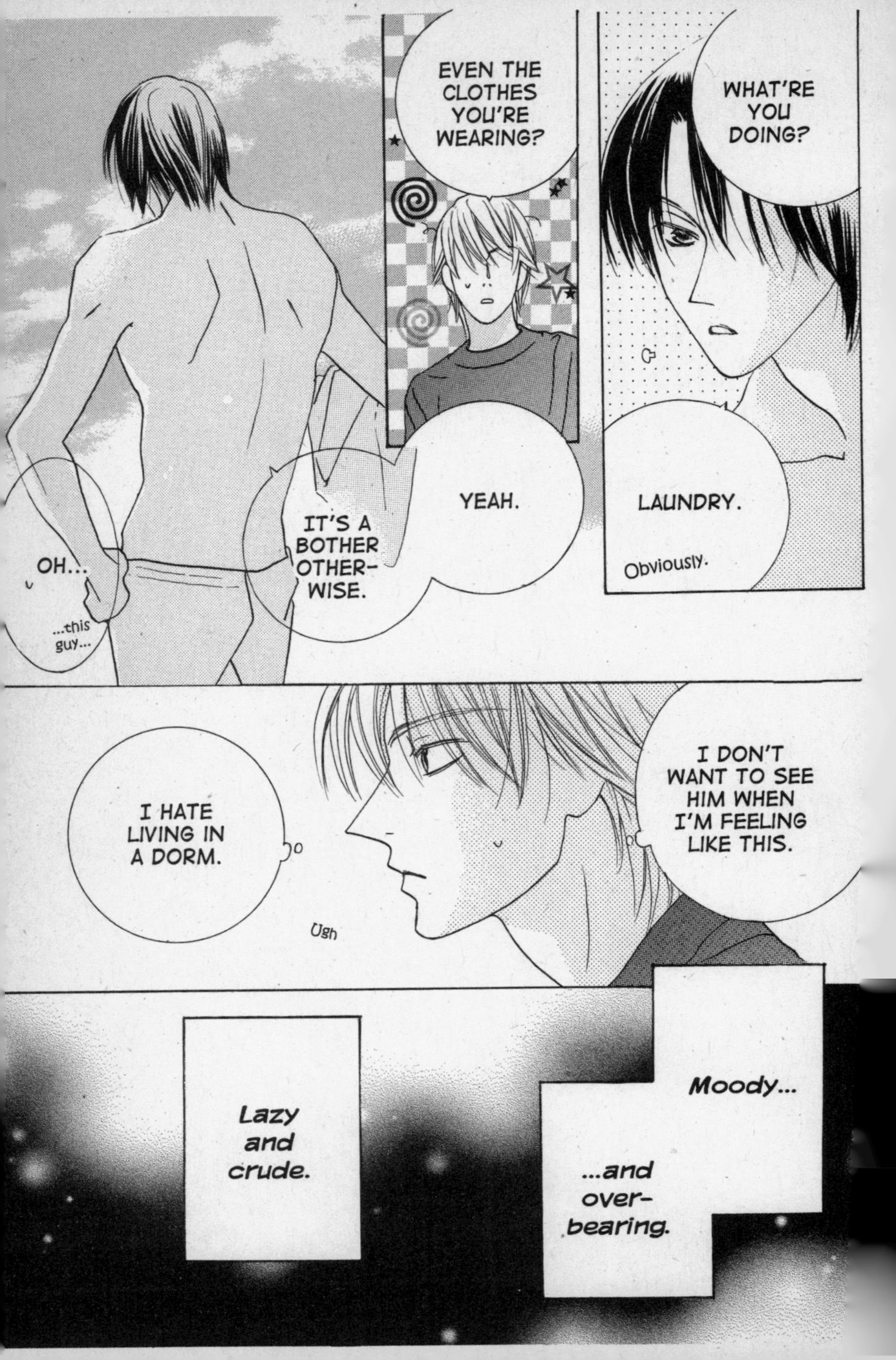
WHAT'RE YOU DOING?
LAUNDRY.
Obviously.
EVEN THE CLOTHES YOU'RE WEARING?
YEAH.
IT'S A BOTHER OTHER-WISE.
OH...
...this guy...
I DON'T WANT TO SEE HIM WHEN I'M FEELING LIKE THIS.
I HATE LIVING IN A DORM.
Ugh
Moody...
...and over-bearing.
Lazy and crude.

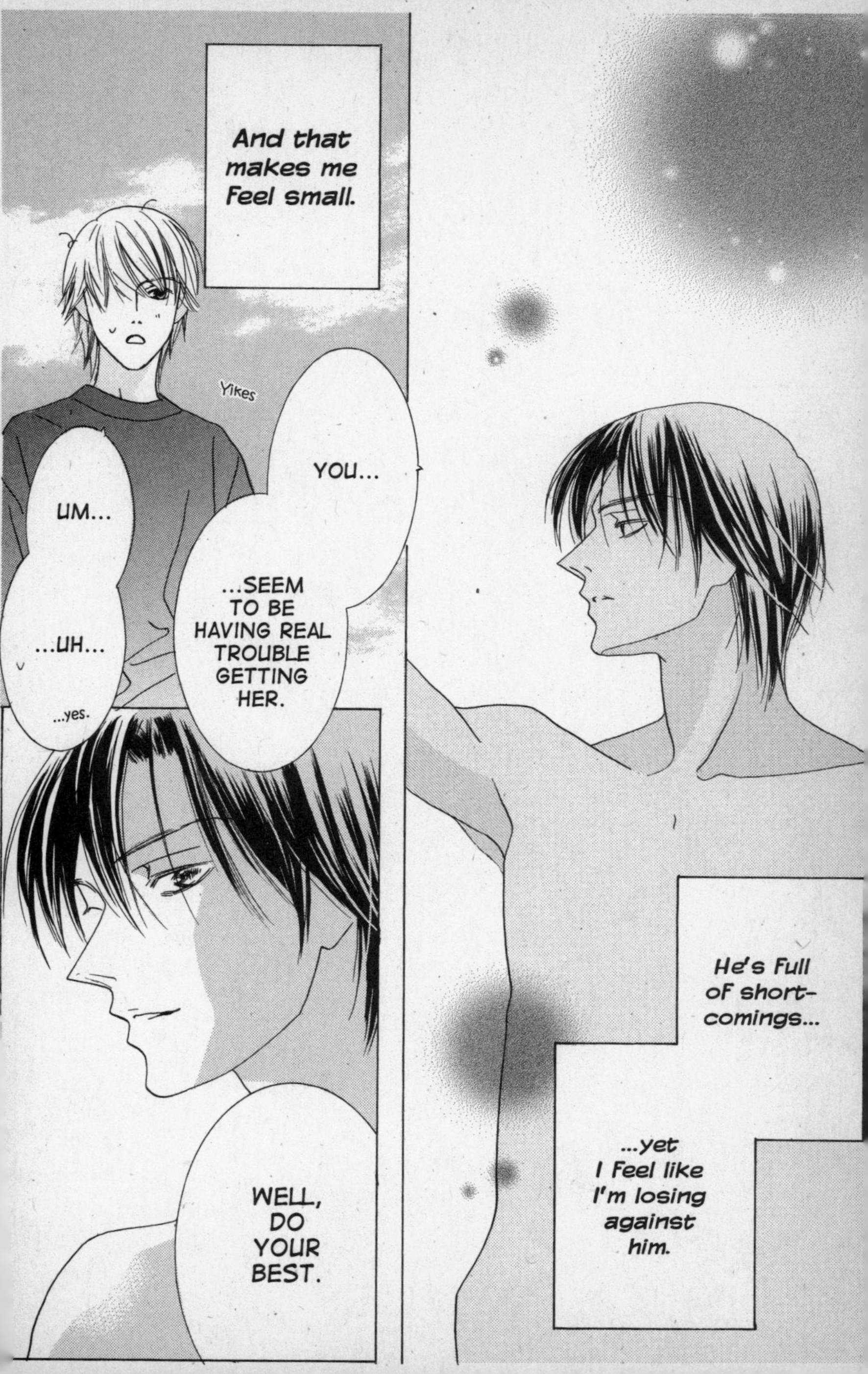
He's Full of short-comings...
...yet I Feel like I'm losing against him.
And that makes me Feel small.
Yikes
YOU...
...SEEM TO BE HAVING REAL TROUBLE GETTING HER.
UM...
...UH...
...yes.
WELL, DO YOUR BEST.

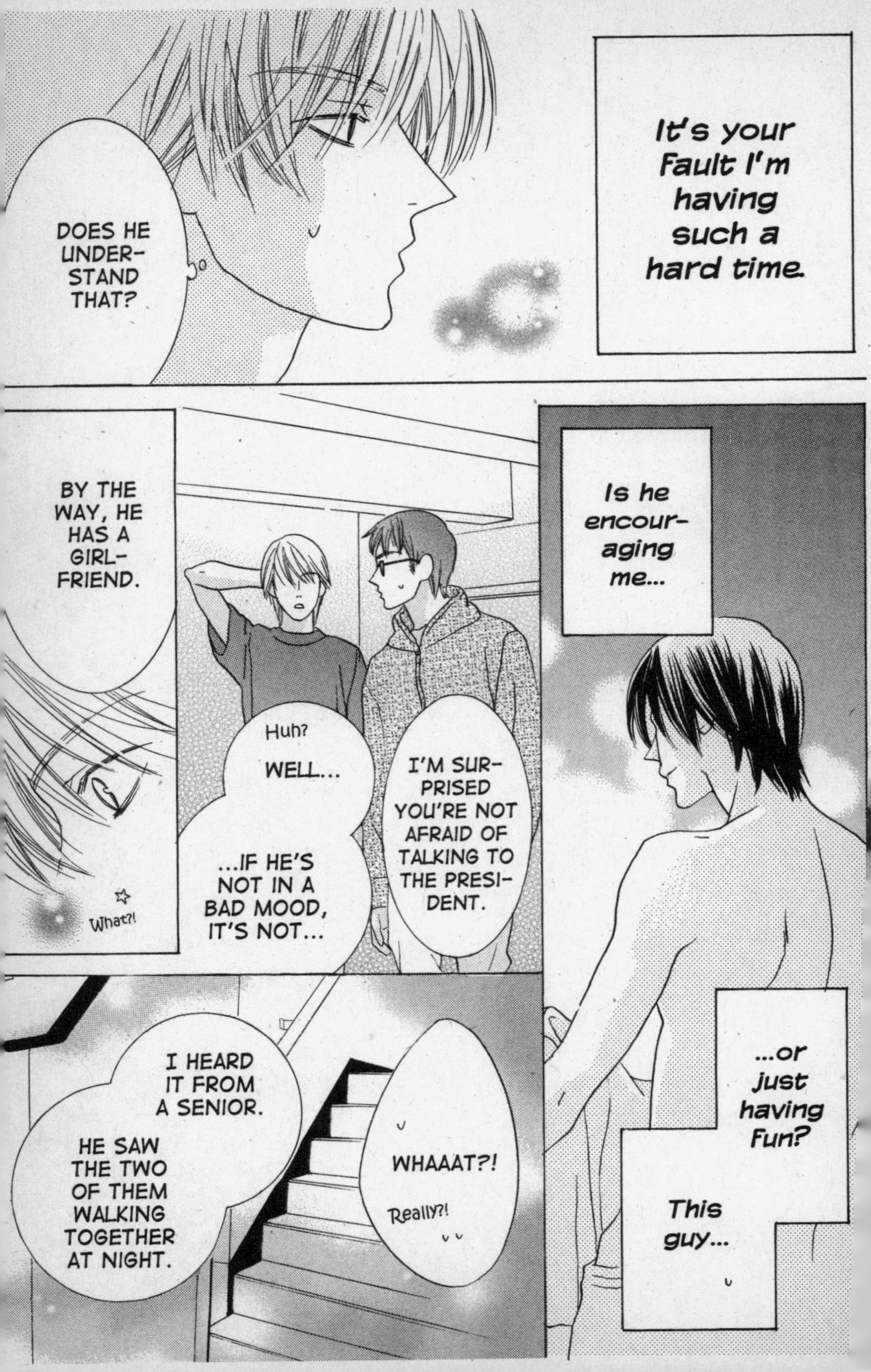
It's your fault I'm having such a hard time.
DOES HE UNDER-STAND THAT?
Is he encour-aging me...
...or just having fun?
This guy...
I'M SUR-PRISED YOU'RE NOT AFRAID OF TALKING TO THE PRESI-DENT.
Huh?
WELL...
...IF HE'S NOT IN A BAD MOOD, IT'S NOT...
BY THE WAY, HE HAS A GIRL-FRIEND.
What?!
WHAAAT?!
Really?!
I HEARD IT FROM A SENIOR.
HE SAW THE TWO OF THEM WALKING TOGETHER AT NIGHT.

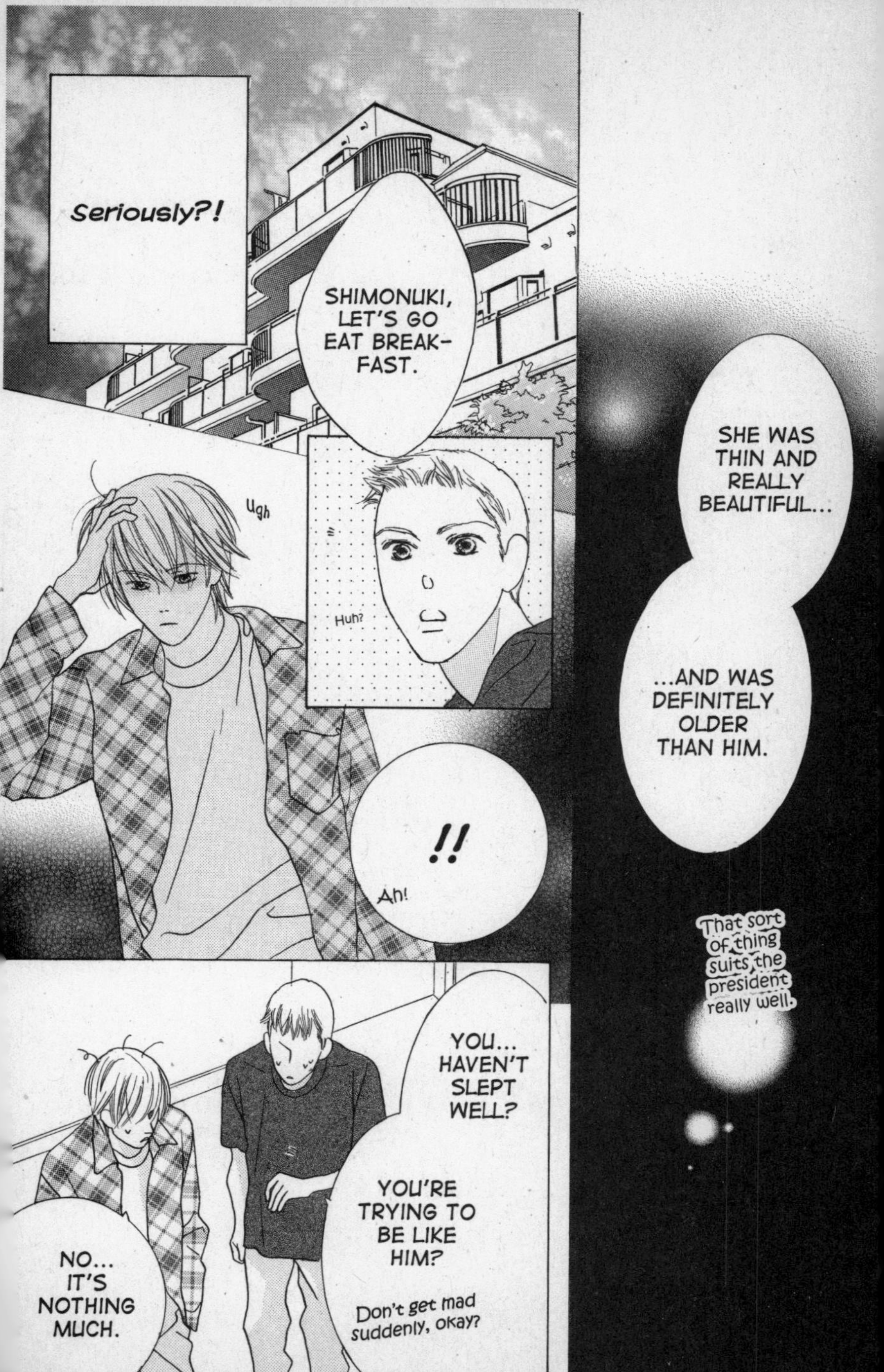
SHE WAS THIN AND REALLY BEAUTIFUL...
...AND WAS DEFINITELY OLDER THAN HIM.
That sort of thing suits the president really well.
Seriously?!
SHIMONUKI, LET'S GO EAT BREAK-FAST.
Huh?
Ugh
!!
Ah!
YOU... HAVEN'T SLEPT WELL?
YOU'RE TRYING TO BE LIKE HIM?
Don't get mad suddenly, okay?
NO... IT'S NOTHING MUCH.

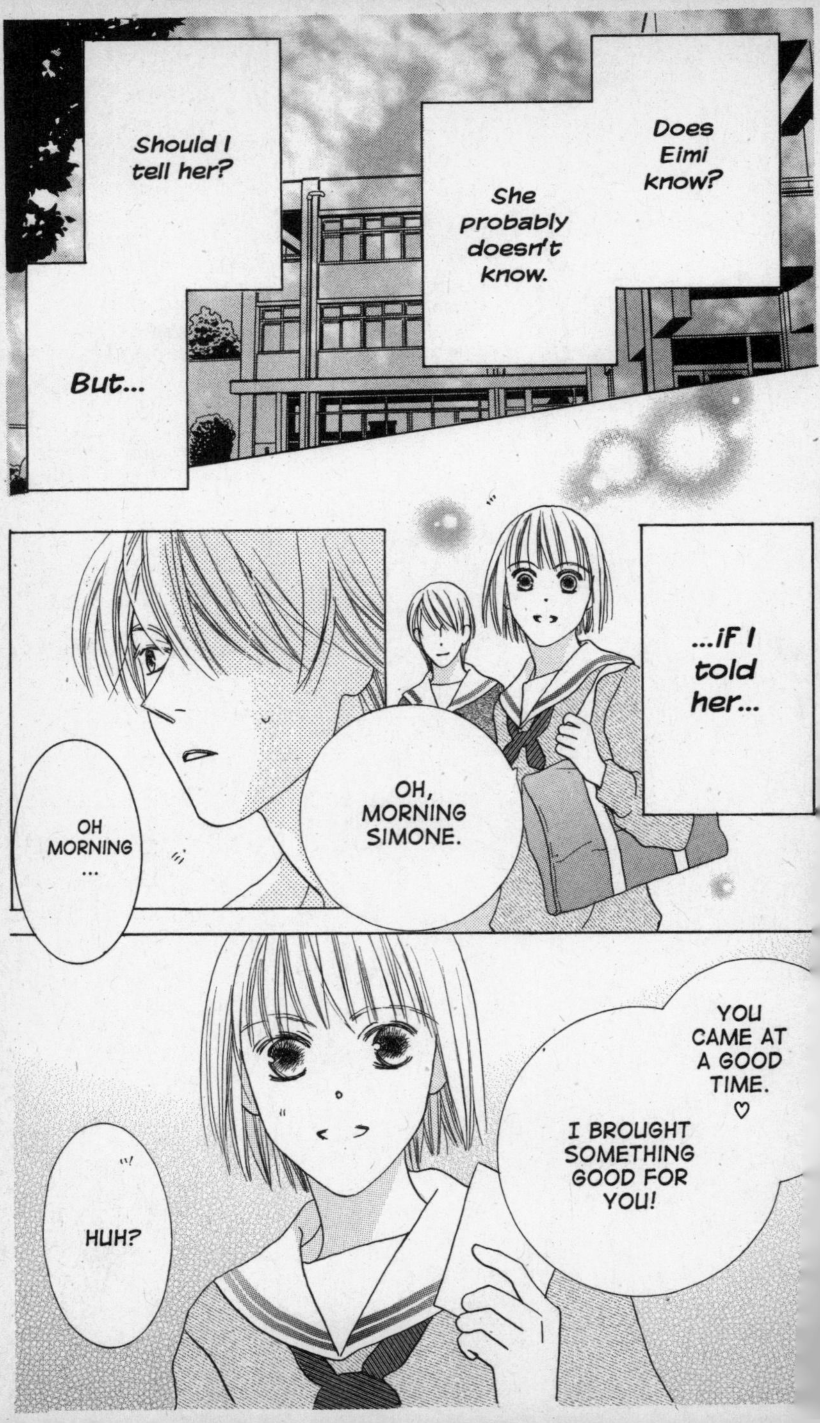
Does Eimi know?
She probably doesn't know.
Should I tell her?
But...
...if I told her...
OH, MORNING SIMONE.
OH MORNING ...
YOU CAME AT A GOOD TIME. ♡
I BROUGHT SOMETHING GOOD FOR YOU!
HUH?

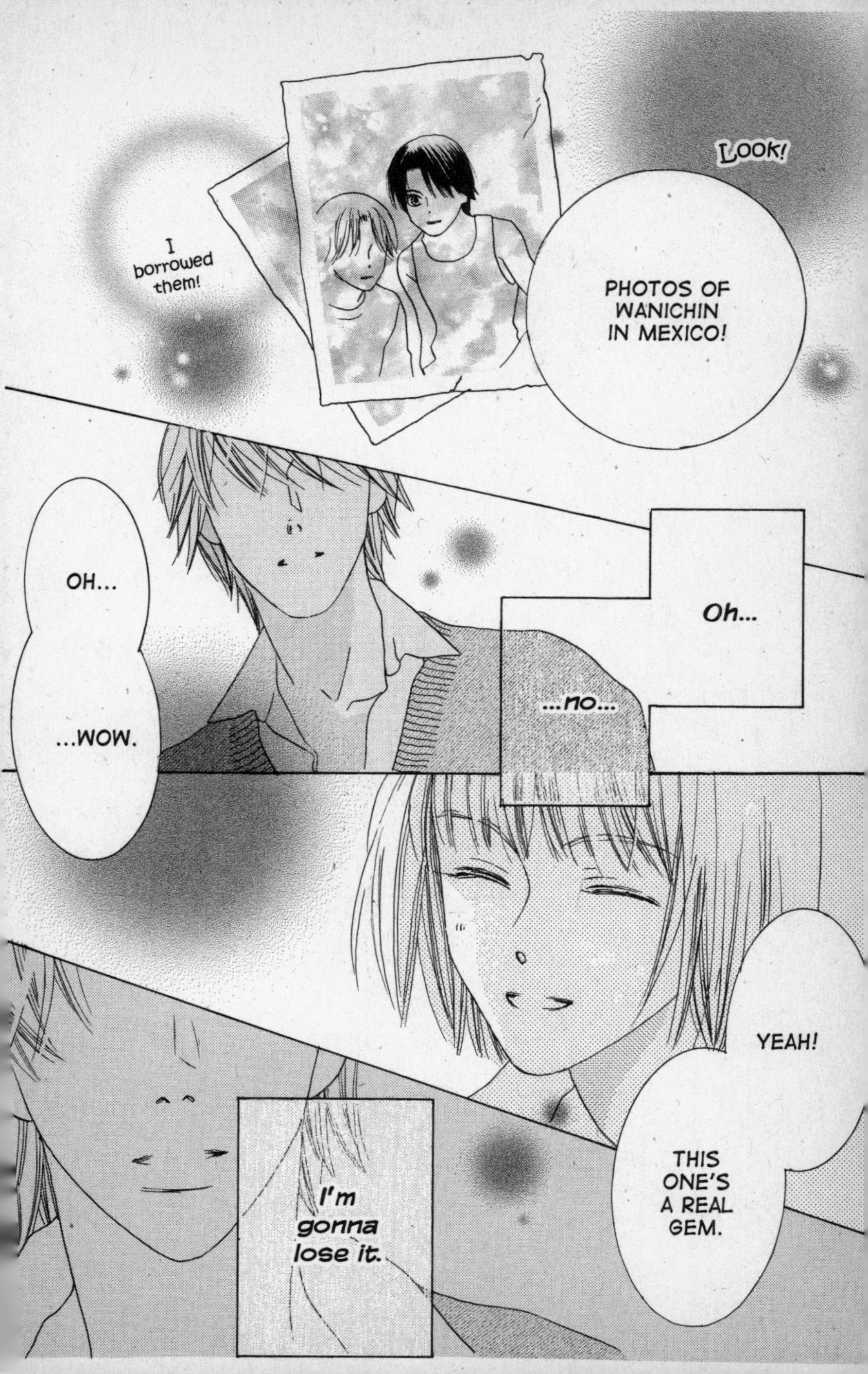
LOOK!
PHOTOS OF WANICHIN IN MEXICO!
I borrowed them!
Oh...
...no...
OH...
...WOW.
YEAH!
THIS ONE'S A REAL GEM.
I'm gonna lose it.

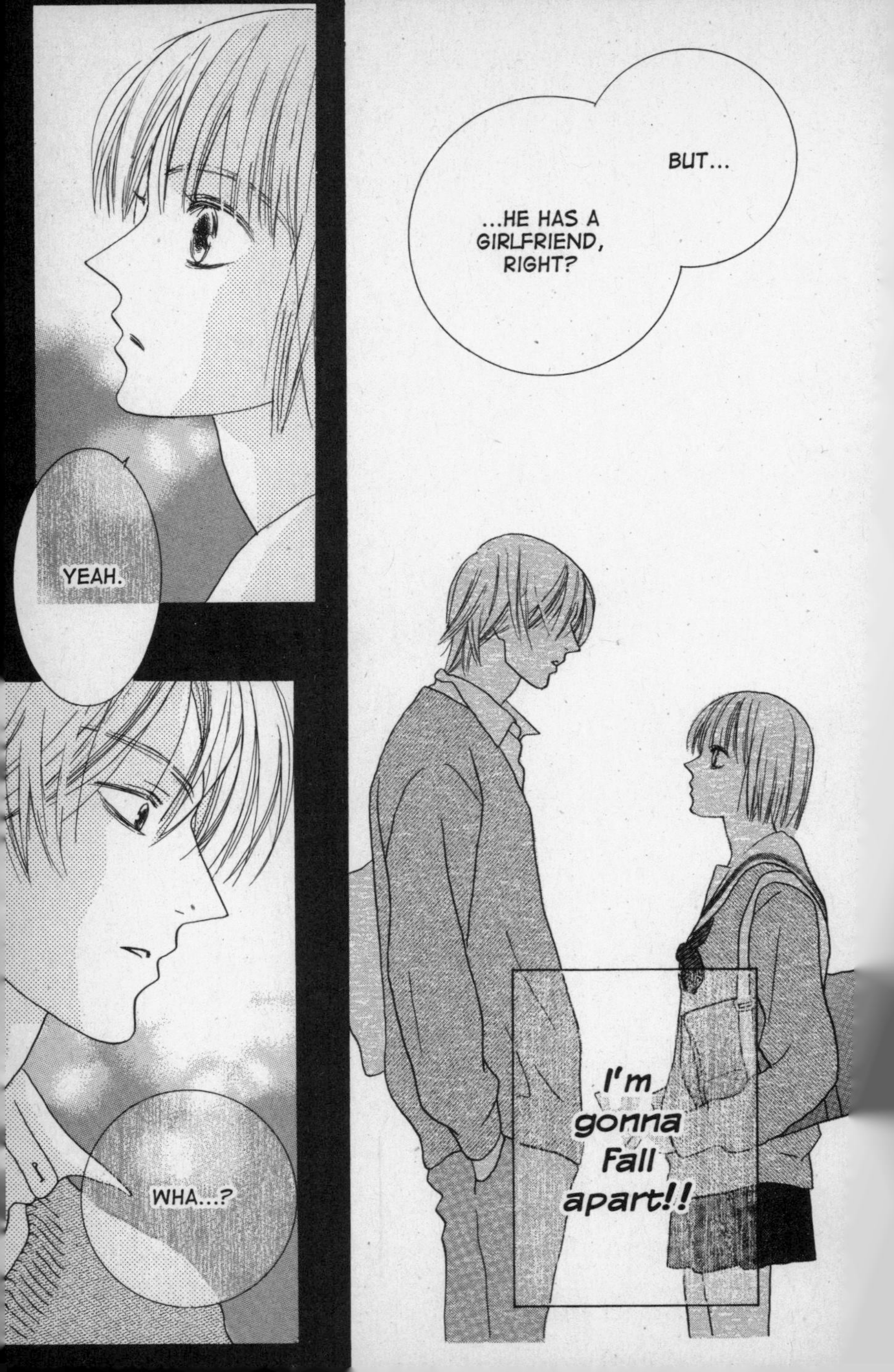
BUT...
...HE HAS A GIRLFRIEND, RIGHT?
I'm gonna Fall apart!!
YEAH.
WHA...?

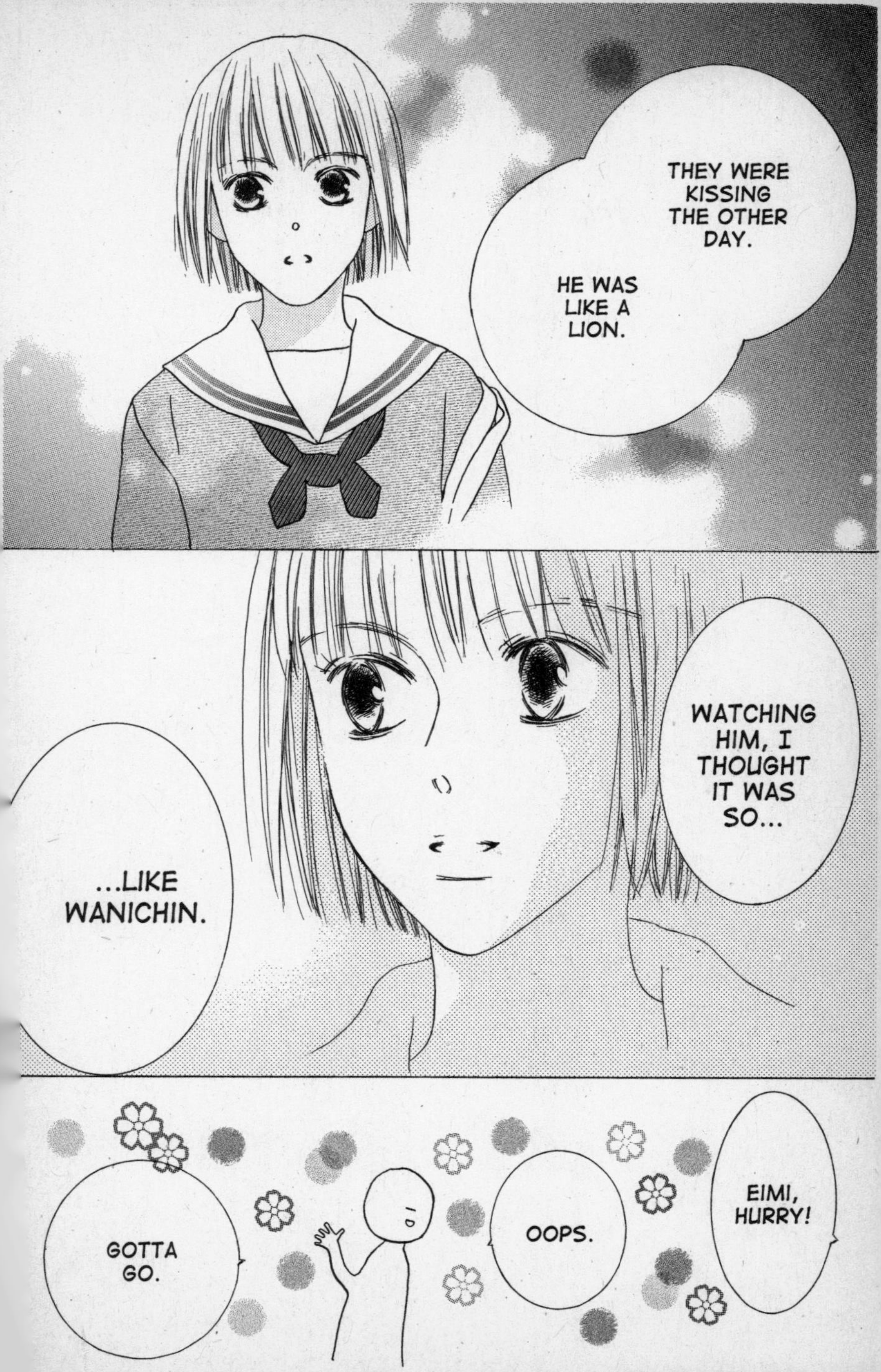
THEY WERE KISSING THE OTHER DAY.
HE WAS LIKE A LION.
WATCHING HIM, I THOUGHT IT WAS SO...
...LIKE WANICHIN.
EIMI, HURRY!
OOPS.
GOTTA GO.

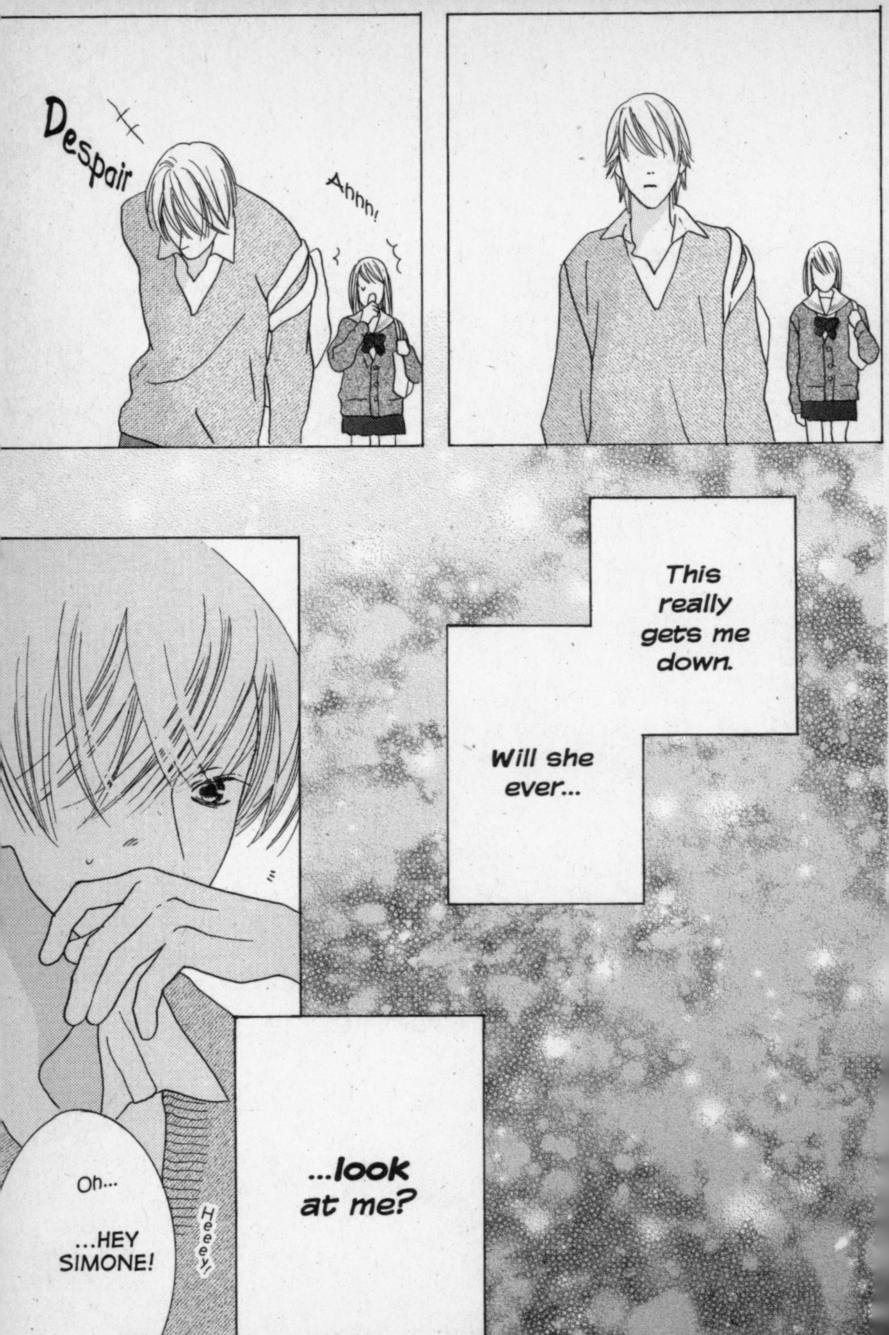
Despair
Annnn!
This really gets me down.
Will she ever...
...look at me?
Heeeey!
Oh... ...HEY SIMONE!

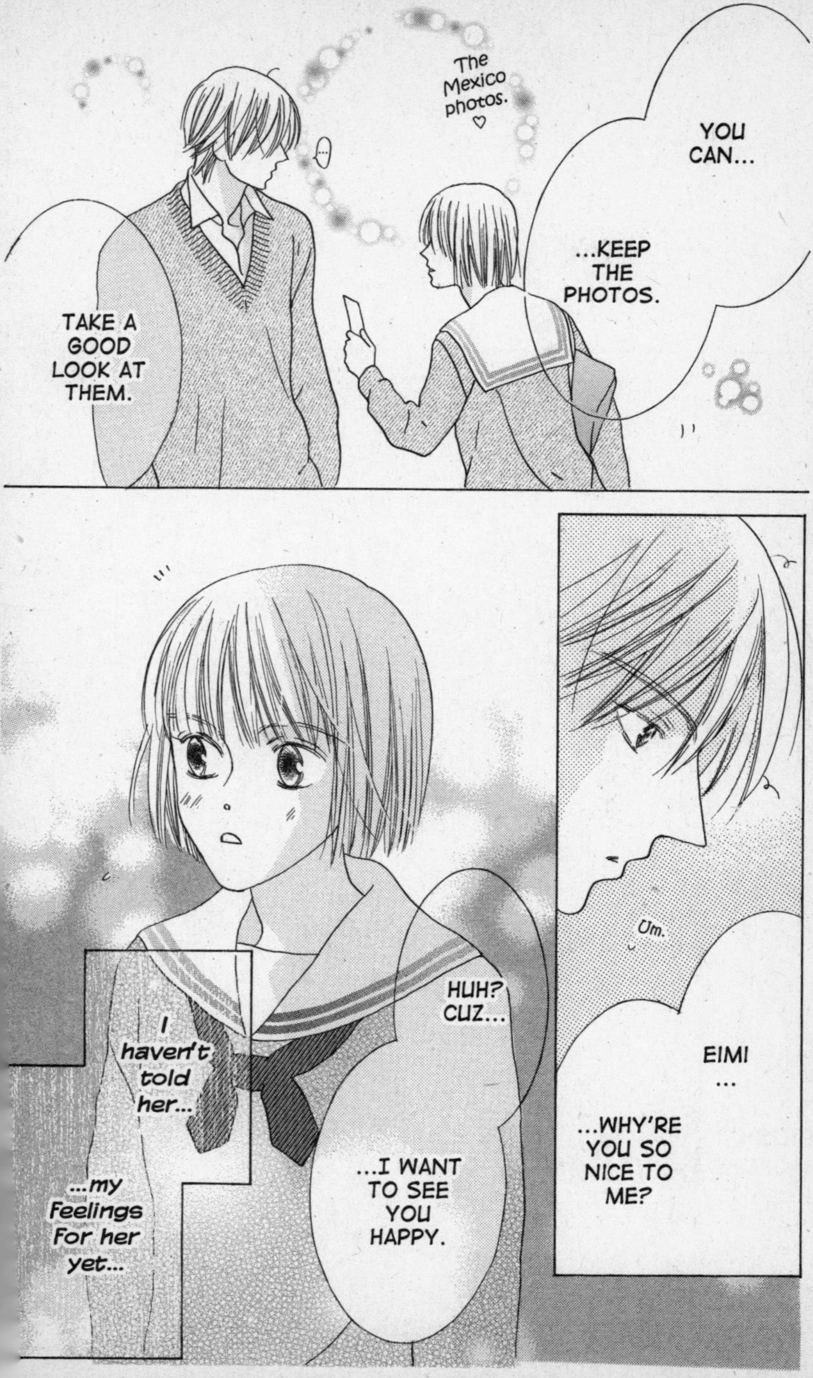
YOU CAN...
...KEEP THE PHOTOS.
The Mexico photos. ♡
...
TAKE A GOOD LOOK AT THEM.
Um.
EIMI...
...WHY'RE YOU SO NICE TO ME?
HUH? CUZ...
...I WANT TO SEE YOU HAPPY.
I haven't told her...
...my Feelings For her yet...

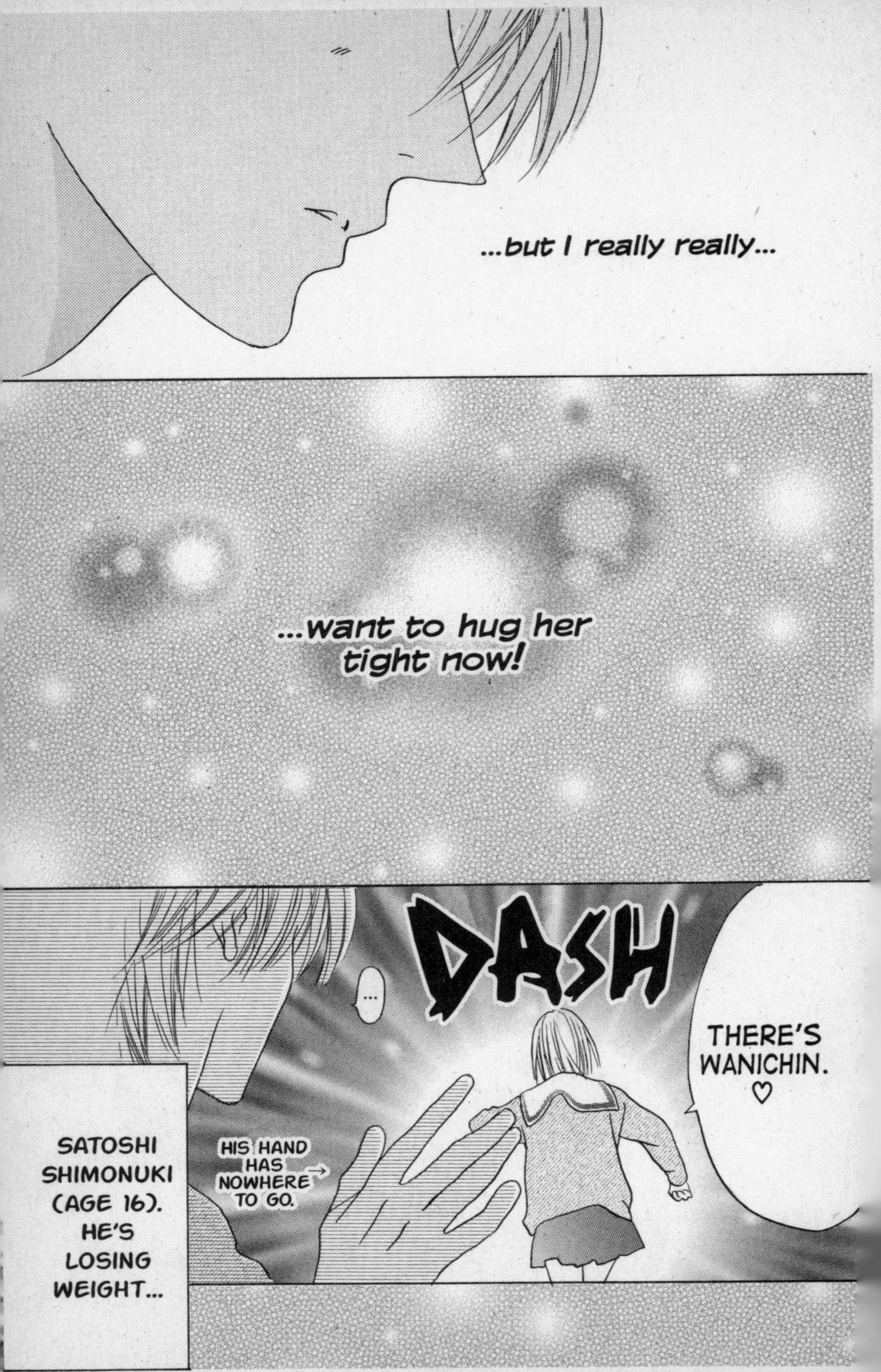
...but I really really...
...want to hug her tight now!
THERE'S WANICHIN. ♡
DASH
...
HIS HAND HAS NOWHERE TO GO.
SATOSHI SHIMONUKI (AGE 16). HE'S LOSING WEIGHT...

BEAUTY IS THE BEAST

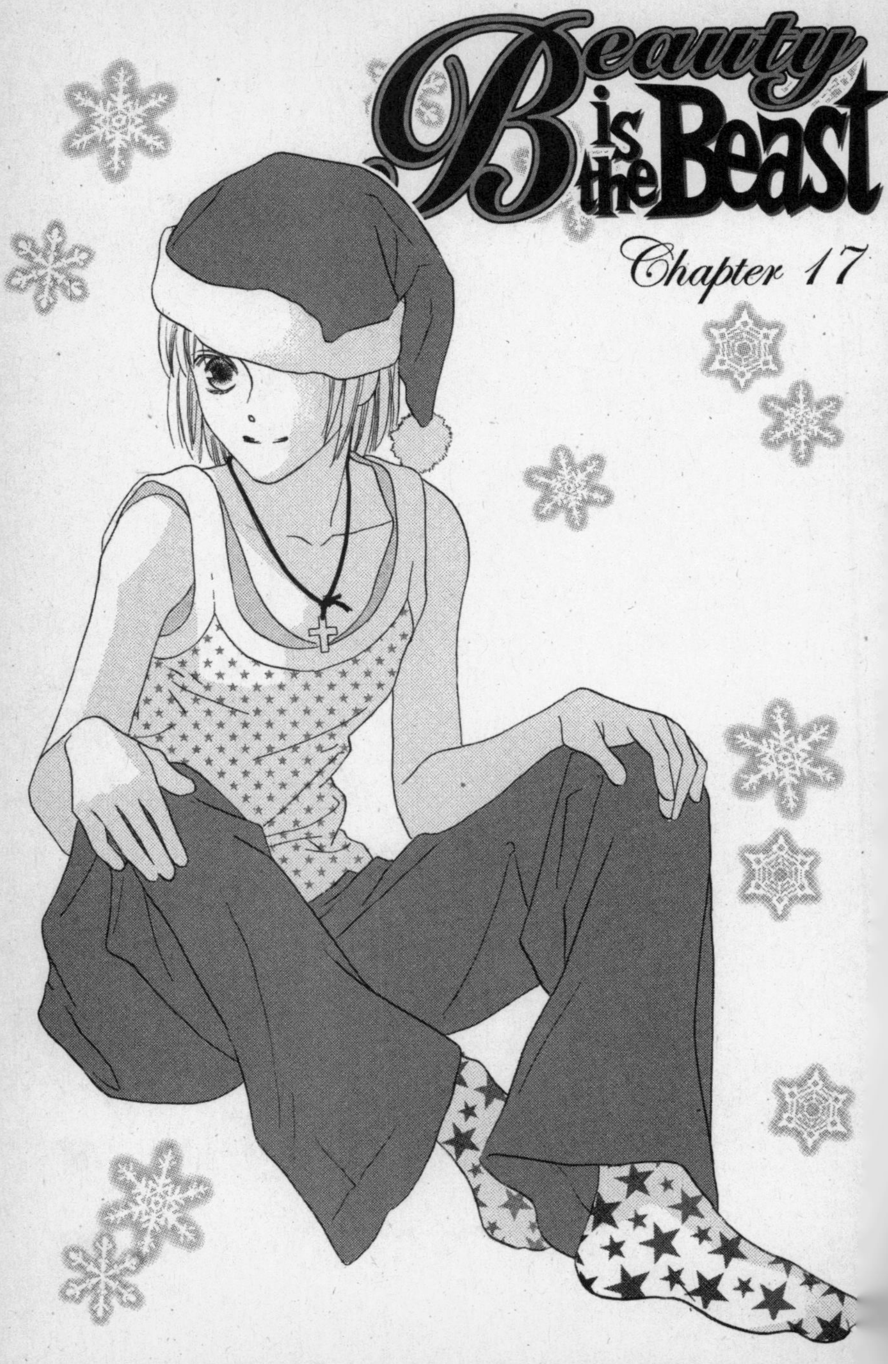
Beauty is the Beast
Chapter 17

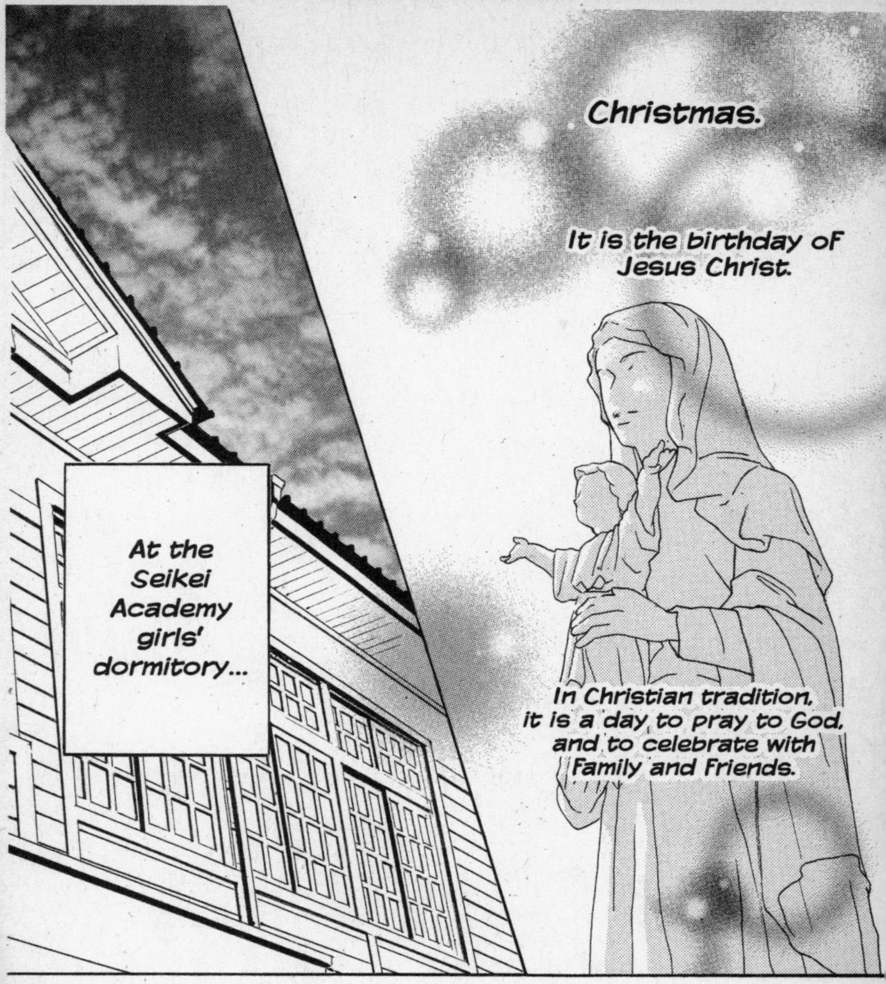
Christmas.
It is the birthday of Jesus Christ.
In Christian tradition, it is a day to pray to God, and to celebrate with Family and Friends.
At the Seikei Academy girls' dormitory...

Looking back, my background music seems to be mainly piano stuff, but actually, I listen to stuff from the MTV charts, and this time... Um... I drew while listening to m-flo, Crystal Kay, AI, Soulhead, and Doji-T.
There's one genre that I can't listen to — when I listen to Trance (does it still exist? I don't know), I fall asleep 100 percent of the time. I can't stand that vague feeling.
I guess I like songs with a definite beat or rhythm.

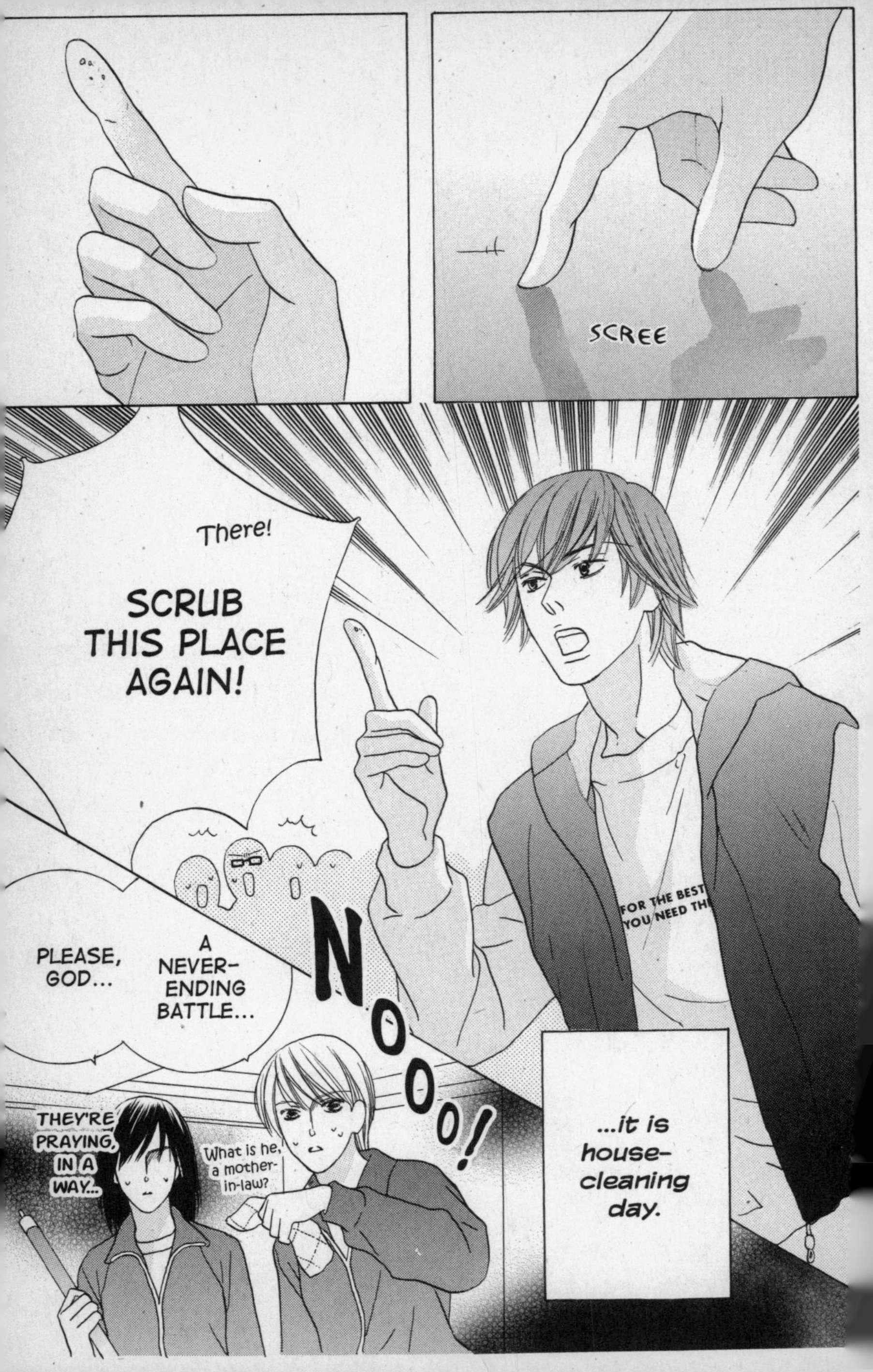
SCREE
There!
SCRUB THIS PLACE AGAIN!
FOR THE BEST
YOU NEED TH
NOOOO!
...it is house-cleaning day.
A NEVER-ENDING BATTLE...
PLEASE, GOD...
What is he, a mother-in-law?
THEY'RE PRAYING, IN A WAY...

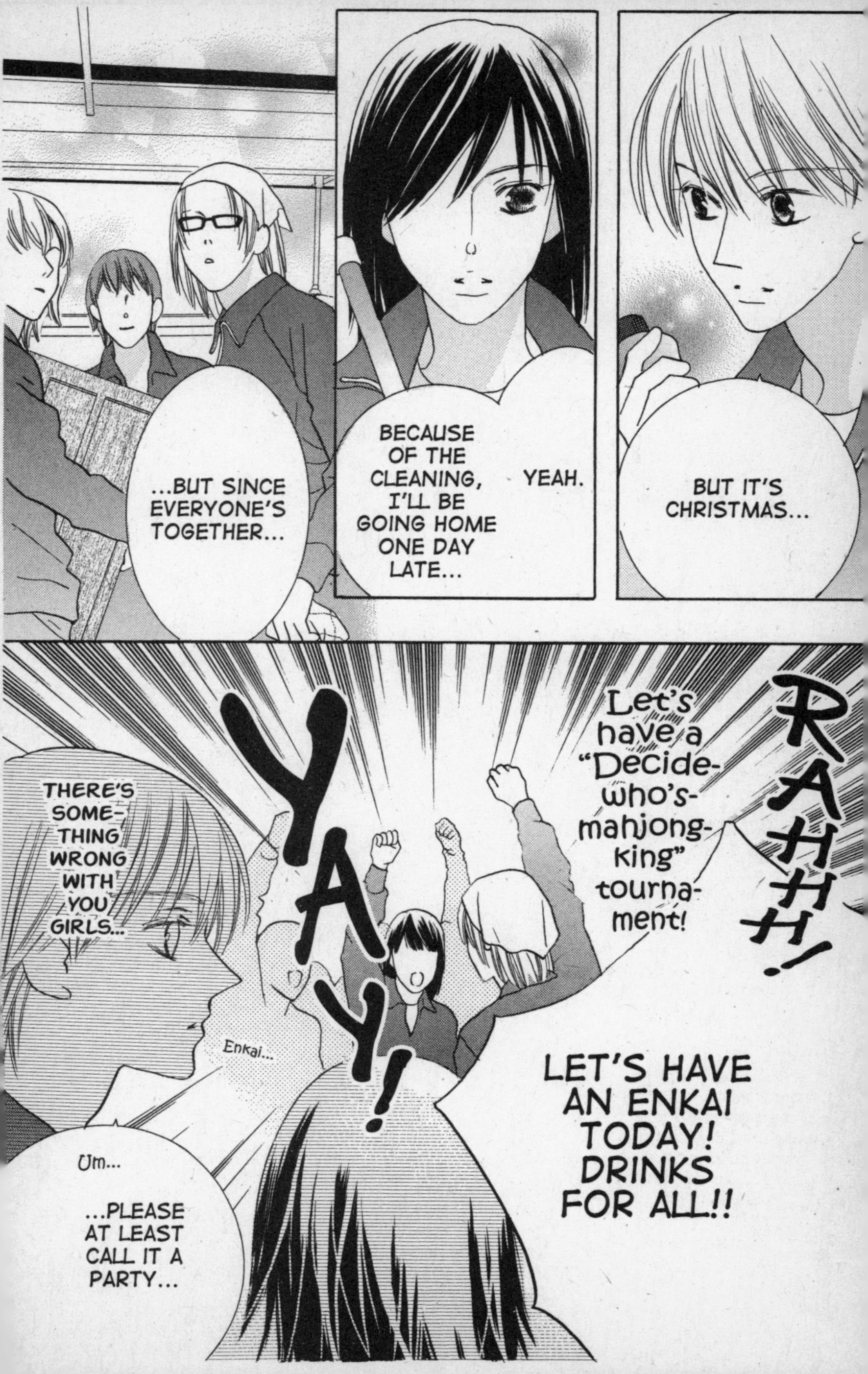
BUT IT'S CHRISTMAS...
YEAH.
BECAUSE OF THE CLEANING, I'LL BE GOING HOME ONE DAY LATE...
...BUT SINCE EVERYONE'S TOGETHER...
RAHHH!
Let's have a "Decide-who's-mahjong-king" tournament!
LET'S HAVE AN ENKAI TODAY! DRINKS FOR ALL!!
YAY!
THERE'S SOMETHING WRONG WITH YOU GIRLS...
Enkai...
Um...
...PLEASE AT LEAST CALL IT A PARTY...

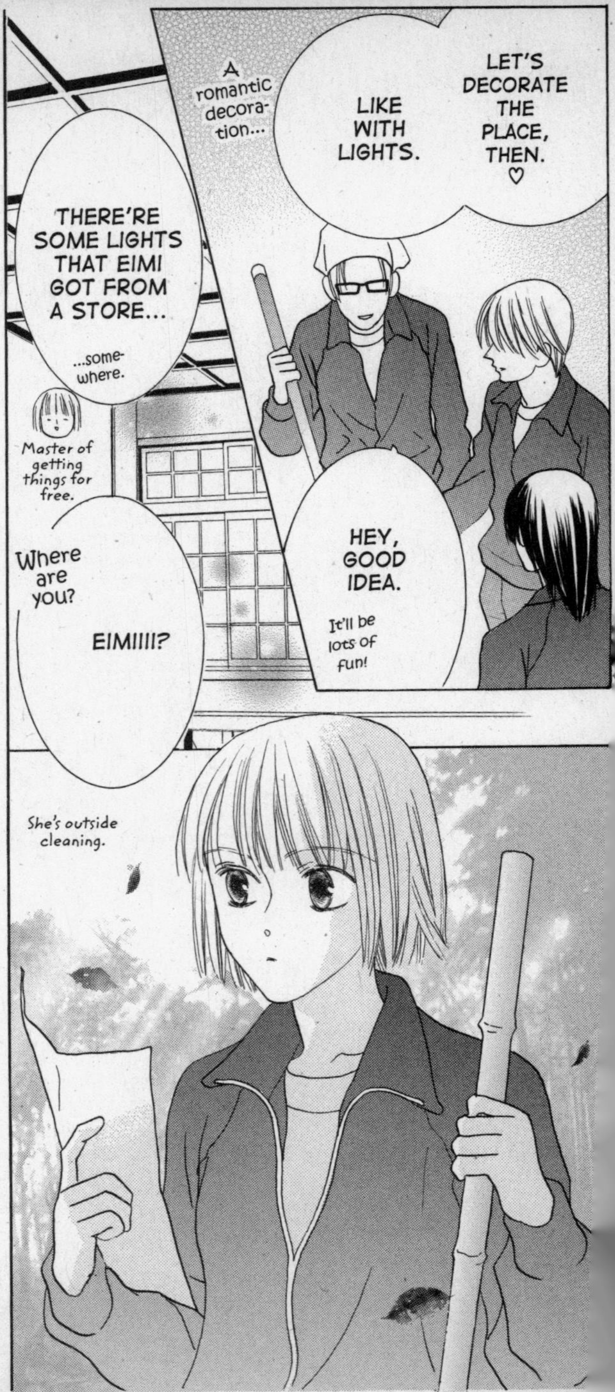
LET'S DECORATE THE PLACE, THEN. ♡
LIKE WITH LIGHTS.
A romantic decoration...
HEY, GOOD IDEA.
It'll be lots of fun!
THERE'RE SOME LIGHTS THAT EIMI GOT FROM A STORE...
...somewhere.
Master of getting things for free.
Where are you?
EIMIIII?
She's outside cleaning.

Recently, because of the number of pages, there hasn't been that much bonus material at the end of the volumes. I feel bad for people who look forward to the volumes. I'm really sorry.

It's the same with the sidebars, but I always have a hard time deciding what to write in these spaces.
About what I like? Well no, no. Something that everyone can understand... no, then... I'm being like Simone. If you have any requests, please tell me.
I really appreciate the letters I receive. I always read them over when I feel like giving up. Even casual words cheer me on.
This year, I'm thinking about replying to them.
Thank you, really.
My appreciation goes out to my staff, who I always give a hard time, and to my editor.
Moreover, thank you from all my heart to everyone who read on until here. I hope we'll be able to see each other again...
Thank you!

Tomo Matsumoto

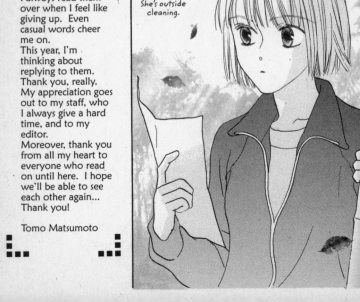

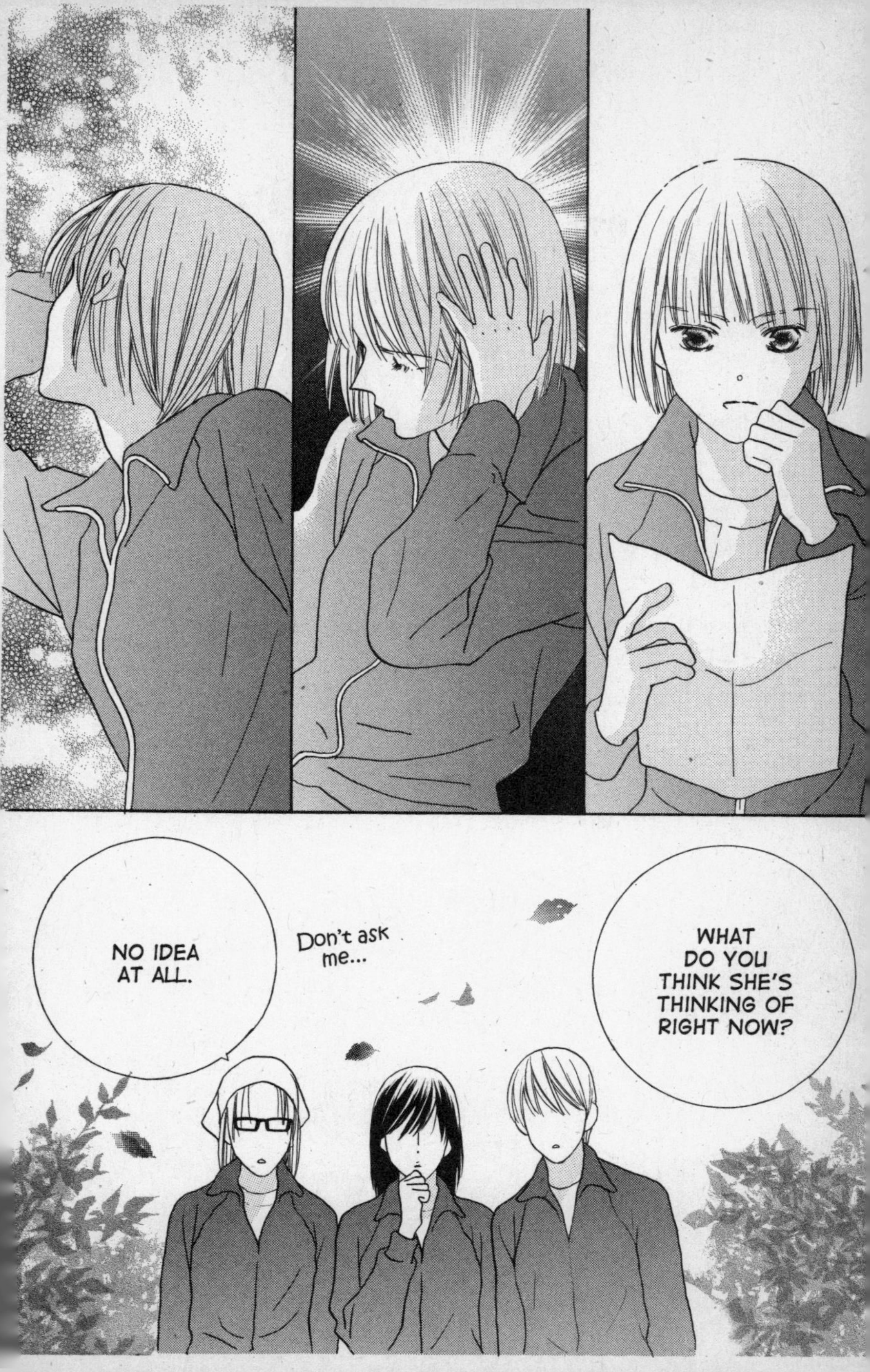
WHAT DO YOU THINK SHE'S THINKING OF RIGHT NOW?
Don't ask me...
NO IDEA AT ALL.

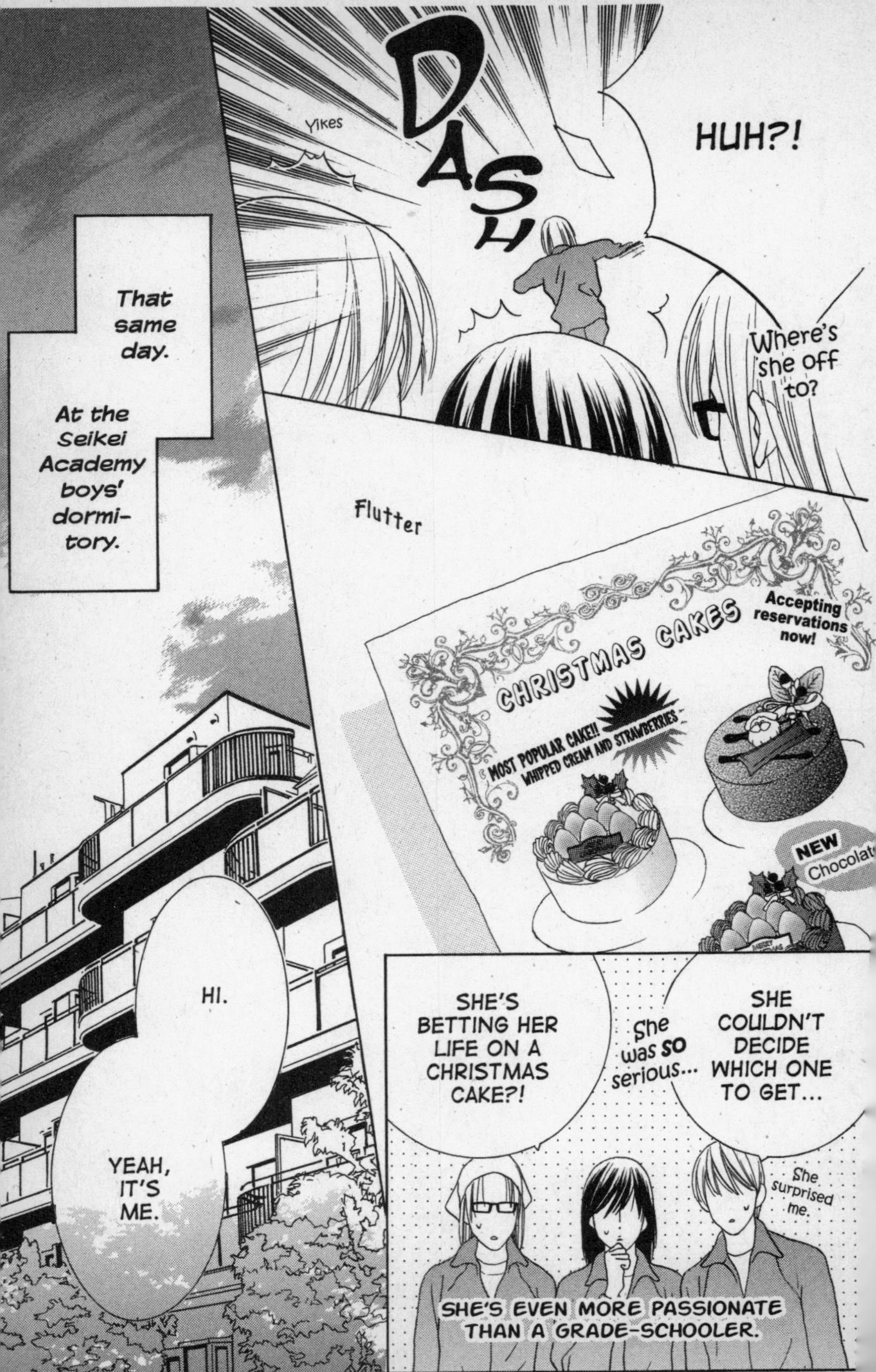
HUH?!
Where's she off to?
DASH
Yikes
Flutter
CHRISTMAS CAKES
Accepting reservations now!
MOST POPULAR CAKE!! WHIPPED CREAM AND STRAWBERRIES
NEW Chocolat
SHE COULDN'T DECIDE WHICH ONE TO GET...
She was SO serious...
SHE'S BETTING HER LIFE ON A CHRISTMAS CAKE?!
She surprised me.
SHE'S EVEN MORE PASSIONATE THAN A GRADE-SCHOOLER.
That same day.
At the Seikei Academy boys' dormitory.
HI.
YEAH, IT'S ME.

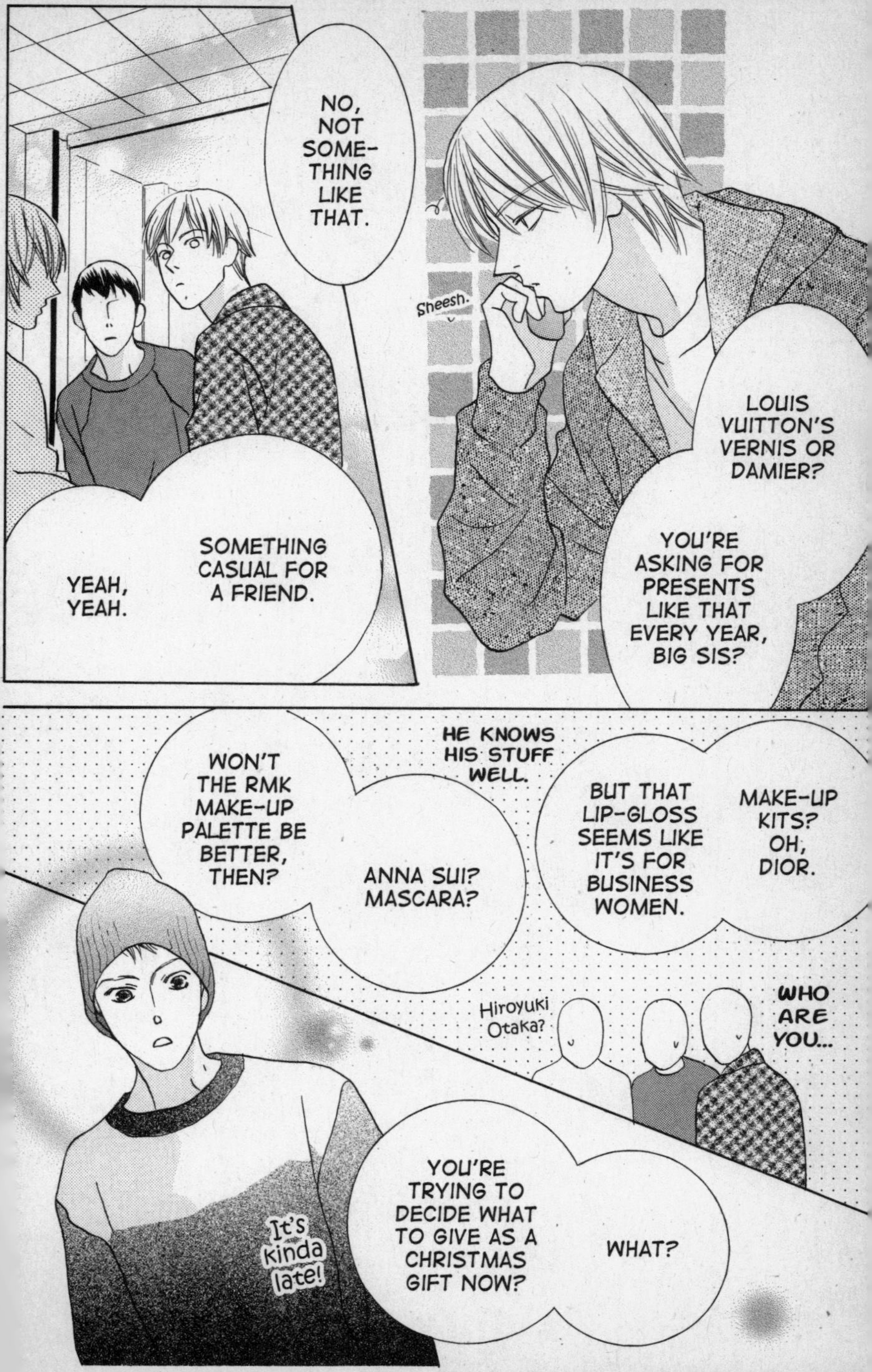
LOUIS VUITTON'S VERNIS OR DAMIER?
YOU'RE ASKING FOR PRESENTS LIKE THAT EVERY YEAR, BIG SIS?
Sheesh.
NO, NOT SOMETHING LIKE THAT.
SOMETHING CASUAL FOR A FRIEND.
YEAH, YEAH.
MAKE-UP KITS? OH, DIOR.
BUT THAT LIP-GLOSS SEEMS LIKE IT'S FOR BUSINESS WOMEN.
HE KNOWS HIS STUFF WELL.
ANNA SUI? MASCARA?
WON'T THE RMK MAKE-UP PALETTE BE BETTER, THEN?
WHO ARE YOU...
Hiroyuki Otaka?
WHAT?
YOU'RE TRYING TO DECIDE WHAT TO GIVE AS A CHRISTMAS GIFT NOW?
It's kinda late!

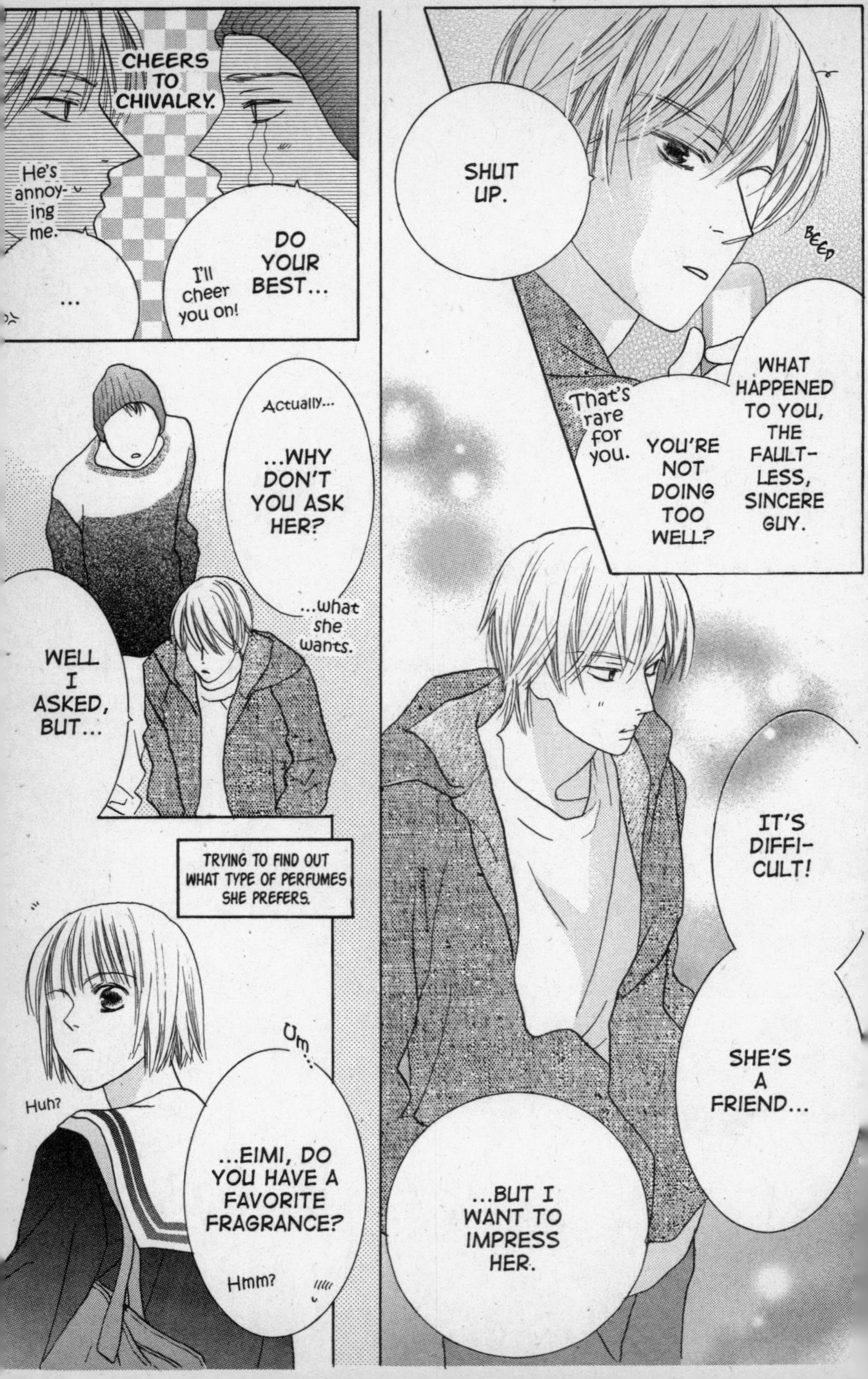
BEEP
WHAT HAPPENED TO YOU, THE FAULTLESS, SINCERE GUY.
YOU'RE NOT DOING TOO WELL?
That's rare for you.
SHUT UP.
IT'S DIFFICULT!
SHE'S A FRIEND...
...BUT I WANT TO IMPRESS HER.
CHEERS TO CHIVALRY.
DO YOUR BEST...
I'll cheer you on!
He's annoying me.
...
Actually...
...WHY DON'T YOU ASK HER?
...what she wants.
WELL I ASKED, BUT...
TRYING TO FIND OUT WHAT TYPE OF PERFUMES SHE PREFERS.
Um...
...EIMI, DO YOU HAVE A FAVORITE FRAGRANCE?
Hmm?
Huh?

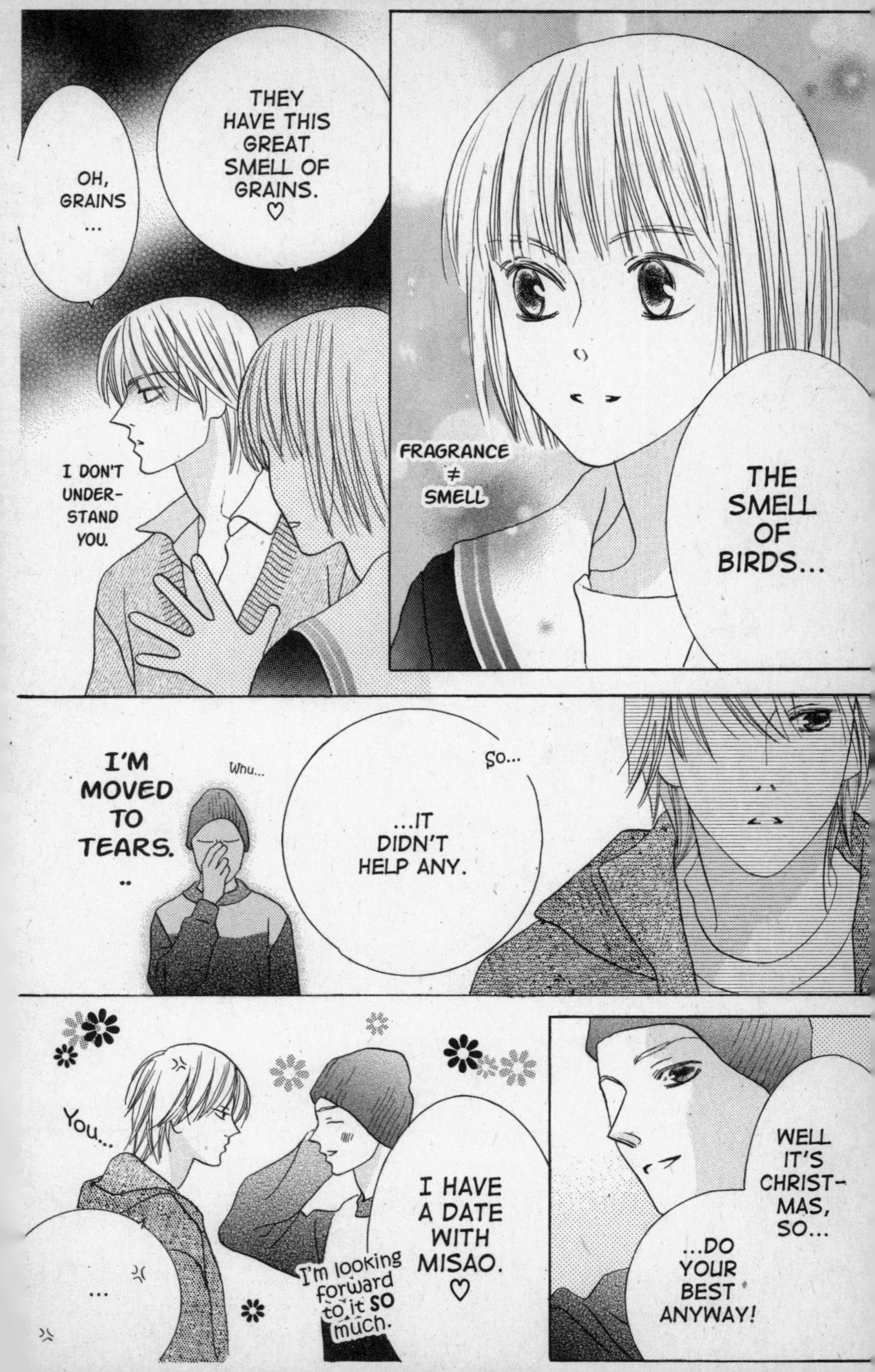
THE SMELL OF BIRDS...
FRAGRANCE ≠ SMELL
THEY HAVE THIS GREAT SMELL OF GRAINS. ♡
OH, GRAINS ...
I DON'T UNDER-STAND YOU.
SO...
...IT DIDN'T HELP ANY.
Whu...
I'M MOVED TO TEARS. ..
WELL IT'S CHRIST-MAS, SO...
...DO YOUR BEST ANYWAY!
I HAVE A DATE WITH MISAO. ♡
I'm looking forward to it SO much.
You...
...

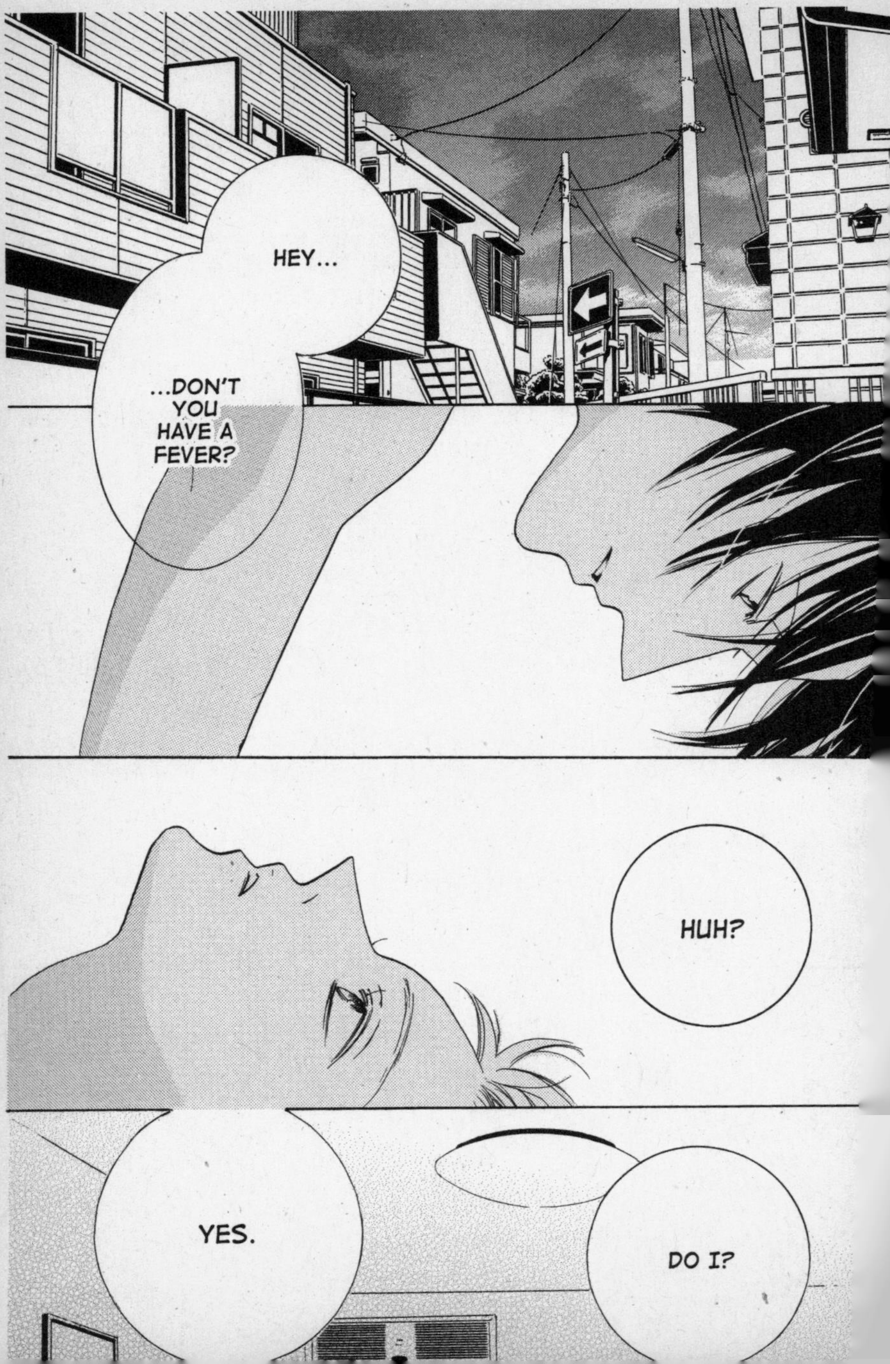
HEY...
...DON'T YOU HAVE A FEVER?
HUH?
DO I?
YES.

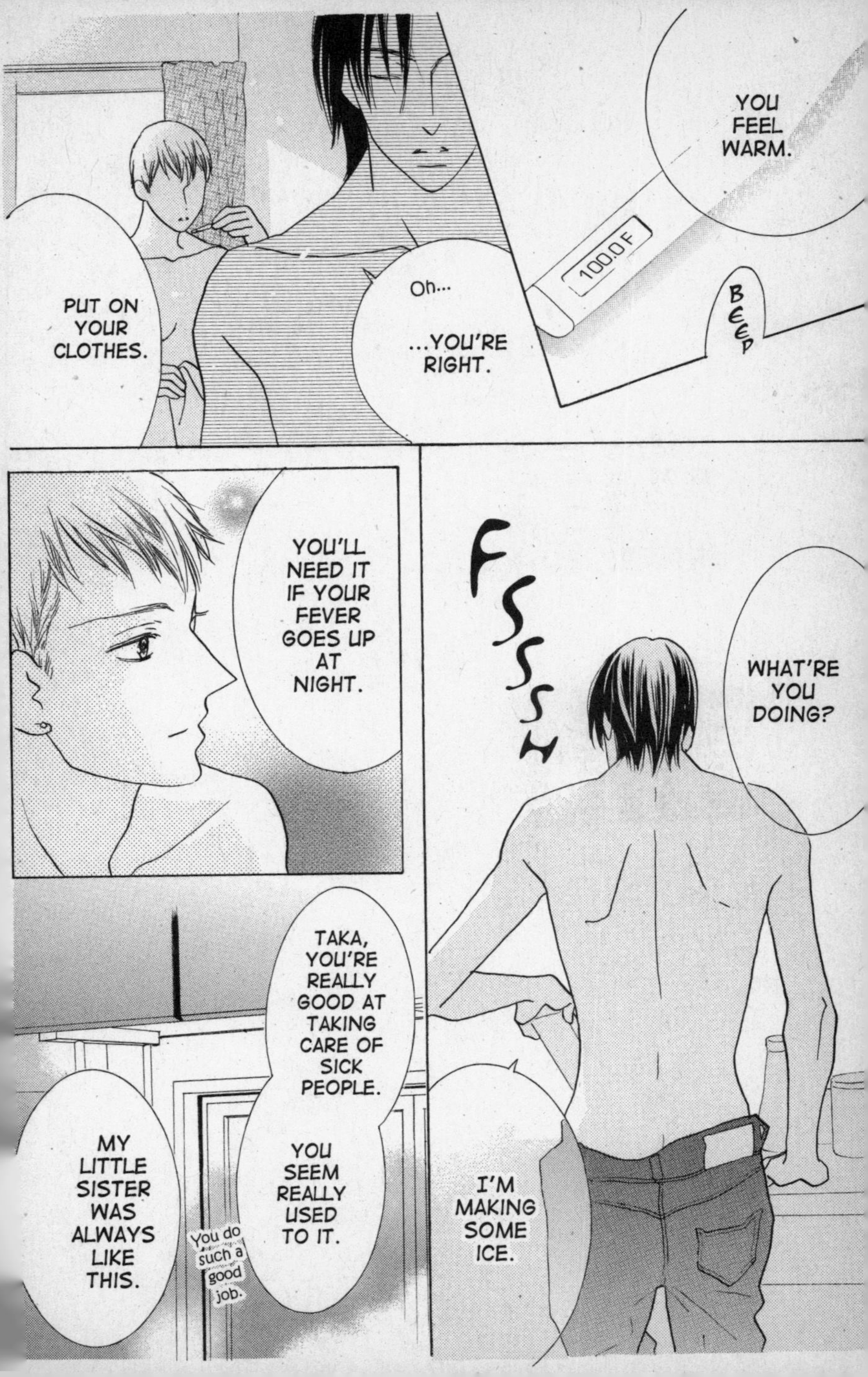
YOU FEEL WARM.
100.0 F
BEEP
Oh...
...YOU'RE RIGHT.
PUT ON YOUR CLOTHES.
FSSH
WHAT'RE YOU DOING?
I'M MAKING SOME ICE.
YOU'LL NEED IT IF YOUR FEVER GOES UP AT NIGHT.
TAKA, YOU'RE REALLY GOOD AT TAKING CARE OF SICK PEOPLE.
YOU SEEM REALLY USED TO IT.
You do such a good job.
MY LITTLE SISTER WAS ALWAYS LIKE THIS.

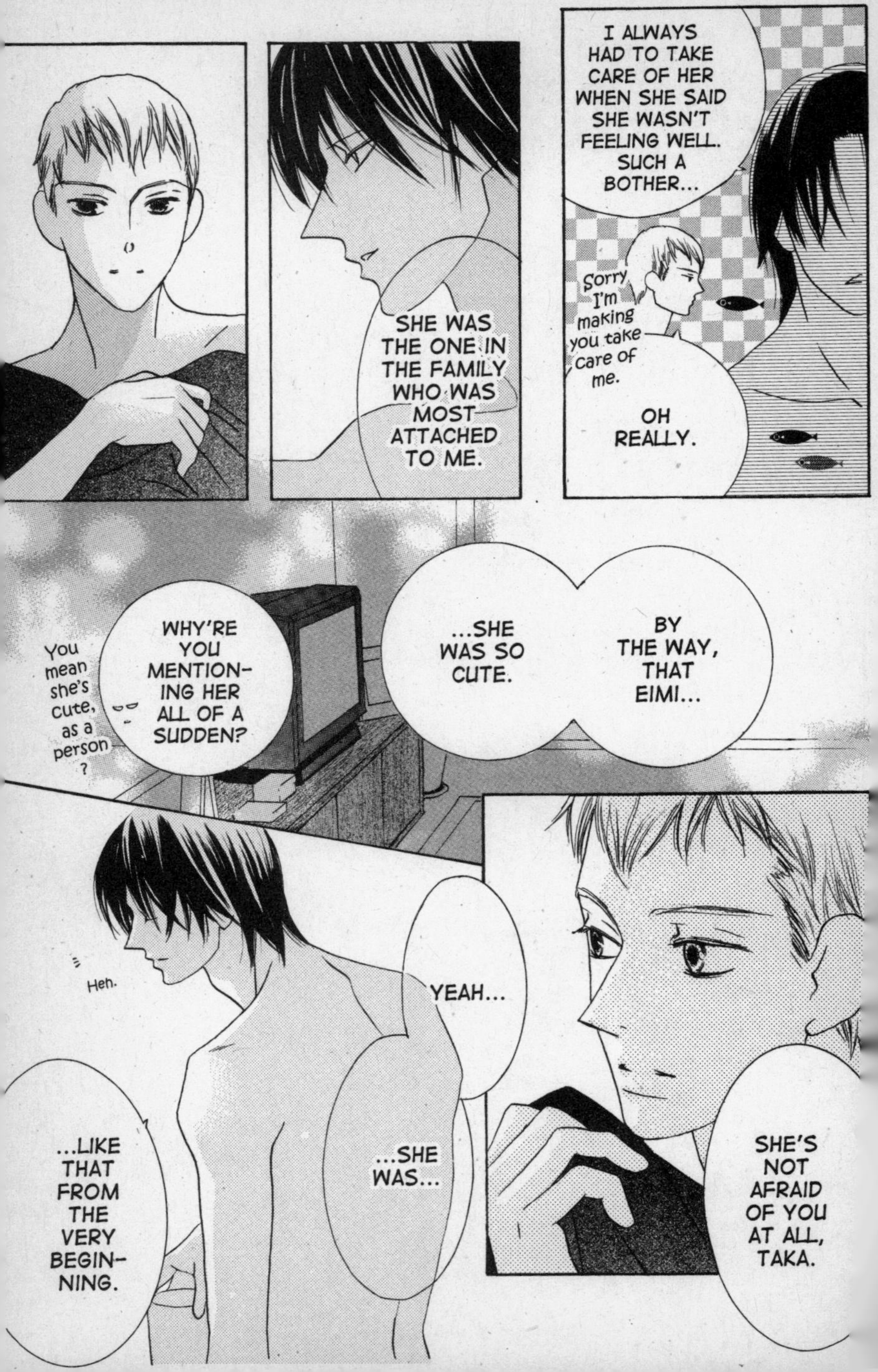
I ALWAYS HAD TO TAKE CARE OF HER WHEN SHE SAID SHE WASN'T FEELING WELL. SUCH A BOTHER...
Sorry I'm making you take care of me.
OH REALLY.
SHE WAS THE ONE IN THE FAMILY WHO WAS MOST ATTACHED TO ME.
BY THE WAY, THAT EIMI...
...SHE WAS SO CUTE.
WHY'RE YOU MENTIONING HER ALL OF A SUDDEN?
You mean she's cute, as a person?
SHE'S NOT AFRAID OF YOU AT ALL, TAKA.
YEAH...
...SHE WAS...
...LIKE THAT FROM THE VERY BEGINNING.
Heh.

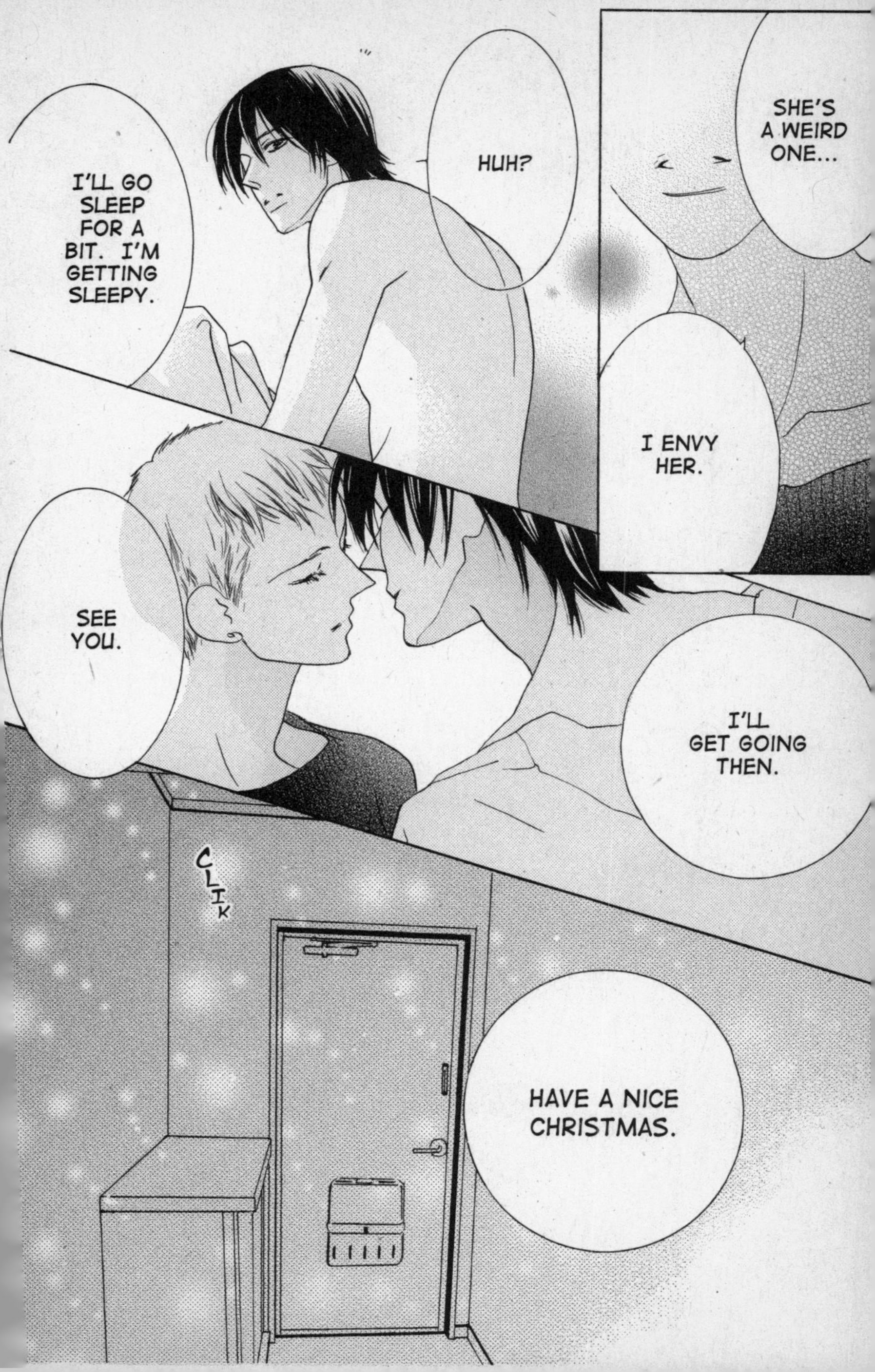
SHE'S A WEIRD ONE...
I ENVY HER.
HUH?
I'LL GO SLEEP FOR A BIT. I'M GETTING SLEEPY.
I'LL GET GOING THEN.
SEE YOU.
HAVE A NICE CHRISTMAS.
CLIK

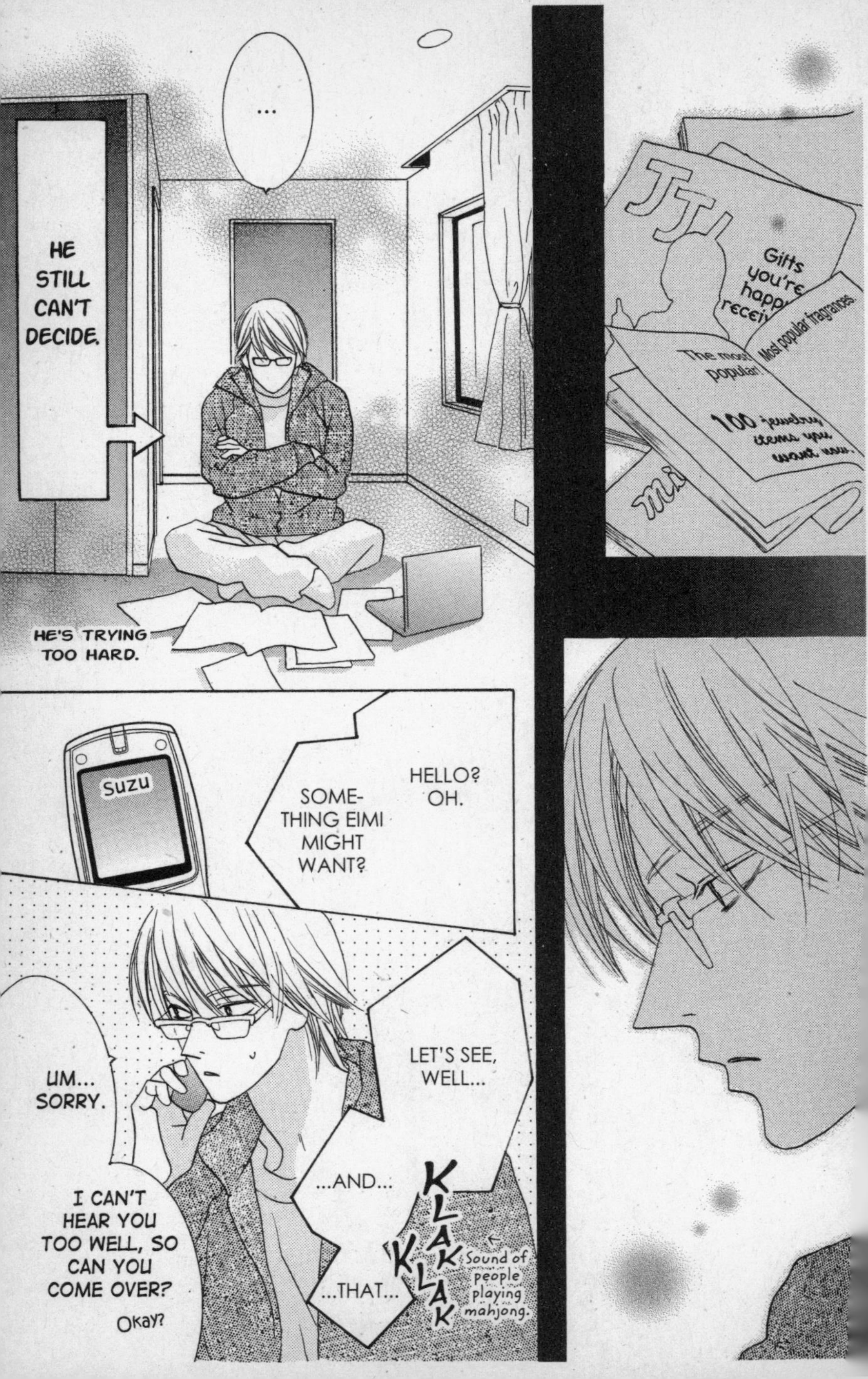
JJ
Gifts you're
Most popular fragrances.
The most popular!
100 jewelry items you want now.
...
HE STILL CAN'T DECIDE.
HE'S TRYING TOO HARD.
HELLO? OH.
SOME-THING EIMI MIGHT WANT?
Suzu
LET'S SEE, WELL...
...AND...
...THAT...
KLAK KLAK KLAK
← Sound of people playing mahjong.
UM... SORRY.
I CAN'T HEAR YOU TOO WELL, SO CAN YOU COME OVER?
Okay?

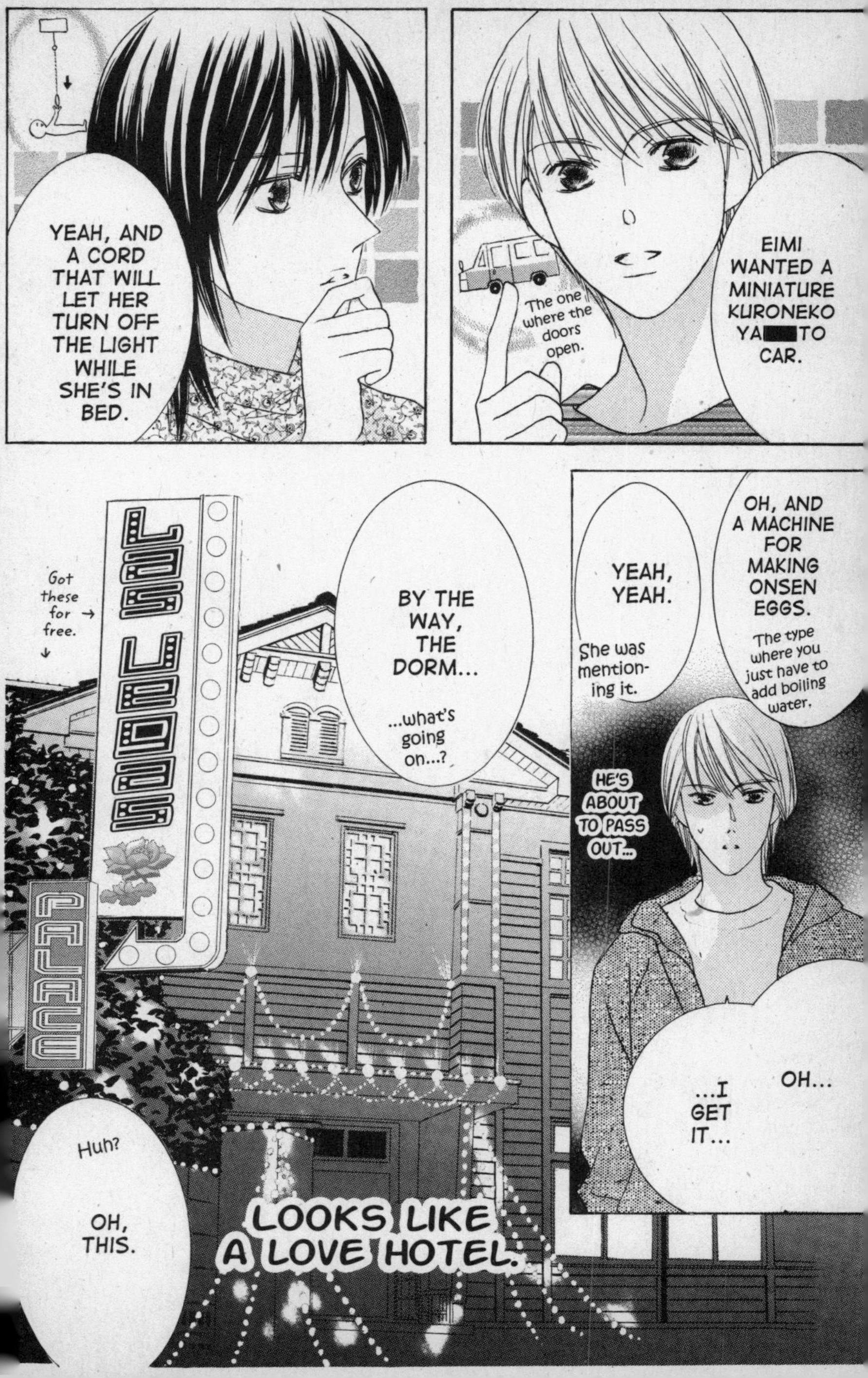
EIMI WANTED A MINIATURE KURONEKO YA[redacted]TO CAR.
The one where the doors open.
YEAH, AND A CORD THAT WILL LET HER TURN OFF THE LIGHT WHILE SHE'S IN BED.
OH, AND A MACHINE FOR MAKING ONSEN EGGS.
The type where you just have to add boiling water.
YEAH, YEAH.
She was mentioning it.
HE'S ABOUT TO PASS OUT...
OH...
...I GET IT...
BY THE WAY, THE DORM...
...what's going on...?
Got these for free.
Las Vegas
PALACE
Huh?
OH, THIS.
LOOKS LIKE A LOVE HOTEL.

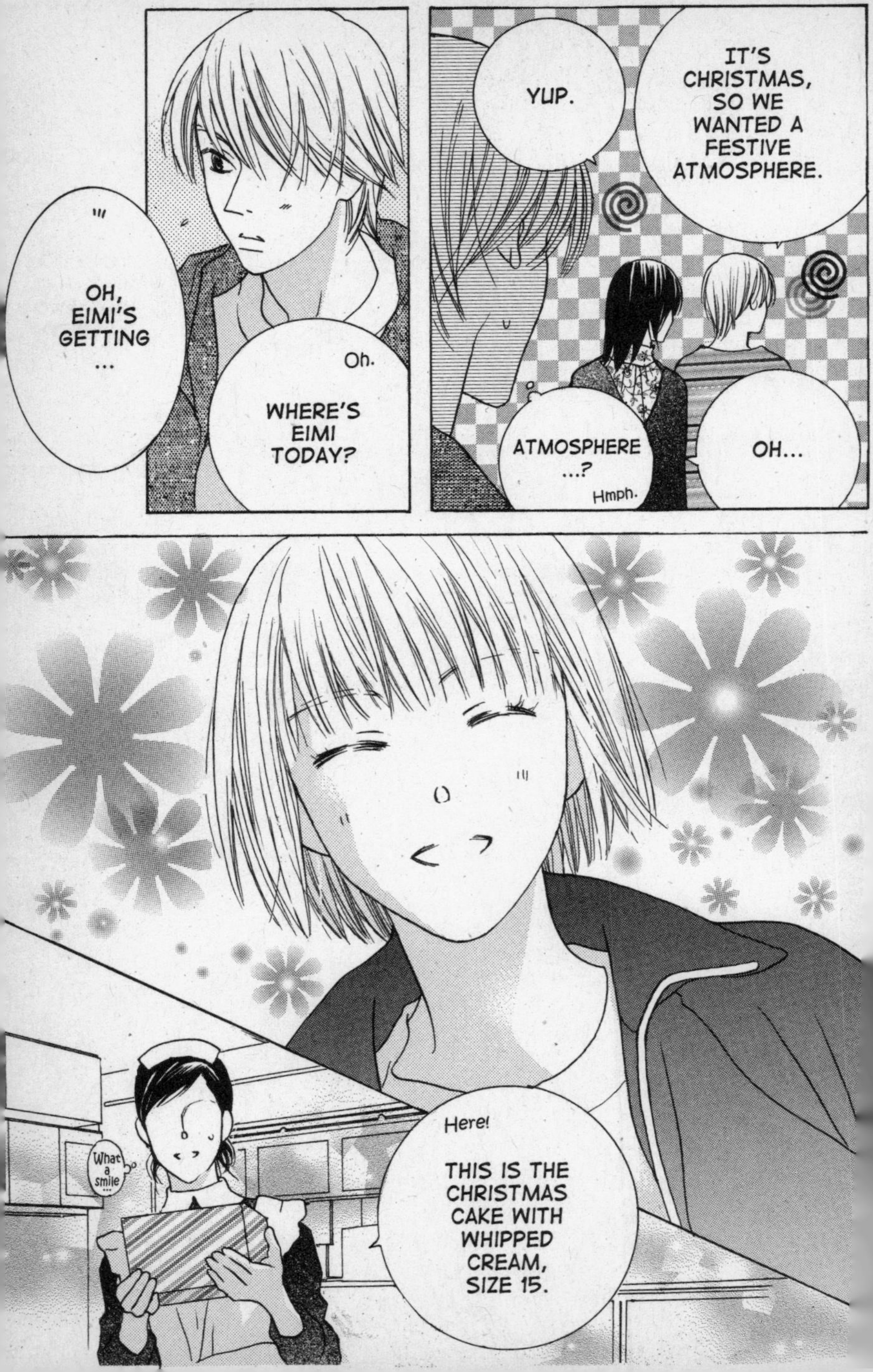
IT'S CHRISTMAS, SO WE WANTED A FESTIVE ATMOSPHERE.
YUP.
OH...
ATMOSPHERE ...?
Hmph.
Oh.
WHERE'S EIMI TODAY?
OH, EIMI'S GETTING ...
Here!
THIS IS THE CHRISTMAS CAKE WITH WHIPPED CREAM, SIZE 15.
What a smile...

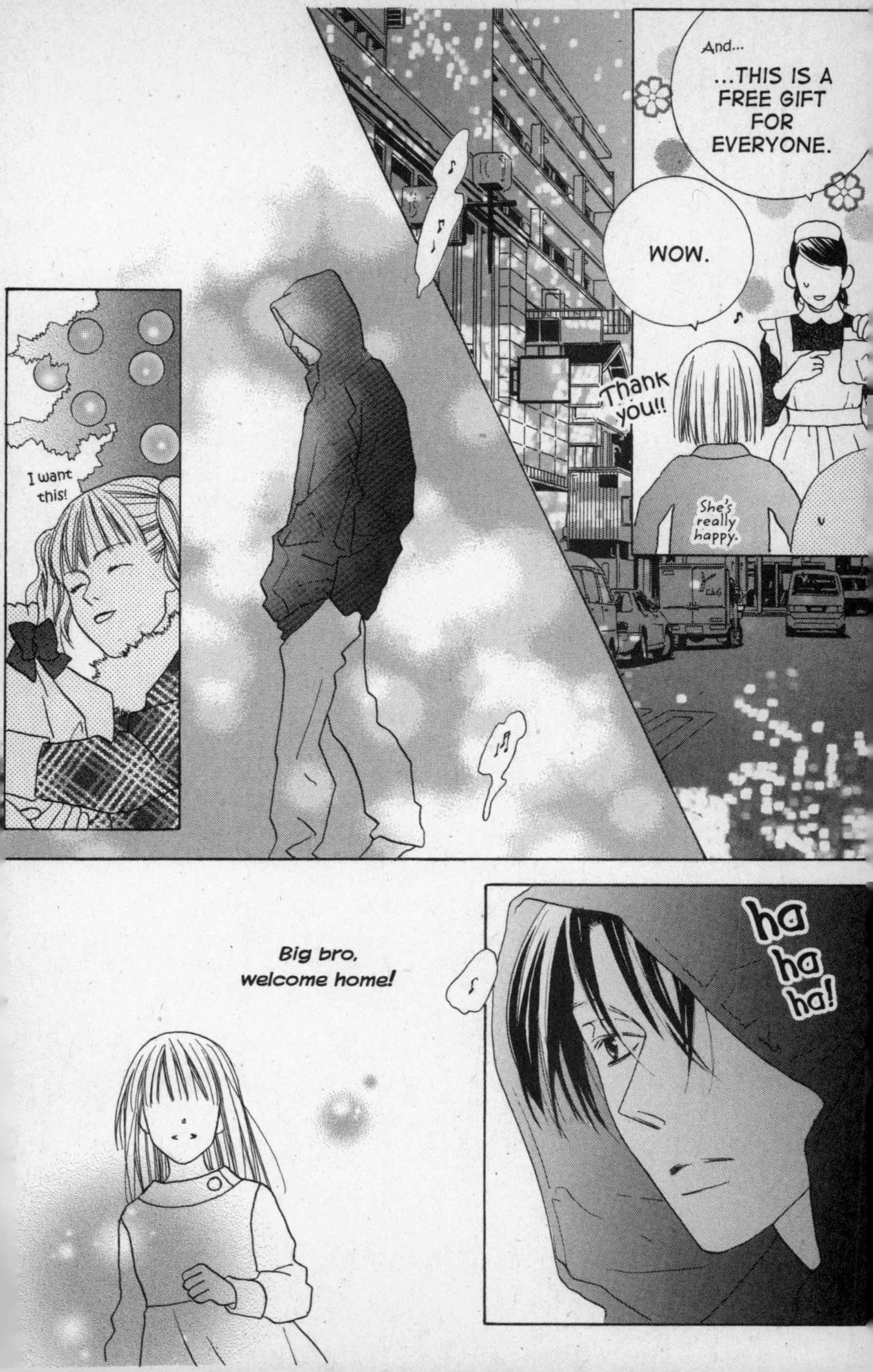
And...
...THIS IS A FREE GIFT FOR EVERYONE.
WOW.
Thank you!!
She's really happy.
I want this!
ha ha ha!
Big bro, welcome home!

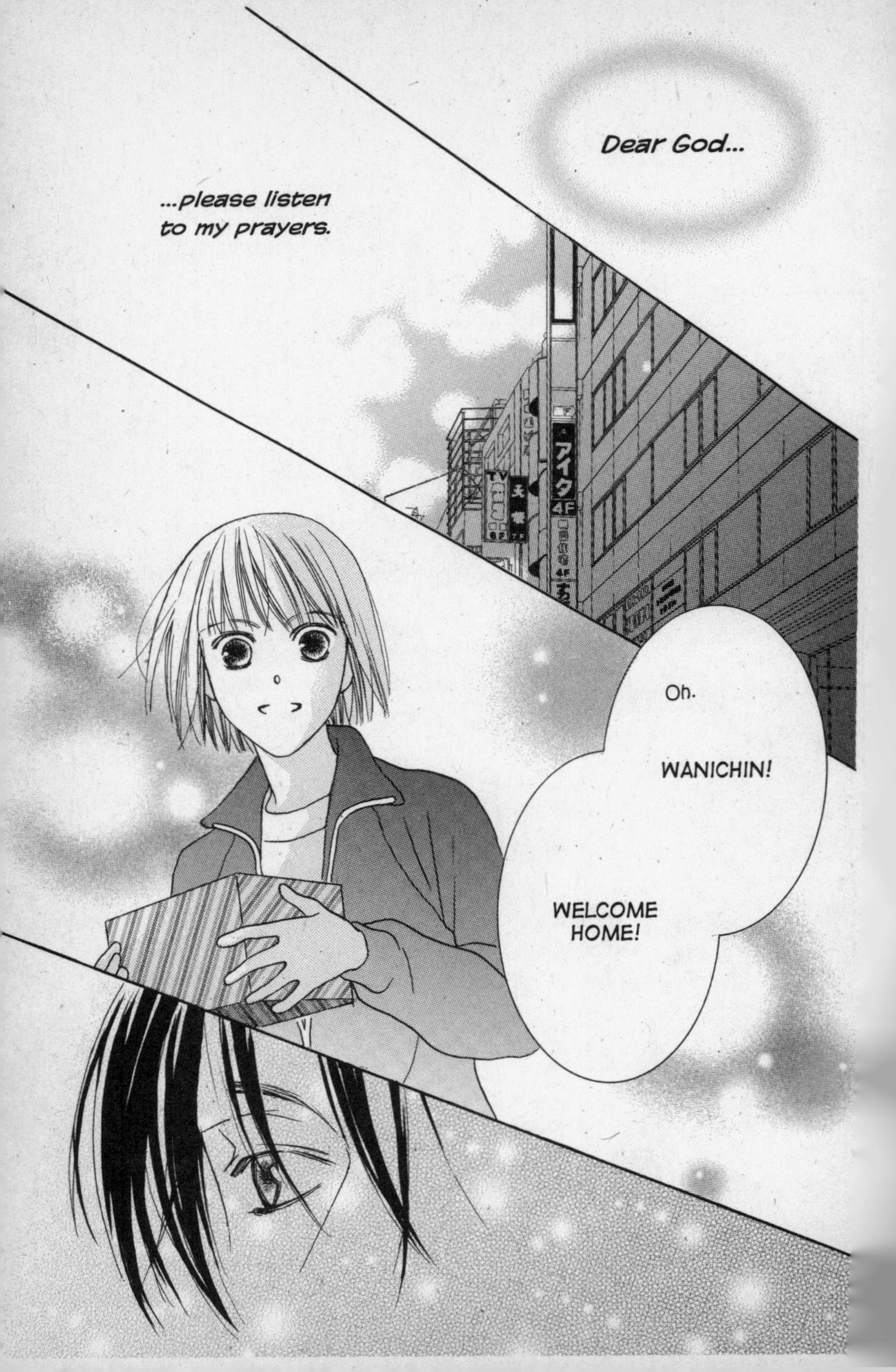
Dear God...
...please listen to my prayers.
アイク 4F
TV
Oh.
WANICHIN!
WELCOME HOME!

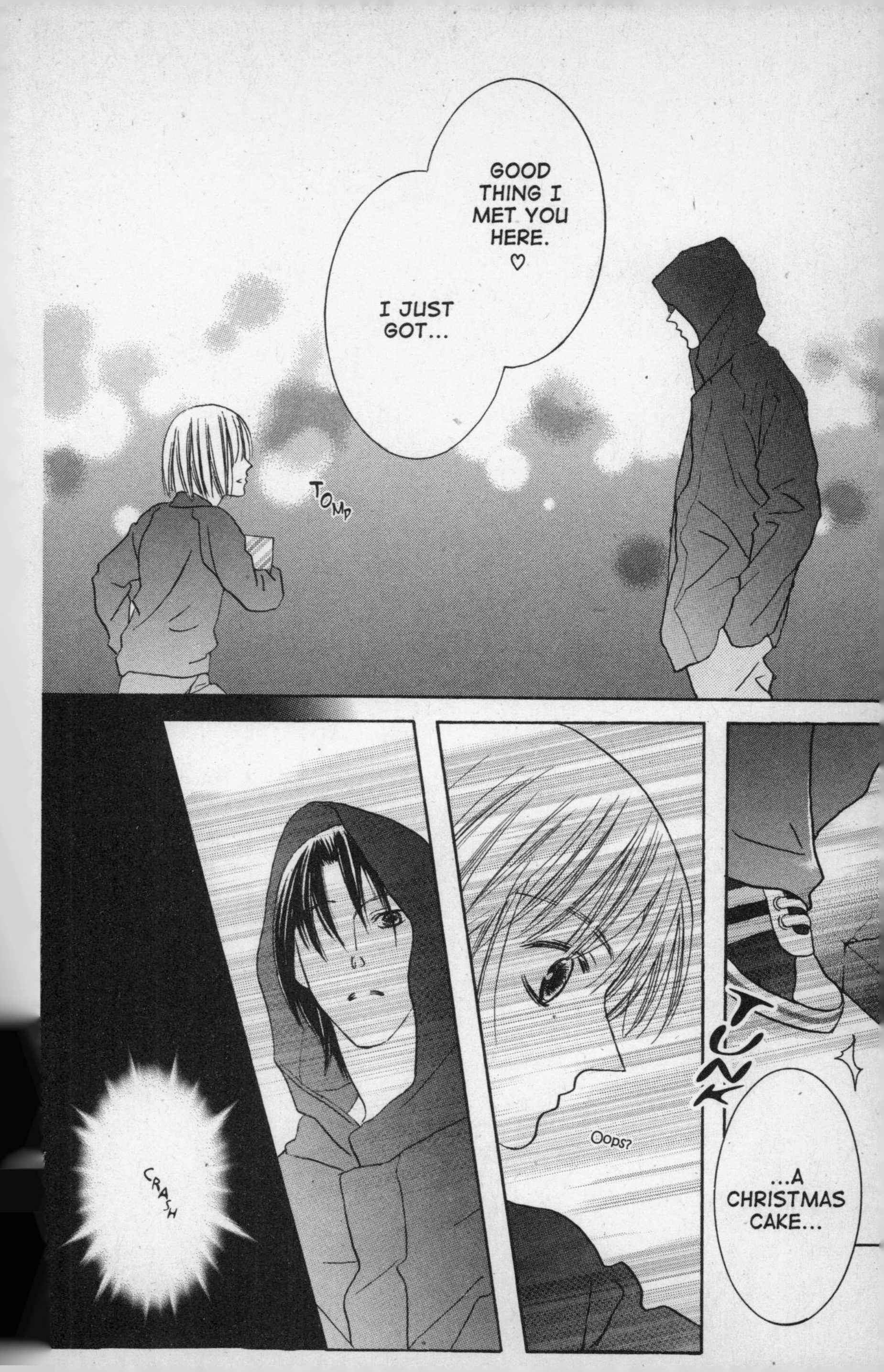
GOOD THING I MET YOU HERE. ♡
I JUST GOT...
TOMP
TUNK
...A CHRISTMAS CAKE...
Oops?
CRASH

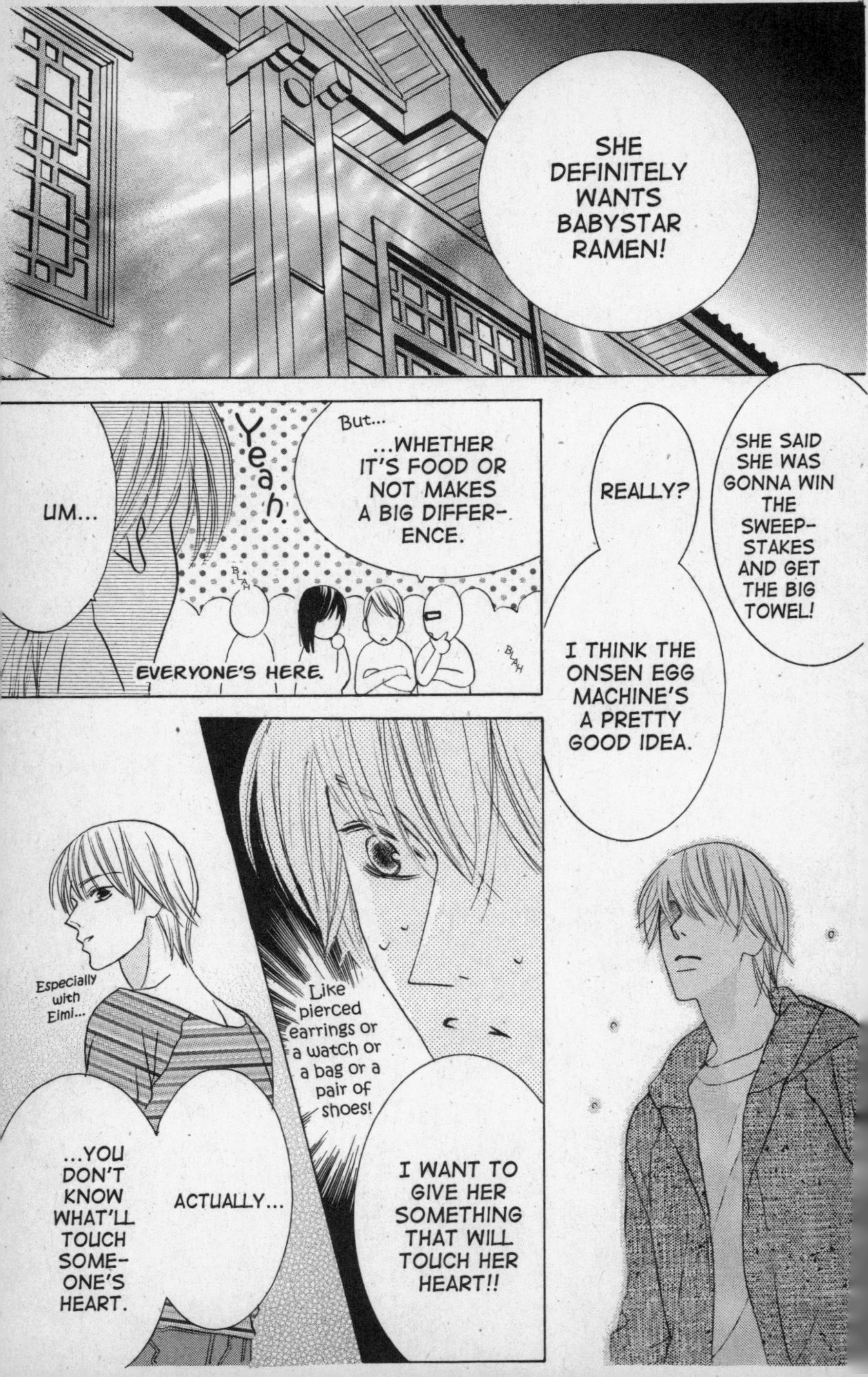
SHE DEFINITELY WANTS BABYSTAR RAMEN!
SHE SAID SHE WAS GONNA WIN THE SWEEPSTAKES AND GET THE BIG TOWEL!
REALLY?
I THINK THE ONSEN EGG MACHINE'S A PRETTY GOOD IDEA.
But...
...WHETHER IT'S FOOD OR NOT MAKES A BIG DIFFERENCE.
Yeah.
BLAH
BLAH
EVERYONE'S HERE.
UM...
I WANT TO GIVE HER SOMETHING THAT WILL TOUCH HER HEART!!
Like pierced earrings or a watch or a bag or a pair of shoes!
Especially with Eimi...
ACTUALLY...
...YOU DON'T KNOW WHAT'LL TOUCH SOMEONE'S HEART.

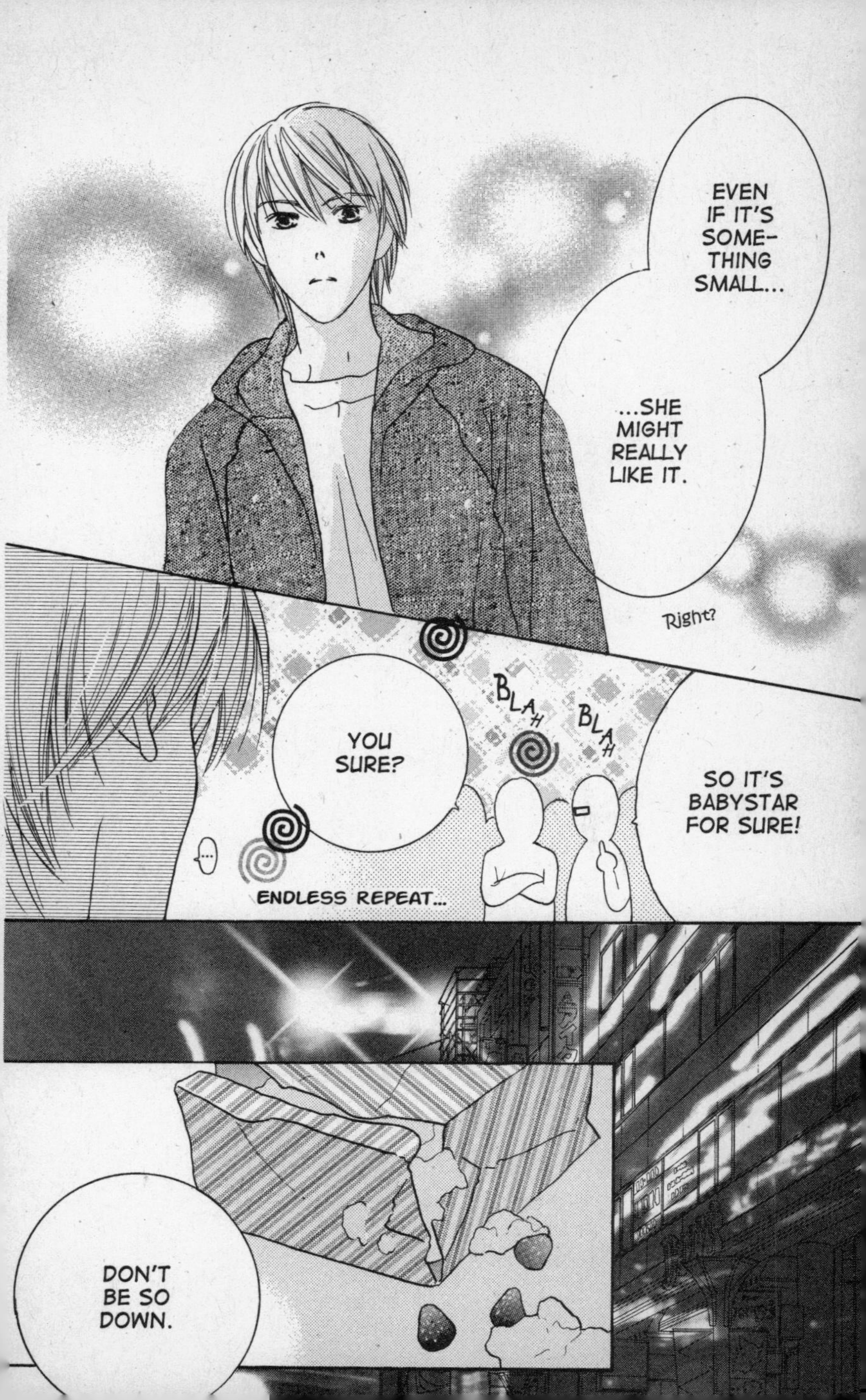
EVEN IF IT'S SOME-THING SMALL...
...SHE MIGHT REALLY LIKE IT.
Right?
SO IT'S BABYSTAR FOR SURE!
BLAH BLAH
YOU SURE?
...
ENDLESS REPEAT...
DON'T BE SO DOWN.

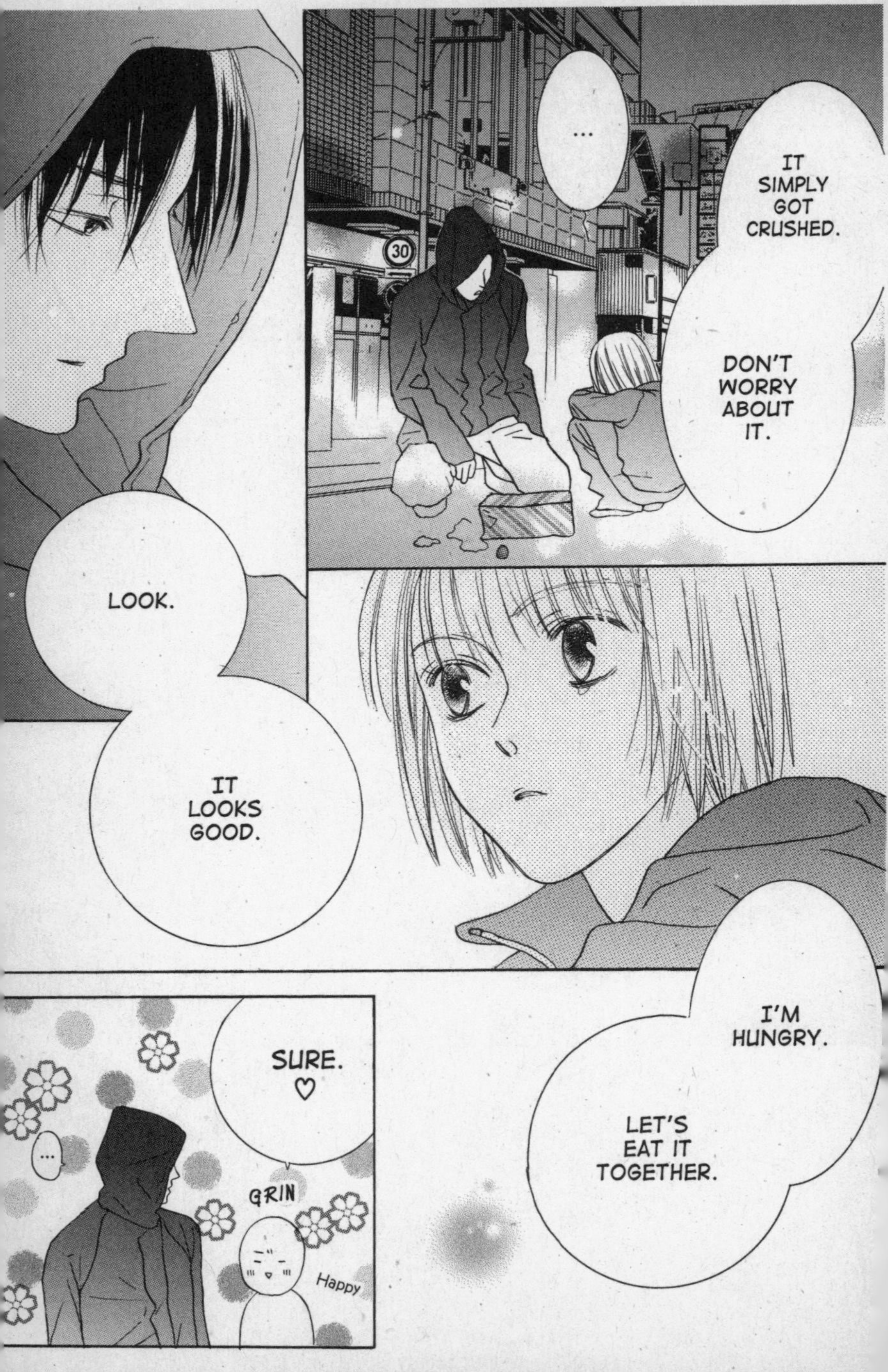
IT SIMPLY GOT CRUSHED.
DON'T WORRY ABOUT IT.
...
LOOK.
IT LOOKS GOOD.
I'M HUNGRY.
LET'S EAT IT TOGETHER.
SURE. ♡
...
GRIN
Happy

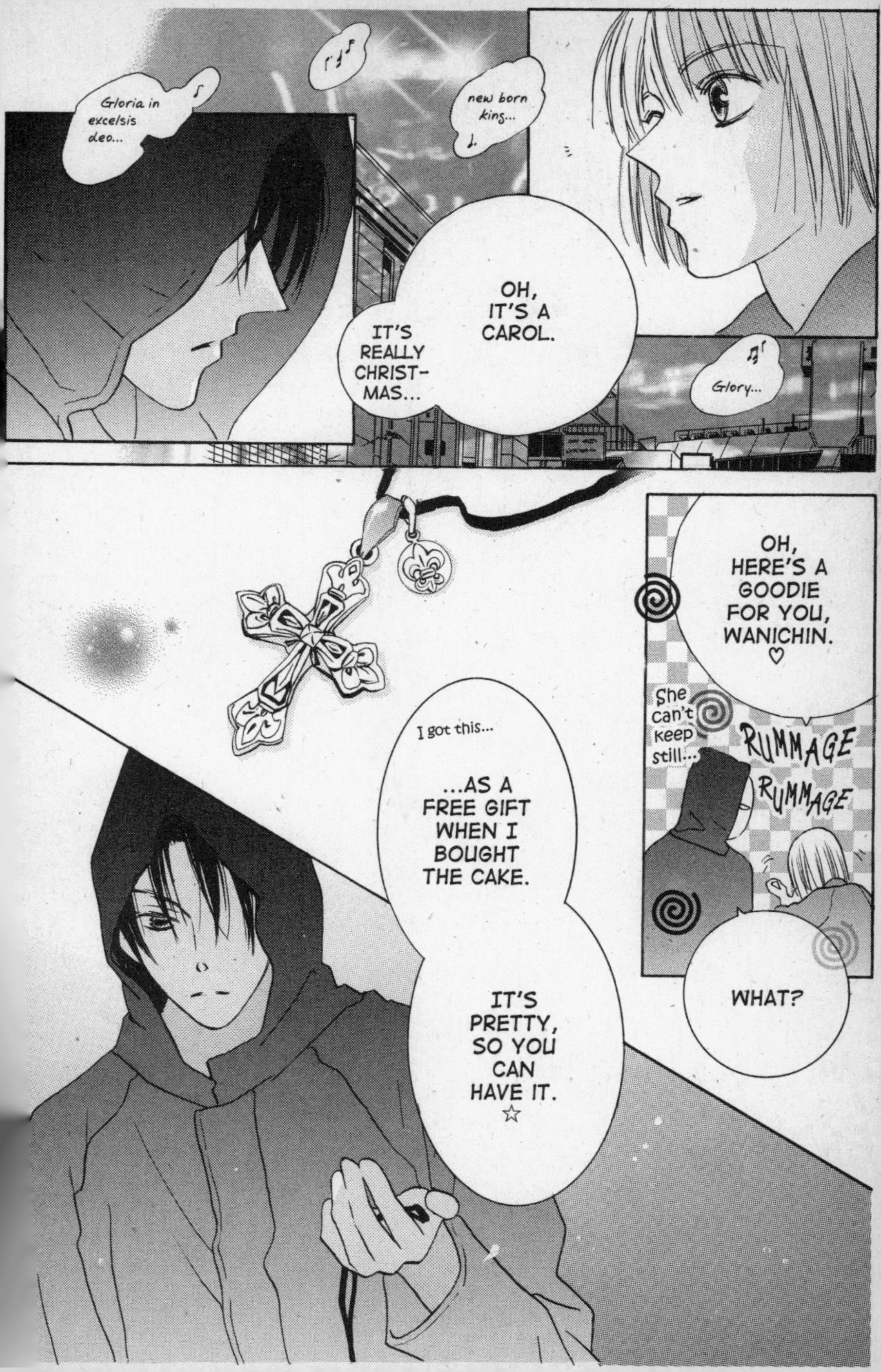
new born king...
Gloria in excelsis deo...
OH, IT'S A CAROL.
IT'S REALLY CHRIST-MAS...
Glory...
OH, HERE'S A GOODIE FOR YOU, WANICHIN. ♡
She can't keep still...
RUMMAGE
RUMMAGE
WHAT?
I got this...
...AS A FREE GIFT WHEN I BOUGHT THE CAKE.
IT'S PRETTY, SO YOU CAN HAVE IT. ☆

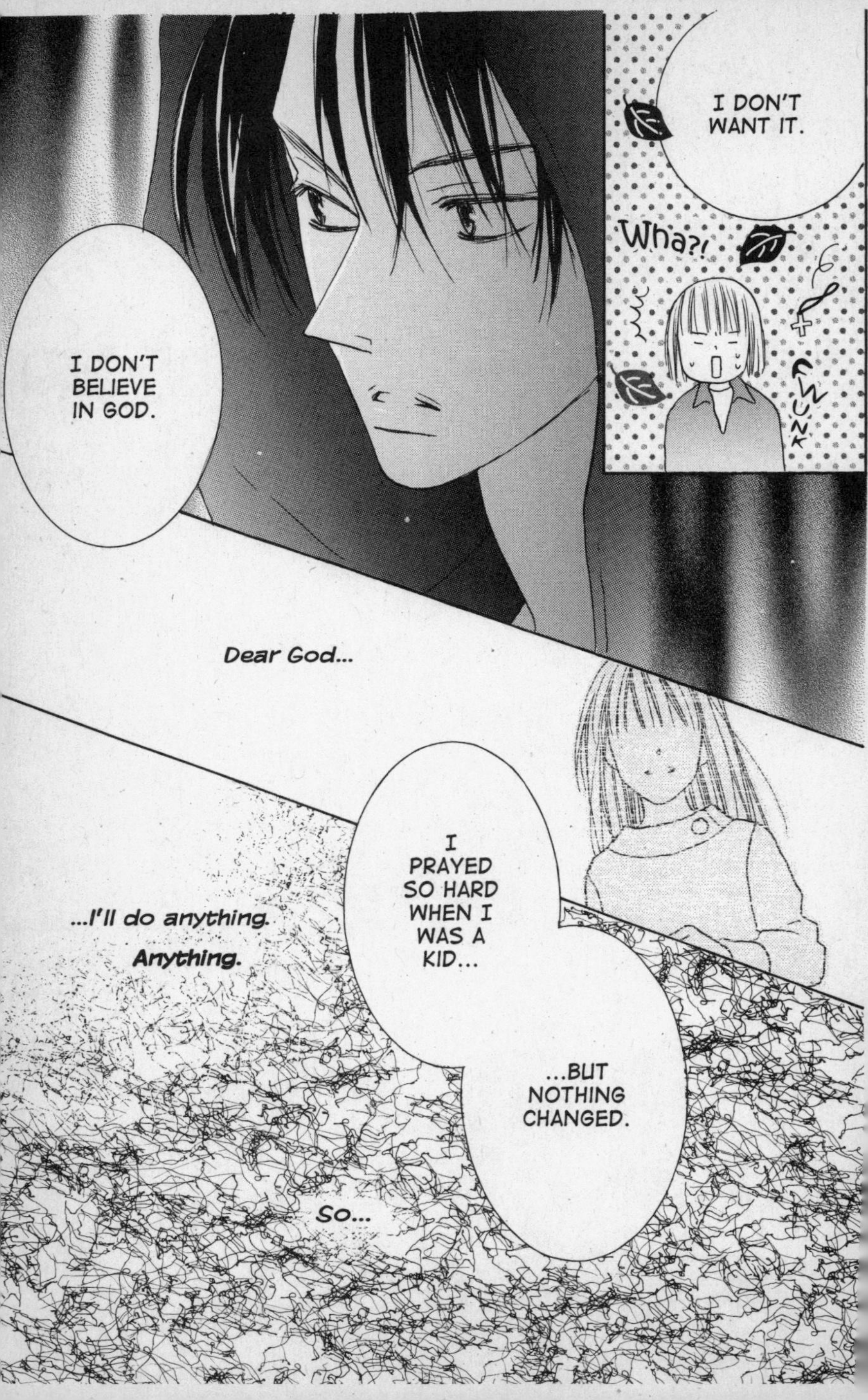
I DON'T WANT IT.
Wha?!
FWUNK
I DON'T BELIEVE IN GOD.
Dear God...
I PRAYED SO HARD WHEN I WAS A KID...
...BUT NOTHING CHANGED.
...I'll do anything.
Anything.
So...

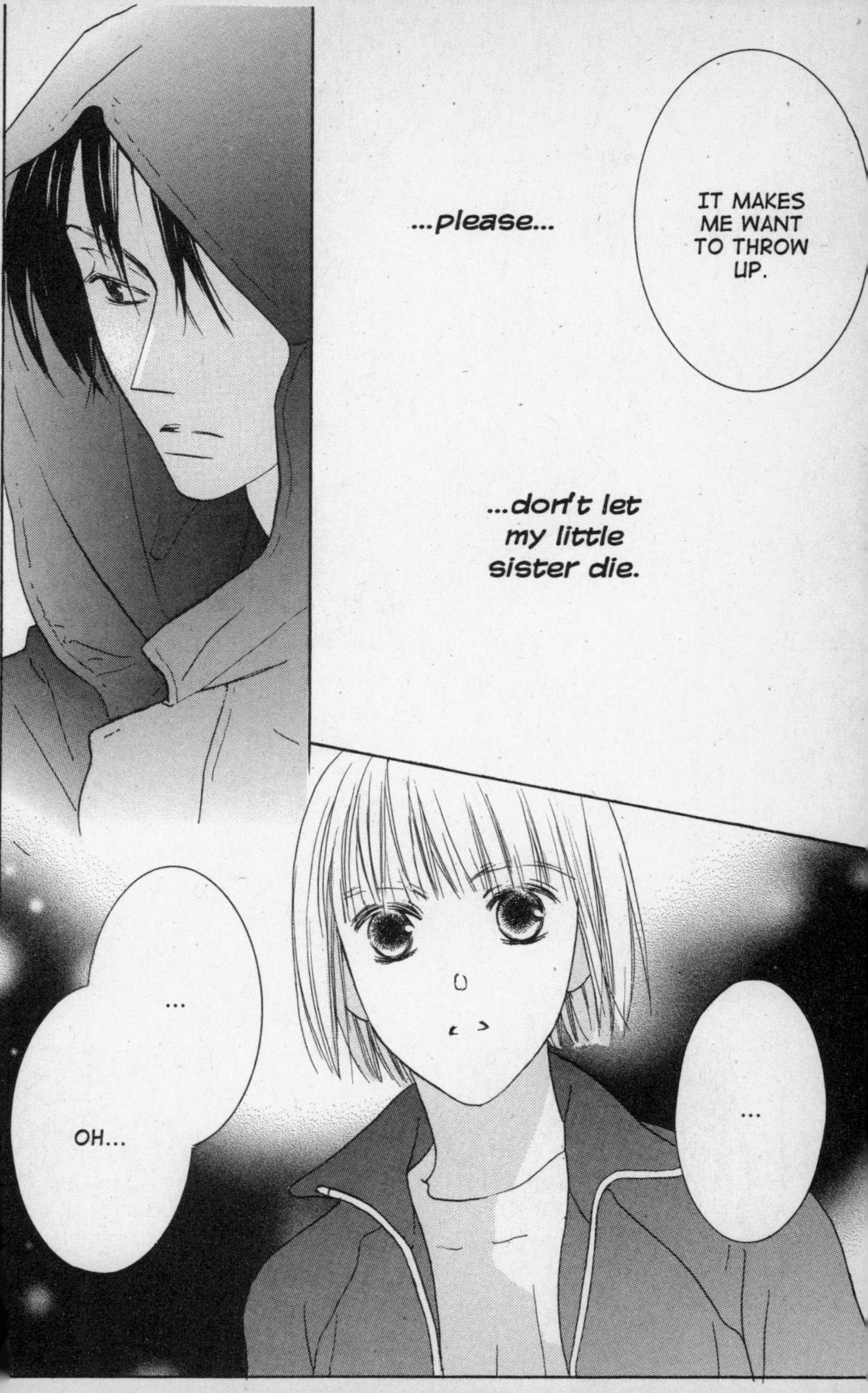
IT MAKES ME WANT TO THROW UP.
...please...
...don't let my little sister die.
...
...
OH...

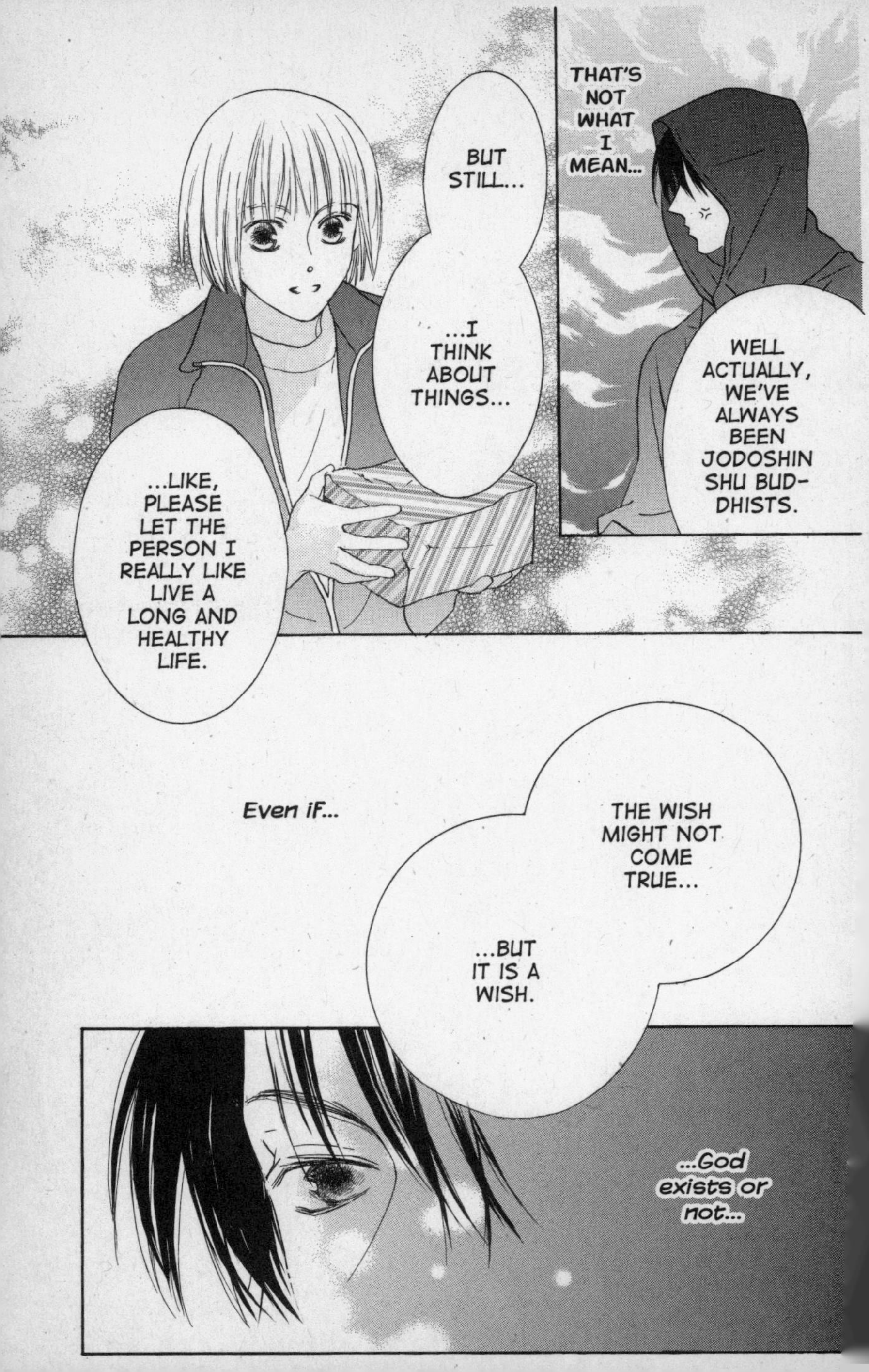
THAT'S NOT WHAT I MEAN...
WELL ACTUALLY, WE'VE ALWAYS BEEN JODOSHIN SHU BUD-DHISTS.
BUT STILL...
...I THINK ABOUT THINGS...
...LIKE, PLEASE LET THE PERSON I REALLY LIKE LIVE A LONG AND HEALTHY LIFE.
THE WISH MIGHT NOT COME TRUE...
...BUT IT IS A WISH.
Even if...
...God exists or not...

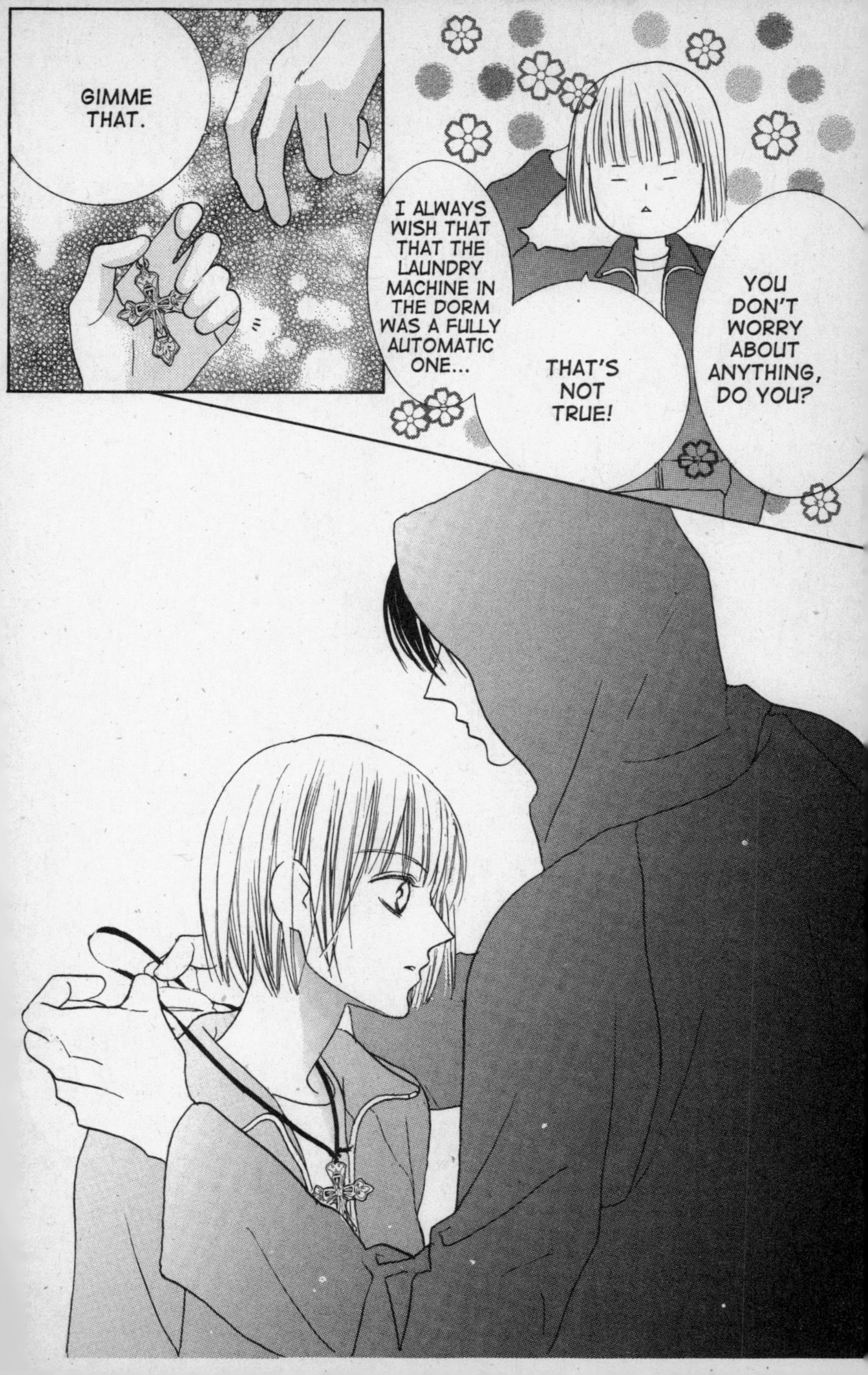
YOU DON'T WORRY ABOUT ANYTHING, DO YOU?
THAT'S NOT TRUE!
I ALWAYS WISH THAT THAT THE LAUNDRY MACHINE IN THE DORM WAS A FULLY AUTOMATIC ONE...
GIMME THAT.

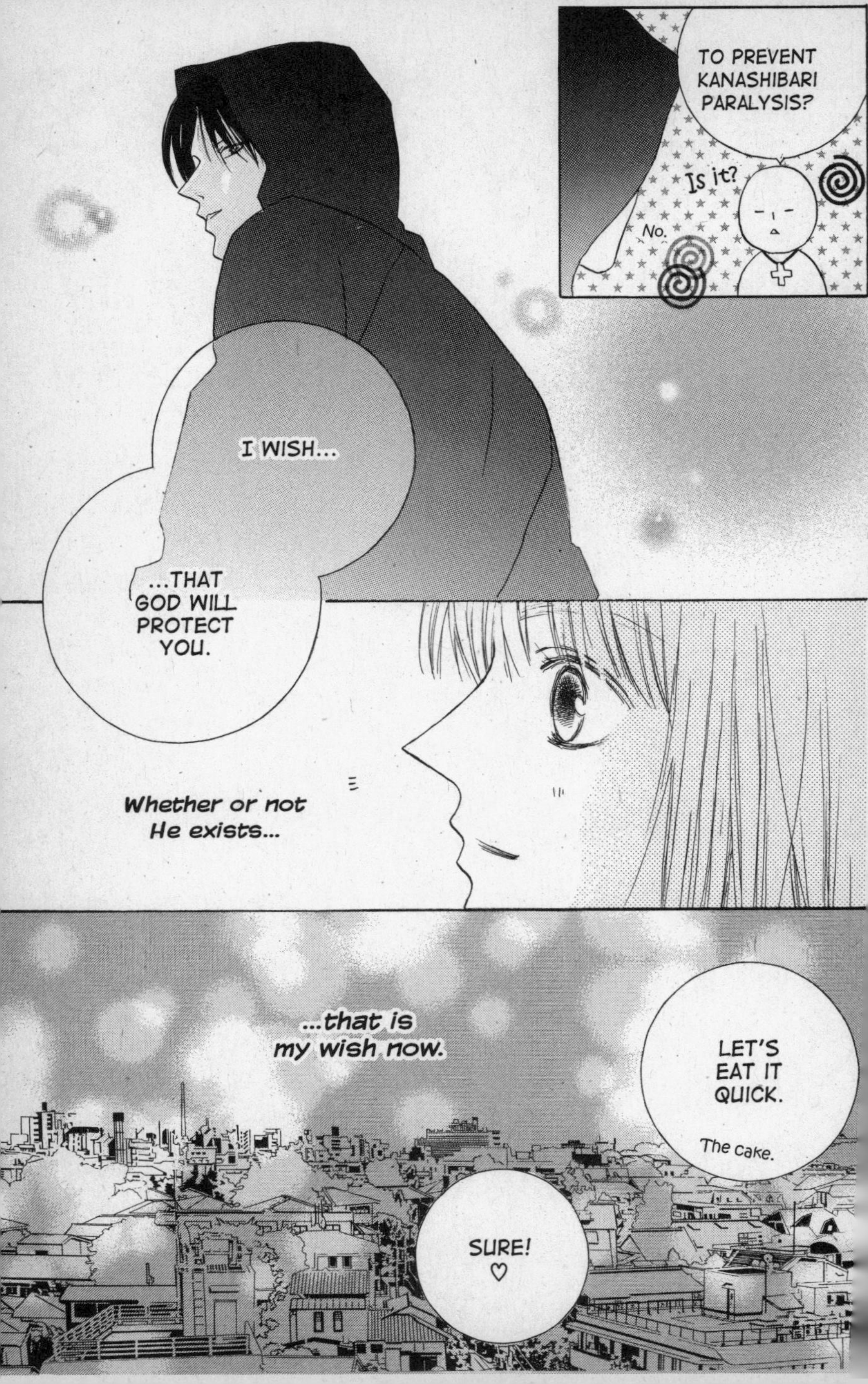
TO PREVENT KANASHIBARI PARALYSIS?
Is it?
No.
I WISH...
...THAT GOD WILL PROTECT YOU.
Whether or not He exists...
...that is my wish now.
LET'S EAT IT QUICK.
The cake.
SURE! ♡

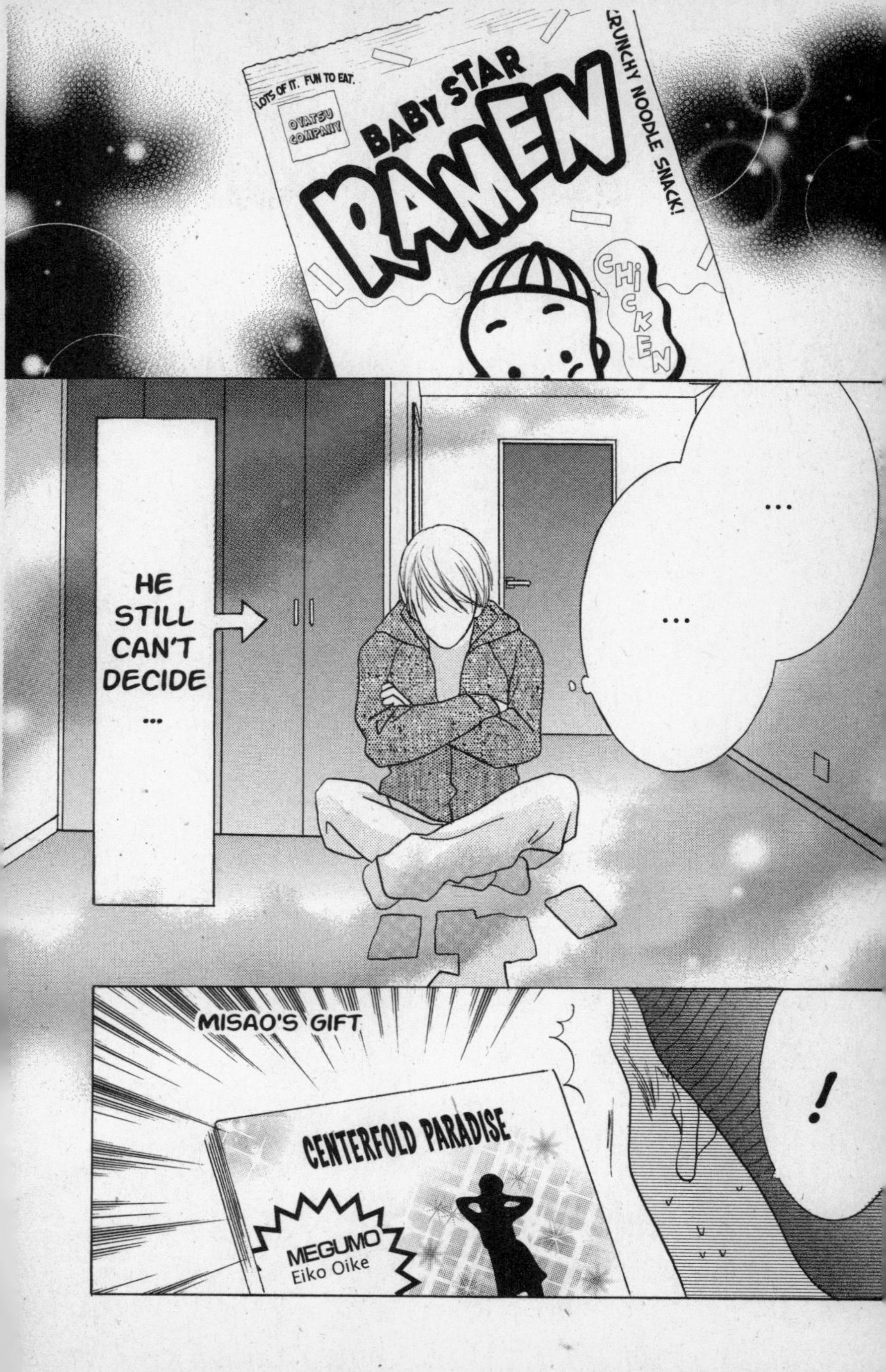
CRUNCHY NOODLE SNACK!
BABY STAR
RAMEN
LOTS OF IT. FUN TO EAT.
OYATSU COMPANY
CHICKEN
...
...
HE STILL CAN'T DECIDE ...
!
MISAO'S GIFT
CENTERFOLD PARADISE
MEGUMO
Eiko Oike

Dorm Information Pamphlet

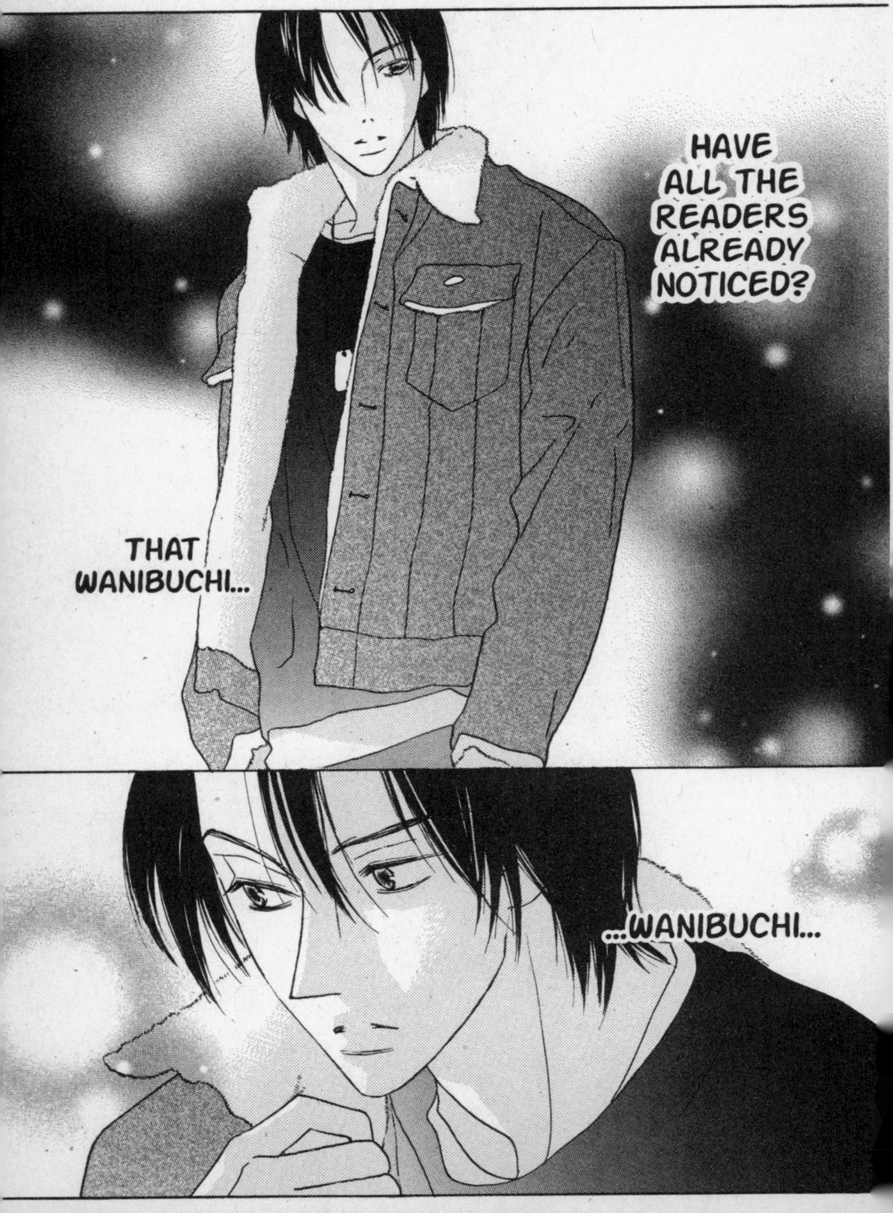
HAVE ALL THE READERS ALREADY NOTICED?
THAT WANIBUCHI...
...WANIBUCHI...

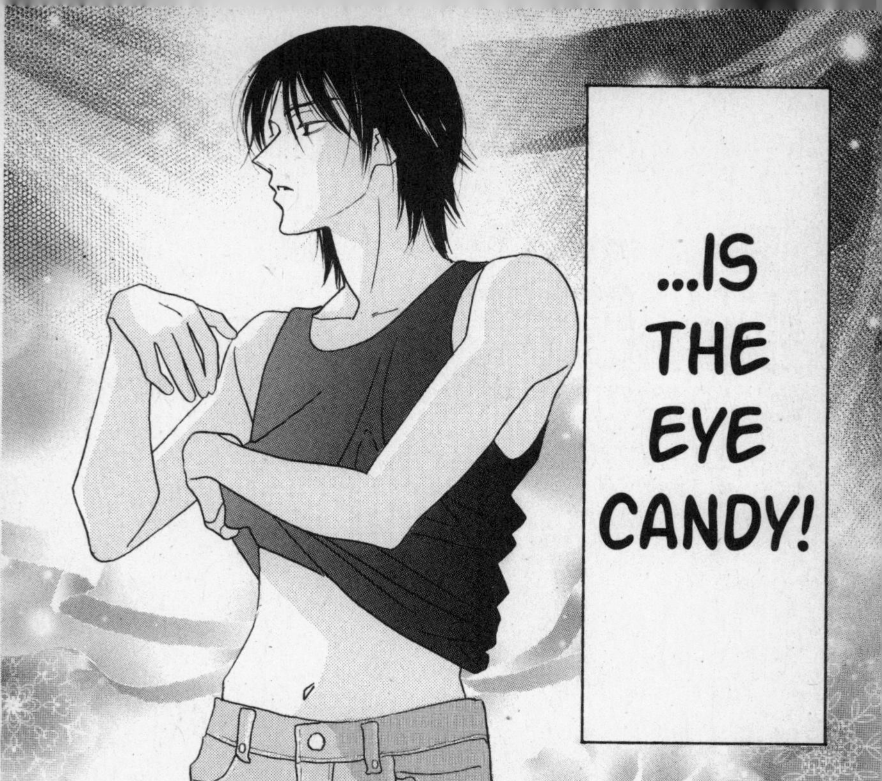
...IS THE EYE CANDY!

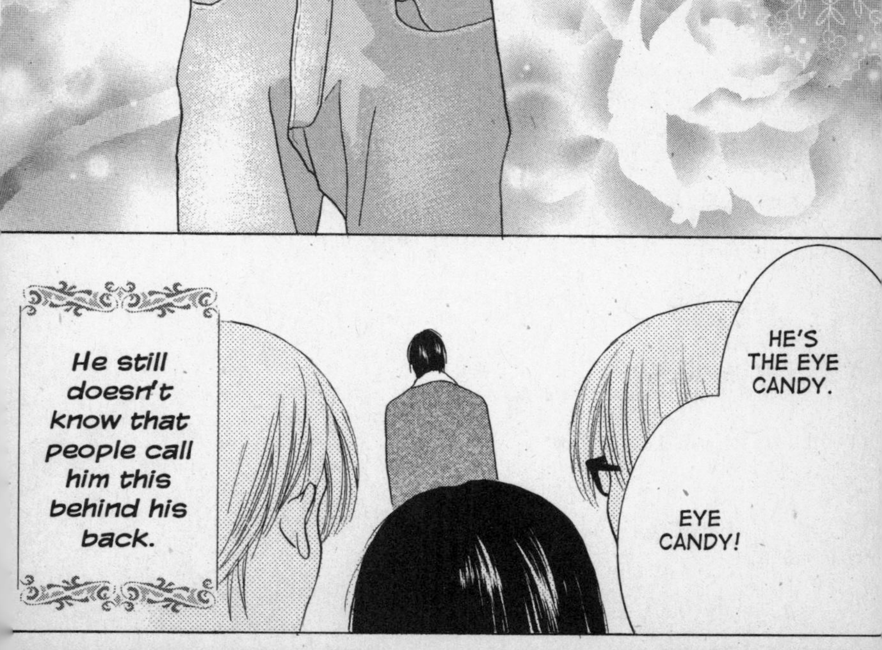
HE'S THE EYE CANDY.
EYE CANDY!
He still doesn't know that people call him this behind his back.

Glossary

Some high school experiences are universal. Others need a little more explanation. In these notes you will find interesting information to enhance your *Beauty Is the Beast* reading enjoyment.

Page 36, panel 1: Shukan Posuto gossip mag style
Shukan Posuto, or Weekly Post, is a Japanese gossip magazine.

Page 42, panel 2: Big Family Special News Report
A reference to the TV specials that focus on large but poor families.

Page 48, panel 2: Hato Subure
This is an actual snack, like a cookie and shaped like a bird. *Hato* means pigeon, hence the name (or the shape).

Page 72, panel 4: Abaranger
The kids' TV show *Bakuryu Sentai Abaranger*, where dinosaurs attack Tokyo and a transdimensional Ranger comes to save the day. It was imported to the U.S. as *Power Rangers Dino Thunder*.

Page 75, sidebar: Cheese tara
Cheese with dried cod.

Page 75, sidebar: Surume
Dried squid or cuttlefish. A classic Japanese bar snack.

Page 75, sidebar: Edamame
Soy bean pods, boiled and salted. A classic Japanese bar snack.

Page 100, panel 4: Iodine Eggs
The chickens that lay these eggs are fed supplements, such as seaweed powder, to increase the iodine levels in their eggs. Iodine is an essential mineral that prevents some goiters and forms of mental retardation.

Page 103, panel 2: Shiso
Shiso is also called perilla or beefsteak plant. It is a spicy herb that tastes like cumin, cilantro, parsley, and cinnamon. Green shiso (aoshiso) has a stronger flavor than red shiso (akashiso).

Page 110, panel 5: Natto
A traditional Japanese staple of fermented soybeans. High in protein and other essential nutrients, *natto* has a rather slimy texture and is an acquired taste.

Page 114, panel 3: Yakitori
Skewered grilled chicken, a common street food.

Page 114, panel 3: Okonomiyaki
Somewhere between a pancake and a pizza, *okonomiyaki* have a base of flour, eggs, and yam or cabbage and are pan-fried. "Okonomi" means "as you like," and refers to the ingredients that can be added on top of the dish. It is often served with a brown okonomiyaki sauce and mayonnaise.

Page 130, panel 3: tatami mat
In Japan, rooms are traditionally measured by how many tatami mats it would take to cover the floor. Tatami mat size varies by region.

Page 131, panel 2: Kyoko Hikawa
The little creature is a Chimo, from Kyoko Hikawa's manga *From Far Away*. Chimos help people teleport.

Page 140, panel 2: Hitoshi
From the quiz show *Discover the Wonders of the World*. Hitoshi is one of the dolls the guests bet when answering questions.

Page 162, panel 4: Enkai
Drinking party for the working stiffs, and not normally a term teenagers use.

Page 165, panel 2: Christmas cakes
In Japan, fruitcake isn't a holiday tradition. Instead, they have sponge cakes decorated with lots of whipped cream and strawberries, or chocolate cream. Cakes can be reserved at cake shops or convenience stores.

Page 166, panel 3: Hiroyuki Otaka
A beauty expert who writes articles about make-up for women's magazines in Japan.

Page 174, panel 1: Kuroneko Ya███to
Kuroneko Yamato is a package delivery service, like UPS.

Page 174, panel 3: Onsen eggs
A special kind of soft-boiled egg traditionally prepared by cooking in a hot spring.

Page 185, panel 1: Jodoshinshu Buddhists
A sect of Buddhism, founded by Kenshin Daishi Shinran Shonin in the 13th century. It adheres to the Amida Buddah of Infinite Light and Life. Part of the tradition includes not practicing prayer, petitioning magic, or superstition.

Page 187, panel 1: Kanashibari paralysis
A state of paralysis just after waking, and is attributed to ghosts or evil spirits appearing in your room.

Tomo Matsumoto was born on January 8th in Osaka and made the switch from nurse to mangaka with her debut story "*Nemuru Hime*" (Sleeping Princess) in *Lunatic LaLa* magazine in 1995. Her other works include *Kiss*, a series about piano lessons and love, *23:00*, a book about street dancing, and *Eikaiwa School Wars* (English School Wars), which is currently serialized in *LaLa Monthly* magazine. Ms. Matsumoto loves dancing and taking English lessons.

BEAUTY IS THE BEAST
Vol. 3
The Shojo Beat Manga Edition

STORY & ART BY
TOMO MATSUMOTO

English Translation & Adaptation/Tomo Kimura
Touch-up & Lettering/Inori Fukuda Trant
Graphics & Cover Design/Yukiko Whitley
Editor/Pancha Diaz

Managing Editor/Megan Bates
Director of Production/Noboru Watanabe
Vice President of Publishing/Alvin Lu
Vice President & Editor in Chief/Yumi Hoashi
Sr. Director of Acquisitions/Rika Inouye
Vice President of Sales & Marketing/Liza Coppola
Publisher/Hyoe Narita

Printed in Canada

Published by VIZ Media, LLC
P.O. Box 77010
San Francisco, CA 94107

Shojo Beat Manga Edition
10 9 8 7 6 5 4 3 2 1
First printing, May 2006

store.viz.com

PARENTAL ADVISORY
BEAUTY IS THE BEAST is rated T for Teen
and is recommended for ages 13 and up.
It contains mature situations.

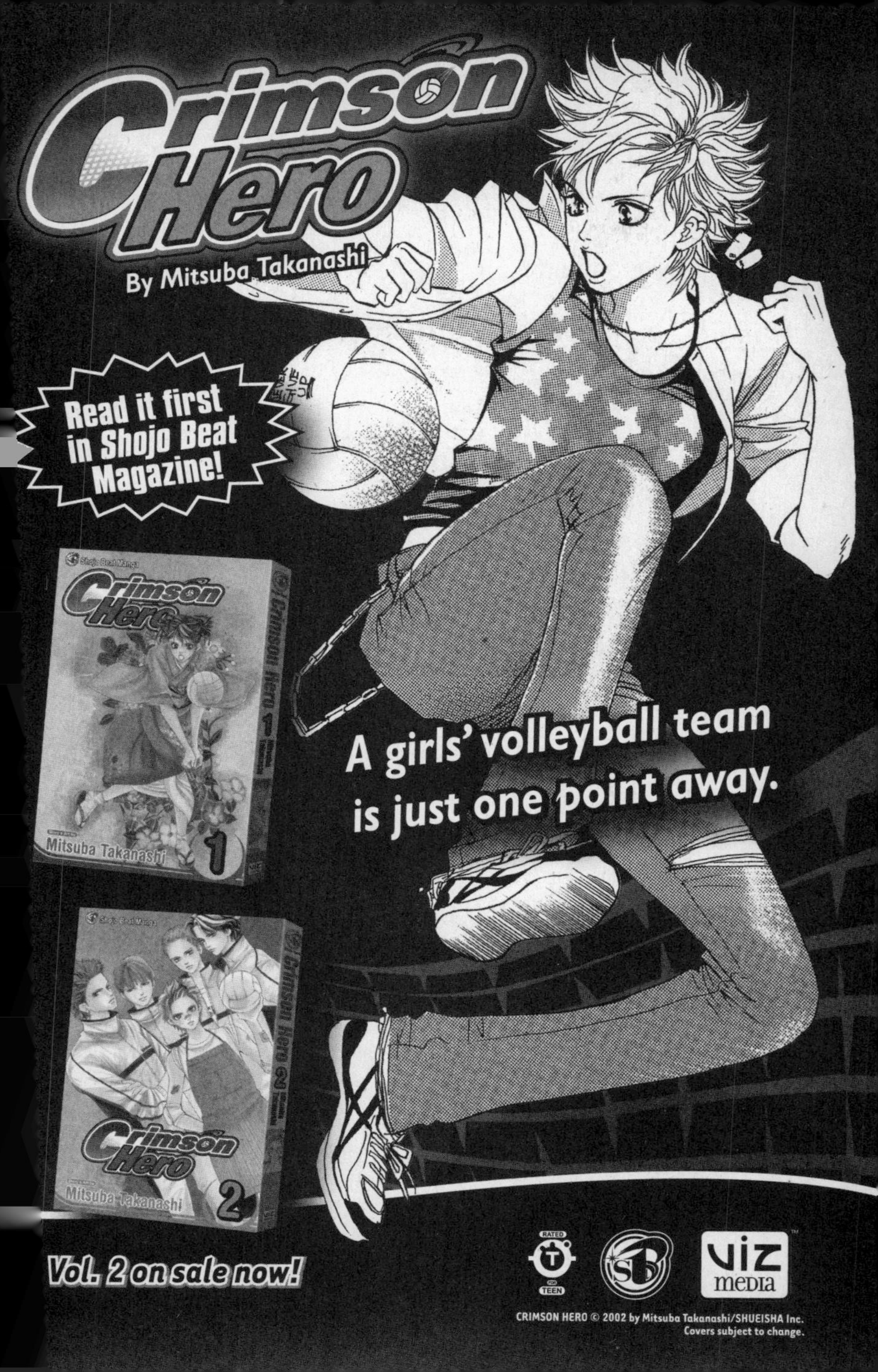
Crimson Hero
By Mitsuba Takanashi
Read it first in Shojo Beat Magazine!
Shojo Beat Manga
Crimson Hero
Mitsuba Takanashi
1
Shojo Beat Manga
Crimson Hero
Mitsuba Takanashi
2
A girls' volleyball team is just one point away.
Vol. 2 on sale now!
RATED T FOR TEEN
viz media
CRIMSON HERO © 2002 by Mitsuba Takanashi/SHUEISHA Inc.
Covers subject to change.

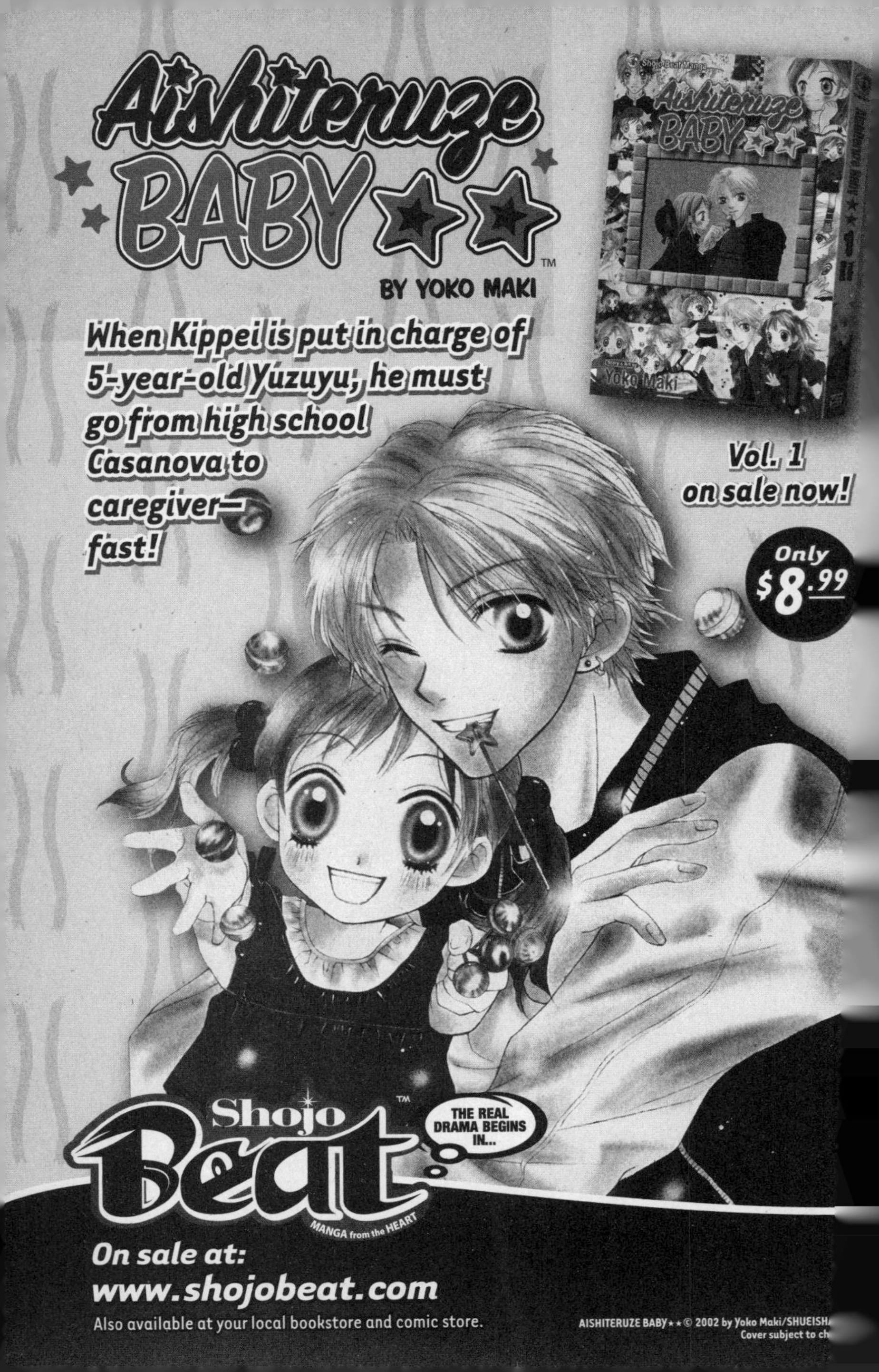
Aishiteruze BABY ★★™
BY YOKO MAKI
When Kippei is put in charge of 5-year-old Yuzuyu, he must go from high school Casanova to caregiver—fast!
Vol. 1 on sale now!
Only $8.99
Shojo Beat™
MANGA from the HEART
THE REAL DRAMA BEGINS IN...
On sale at:
www.shojobeat.com
Also available at your local bookstore and comic store.
AISHITERUZE BABY ★★ © 2002 by Yoko Maki/SHUEISHA
Cover subject to ch

Save OVER 50% OFF the cover price!

D0956578

Six of the most addictive Shojo Manga from Japan: Nana, Baby & Me, Absolute Boyfriend (by superstar creator Yuu Watase!), and more! Plus the latest on what's happening in Japanese fashion, music, and culture!

Save 51% OFF the cover price PLUS enjoy all the benefits of the 🌸 Sub Club with your paid subscription - your issues delivered first, exclusive access to ShojoBeat.com, and gifts mailed with some issues.

✓ YES! Please enter my 1-year subscription (12 GIANT issues) to *Shojo Beat* at the special subscription rate of only $34.99 and sign me up for the 🌸 Sub Club.

only $34.99 for 12 HUGE issues!

NAME

ADDRESS

CITY   STATE   ZIP

E-MAIL ADDRESS   P5GN03

☐ MY CHECK, PAYABLE TO SHOJO BEAT, IS ENCLOSED

CREDIT CARD: ☐ VISA   ☐ MASTERCARD

RATED T+ FOR OLDER TEEN

ACCOUNT #   EXP. DATE

SIGNATURE

☐ BILL ME LATER PLEASE

CLIP AND MAIL TO ➤

SHOJO BEAT
Subscriptions Service Dept.
P.O. Box 438
Mount Morris, IL 61054-0438

Canada add $12 US. No foreign orders. Allow 6-8 weeks for delivery.